GERM MEANS BUSINESS

A multi-media language course in business German

KATRIN KOHL

Fellow in German, Jesus College, Oxford

TRISTAM CARRINGTON-WINDO

Technical translator, visiting lecturer,
University of Surrey and University of Westminster

BBC BOOKS

This book is based on material specially recorded in Germany and on material filmed for the BBC Continuing Education television series *Germany means Business*, first broadcast from January 1993. The three C75 cassettes are available for sale from booksellers: ISBN 0 563 36401 7. A business pack containing the course book and three cassettes is also available from booksellers: ISBN 0 563 36754 7. A video language pack containing the TV programmes, an additional tutor video and a video handbook, together with the course book and three cassettes, is available from Autumn 1993 to businesses and educational institutions from BBC Training Videos, BBC Enterprises Ltd, 80 Wood Lane, London W12 0TT. UK Sales Office and world sales: 081 576 2361   Canada: 416 469 1505   Australia: 02 331 7744

For information on the full range of BBC language books and cassettes, write to BBC Books, Language Enquiry Service, Room A3116, Woodlands, 80 Wood Lane, London W12 0TT.

PROJECT EDITOR: MADDALENA FAGANDINI
DESIGNED BY ANN SALISBURY
COVER ILLUSTRATION BY PAUL DAVIS
PRODUCER, BBC TV SERIES *GERMANY MEANS BUSINESS*: BERNARD ADAMS
INTERVIEWERS: PETER SAHLA, KERSTIN WACHHOLZ

ISBN 0 563 36342 8

Published by BBC Books, a division of BBC Enterprises Ltd
Woodlands, 80 Wood Lane, London W12 0TT
First published 1993

Typeset in 10/12pt Bembo by Selwood Systems Ltd, Midsomer Norton
Printed and bound in Great Britain by Butler & Tanner Ltd, Frome and London
Cover printed by Clays Ltd, St Ives plc

The authors and publisher wish to thank the following for their assistance and for permission to reproduce copyright and photographic material:
Allgemeiner Deutscher Automobil-Club e. V.; AMK Berlin; Bild-Zeitung, Axel Springer Verlag; Otto Bosse GmbH & Co. KG; Bundesverband deutscher Banken e. V.; Berliner Verkehrs-Betriebe (BVG); Deutsche BP AG; Deutsche Bundespost Telekom; Deutsches Institut für Normung e. V.; Dresdner Bank AG; Düsseldorfer Messegesellschaft mbH; The English Pot Pourri Company; Funk-Restaurant; Globus Kartendienst GmbH; Ibis Hotels Deutschland; W. Kaiser Fenster GmbH & Co. KG; Münchener Messe- und Ausstellungsgesellschaft mbH; Northshore Yachts Ltd; Okuma Europe GmbH; Pan Imperial GmbH; Price Waterhouse GmbH; Psion UK plc; Schering AG; Schott Glaswerke; Stahlgruber Otto Gruber GmbH & Co.; Süddeutscher Verlag GmbH; Tradecom GmbH; Ultimar GmbH & Co. KG; Verband der Technischen Überwachungs-Vereine e. V.; Herbert Walter Werkzeug- und Maschinenbau GmbH.

Every effort has been made to trace all copyright holders, but the publisher will be pleased to make the necessary arrangements at the earliest opportunity if there are any omissions.

Photograph credits: Allsport *66*; Art Directors Photo Library *1*; Klaus Barisch *51 (bottom)*; BBC *67, 81, 100, 113 (bottom), 114, 121, 134 (top)*; Gerrit Buntrock/Anthony Blake Photo Library *62*; Tristam Carrington-Windo *5, 18, 24, 38 (bottom), 82, 105, 115, 132 (top)*; Petra Hirst *57 (bottom)*, *58, 87, 91, 104, 106, 111, 116, 117, 118, 125, 127, 128, 130*; Mike Schroder/Katz Pictures *123*; Günter Kohl *60*; Picture Bank *99*; Peter Sahla *3 (left)*, *25, 44, 47, 51 (top)*, *73, 74, 78, 122*; Spectrum *15*; Telegraph Colour Library *57 (top)*; Barbara Weber *4 (left)*.

CONTENTS

INTRODUCTION

To succeed in business in Europe's most demanding market you'll need to be able to communicate effectively and understand German business culture.

German means Business is a course for beginners based on recordings carried out in companies throughout Germany. It looks at one of the big trade fairs, at Germany's training system, and at a traditional medium-sized machine-tool company now teaming up with a Japanese corporation. You'll also be introduced to a newly privatized healthcare company in the former East Germany, follow a product being launched by a foreign company, and go on a factory tour.

In the recordings, you'll hear conversations, presentations, meetings and phone calls; you'll get pronunciation practice and plenty of opportunities to speak. The course book sets the recordings in context and gives you a thorough grounding in business German. In addition, it offers written material taken from company brochures, letters, press releases, trade-fair catalogues, newspapers, etc.

Many of the recordings are taken from the BBC television programmes *Germany means Business* – a series of five documentaries on the business world in Germany. These are invaluable for cultural background, while the book and the cassettes provide the complete language course.

HOW TO USE THE COURSE

German means Business assumes you're not already using German in your work. It begins with the basics, essential to start you off or to refresh any knowledge of German you may already have. Straight away you'll be dealing with real-life situations and German speakers in their normal working contexts. This means that from the start you get used to tackling complex language, and in doing so you learn to cope with the actual language you'll encounter in Germany. Each unit covers a different area of the language and introduces you to a variety of transactions and business situations. The course has been designed to allow you to work at your own pace. The wide variety of activities are intended to assist learning rather than test what you know. Use the recordings with the course book so that you get plenty of practice in listening to and speaking the language. The listening symbol 🎧 or 🎧 with track number indicates that there's a related recording.

The recordings were made in different parts of Germany, and you'll need to get used to a variety of regional accents. Listen first, to tune in to the way people speak, then concentrate on getting the main points before going into detail. Listen to a recording several times without looking at the book and try doing the listening activities. Then use the questions marked ▶ to help you get the gist of what you hear, or direct you to specific facts. Answers to ▶ are always in English, unless otherwise stated. Listen to the conversations several times and repeat what you hear out loud until you feel you could take part in them yourself. The more you do this, the more natural the language will become. The cassettes include explanations, exercises and additional conversations, and a list of contents is enclosed with each cassette.

In the book, a **translation key** is given after each piece of German with translations of selected phrases and expressions in context. **Word lists** in the margin provide English equivalents for useful words used in the German alongside. They also include extra words related to the topic, which you may find helpful to learn as you go along. And **learning strategies** give you hints on how to make best use of your German.

Quotes in German from the people interviewed offer personal insight into the German business scene. No help is given with these, although you'll find translations of the individual words in the *Glossary*. You could either work them out immediately or come back to them later.

Cultural information, in English, will make your dealings with Germany more interesting and effective.

Business file provides background information on the German business scene.

Nuts and bolts presents important grammar points to help you understand the German you're learning. By familiarizing yourself with the patterns of the language, you can make your learning more efficient. If you want to know more about a particular point introduced in *Nuts and bolts*, look up the page references to the *Grammar* section.

Practice provides activities specially designed to help you understand and practise the German you've been listening to and reading. Don't be discouraged if you can't get to grips with something first time round. Go over the material again or come back to it later – you'll find that gradually everything will fit into place. These exercises usually require answers in German. Some will be single words or phrases, but try to make complete sentences whenever possible. For some activities you may need to use the *Glossary* at the end of the book, or an English/German dictionary. Remember that the *Answers* section is there to help you.

Checklist offers key phrases for use in everyday business situations and should give you flexibility for your transactions in German. Practise *Checklist* on your own or with a fellow student or colleague until you feel confident. *Review* consists of optional revision exercises for additional practice. *Structures* summarizes important grammar points and fills in the detail. It puts some of the points in *Nuts and bolts* into a wider context and helps you get an overview of the patterns of the language.

Towards the end of each unit there are additional recordings for you to listen to. Although a transcript of these recordings is given in the *Answers* section, you should try to get used to understanding spoken German without written support.

This section will help you develop reading skills. It presents extracts of written German from company brochures, newspapers, letters, etc., related to the subject of each unit.

When you've worked your way to the end of a unit, keep coming back to it and see how you've progressed.

At the end of the book you'll find three sections that will support your learning:

Grammar begins with a guide to pronunciation and spelling, followed by a comprehensive summary of the language structures in *German means Business*. You can refer back to relevant points in the book by using the page references provided.

Answers provide a key for all tasks.

The *Glossary* contains the German words in *German means Business*, translated in context.

1

MEIN NAME IST . . .

GREETINGS, INTRODUCTIONS, JOBS

Read through the conversations and interviews and listen to them until you feel you could take part in them yourself. Then go over them again and do just that!

ALLES KLAR?

 The first four conversations are over the telephone and the last one is in a bank. Notice how people greet each other and identify themselves.

die Firma *firm, company*
die Gesellschaft *company*
der Hersteller *manufacturer*
die Messe *trade fair*
die Ausstellung *exhibition*
die Pressestelle *press office*
das Reisebüro *travel agent*
AG (comparable with) *Plc*
GmbH (comparable with) *Ltd*

PSION GMBH, HAND-HELD-COMPUTERHERSTELLER, BAD HOMBURG

Frau Weidemann Miko Data, Weidemann, guten Tag!
Herr Grodtke Guten Tag, Frau Weidemann! Grodtke, Firma Psion. Ich hätte gerne Herrn Mischke gesprochen.

NEUHAUS & NEUHAUS GMBH, FILMGESELLSCHAFT, MÜNCHEN

Frau Wagner Firma Neuhaus und Neuhaus, Wagner, guten Tag!
Frau Müller Guten Tag! Hier Müller, Firma Atelier GmbH.
Frau Wagner Ach, die Frau Müller, guten Tag!

MÜNCHENER MESSE– UND AUSSTELLUNGSGESELLSCHAFT MBH

Frau Schwamm Pressestelle, Schwamm, grüß Gott!

PAN IMPERIAL GMBH, REISEBÜRO, MÜNCHEN

Frau von Asen Pan Imperial, grüß Gott!
Herr Gräter Ja. Guten Tag! Mein Name ist Günther Gräter . . .
Frau von Asen Ja, grüß Gott, Herr Gräter!
Herr Gräter . . . und ich wollt' mich bei Ihnen erkundigen . . .

die Bank	*bank*
das Konto	*account*
das Geld	*money*
die Währung	*currency*
die Mark	*mark (German currency)*
überweisen	*to transfer (money)*
wechseln	*to change (money)*

DRESDNER BANK AG, DRESDEN

Herr Kreimeier Tag!
Herr Teufel Guten Tag, Herr Kreimeier!
Herr Kreimeier Ich möcht' gern 250 Mark überweisen . . .
(And on concluding the transaction:)
Herr Kreimeier Alles klar? Danke schön! Wiedersehen!
Herr Teufel Wiedersehen! Kommen Sie bald wieder.
Herr Kreimeier Ja.

alles klar? *understood?, OK?*
ich wollt' mich . . . erkundigen *I wanted to enquire . . . (lit. inform myself)*
bei Ihnen (lit.) *from you*
ich möcht' gern . . . überweisen *I'd like to transfer . . .*

NUTS AND BOLTS ▶

Notice the German equivalent of the English *is*:
Mein Name **ist** Günther Gräter.
For other forms of the verb **sein** (*to be*), see p 144.

In case you've noticed some unfamiliar letters: listen to the recordings to hear the pronunciation of **ä**, **ö** and **ü**, which are variations of the vowels **a**, **o** and **u**. The letter **ß** is sometimes used instead of **ss**. Nouns are always written with a capital letter, which makes them easy to recognize when reading.

Greetings

How you greet people in Germany depends on the time of day and where you are. **Guten Tag!** – sometimes just **Tag!** – is standard throughout Germany during the working day. **Guten Morgen!** is for early in the morning and **Guten Abend!** for the evening. **Grüß Gott!** is a catch-all greeting in southern Germany, which can be used at any time. The more informal **Hallo!** is universal.

Auf Wiedersehen! – often shortened to **Wiedersehen!** – is the German for *goodbye* and literally means *until we meet again*. In the north, the informal **Tschüs!** is common, though in business contexts it's safer to stick to **Auf Wiedersehen!** On the phone, you say **Auf Wiederhören!**, *until we speak* (lit. *hear*) *again*.

The word lists in the margin give you useful vocabulary to learn. Most of the words appear in the recordings or written German, but occasionally related words are added to give you flexibility.

PRACTICE ▶

Learning a language is a gradual process, and it's best to do a little every day rather than a big stint once a week. And remember that passive learning also helps, so listen to the recordings as often as you can.

Practise answering the questions out loud, then try writing the answers down. You can check them with the recorded answers on track 2 and in the *Answers* section.

a How would you greet Mr Grodtke mid-morning?
b How would you greet Mr Teufel in the afternoon?
c And Ms Wagner first thing in the morning?
d How would you greet Mr Gräter in the evening?
e How could you greet Ms von Asen if you wanted to make a point of feeling at home in southern Germany?

WIE IST IHR NAME?

 Peter Sahla asked some business people their names. Listen to the recordings, then try asking the questions yourself.

Gerrit Neuhaus

Rüdiger Linde

Alessandra Folco

der Name *name*
der Nachname *surname*
heißen *to be called*
können *to be able to, can*
sagen *to say, to tell*
buchstabieren *to spell*

NEUHAUS & NEUHAUS GMBH, MÜNCHEN
Herr Sahla   Wie ist Ihr Name?
Herr Neuhaus   Mein Name ist Gerrit Neuhaus.

ADAC, ALLGEMEINER DEUTSCHER AUTOMOBILCLUB, MÜNCHEN
Herr Sahla   Wie heißen Sie, bitte?
Herr Linde   Ich heiße Rüdiger Linde.

DEUTSCHE BP AG, MINERALÖLGESELLSCHAFT, HAMBURG
Herr Sahla   Könnten Sie mir bitte sagen, wie Sie heißen?
Frau Folco   Ich heiße Alessandra Folco.

Make a note of any words you think will be particularly useful to you. Keep them in a notebook or, better still, on separate cards with the translation on the back, and check them through at regular intervals.

Herr Sahla   Könnten Sie bitte mal sagen, wie Sie heißen?
Frau Heuck   Mein Name ist Elke Heuck.
Herr Sahla   Wie buchstabiert man das?
Frau Heuck   Heuck? Den Nachnamen? H – E – U – C – K.

wie ist . . . ? *what* (lit. *how*) *is . . . ?*
könnten Sie mir bitte sagen . . . ? *could you please tell me . . . ?*
wie heißen Sie? *what's your name?* (lit. *how are you called?*)
wie buchstabiert man das? *how do you spell that?*

NUTS AND BOLTS

Notice how the verb ending changes:
    ich heiß**e** *I'm called*
    Sie heiß**en** *you're called*
In dictionaries, verbs are normally listed in their infinitive form, eg **heißen** (*to be called*). You can find out more about verb endings on p 145.

Sooner or later you're bound to be asked to spell your name, company or address, so get to know the German alphabet. It's listed on p 138 and recorded on track 3.

Notice also how the word order changes (see p 147):
    Wie **heißen Sie**?
    Könnten Sie mir bitte sagen, wie **Sie heißen**?

DARF ICH VORSTELLEN?

Peter Sahla

 When meeting someone for the first time, give your name, shake hands and, if appropriate, introduce a colleague.

Herr Sahla	Guten Tag! Mein Name ist Peter Sahla.
Herr Yenal	Guten Tag, Herr Sahla! Yenal ist mein Name.
Herr Sahla	Darf ich vorstellen? Das ist Frau Wachholz.
Herr Yenal	Guten Tag, Frau Wachholz!
Frau Wachholz	Guten Tag!

darf ich vorstellen? *may I introduce?*
das ist ... *this is ...*

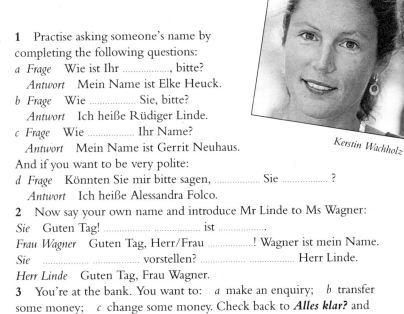

Kerstin Wachholz

PRACTICE ▶

1 Practise asking someone's name by completing the following questions:
a Frage Wie ist Ihr ...., bitte?
  Antwort Mein Name ist Elke Heuck.
b Frage Wie .... Sie, bitte?
  Antwort Ich heiße Rüdiger Linde.
c Frage Wie .... Ihr Name?
  Antwort Mein Name ist Gerrit Neuhaus.
And if you want to be very polite:
d Frage Könnten Sie mir bitte sagen, ... Sie .... ?
  Antwort Ich heiße Alessandra Folco.

2 Now say your own name and introduce Mr Linde to Ms Wagner:
Sie Guten Tag! .... ist ....
Frau Wagner Guten Tag, Herr/Frau .... ! Wagner ist mein Name.
Sie .... vorstellen? .... Herr Linde.
Herr Linde Guten Tag, Frau Wagner.

3 You're at the bank. You want to: *a* make an enquiry; *b* transfer some money; *c* change some money. Check back to ***Alles klar?*** and work out what to say.
a Ich .... bei Ihnen erkundigen ...
b Ich .... 250 .... überweisen.
c Ich .... 400 .... wechseln.

Shake hands!
When meeting a business contact for the first time you'll be expected to shake hands and exchange business cards. In some German offices, shaking hands is part of the daily ritual, so don't be surprised if a round of hand-shaking precedes a day's work. And of course **Guten Morgen**! is a must.

Checklist provides key phrases for use in business situations. You can adapt them to your own needs. Practise by listening to the recorded summary to see how these phrases are spoken, and then try imitating the sounds and intonation.

It's best to learn nouns with the appropriate definite article: **der**, **die** or **das**. You'll find it's given with each noun in the *Glossary*. Knowing whether a noun is *masculine, feminine* or *neuter* will help you get to grips with German grammar.

Greet people
Guten Morgen!
Guten Tag!
Guten Abend!
Grüß Gott!
Hallo!

Say goodbye
Auf Wiedersehen!
Auf Wiederhören!
Tschüs!

Give your name
Mein Name ist . . .
Ich heiße . . .

Introduce someone
Darf ich vorstellen?
Das ist Herr/Frau/
    Herr Doktor/Frau Doktor . . .

Ask someone their name
Wie ist Ihr Name?
Wie heißen Sie, bitte?
Könnten Sie mir bitte sagen,
    wie Sie heißen?

Ask someone to spell a word
Wie buchstabiert man das?

Ask for information
Ich wollte mich erkundigen . . .

Say you want to transfer/ change some money
Ich möchte gern(e) 250 Mark
    überweisen.
Ich möchte gern(e) 250 Pfund
    wechseln.

Say please and thank you
Bitte.
Danke schön.

Use *Checklist* to practise greetings and introductions.

DAS BERUFSBILD

Here Peter Sahla asks people what their job is.

▶ Give a profile of them in English, listing:
a name;   *b* job;   *c* company.

Gerrit Neuhaus tells Peter Sahla what he does.

NEUHAUS & NEUHAUS GMBH, MÜNCHEN

Herr Sahla   Wie ist Ihr Name?
Herr Neuhaus   Mein Name ist Gerrit Neuhaus.
Herr Sahla   Und was sind Sie von Beruf?
Herr Neuhaus   Ich bin von Beruf Filmregisseur, Fernsehregisseur und
Fernsehproduzent.

When dealing with German, listen out for the main points. ▶ indicates questions to be answered in English. They're intended to help you locate specific information.

Pressestelle, Deutsche BP

der Beruf   *job, trade, profession*
die Bürokraft   *secretary*
die Sekretärin   *secretary (f.)*
der Assistent   *assistant*
die Assistentin   *assistant (f.)*
das Büro   *office*
der Regisseur   *(film) director*
die Regisseurin   *(film) director (f.)*
der Produzent   *producer*
die Produzentin   *producer (f.)*
der Film   *film*
das Fernsehen   *television*

Uwe Reif and Alessandra Folco work in the BP press department. They talk about the company and their positions.

Herr Sahla   Wie heißen Sie?
Herr Reif   Ich heiße Uwe Reif.
Herr Sahla   Und was ist Ihre Funktion innerhalb der Firma?
Herr Reif   Ich bin Pressesprecher bei der Deutschen BP AG in Hamburg.
Herr Sahla   Könnten Sie mir bitte sagen, wie Sie heißen?
Frau Folco   Ich heiße Alessandra Folco.
Herr Sahla   Und Sie arbeiten bei welcher Firma?
Frau Folco   Ich arbeite bei der Deutschen BP AG in Hamburg.
Herr Sahla   Und was ist Ihre Funktion?
Frau Folco   Ich bin in einem Zweier-Sekretariat als Zweit-Sekretärin angestellt, und das ist das Berufsbild Büro-Assistentin.
Herr Sahla   Was für eine Firma ist die Deutsche BP?
Herr Reif   Die Deutsche BP ist eine der führenden Mineralölgesellschaften in Deutschland.

Michaela von Asen talks about her job, her company and her area of responsibility.

PAN IMPERIAL GMBH, MÜNCHEN

Herr Sahla   Wie ist Ihr Name?
Frau von Asen   Mein Name ist Michaela Josefa von Asen.
Herr Sahla   Und was sind Sie von Beruf?
Frau von Asen   Und mein Beruf ist Reisebürokauffrau.
Herr Sahla   Und für welche Firma arbeiten Sie?
Frau von Asen   Ich arbeite für die Firma Pan Imperial Reisen GmbH in München und bin dort größtenteils zuständig für den Individualtourismus.

was sind Sie von Beruf?   *what's your job/profession?*
innerhalb   *within, in*
was für eine . . . ?   *what kind of . . . ?*
eine der führenden Mineralölgesellschaften   *one of the leading oil companies*
Reisebürokauffrau   *travel agent (f.)*
für welche . . . ?   *for which . . . ?*
größtenteils   *mainly*
zuständig für   *responsible for*

Frau/Fräulein

Although you'll find that **Fräulein** is still sometimes used, it's now normal to address all women as **Frau**. The use of **Fräulein** has been abolished in official communications.

When asking for yes/no information, the order of words changes:

Sie sind Pressesprecher bei der Deutschen BP.
Sind Sie Pressesprecher bei der Deutschen BP?

For more detailed information, start with a question word like **was**? (*what?*), **was für**? (*what kind of?*) or **wie**? (*how?*) (see p 147):

Was ist Ihre Funktion innerhalb der Firma?
Was für eine Firma ist die Deutsche BP?
Wie ist Ihr Name?

Welche? (*which?*) is often preceded by a preposition:

Für **welche** Firma arbeiten Sie?

German distinguishes between male and female forms of job designations:

der Assistent (*m.*), **die Assistentin** (*f.*)

With a few jobs, you'll find the endings **–mann** and **–frau**: **der Kaufmann** (*salesman*), **die Kauffrau** (*saleswoman*) (see p 139).
The masculine form is also used as the 'neutral' form.

PRACTICE ▶

Wir sind ein erfolgreicher Automobil-Importeur im Norden von München. Für unsere Abteilung **Vertriebsinnendienst** suchen wir eine(n)

Folgende Hauptaufgaben erwarten Sie:

– Bearbeitung von Händleranfragen
– Führen der Händlerakten
– Überwachung der Händlerentwicklung

Unser neuer Mitarbeiter sollte eine abgeschlossene kaufmännische Ausbildung – möglichst im Automobilbereich –, Verantwortungsbewußtsein, Selbständigkeit, Erfahrung mit Online-Datenverarbeitung und gute Umgangsformen haben, kontaktfreudig und an genaues Arbeiten gewöhnt sein.

Bitte bewerben Sie sich bei

Suzuki Auto GmbH Deutschland & Co. KG

Personalabteilung
Postfach 12 46
80422 Oberschleißheim

Suzuki. Anders als alle anderen.

 In which category in **1d** does this job belong?

1 These job titles appeared in advertisements in the *Süddeutsche Zeitung*: Telefonistin, Kundendienst-Techniker/in, Diplom-Ingenieur/in, Produktmanager/in, Marketing-Leiter(in), Sachbearbeiter/in, Vertriebs-Assistent/in, Buchhalter/in, Vorstandsassistentin, Vorstandssekretärin, Telefon-/Empfangssekretärin, Techniker(in), Industriekaufmann/frau, Bürokauffrau/-mann, Bankkaufmann, Verkaufsprofi, Diplom-Kaufleute, Steuerberater, Wirtschaftsprüfer, Ingenieur(in)

a Which jobs encourage both men and women to apply?
b Which jobs are advertised for women only?
c Which jobs are probably for men only?
d Match the jobs with these categories, using the *Glossary* to help you: *i* reception/secretarial; *ii* clerical/sales; *iii* marketing; *iv* customer service; *v* accountancy/book-keeping; *vi* banking; *vii* technical/ engineering.

2 Try presenting yourself in the various jobs listed below, eg:

Frage Was sind Sie von Beruf?
Antwort **Ich bin Reisebürokauffrau.**

a Pressereferent(in); *b* Sekretärin; *c* Manager(in); *d* Geschäftsführer(in); *e* Sachbearbeiter(in); *f* Werbeleiter(in); *g* Vertreter(in); *h* Vertriebsassistent(in).

3 Use the same jobs to answer in a different way, eg:

Frage Was sind Sie von Beruf?
Antwort **Mein Beruf ist Reisebürokauffrau.**

4 Use the companies listed to say who you work for, eg:

Frage Für welche Firma arbeiten Sie?
Antwort **Ich arbeite für die Firma Pan Imperial Reisen GmbH.**

a Psion GmbH; *b* Neuhaus & Neuhaus GmbH; *c* Price Waterhouse; *d* Telekom.

5 Practise asking someone else which company they work for.

6 Use the information on the business cards to work out how these people might introduce themselves, giving name, job and company. (Elke Heuck is a **Sachbearbeiterin**.)

Now practise presenting yourself!

CHECKLIST ▶

Present your job and responsibilities
Ich bin (von Beruf) Regisseur(in).
Mein Beruf ist Reisebürokauffrau/-kaufmann.
Ich bin bei der Firma X.
Ich arbeite bei der Firma X.
Ich arbeite für die Firma X.
Ich bin zuständig für den Individualtourismus.

Ask someone about their job and responsibilities
Was sind Sie von Beruf?
Was ist Ihre Funktion?
Für welche Firma arbeiten Sie?

Use *Checklist* to practise discussing jobs and responsibilities.

NUTS AND BOLTS ▶ Have you noticed that people say **für die Firma**, but **bei der Firma**? This is an example of how the form of German words can change, depending on a number of different factors (see p 139 and 142). But don't let this put you off. For now, just get used to how the words go together.

8

1   Was sind Sie von Beruf? Practise answering the question giving the following jobs: *a* Vertreter(in);   *b* Geschäftsführer(in);   *c* Sachbearbeiter(in);   *d* Ingenieur(in).   Add the ending **-in** if you're a woman! If your own job hasn't appeared yet, look it up in your dictionary and practise using it.

Frage   Was sind Sie von Beruf?

Antwort   Ich ....

2   If you don't catch someone's name, ask them to tell you.

a Frage   Wie .... Name, bitte?

   Antwort   Mein Name ist Günther Gräter.

b Frage   .... Sie, ...?

   Antwort   Ich heiße Sabine Wagner.

c Frage   .... Ihr ....?

   Antwort   Mein Name ist Axel Kreimeier.

Kooperation miteinander

„Die Zusammenarbeit in einem multi-nationalen, multi-europäischen Unternehmen funktioniert durch Kooperation, Abstimmung untereinander. Ein Hin und Her, Geben und Nehmen zwischen den Zentralen hier in Hamburg und BP Europa, und dann natürlich auch BP London als übergeordneter Stelle – weltweite Kooperation." (Uwe Reif, *Deutsche BP*)

3   Complete questions and answers, giving your own name.

a Frage   .... Name, bitte?

   Antwort   .... ist ....

b Frage   .... Sie, ...?

   Antwort   ....

c Frage   Könnten .... mir bitte sagen, ... Sie ....?

   Antwort   ....

4   Can you complete the following?

a   You want to introduce a colleague.

   ....? Das .... Herr Wolf.

b   You're not sure how to spell someone's name. Ask.

   .... buchstabiert man ....?

c   Say which company you work for ...

   Ich .... die Firma ....

d   ... and what you're responsible for.

   .... für Marketing.

5   What questions would produce the following answers?

a Frage   .... , ...?

   Antwort   Ich heiße Elke Heuck.

b Frage   .... , ...?

   Antwort   Mein Name ist Grodtke.

c Frage   ....?

   Antwort   G – R – O – D – T – K – E.

d Frage   ....?

   Antwort   Mein Beruf ist Reisebürokauffrau.

e Frage   ....?

   Antwort   Ich arbeite für die Firma BP.

Gender

In German, a noun is either masculine (*m.*), feminine (*f.*) or neuter (*n.*), and this affects the form of the definite article (equivalent to *the*): **der** (*m.*), **die** (*f.*), **das** (*n.*). With some nouns the *gender* is obvious, eg **der Mann**, **die Frau**, but with most nouns the gender is arbitrary, eg **der Beruf**, **die Firma**, **das Büro**, and **der Dollar**, **die Mark**, **das Pfund**. That's why it's important to learn a noun with its definite article (see p 139).

Nouns

Concentrate on nouns for the main information in a sentence. In written German, all nouns start with a capital; in the spoken language, they're usually stressed.

You'll often find two, three or even more words joined to form a compound noun (see p 138):

die Presse + der Sprecher = der Pressesprecher
das Mineral + das Öl + die Gesellschaft = die Mineralölgesellschaft
die Ausstellung + die Gesellschaft = die Ausstellungsgesellschaft

The gender is always that of the last noun.

Verbs

Dictionaries list verbs in the infinitive form: **heißen** (*to be called*), **sagen** (*to say*), **buchstabieren** (*to spell*), **arbeiten** (*to work*).

Verb endings change according to the person or persons doing the activity. The regular pattern is that of verbs like **sagen** and **arbeiten**, where standard endings replace **-en**. **Sein** and **haben** are irregular. These are the forms of the present tense (see p 144–145):

	sein	haben	sagen	arbeiten	
ich	**bin**	habe	sage	arbeite	*I*
er/sie/es/man	**ist**	hat	sagt	arbeitet	*he/she/it/one*
wir	**sind**	haben	sagen	arbeiten	*we*
sie/Sie	**sind**	haben	sagen	arbeiten	*they/you (formal)*

⑩ AMK Berlin

Rainer Knopf
Projektleiter

AMK Berlin Ausstellungs-Messe-Kongress-GmbH
Messedamm 22, D-14055 Berlin
Telefon: (030) 30 38-0, Durchwahl: (030) 30 38 20 31
Telex: 1 82 908 amkb d, Telefax: (030) 30 38-23 25

? **1** What is Mr Knopf's job?
2 What is his direct line?

EIN EIGENES AUFGABENGEBIET

 Elke Heuck is employed in the BP press office as a clerk with her own specialist area of responsibility. Listen to her describing her job.

Listen to the next two conversations without following them in print. This will help you get used to the rhythm and sounds of the language, and to understand spoken German. Listen first to the recordings, check the explanations of words and expressions, then listen again and see if you can answer the ▶ questions in English. If you want to read what's said, look up the conversations in **Answers**.

der Fall   *case*
die Aufgabe   *task, job*
das Gebiet   *area*
der Bereich   *area*
die Produktion   *production*
die Herstellung   *manufacture*
die Broschüre   *brochure*
die Öffentlichkeit   *(general) public*
die Schule   *school*
verteilen   *to distribute*

▶ **1** What is Ms Heuck's area of responsibility?
2 Who are the brochures intended for?

in diesem Fall   *in this case*
ein eigenes Aufgabengebiet   *my own area of responsibility*
darf man fragen . . .?   *may I (lit. one) ask . . . ?*
was für ein . . . das ist   *what type of . . . it is*
die wir dann verteilen   *which we then distribute*

NUTS AND BOLTS ▶

Check back and listen to the way Elke Heuck shortens **ich habe** to **ich hab'**. Get used to recognizing this type of short form when listening to people talking. A final **-e** on verbs is often dropped in conversation:

Ich **wollt'** mich bei Ihnen erkundigen . . .
Ich **möcht'** gern 250 Mark überweisen . . .

PRACTICE ▶

1 You're not sure how to spell someone's name. What do you say?
2 You want to make sure your question won't offend. What do you say?

You'll find that some people talk slowly and clearly, others rush and swallow half their words. Listen to the recordings several times to get used to individual styles of speaking.

EIN JAHRESUMSATZ VON ZWEIEINHALB MILLIONEN MARK

Gerrit Neuhaus is a film and television producer in Munich who runs his own production company and has recently expanded into east Germany.

1 Work out the order in which Peter Sahla asks about the following topics: *a* company turnover; *b* his profession; *c* company subsidiaries; *d* his name; *e* his area of responsibility; *f* head office.

2 What's the name of Mr Neuhaus' company?

3 Who else does he work for?

4 What are his responsibilities in the company?

5 What is the company's annual turnover?

6 Where in east Germany does Mr Neuhaus have an office?

die Sendeanstalt *broadcasting network/station*
der Hauptsitz *head office*
die Niederlassung *branch*
die Zweigstelle *branch office*
der Umsatz *turnover*
das Jahr *year*
die Tätigkeit *activity*
die Verantwortung *responsibility*
zum Beispiel *for example*
zuständig für *responsible for*
verantwortlich *responsible*
herstellen *to manufacture*

in erster Linie *primarily*
darüber hinaus *additionally*
im Bereich einer Tätigkeit eines Producers *within the area of activity of a producer*
irgendwelche Niederlassungen *any branches*
in den neuen Bundesländern *in the new Länder*

EUROPAS GRÖSSTER SPEZIALGLAS-HERSTELLER

The Schott Group is Europe's largest manufacturer of specialist glass, including materials for electronic components, which they exhibited at the Productronica trade fair in Munich. Read their catalogue entry and press release.

Find the following information from the catalogue entry: *a* product area covered by the fair; *b* opening times during the week; *c* opening times on Saturday; *d* date of the fair; *e* location of the fair; *f* location of the Schott Group stand.

PRODUCTRONICA 91
9. Internationale Fachmesse der Elektronik-Fertigung

München Messegelände
12.–16. November 1991
Geöffnet 9.00–18.00 h
Samstag 9.00–16.00 h

Schott Gruppe auf der Productronica/München Halle 5, Stand B 01
Werkstoffe für Bauelemente

(Offizieller Katalog, Productronica 91)

 SCHOTT

DIE SCHOTT GRUPPE

Die Schott Gruppe entwickelt, fertigt und vertreibt weltweit mit ca. 18.000 Mitarbeitern rund 50.000 Artikel. Das Angebot umfaßt Spezialgläser und Glaskeramiken als Komponenten für Spitzentechnologien, Apparate und elektronische Geräte sowie komplette Problemlösungen. Der Weltumsatz beträgt über 2 Milliarden D-Mark.

Drei Sparten (Chemie/Pharma, Fernsehen/Haustechnik, Optik/Optoelektronik) koordinieren die unternehmerischen Aktivitäten von über 40 Produktionsstätten. Das Vertriebsnetz umfaßt mehr als 20 eigene Vertriebsgesellschaften und rund 280 Vertretungen in mehr als 100 Ländern.

Schott ist Europas größter Spezialglas-Hersteller. Schott Glaswerke, Mainz, Bundesrepublik Deutschland, sind das Hauptwerk und die Forschungs- und Vertriebszentrale der Schott Gruppe. In Mainz befindet sich auch der Sitz der Gruppenleitung.

(Presse-Information, SCHOTT)

When reading German, see how much you can understand with guess-work. Don't expect to recognize every word right away, but concentrate on looking for important facts and on getting the gist.

1	eins	11	elf
2	zwei	12	zwölf
3	drei	13	dreizehn
4	vier	14	vierzehn
5	fünf	15	fünfzehn
6	sechs	16	sechzehn
7	sieben	17	siebzehn
8	acht	18	achtzehn
9	neun	19	neunzehn
10	zehn	20	zwanzig

entwickelt, fertigt und vertreibt   *develops, manufactures and sells*
das Angebot umfaßt   *the range includes*
der Weltumsatz beträgt   *world turnover amounts to*
Sparten   *product groups*
die unternehmerischen Aktivitäten   *corporate activities*
das Vertriebsnetz umfaßt   *the sales network includes*
Vertriebsgesellschaften   *distributors/sales companies*
Vertretungen   *agents*
mehr als   *more than*
befindet sich   *is based*

PRACTICE ▶

1 Put the following summaries of the three paragraphs in the Schott Group press release in the order in which they appear: *a* description and location of the company;   *b* the company's products;   *c* product groups and sales organization.
2 The press release contains a number of facts. Find the following:
a number of employees;   *b* number of products;
c materials comprising the products;   *d* world turnover;
e number of production facilities;   *f* number of sales companies;
g number of agencies;   *h* number of countries with representation;
i location of the company's main plant;   *j* location of group head office.
3 Put these in the order in which they appear: *a* applications for the range of glasses and ceramics;   *b* location of company headquarters;
c position of Schott within Europe;   *d* structure of the sales network;
e number of employees and products;   *f* function of the divisions.

der Geschäftsführer *managing director*
die Geschäftsführerin *managing director (f.)*
der Mitarbeiter *employee, colleague*
die Mitarbeiterin *employee, colleague (f.)*

der Staat *nation, state*
die Republik *republic*
der Bund *federation*
das Land *Land, state, country*
das Königreich *kingdom*
die Identität *identity*
die Minderheit *minority*
die Europäische Gemeinschaft
the European Community
der Binnenmarkt *the single market*
der Bundestag *lower house*
der Bundesrat *upper house*
die Kultur *culture, heritage*
die Sprache *language*
der Humor *humour*

Der lokale Markt

„Daß es immer einen lokalen Markt geben wird, das ist klar; der lokale Markt muß auch speziell bearbeitet werden, weil die Emotionalität in dem lokalen Markt ganz eigen ist. Man kann in Deutschland nicht mit der gleichen Konzeption vorgehen wie auf einem französischen Markt." (Claude Heinz, *Mach Eins Werbeagentur*)

Over one hundred million people worldwide speak German as their mother tongue. German-speaking peoples existed as a patchwork of minor kingdoms and princedoms for hundreds of years. Today, German is the main language in Germany, Austria, the German-speaking part of Switzerland, and Liechtenstein.

Germany only came into being as a unified state with a sense of national identity in 1871. After the collapse of the Third Reich, two separate states were founded in 1949: the Federal Republic of Germany (**BRD** – **Bundesrepublik Deutschland**) and the German Democratic Republic (**DDR** – **Deutsche Demokratische Republik**). The Federal Republic of Germany went on to become one of the founders of the European Community, and West Germans endeavoured to be Europeans while retaining a strong sense of local identity. The fall of the Berlin Wall in November 1989 created a new Germany, the largest country in western Europe. It put the question of identity back on the agenda as Europe entered the single market.

Germany has a federal structure and is divided into 16 *Länder*, including the three city states Hamburg, Bremen and Berlin. Each *Land* is represented at national level in the **Bundesrat**, which has to approve many bills passed by the elected assembly, the **Bundestag**, before they become law. The *Länder* have considerable autonomy. They collect their own taxes and have holdings in companies. They are also responsible for education, although they have to confer with the federal education minister.

Germans are proud of their local cultural heritage and think of themselves as Bavarians, Saxons, Rhinelanders, . . . Your hosts will be impressed if you know something about local geography and history.

Ideas of what people in Germany are like generally take little account of regional divergences. People in the north have a reputation for Prussian formality, while Rhinelanders and Bavarians let their hair down in a long series of partying during the carnival period. Southern Bavaria is the country of **Biergärten** *(beer gardens),* while Franconia and the Rhineland go in for **Weinfeste** *(wine festivals).* Even the sense of humour can vary – dry in the north, bawdy in the south. It is a country of contrasts. And remember that most Germans wouldn't be seen dead in leather breeches!

2

GUTE FAHRT!

RESERVATIONS, BOOKINGS, REQUESTS

Buying rail tickets to Hamburg, booking into a hotel in Düsseldorf and paying the bill in Munich. Hiring a car is also on the agenda.

RAUCHER ODER NICHTRAUCHER?

Peter Sahla books rail tickets to Hamburg for next Monday.

der Zug *train*
die Karte *ticket*
die Platzkarte *seat reservation*
der Zuschlag *supplement*
der Raucher *smoking, smoker*
der Nichtraucher *no smoking, non-smoker*
erster/zweiter Klasse *first/second class*
(der/die/das) nächste *(the) next*
gut *good*
schlecht *bad, poor*
früh *early*
spät *late*
zurückkommen *to return*
reservieren *to reserve*

Find the following facts about the trip: *a* destination; *b* number of tickets; *c* day of travel; *d* date; *e* time of day; *f* seat reservation/no reservation; *g* smoking/no smoking; *h* day of return; *i* times of departure and arrival.

AMTLICHES BAYERISCHES REISEBÜRO GMBH, MÜNCHEN

Herr Reisinger Grüß Gott! Bitte schön?
Herr Sahla Guten Tag! Ich hätte gern zwei Karten nach Hamburg: München-Hamburg.
Herr Reisinger Ja, gerne. Für wann?
Herr Sahla Nächsten Montag. Das ist der . . .
Herr Reisinger Sechste April.
Herr Sahla . . . sechste April, ja. Wenn es geht also sehr früh.
Herr Reisinger Wie lang würden Sie denn in Hamburg bleiben?
Herr Sahla Ich möchte zurückkommen am Freitag.
Herr Reisinger Am Freitag. Zweiter oder erster Klasse?
Herr Sahla Erster Klasse.

10	zehn
20	zwanzig
30	dreißig
40	vierzig
50	fünfzig
60	sechzig
70	siebzig
80	achtzig
90	neunzig
100	(ein)hundert

Montag	*Monday*
Dienstag	*Tuesday*
Mittwoch	*Wednesday*
Donnerstag	*Thursday*
Freitag	*Friday*
Samstag/Sonnabend	*Saturday*
Sonntag	*Sunday*

Herr Reisinger Erster Klasse. Möchten Sie Platzkarten auch reservieren dazu, oder...?

Herr Sahla Ja, bitte.

Herr Reisinger Und soll's im Raucher oder im Nichtraucher sein?

Herr Sahla Nichtraucher, bitte.

Herr Reisinger Nichtraucher. Also, dann hätt' ich für Sie einen Zug – der erste Intercity, der da fährt, wär' um fünf Uhr fünfundvierzig und wär' um elf Uhr sechsundvierzig in Hamburg.

Herr Sahla Gut.

Herr Reisinger (*Adds up the cost*) Ja, das käme dann auf achthundertzweiundfünfzig Mark in der ersten Klasse, plus die Zuschläge.

der sechste April	*the sixth of April*
wenn es geht	*if possible*
wie lang...?	*how long...?*
würden Sie ... bleiben?	*would you be staying...?*
möchten Sie...?	*would you like...?*
auch ... dazu	*also...*
soll's ... sein?	*should that be...?*
also, dann hätt' ich	*right, then I have*
der da fährt	*which goes*
wär' um	*would be at*
das käme dann auf	*that would then come to*

Notice how Mr Reisinger asks questions starting with the verb:

Möchten Sie Platzkarten reservieren?

In a statement, the verb comes second (see p 147):

Ich **möchte** zurückkommen am Freitag.

Notice also the vowel change in the verb **fahren** (see p 143):

Der Intercity **fährt** um 5.45 Uhr.

1 Der erste Intercity fährt um 5.45 Uhr. Practise giving departure times for *a* der Bus, *b* der Zug, *c* der Intercity:

5.20   9.45   13.20   6.00   16.15   7.00

2 Practise saying that you'd like two tickets to:

a Munich; *b* Berlin; *c* Hamburg; *d* Dresden; *e* London.

3 You're at the station and have a number of requirements. Use **ich möchte** or **ich möchte gerne** to say you'd like the following:

a eine Fahrkarte nach Berlin; *b* einen Sitzplatz reservieren; *c* einen Wagen mieten; *d* ein Taxi.

U-Bahn/S-Bahn

The underground **U-Bahn** and overground **S-Bahn** railway systems in German cities operate with automatic ticket machines and ticket validators. You have to purchase and validate a ticket before entering the system.

KANN ICH IHNEN HELFEN?

 Katherine Baltaci calls into the Sixt office at Munich airport to hire a car. Although she didn't book, there's one available.

1 What kind of car would Ms Baltaci like?

2 Which of the following is she asked for, and in what order?
a passport; *b* driving licence; *c* keys; *d* address; *e* cash;
f credit card; *g* reservation; *h* ID card.

3 Which five facts will help her locate the car?

die Adresse *address*
die Reservierung *reservation*
das Auto *car*
der Wagen *car*
die Autovermietung *car hire*
das Parkhaus *multi-storey car park*
der Führerschein *driving licence*
die Autopapiere *car papers*
die Versicherung *insurance*
die Vollkaskoversicherung *fully-comprehensive insurance*
der Personalausweis *ID card*
der Paß *passport*
der Schlüssel *key*
die Nummer *number*
bitte (schön) *you're welcome*
fahren *drive, go (by vehicle)*
mieten *to rent*

21 einundzwanzig
22 zweiundzwanzig
23 dreiundzwanzig
24 vierundzwanzig
25 fünfundzwanzig
26 sechsundzwanzig
27 siebenundzwanzig
28 achtundzwanzig
29 neunundzwanzig
30 dreißig

SIXT AG, AUTOVERMIETUNG, FLUGHAFEN MÜNCHEN

Herr Tuebner   Guten Tag! Kann ich Ihnen helfen?

Frau Baltaci   Ja, grüß Gott! Mein Name ist Baltaci. Ich hätt' gern 'nen Wagen, hab' aber leider keine Reservierung.

Herr Tuebner   Was würden Sie denn gerne fahren für'n Wagen?

Frau Baltaci   Ich denke so Opel Vectra . . .

Herr Tuebner   Mhm. Kein Problem. Ein Opel Vectra . . . vollversichert – für Sie? Das heißt inklusive Vollkasko- und Personen-, Insassen-versicherung?

Frau Baltaci   Vollkasko für den Wagen, Personen – nein.

Herr Tuebner   Haben Sie Ihren Personalausweis, Führerschein und Kreditkarte dabei?

Frau Baltaci   Moment, bitte . . . (*Gives him the documents*)

Herr Tuebner   Und Ihre Privatadresse bräucht' ich noch, oder ist die noch aktuell auf dem Führerschein?

Frau Baltaci   Die ist noch aktuell.

Herr Tuebner   (*Fills in the form*) So, das ist der Schlüssel. Das ist ein schwarzer Opel Vectra mit Münchner Kennzeichen. Der befindet sich in unserem Parkhaus gegenüber, im dritten Stock, auf der Parkplatz-Nummer 45.

Frau Baltaci   Danke schön.

Herr Tuebner   Bitte schön. Gute Fahrt wünsch' ich Ihnen!

Frau Baltaci   Vielen Dank. Wiedersehen!

(ich) hab' . . . keine Reservierung   . . . *I don't have a reservation*
was . . . für'n Wagen?   *what kind of car . . . ?*
haben Sie . . . dabei?   *do you have . . . with you?*
. . . bräucht' ich noch   *I'll need . . .*
ist die noch aktuell . . . ?   *is that still up-to-date . . . ?*
der befindet sich in   *it's in*
gegenüber   *opposite*
im dritten Stock   *on the third floor*
. . . wünsch' ich Ihnen   *I wish you . . .*

The definite article **der/die/das** (*the*) can also be used to stand for a noun, like *it* or *this/that* in English:

> **Ein** schwarzer **Opel Vectra** (*m.*) ... **Der** befindet sich in unserem Parkhaus.
>
> **Ihre Privatadresse** (*f.*) ..., oder ist **die** noch aktuell?

The gender of **der/die/das** is the same as that of the noun it refers to, although **das** is often used generally to mean *this/that* (see p 140):

> **Das** ist der Schlüssel.

And you may have noticed how the main point of a sentence can be emphasized by being put at the beginning, before the verb:

> **Gute Fahrt** wünsche ich Ihnen!

A more neutral way of saying this would have been:

> Ich wünsche Ihnen (eine) **gute Fahrt**!

1 How does Mr Tuebner say *no problem*?

2 Complete the sentences with the correct preposition:

auf auf in am (an + dem) nach in mit im (in + dem)

a Die Adresse ist .... dem Führerschein; *b* Das Auto befindet sich .... dem Parkhaus. *c* Das Auto ist .... dritten Stock .... dem Parkplatz 65; *d* Es ist ein Ford .... Berliner Kennzeichen; *e* Ich möchte zwei Karten .... München; *f* Ich werde zwei Tage .... Hamburg bleiben; *g* Ich möchte .... Freitag zurückkommen.

3 Der, die or **das**? Give the definite article for the following nouns: *a* Karte; *b* Zug; *c* Taxi; *d* Wagen; *e* Auto; *f* Name; *g* Firma; *h* Hersteller; *i* Bank.

Remember your papers!

There's a legal requirement in Germany for everybody to carry their ID card or passport at all times. You must also have your driving licence and car papers with you when driving anywhere.

? What does this sign indicate? *a* motorway; *b* dual carriageway; *c* one-way street; *d* cul-de-sac.

ICH HÄTTE GERN ZWEI ZIMMER RESERVIERT

Januar	*January*
Februar	*February*
März	*March*
April	*April*
Mai	*May*
Juni	*June*
Juli	*July*
August	*August*
September	*September*
Oktober	*October*
November	*November*
Dezember	*December*

das Zimmer	*room*
das Bad	*bath(room)*
die Dusche	*shower*
das WC	*toilet*
die Toilette	*toilet*
die Nacht	*night*
der Empfang	*reception*
lieber	*preferably*
brauchen	*to need, require*
kosten	*to cost*
schauen	*to look*

1 How many rooms does Alessandra Folco want to book and for when?
2 What combination of the following is Kerstin Wachholz looking for? *a* single room; *b* shower; *c* bath; *d* double room; *e* one night; *f* two nights.

DEUTSCHE BP AKTIENGESELLSCHAFT, HAMBURG

Frau Folco Ja, Folco ist mein Name, von der Deutschen BP. Schönen guten Tag! Ich hätte gern zwei Zimmer bei Ihnen reserviert. Und zwar vom 13. auf den 14. Dezember . . .

HOTEL GROSSER KURFÜRST, DÜSSELDORF

Frau Wachholz	Guten Tag!
Empfang	Schönen guten Tag! Kann ich Ihnen helfen?
Frau Wachholz	Haben Sie noch ein Zimmer für zwei Nächte?
Empfang	Was brauchen Sie, ein Einzel- oder ein Doppelzimmer?
Frau Wachholz	Ein Einzelzimmer, bitte.
Empfang	Und möchten Sie Dusche, WC oder Bad?
Frau Wachholz	Lieber Bad, wenn's geht.
Empfang	Dann muß ich mal schauen . . . Für zwei Nächte, das hab'

ich noch frei. Das ginge gut.

Frau Wachholz	Wieviel kostet das?
Empfang	115 Mark.

kann ich Ihnen helfen? *can I help you?*
haben Sie noch . . .? *do you still have . . .?*
wenn's geht *if that's OK*
das ginge gut *that would be fine*
wieviel . . .? *how much . . .?*

NUTS AND BOLTS

Können (*to be able to/can*) and **müssen** (*to have to/must*) are known as modal verbs. The verb that expresses what you can or must do comes at the end of the clause, in its infinitive form (see p 144).

Kann ich Ihnen **helfen**?
Dann **muß** ich mal **schauen**.

PRACTICE

1 You're in reception and a client walks in. Ask if you can help him.
2 Use the verb **möchten** to ask a guest if she would like:
a a room; *b* a single room; *c* a double room; *d* bath; *e* toilet; *f* shower.
3 Now ask the receptionist the price of: *a* a double room; *b* a room with bath; *c* a room with shower.

19

ANGENEHMEN AUFENTHALT!

Hotel Ibis, München

Rémy Schaff comes from Alsace. He's in Munich for the Systems trade fair and checks into the Hotel Ibis before going into town. He returns later in the evening and arranges for an early-morning call.

1 Which floor is Mr Schaff's room on?
2 What does he ask for when he returns in the evening?
3 At what time does he want to be called in the morning?
4 What time's breakfast?
5 How does Mr Schaff want to pay?

HOTEL IBIS, MÜNCHEN

Herr Schaff Guten Tag! Ich hab' ein Zimmer bestellt.
Empfang Schönen guten Tag! Auf welchen Namen, bitte?
Herr Schaff Schaff.
Empfang Herr Schaff. Kleinen Moment. Würden Sie sich schon mal eintragen?
Herr Schaff Ja, danke. (*He fills in the registration card.*)
Empfang Okay. Da haben wir das Zimmer 432.
Herr Schaff Wie finde ich das?
Empfang Das ist in der vierten Etage. Der Aufzug ist bitte gleich hier vorn. Ich wünsch' Ihnen einen angenehmen Aufenthalt.
Herr Schaff Danke schön!

(*Later that evening*)
Herr Schaff Guten Abend! Ich möchte meinen Schlüssel, bitte! 432.
Empfang Schönen guten Abend, Herr Schaff! Ja, bitte schön! Herr Schaff, möchten Sie sich wecken lassen?
Herr Schaff Oh ja, bitte, ja. Um sechs Uhr wäre mir ganz recht.
Empfang Gut, Herr Schaff.
Herr Schaff Frühstück ist ab halb sieben?
Empfang Halb sieben, das ist richtig, bis zehn Uhr.
Herr Schaff Das wär's schon. Schönen Abend noch!

(*The following morning*)
Empfang Schönen guten Morgen, Herr Schaff!
Herr Schaff Guten Morgen! Ich möchte gerne zahlen.
Empfang Okay. Das war das Zimmer 432 . . .
Herr Schaff Ich hätte da noch eine Frage: Nehmen Sie auch Kreditkarten?
Empfang Ja, wir akzeptieren Kreditkarten jeder Art. Mit welcher möchten Sie denn bezahlen?
Herr Schaff Mit der Eurocard.
Empfang Ist kein Problem. Mit Eurocard können Sie bei uns zahlen.

der Morgen *morning*
der Vormittag *morning*
der Nachmittag *afternoon*
der Abend *evening*
der Aufzug *lift*
das Frühstück *breakfast*
der Aufenthalt *stay*
richtig *correct*
gut *good*
schön *beautiful, nice, good*
bestellen *to book*
sich eintragen *to sign, register*
zahlen *to pay*

der/die/das erste *first*
der/die/das zweite *second*
der/die/das dritte *third*
der/die/das vierte *fourth*
der/die/das fünfte *fifth*
der/die/das sechste *sixth*
der/die/das siebte *seventh*
der/die/das achte *eighth*
der/die/das neunte *ninth*
der/die/das zehnte *tenth*
der/die/das zwanzigste *twentieth*

ich hab' . . . bestellt   *I have booked . . .*
würden Sie . . . ?   *would you . . . ?*
gleich hier vorn   *just over there*
ich wünsch' Ihnen einen angenehmen Aufenthalt   *I wish you a pleasant stay*
möchten Sie sich wecken lassen?   *would you like to be woken?*
um sechs Uhr   *at six o'clock*
ab halb sieben   *from half past six*
das wär's schon   *that's all*
nehmen Sie auch Kreditkarten?   *do you also take credit cards?*
jeder Art   *of all kinds*

NUTS AND BOLTS

You can often communicate quite effectively without bothering too much about endings and such matters as 'gender' and 'case'. Eventually, though, you'll need to know how they work, so it's worth getting used to them gradually. Check unfamiliar terms in the **Grammar** section.

PRACTICE

The equivalent of the English indefinite article *a* or *an* is **ein**. The form of **ein** varies according to the gender of the noun: **ein** (*m.*), **eine** (*f.*), **ein** (*n.*): **ein Zug** (*m.*), **eine Frage** (*f.*), **ein Zimmer** (*n.*). The form can also vary according to the part played by the noun in the sentence:

  Ich wünsche Ihnen ein**en** angenehm**en** Aufenthalt (*m.*).
This kind of variation is called *case* (see p 139).

Note also that when writing eg 1st, 2nd, 3rd in figures in German, you simply put a dot after the number: **1.**, **2.**, **3.**

1   If **wieviel** is *how much* and **Uhr** is *time*, how would you ask someone *What (how much?) time is it?* Check **Answers** and then practise asking the time.
2   Practise giving these times: *a* seven o'clock;   *b* ten o'clock;   *c* six thirty (check how Mr Schaff asks about breakfast);   *d* six o'clock;   *e* ten thirty.   Do this with a partner if possible.
3   Say you've booked a room.
4   How does the receptionist ask Mr Schaff to wait?
5   See how Mr Schaff asks where his room is, and practise asking for directions to: *a* the room;   *b* the toilet;   *c* the travel agent;   *d* the exhibition (**die Ausstellung**);   *e* the telephone (**das Telefon**).
6   There are 17 different nouns in Mr Schaff's conversation with the receptionist. Note them down, then use the **Glossary** to find their gender (**der, die** or **das**).
7   Practise referring to the past. Use **bestellen** to say you've booked the following: *a* ein Zimmer;   *b* zwei Karten;   *c* ein Auto.   Then do the same with **reservieren**.

Wenige Hotels
„In der ehemaligen DDR gibt es sehr wenige Hotels. Wir haben festgestellt, daß auch außerhalb der Messezeiten zum Beispiel in Dresden oder Leipzig kaum Zimmer zu bekommen sind." (Michaela von Asen, *Pan Imperial*)

Good timing
German business demands punctuality, so if you have an appointment be careful with **halb**: it's not half *past* but half *to*. **Halb sieben** is literally *half to seven*, ie *half past six*. You can always double-check by repeating the time like this: **sechs Uhr dreißig**. Should you be late, the phrase you need is **Ich habe mich leider verspätet.**

You should now be able to buy a ticket, rent a car and book a hotel room.

Ask for something
Haben Sie . . . ?
Haben Sie ein Zimmer?

Say you would like (to do) something
Ich hätte gern(e) einen Wagen.
Ich möchte meinen Schlüssel, bitte.
Ich möchte gern(e) zahlen.
Ich möchte Platzkarten reservieren.

Say something would be fine
Um sechs Uhr wäre mir ganz recht.
Das wäre mir recht.

Ask for the time
Wieviel Uhr ist es?

Give the time
Es ist sechs Uhr.
Es ist halb neun.
Der Zug fährt um fünf Uhr fünfundvierzig.
Frühstück ist ab halb sieben.

Ask someone to wait a moment
(Einen) kleinen Moment.

Give a location
Der Wagen/das Auto befindet sich in . . .
Der Aufzug ist gleich hier vorn(e).

Ask the price and if you can pay by credit card
Wieviel kostet das?
Nehmen Sie Kreditkarten?

Reserve a room, or say you've booked one
Haben Sie ein Zimmer?
Ich hätte gern(e) ein Zimmer reserviert.
Ich habe ein Zimmer bestellt.

Ask if you can help
Kann ich Ihnen helfen?
Bitte schön?

Wish someone a good stay or journey
Ich wünsche Ihnen einen angenehmen Aufenthalt!
Gute Fahrt wünsche ich Ihnen!

Practise making arrangements for travel and accommodation with **Checklist**.

der Fremdenverkehr   *tourism*
das Hotel   *hotel*
die Pension   *boarding house, pension*
der Gasthof   *inn*
das Verkehrsamt   *tourist office*
der Verkehrsverein   *tourist office*
der Fremdenverkehrsverein   *tourist office*
die Vollpension   *full board*
die Halbpension   *half board*

1 How would you ask for the price of something?
2 Wish someone   *a* a good journey;   *b* a pleasant stay.
3 Give the **er/sie/es/man** form in the present for the verbs   *a* können;   *b* fahren;   *c* machen;   *d* sein.
4 Now make sentences using the verbs *a–d* in question 3 and the following words: *a* ich/helfen/Ihnen;   *b* siebzehn/um/der/Uhr/Zug;   *c* einen/Millionen/Reisebüro/von/das/Umsatz/zwei;   *d* Name/mein/Müller.
5 Nouns ending in **-ung** are generally derived from a verb. What verbs are these derived from?   *a* Ausstellung;   *b* Reservierung;   *c* Herstellung;   *d* Leitung.

Whenever you come across a noun ending in **–ung**, make a note of the related verb too. These nouns are all feminine.

6 Pick the correct preposition from the list to fill the gaps:

innerhalb   in   bei   auf   bei   von   für   für

a Ich bin Ingenieur .... der BP;   b .... Wiedersehen;
c Ich bin .... Beruf Filmregisseur;   d .... diesem
Fall;   e Ich bin zuständig .... die Öffentlichkeitsarbeit;   f Ich
arbeite .... die Firma Pan Imperial;   g Ich wollte mich ....
Ihnen erkundigen;   h Was ist Ihre Funktion .... der Firma?

? Can you supply the missing English translations? See how far you can get without help, then check the **Glossary**.

hotel ibis

ZIMMERPREISE

....

1992

EINZELZIMMER	DM 135,00 / 165,00*
DOPPELZIMMER	DM 165,00
Frühstücksbuffet pro Person	DM 14,00
Hund	DM 8,00
hoteleigene Tiefgarage	DM 8,00

(Preisänderungen vorbehalten)

....

(Preise inklusive MwSt.)

....

* gültiger Preis für Messezeiten

....

Plurals

It's sometimes difficult to tell whether a noun is singular or plural in German, because the plural can be formed in several ways:

Singular		Plural
Hersteller	**–**	Hersteller
Gerät	**-e**	Ger**ä**t**e**
Karte	**-(e)n**	Kart**en**
Vertretung		Vertretung**en**
Geld	**-er**	Geld**er**
Büro	**-s**	Büro**s**

Some nouns also have a vowel change in the plural, eg **der Zug – die Züge**. In the *Grammar* section, you'll find some hints on which type of noun has which plural ending (see p 139). And in the *Glossary* you'll find the plural indicated after each noun.

Case

The form of German nouns (or pronouns) and any accompanying words like articles can vary depending on the part they play in a sentence (see p 146). The base form is that of the *nominative case*, and this is used for the person or thing carrying out the action of the verb. This is the *subject* of the sentence:

> **Die Firma** macht einen Umsatz von 2 Millionen Mark.
> **Ich** hätte gerne einen Wagen.

Some verbs are followed by an *object* which is directly affected by the 'action'. This is in the *accusative case*:

> Die Firma macht **einen Umsatz** von 2 Millionen Mark.
> Ich hätte gerne **einen Wagen**.
> Ich hätte gern **eine Karte** nach Berlin.

Strong verbs

Some very common German verbs have a vowel change in some forms, eg **fahren** and **betragen** (see p 143):

> Der erste Intercity **fährt** um 5.45 Uhr.
> Der Weltumsatz **beträgt** über 2 Milliarden DM.

Have a look at the entries for these verbs in the *Glossary* to see how vowel changes are listed.

? What is the function of the **Parkscheinautomat?**

If you haven't read the *Introduction*, do so now and find out how best to use the course!

EIN GROSSES VERKEHRSUNTERNEHMEN

 Hartmut Schmidt is an engineer with Berlin's public transport system. Listen as he defines his job and outlines the history of the company's name, and answer the questions in English.

Dipl.-Ing.
Hartmut Schmidt
Direktionsabteilungsleiter
Betriebs- und Absatzplanung (BAP)

Berliner Verkehrs-Betriebe (BVG)
Eigenbetrieb von Berlin
Potsdamer Straße 188 · 10783 Berlin
Telefon (030) 256 90 11
Telefax (030) 256 90 33

▶ 1 What is Mr Schmidt's profession?
2 What is his specialist area?
3 Which company does he work for?
4 When was this company founded?
5 What was the company called then?
6 When was the company renamed?

der Leiter   *head*
der Sektor   *sector*
der Verkehr   *traffic*
das Unternehmen   *company*
der Betrieb   *business, company*
der Bus   *bus*
die Straßenbahn   *tram*
die U-Bahn   *underground (train)*

Bau- und Verkehrswesen   *construction and transport*
beziehungsweise   *or (rather)*
Betriebs- und Haushaltsplanung   *operations and budget planning*
ist entstanden   *came into being*
haben sich zusammengeschlossen   *amalgamated*
zu einem großen   *to form a large*
sie nannten sich damals   *at that time they were called*

NUTS AND BOLTS ▶ The German word for *of* is **von**, eg **die Produktion von Broschüren**, but it's very common to use the article for *of the/a* . . . :
    Ich arbeite als Leiter **der Direktionsabteilung** (*f.*).
    im Bereich **einer Tätigkeit** (*f.*) **eines Producers** (*m.*)
The articles and nouns in bold type are in the *genitive case* (see p 146).

PRACTICE ▶ 1 Build up a profile in German of Hartmut Schmidt and his organization: *a* profession; *b* name of company; *c* position in his company; *d* date of foundation; *e* four types of transport in the new company; *f* event in 1938.
2 Give an outline of the organization using the following verbs:
a heißt; *b* entstand; *c* nannte sich; *d* umfaßte; *e* wurde umbenannt.

DER ADAC

Rüdiger Linde works at the headquarters of the ADAC, the German Automobile Club, in Munich.

der Verband *association*	▶
die Stadt *town, city*	
der Ort *place*	
zum Beispiel *for example*	
wichtig *important*	
sprechen *to say, speak*	

Listen for the following facts about Rüdiger Linde and his organization: *a* profession; *b* ranking of ADAC in Europe; *c* location of head office; *d* number of regional offices in Germany.

größte *biggest*
darüber hinaus *in addition*
wichtigsten *most important*
bisher *up to now*

NUTS AND BOLTS ▶

Prepositions can become fused with the definite article that follows:

in den wichtigsten Städten
im (in dem) Sommer oder **im** Winter
Ich arbeite **beim (bei dem)** ADAC.

Look out for the forms **am (an dem)**, **beim (bei dem)**, **im (in dem)**, **zum (zu dem)**, **zur (zu der)** (see p 142).

PRACTICE ▶

1 How does Mr Linde say *I am an engineer*?
2 Find the six countries he mentions and match them to these nationalities: *a* der Spanier/die Spanierin; *b* der Franzose/die Französin; *c* der Engländer/die Engländerin; *d* der Deutsche/die Deutsche; *e* der Italiener/die Italienerin; *f* der Grieche/die Griechin.
3 And what are these countries in English? *a* Kanada; *b* Polen; *c* Brasilien; *d* Australien; *e* Argentinien; *f* China; *g* Irland; *h* Schottland; *i* die Schweiz; *j* Belgien; *k* Dänemark; *l* Norwegen; *m* Rußland; *n* Österreich; *o* die Vereinigten Staaten.

KONFERENZEN, TAGUNGEN UND SEMINARE

 Hotel Ibis is Europe's biggest chain of two-star hotels. Read through this section of one of their leaflets on conference facilities.

 What services and facilities does Ibis provide for business people?

die Konferenz *conference*
die Tagung *conference*
das Seminar *seminar*
die Planung *planning*
die Organisation *organization*
die Anforderung *requirement*
unterstützen *to support*
zeitgemäß *modern*
freundlich *friendly*
erfolgreich *successful*

IBIS unterstützt Sie bei der Planung und Organisation von Konferenzen, Tagungen und Seminaren. Mit modern ausgestatteten Konferenzräumen in variablen Größen. Maßgeschneidert auf Ihre Anforderungen. Mit zeitgemäßer Konferenztechnik und freundlichem Service, der einen erfolgreichen Tagungsverlauf garantiert. Sprechen Sie mit uns. Gerne sind wir Ihnen bei der Planung Ihres nächsten Seminars behilflich.

(Hotel Ibis, München)

maßgeschneidert *tailored*
auf Ihre Anforderungen *to your requirements*
der ... garantiert *which guarantees ...*
gerne sind wir ... behilflich *we shall be pleased to help ...*

NUTS AND BOLTS ▶ Requests are often made using what's called the *imperative* form:
Sprechen Sie mit uns!
Notice how it's formed with the **Sie** (formal *you*) form of the verb plus **Sie** (see p 147). The imperative is used a lot in advertising language.

PRACTICE ▶ **1** Only one of the first three sentences in the leaflet is a complete sentence with a main verb and a subject. Can you spot both subject and verb?
2 Which is the verb in the last sentence, and which the subject? (Hint: it's not a noun.)
3 Look at the plan showing part of Berlin's transport system and find the German for: *a* street; *b* village (appears as the second part of a compound noun); *c* zoo; *d* square (appears five times as the second part of compound nouns); *e* town hall (compound noun – nothing to do with rats!); *f* lake (second part of a compound noun); *g* east (first part of a compound noun); *h* direction; *i* garden; *j* beautiful (first part of a compound noun); *k* house (second part of a compound noun); *l* the abbreviation for *station*.

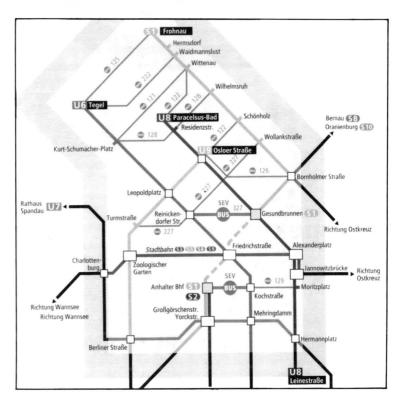

BUSINESS FILE

die Autobahn *motorway*
die Landstraße *trunk road*
der Spediteur *freight forwarder*
die Spedition *freight forwarder*
die Fracht *freight*
der Hauptbahnhof *main station*
die Bahn *train, railway*
die Deutsche Bundesbahn
  Federal German Railway
der Flughafen *airport*
das Flugzeug *aeroplane, aircraft*
das Taxi *taxi*
die Fahrkarte *ticket*
der Fahrausweis *ticket*
der Entwerter *validator*
entwerten *to validate*

Germany lies at the centre of Europe and has borders with nine different countries, so development of a sophisticated transport infrastructure has long been a priority. Both road and rail networks in the east are gradually being upgraded to meet the needs of the economy. The powerful car lobby has ensured that despite environmental concerns, the country's motorways have no speed limit.

Frankfurt Airport is the hub of Germany's air transport and claims to be Europe's busiest airport. In 1992, a new airport opened in Munich to cater for the steady increase in air traffic.

Major cities in Germany have an integrated system of transport combining railways, buses, often trams and in many cases an underground. All these modes of transport run to a strict timetable, and outlying areas are well-served by bus connections to overground services. Cream-coloured taxis are plentiful and can be hailed in the street or hired at one of the many taxi ranks.

For a comprehensive travel guide to the German business scene, read *The Economist Business Traveller's Guide to Germany*.

Abdul-Rahman Adib

EINE GUTE ÜBERSICHT

INFORMATION, ENQUIRIES, EXPLANATIONS

Germany's trade fairs attract visitors from all over the world. In 1992, an estimated two million visitors flocked to Düsseldorf, which organizes fairs ranging from fashion and footwear to boats.

WIE SIEHT'S AUS?

Project manager Abdul-Rahman Adib is satisfied with the preparations for Boot Düsseldorf, the world's biggest boat show under one roof.

1 Where are most of the boats two days before the opening?
2 What's happening to them and who's arriving at the fair now?

DÜSSELDORFER MESSEGESELLSCHAFT MBH, DÜSSELDORF

Frau Wachholz   Herr Adib, es sind jetzt nur noch zwei Tage bis zum Beginn der Messe. Wie sieht's aus? Was ist so der neueste Stand?
Herr Adib   Ja, insgesamt sieht's gut aus. Die meisten Boote, vor allem schweren Boote, sind schon in den Hallen. Die stehen schon. Die werden poliert und saubergemacht. Zur Zeit reisen noch die Kleinaussteller intensiv an, planen schnell ihre Stände, gerade im Bereich Ausrüstung und Zubehör aufbauen. Wir liegen sehr gut mit den Vorbereitungen.

es sind   *it's*
bis zum Beginn   *to the start*
wie sieht's aus?   *how are things looking?*
der neueste Stand   *the latest position*
reisen noch die Kleinaussteller ... an   *the small exhibitors are still arriving . . .*
wir liegen sehr gut mit   *we're well-placed with*

die Messe   *(trade) fair*
die Messegesellschaft   *(trade) fair company*
der Beginn   *beginning, start*
die Vorbereitung   *preparation*
der Stand   *position, exhibition stand*
die Ausrüstung   *equipment*
das Zubehör *(sing.)*   *accessories*
vor allem   *above all*
stehen   *to stand*
planen   *to plan*
aufbauen   *to build (up), erect*

NUTS AND BOLTS

See how Mr Adib says that the boats **are** being polish**ed** and clean**ed**:
Die **werden** poliert und sauber**ge**macht.
These sentences are in the *passive*, which is formed using the verb **werden**

gut	*good*	schlecht	*bad*
schnell	*fast*	langsam	*slow*
leicht	*light*	schwer	*heavy*
klein	*small*	groß	*large*
sauber	*clean*	schmutzig	*dirty*

and a past participle (eg **poliert, saubergemacht**) (see p 143–145). The passive is very useful for describing processes.

Notice also Mr Adib's use of the verbs **aussehen** and **anreisen**:
> Insgesamt **sieht**'s gut **aus**.
> Zur Zeit **reisen** die Kleinaussteller **an**.

These are called *separable* verbs. They have a prefix which may be shunted to the end of the clause or sentence (see p 143).

(see p 143–145)

(see p 143)

PRACTICE ►

Remember to make a note of words that you think will be useful to you, eg **das Zubehör, die Ausrüstung**.

Construct sentences to explain what happens to the boats (check the interview with Mr Adib for the correct form of the verbs):
a Boote + saubermachen;   *b* Boote + polieren;   *c* Boote + in England + bauen;   *d* Boote + in Großbritannien + produzieren; *e* Boote + auf der Messe + präsentieren.

WO BEKOMMEN WIR DIE KARTEN?

► Where's the ticket office?

BOOT DÜSSELDORF

Besucher   Wo bekommen wir die Karten?
Information   Wenn Sie bitte aus der Tür rausgehen, nach rechts zehn Meter, da ist die Kasse.
Besucher   Vielen Dank!
Information   Bitte!

der Besucher   *visitor*
die Kasse   *ticket office, cash desk*
die Tür   *door*
rechts   *(on the) right*
links   *(on the) left*
bekommen   *to get*

wo bekommen wir . . . ?   *where do we get . . . ?*
wenn Sie . . . rausgehen   *if you go out . . .*

NUTS AND BOLTS ►

Notice how visitors are directed *to the right*:
> **nach rechts**

To the left and *straight on* would be:
> **nach links**   **geradeaus**

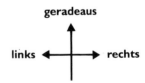

,,Wir haben uns überlegt, was wir für dieses Jahr neu und besser machen können, und sind dann nach vielen Forschungen auf einen Bazillus gestoßen, auf den Virus Nauticus." (Herr Köhler, *Düsseldorfer Messegesellschaft mbH*)

? 1 What did the advertising department do before making a decision on the logo?
2 What is another name for the **boot-Bazillus**?
3 When does the **boot-Bazillus** always appear and on what occasion?
4 How should the **boot-Bazillus** be spread around?

Ich hab' den boot-Bazillus
I like Wassersport

Taucht jedes Jahr im Januar zur boot Düsseldorf auf. Befällt alle, die vom Wassersport träumen.

Wer vom boot-Bazillus erwischt wird, sollte ihn mit diesem Aufkleber weiter verbreiten.

30

1   How could you ask for the ticket office using the verb **sein**?

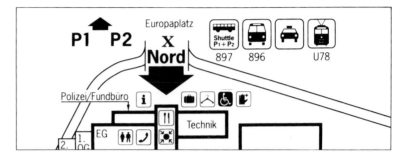

2   Supply a key to the plan of the north entrance by matching the German to the symbols: *a* Gepäckaufbewahrung;   *b* Information + Katalogverkauf;   *c* Garderobe;   *d* Behinderten-Einrichtungen;   *e* Meeting-Point;   *f* Erste Hilfe;   *g* Restaurant;   *h* Telefon;   *i* Toiletten.

3   Try asking for these facilities, using the verbs indicated: *a* sein + die Informationsstelle;   *b* sich befinden + der Meeting-Point;   *c* bekommen + Information;   *d* sein + die Behinderten-Einrichtungen (*pl.*);   *e* sich befinden + die Garderobe;   *f* finden + ein Restaurant;   *g* sein + die Erste Hilfe;   *h* bekommen + einen Katalog;   *i* sein + die Toiletten (*pl.*).

4   Now you're standing at the north entrance to Boot 92, at the spot marked **X.** Could you give directions if asked **Wo ist/sind...?**   *a* die Informationsstelle;   *b* der Meeting-Point;   *c* das Restaurant;   *d* die Behinderten-Einrichtungen (*pl.*);   *e* die Garderobe;   *f* die Telefone (*pl.*);   *g* die Gepäckaufbewahrung;   *h* die Toiletten (*pl.*).

Konsequenzen ziehen

„Ich glaube, es ist wesentlich, daß ein Erstaussteller sich auf Messen umschaut und versucht, aus den Fehlern anderer Konsequenzen zu ziehen." (Thomas Bley, *Ultimar GmbH*)

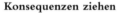

DÜSSELDORF IST OKAY!

On the opening day of Boot Düsseldorf, Kerstin Wachholz talked to an exhibitor and a visitor.

1   How many times has each of them been to the fair?
2   Why do they like the fair?

BOOT DÜSSELDORF

Frau Wachholz   Sind Sie heute das erste Mal auf der Boot Düsseldorf?
Besucherin   Nein. Ich bin jetzt mindestens das vierte oder fünfte Mal auf der Boot.
Frau Wachholz   Und wie gefällt Ihnen die Messe hier?
Besucherin   Ausgesprochen gut, weil man eine sehr gute Übersicht bekommt.

der Aussteller	*exhibitor*
die Besucherin	*visitor (f.)*
größer	*bigger*
besser	*better*
mehr	*more*
heute	*today*
mindestens	*at least*
kommen	*to come*

Frau Wachholz Sie sind als Aussteller hier. Ist es das erste Mal auf der Boot Düsseldorf?

Aussteller   Nein, zirka das zwanzigste Mal.

Frau Wachholz Und wie gefällt es Ihnen hier?

Aussteller   Eigentlich immer besser. Kommen immer mehr Besucher, wird immer internationaler, Messe wird größer, Organisation wird besser. Düsseldorf ist okay!

das erste Mal   *(for) the first time*
das fünfte Mal   *(for) the fifth time*
wie gefällt Ihnen . . . ?   *how do you like . . . ?*
ausgesprochen gut   *really well*
weil man . . . bekommt   *because you get . . .*
kommen immer mehr Besucher   *more and more visitors are coming*

NUTS AND BOLTS ▶

You've seen how **werden** is used with the past participle of another verb to form the passive (see p 144 and 145). **Werden** can also be used in its own right as a main verb, meaning *to become*:

(Die) Messe **wird** größer.

Notice also how the exhibitor makes a comparison. If you want to say that something is *bigger/more international* you add **-er** to the adjective; with some German adjectives you also modify the vowel (see p 141):

international – international**er**   groß – gr**ö**ß**er**

Some comparatives are irregular:

gut – **besser**   viel – **mehr**

Immer can be used to say *more and more*:

Es wird **immer** international**er**.

PRACTICE ▶

1   Notice how Kerstin Wachholz confirms a fact using **Sie sind . . .** Practise doing the same with the following: *a* exhibitor;   *b* visitor;   *c* manufacturer;   *d* secretary;   *e* engineer;   *f* managing director.

2   How would you ask, rather than confirm, what somebody is? Practise using the words in **1** *a–f*.

3   How could you ask someone: *How do you like it?* Now ask them how they like: *a* the fair;   *b* Düsseldorf;   *c* the boat;   *d* the exhibition;   *e* Munich.

4   You regularly visit trade fairs. Practise saying you're at these fairs for the Xth time: *a* 5th time, Boot;   *b* 4th time, Systems;   *c* 10th time, Productronica;   *d* 8th time, Analytika;   *e* 3rd time, here.

5 How would you say that the following are getting *bigger, faster, more international* in that order? *a* trade fair; *b* boats; *c* visitors.

6   Using the following adjectives, practise saying that the product (**das Produkt**) is getting more and more: *a* modern;   *b* exklusiv;   *c* schön;   *d* gut.

Flexibel

,,Man muß sehr flexibel sein. Man muß internationale Sprachen beherrschen. Es gibt italienische Kunden, deutsche Kunden, englische Kunden. Und im großen und ganzen haben wir innerhalb des Betriebes genügend Leute, die fast alle wichtigen Sprachen beherrschen.‟ (Peter Gruber, *Sunseeker Ltd.*)

HANDELN MIT VERSPRECHEN

Rudolf Grospitz

der Dienstleister *service company*
der Quadratmeter *square metre*
das Exponat *exhibit*
die Qualität *quality*
es gibt *there is*
gang und gäbe *usual*
verkaufen *to sell*
versprechen *to promise*

Rudolf Grospitz is events and entertainments director at the Düsseldorf Fair. He outlines the exhibition company's philosophy.

▶ 1 When did Boot start up and how many exhibitors did it have?
2 What do exhibitors have to pay for in order to participate?
3 What two promises do the exhibition organizers make?

DÜSSELDORFER MESSEGESELLSCHAFT MBH, DÜSSELDORF

Frau Wachholz   Was sind die wichtigsten Messen in Düsseldorf?
Herr Grospitz   Es gibt keine wichtigste! Jede Messe ist wichtig. Und wenn Sie sich vorstellen, daß die Boot mal bei Null angefangen hat mit 50 Ausstellern vor 20 Jahren und heute die größte Bootmesse der Welt ist! Wir sind Dienstleister. Wir verkaufen den Ausstellern die Quadratmeter und versprechen, daß die Besucher hier auch in ausreichender Zahl kommen und die Besucher dann auch gute Exponate finden. Wir handeln ja nur mit Versprechen.
Frau Wachholz   Gibt es etwas, was das Düsseldorfer Messe-Unternehmen bietet, was anderswo vielleicht nicht so gang und gäbe ist?
Herr Grospitz   Menschen! Eine perfekte Infrastruktur und Menschen, gute Mitarbeiter, gute Kollegen. Wie selten auf der Welt!

wenn Sie sich vorstellen, daß *when you think that*
versprechen, daß *promise that*
in ausreichender Zahl *in sufficient numbers*
wir handeln ja nur mit Versprechen *after all, we only deal in promises*
gibt es etwas, was...? *is there anything that...?*

NUTS AND BOLTS ▶

Notice how **-st-** is added to the adjective **wichtig** (followed by a case ending) to form the superlative *the most important* (see p 141):
   Was sind die wichtig**st**en Messen?

Some superlatives are irregular:
   groß – der/die/das **größte**
   gut – der/die/das **beste**
   viel – der/die/das **meiste**

PRACTICE ▶

1 How would you say: *We deal in...?*
2 How would you ask someone *What are the most important...?* *a* trade fairs; *b* cities; *c* manufacturers; *d* companies; *e* exhibitors.
3 **Diese Produkte sind die wichtigsten auf dem Markt**. How would you say *These products are the .... on the market?* *a* smallest; *b* fastest; *c* most beautiful; *d* biggest; *e* best; *f* newest.

England or Great Britain?
Germans often say **England** when in fact they're referring to **Großbritannien**, and **englisch** is frequently used instead of **britisch**.

EIN VERKAUFSPREIS VON 3,8 MILLIONEN

Thomas Bley is presenting the Ultimar 62 – a futuristic catamaran.

▶ 1 What would the delivery time and purchase price be?
2 How should Ms Wachholz contact Dr Bley if she's interested?

Ultimar 62

die Zeit *time*
die Lieferzeit *delivery time*
der Preis *price*
der Verkaufspreis *purchase/retail price*
das Konzept *concept, design*
der Termin *appointment*
die Visitenkarte *business card*
die Daten (*n. pl.*) *facts*
das Telefon *telephone*
das Telefax/Fax *fax*
rechnen (mit) *to reckon (with)*
geben *to give*
sich melden *to get in touch*
anrufen *to ring up*

ULTIMAR GMBH & CO. KG, BOOT DÜSSELDORF
Frau Wachholz Wie lange wäre die Lieferzeit?
Dr. Bley Also, Sie müßten mit einer Lieferzeit von ungefähr 11 Monaten rechnen. Wenn wir also relativ schnell uns über das Konzept und Ihre Wünsche im Klaren wären, dann könnten wir eigentlich anfangen zu bauen.
Frau Wachholz Und wieviel würde das ungefähr kosten?
Dr. Bley Nun, wir gehen – je nachdem, welche Sonderwünsche Sie einbringen – von einem momentanen Verkaufspreis von 3,8 Millionen D-Mark aus.
Frau Wachholz Haben Sie vielleicht irgendwie 'ne Visitenkarte, daß ich nochmal ...?
Dr. Bley Natürlich, ich kann Ihnen meine Visitenkarte geben. Bitte schön. Da sind alle Daten drauf.
Frau Wachholz Ja, danke. Dann werd' ich mich nochmal bei Ihnen melden und einen Termin machen ...
Dr. Bley Gut. Wenn Sie wünschen, dann schicken Sie uns 'n Fax oder rufen Sie an.

wie lange wäre ...? *how long would ... be?*
wenn wir ... uns ... im Klaren wären *if we were clear ......*
anfangen zu bauen *begin to build*
wir gehen ... von ... aus *... we start from ...*
je nachdem, welche *depending on which*
werd' ich mich nochmal bei Ihnen melden *I'll contact you again*

NUTS AND BOLTS ▶

Remember that all the material in *German means Business* was collected in Germany. This means you'll come across different accents, the short forms that are characteristic of informal speech (eg **ich hab'**), and word order that may not correspond to the rules. But you'll get used to the way people talk in their everyday work.

Notice the position of the verb used with **können** and **müssen** (see p 144):
> Sie **müßten** mit einer Lieferzeit von 11 Monaten **rechnen**.
> Ich **kann** Ihnen meine Visitenkarte **geben**.

Ms Wachholz talks about the future with **werden** plus an infinitive:
> Dann **werde** ich mich nochmal bei Ihnen **melden**. (see p 145)

And have you noticed how speakers often shorten the indefinite article?
> **'ne (eine) Visitenkarte** **'n (ein) Fax**
You'll also meet **'n** (for **einen**), **'nem (einem)**, **'nen (einen)** and **'ner (einer)**.

1 Ask someone to: *a* send a fax; *b* ring you up.
2 **Kann ich Ihnen meine Visitenkarte geben?** Ask someone if you can: *a* give them your business card; *b* ring them up; *c* fax them; *d* give them your telephone number.

ICH INTERESSIERE MICH FÜR IHR SCHIFF

Peter Gruber is the European agent for Sunseeker, a small British boatyard based in Poole. Mr Ciotti is interested in one of the company's boats.

1 What kind of boat has Mr Ciotti sailed previously?
2 How many boats does Sunseeker produce?
3 What types of power unit can Sunseeker offer?

SUNSEEKER LTD., BOOT DÜSSELDORF

Herr Ciotti   Schönen guten Tag!
Herr Gruber   Guten Tag!
Herr Ciotti   Ciotti ist mein Name.
Herr Gruber   Gruber. Wie kann ich Ihnen helfen?
Herr Ciotti   Eh ... Ich interessier' mich für eines Ihrer Schiffe. Ich hab' bis jetzt Italiener gefahren. Und ich finde eigentlich Ihre Modellpalette sehr interessant. Und gerad' dies Boot würde mich sehr interessieren. Wo werden die Schiffe eigentlich gebaut? Sind das Amerikaner, oder ...?
Herr Gruber   Das sind englische Schiffe. Die werden in England produziert. Das ist 'ne relativ kleine Werft. Wir produzieren 400 bis 450 Boote in allen Größen jetzt. Und wir können Ihnen das Boot natürlich mit diversen Motorisierungsmöglichkeiten anbieten – Diesel- oder Benzinmotorisierung.
Herr Ciotti   Ich würd' mir natürlich jetzt das Boot auch mal von innen angucken.
Herr Gruber   Können wir gerne machen.
Herr Ciotti   Ja?
Herr Gruber   Ja. Okay, dann lassen wir uns an Bord gehen ...
Herr Ciotti   Okay.

das Boot	*boat*
das Schiff	*ship*
die Größe	*size*
die Palette	*range*
interessant	*interesting, important*
sich interessieren für	*to be interested in*
anbieten	*to offer, to sell*
gehen	*to go*

Besonderheiten
„Ich glaube, es gibt in jedem Markt Besonderheiten in den Nuancen. Und wenn man erfolgreich sein will, muß man sich dort vorher schon mal informieren. Das fängt mit solchen banalen Sachen an wie mit den Polsterstoffen. In England ist man auf den praktischen Aspekt aus, daß es abwaschbar sein soll. Und hier in Deutschland muß es schon ein Stoff sein." (Peter Deichgräber, *Northshore*)

ich interessier' mich für	*I am interested in*
eines Ihrer Schiffe	*one of your boats*
ich hab' ... gefahren	*I've sailed ...*
wo werden ... gebaut?	*where are ... built?*
sind das ...?	*are they ...?*
'ne relativ kleine Werft	*a relatively small shipyard*
wir können Ihnen ... anbieten	*we can offer you ...*
lassen wir uns	*let's*

The verb **haben** can be used in its own right as a main verb:
> Ich **habe** eine Visitenkarte.

or with the past participle of another verb to talk about the past:
> Ich **habe** ein Zimmer **bestellt**.

The past participle goes to the end of the clause or sentence (see p 144).

Remember that the definite article can be used to mean *this/that/it* or *these/those/they*:
> **Das** ist eine relativ kleine Werft.
> **Das** sind englische Schiffe.
> **Die** werden in England produziert.

Another word for *this/these* is **dies** (sometimes with an ending, **dieser**, **diese**, **dieses**) (see p 140):
> **Dies** Boot würde mich sehr interessieren.

Ein Jahr vorher

„Ich kann eigentlich nur jedem empfehlen, sich eine Messe in dem Land anzusehen, in dem man verkaufen will. Damit man sieht, wer ist dort erfolgreich und warum. Nur dann hat es Sinn, das viele Geld für Transporte, Stand und all solche Geschichten auszugeben." (Peter Deichgräber, *Northshore*)

1 Ask someone how you can help them.
2 Ask how much something costs.
3 **Ich interessiere mich für . . .** Say you're interested in these (**diese**):
a products; *b* ships; *c* trade fairs; *d* exhibits; *e* brochures;
f machines (**Maschinen**); *g* computers (**Computer**).
4 Now say you're interested in the items listed in **3** *a–g* using **ich finde
. . . interessant**.
5 Use **werden . . . produziert** to present the country of production for different products: *a* Schiffe/England; *b* Maschinen/Frankreich; *c* Computer/Deutschland; *d* Autos/Italien; *e* Broschüren/Kanada.
6 You're visiting a trade fair for machine tools and are interested in a particular machine. Complete the following conversation.

Sie ....!
Aussteller Schönen guten Tag!
Sie ....
Aussteller Meyer. Wie kann ich Ihnen helfen?
Sie .... diese Maschine.
Aussteller Ja, das ist unser neuestes Modell.
Sie ....?
Aussteller Ja, ich kann Ihnen gerne eine Broschüre geben.
Sie ....
Aussteller Auf Wiedersehen!

VIP-Kunden und Alt-Kunden

„Es ist sehr wichtig für uns, schon vor der Messe potentielle Kunden zu kontaktieren. Wir laden unsere VIP-Kunden ein. Und auch unsere Alt-Kunden, die eventuell von ihrem Boot aufsteigen oder umsteigen möchten." (Peter Gruber, *Sunseeker Ltd.*)

Long-term investment

The German market is considered one of the most difficult to penetrate, but its size and wealth make long-term investment worthwhile. Expect a formal approach to business and show your commitment with knowledge of the language, culture and country.

WIRKLICH POSITIV

As the boat show draws to a close, Kerstin Wachholz asks Mr Adib for his impressions.

1 How does he personally feel about the way things have gone?
2 What's the atmosphere like at the fair?
3 What are the prospects for the coming season?

die Stimmung *atmosphere, morale*
die Mannschaft *crew, team*
das Team *team*
der Partner *partner*
das Ergebnis *result*
das Zwischenergebnis *interim result*
die Auswertung *analysis*
die Befragung *survey*
froh *happy, happily*
beeindruckt *impressed*
erfreulich *pleasing*
wirklich *real(ly)*
schauen *to look*

DÜSSELDORFER MESSEGESELLSCHAFT MBH, DÜSSELDORF

Frau Wachholz Herr Adib, heute ist der fünfte Messetag. Wie läuft es?
Herr Adib Ja, erfreulicherweise sehr gut. Ich bin persönlich sehr froh und beeindruckt von dem, was sich in diesen Tagen in den Hallen getan hat. Die Stimmung in der Mannschaft, beim Team – aber auch bei unseren Partnern in den Hallen und bei den Besuchern – scheint gut zu sein. Die Zwischenergebnisse, Auswertungen – persönliche Befragungen aus den Hallen geben mir Anlaß, wirklich positiv in die kommende Wassersportsaison zu schauen.

wie läuft es? *how's it going?*
von dem, was sich ... getan hat *by what has been happening...*
scheint gut zu sein *seems to be good*
geben mir Anlaß, wirklich positiv in ... zu schauen *give me grounds to look forward confidently to...*

PRACTICE

1 Ask someone how things are going.
2 Say that you're: *a* happy; *b* impressed; *c* interested; *d* optimistic (**optimistisch**); *e* satisfied (**zufrieden**).

CHECKLIST

Practise gathering information, making enquiries and saying things are looking good.

Ask where you can get something
Wo bekommen wir die Karten?
Wo bekomme ich einen Katalog?

Ask someone what they do
Sind Sie Aussteller?

Ask how things are
Wie sieht's aus?
Was ist der neueste Stand?
Wie läuft es?

Ask someone if they like something
Wie gefällt es Ihnen?
Wie gefällt Ihnen die Messe?

Southerly 101, Northshore

Die Ernte dieser Messe

„Es ist hier auf deutschen Messen fast nicht möglich, eine *snap decision* beim Kunden zu erreichen. Man muß so eine Geschichte vorbereiten. Und die Ernte dieser Messe wird im Laufe des Jahres kommen." (Peter Deichgräber, *Northshore*)

REVIEW ▶

❓ What can you do on the right?
What must you do on the left?

Say you're interested in something
Ich interessiere mich für Ihr Schiff.
Ich finde Ihre Modellpalette sehr interessant.

Ask what are the most important . . .
Was sind die wichtigsten . . . ?

Ask about delivery times
Wie lange wäre die Lieferzeit?

Ask someone for their business card
Haben Sie eine Visitenkarte?

Ask someone to send a fax or ring up
Schicken Sie uns ein Fax.
Rufen Sie uns an.

Say things are looking good
Insgesamt sieht es gut aus.
Wir liegen sehr gut mit . . .

Say something's fine
Das ist okay!

Say you'll contact someone and make an appointment
Ich werde mich bei Ihnen melden.
Ich werde einen Termin machen.

Use **Checklist** to gather information and make enquiries relevant to your job.

1 Can you remember how to obtain the following information?
a .... ?   Das kostet DM 120.
b .... ?   Mein Name ist Schmidt.
c .... ?   S – C – H – M – I – D – T.
d .... ?   Ich arbeite für die Firma System.
e .... ?   Unsere Firma macht einen Jahresumsatz von 3,5 Millionen.

2 Remember that you can form nouns from verbs using the suffix **-ung**. What verbs do the following nouns come from?   *a* Forschung; *b* Vertretung;   *c* Lösung;   *d* Vermietung. You can check the meaning of both nouns and verbs in the **Glossary**.

3 Find in this unit nouns related to these verbs: *a* versprechen; *b* ausstellen;   *c* beginnen;   *d* vorbereiten;   *e* stehen.

4 You want to ask a colleague how things are going. Look back over the interviews and find three ways of doing so using: *a* wie/aussehen; *b* was/sein/Stand;   *c* wie/laufen.

5 You're at the **Systems** trade fair, gathering information on terms and conditions for a computer you're interested in. Complete the conversation:

Sie ....?

Vertreter Sie müßten mit einer Lieferzeit von zwei Wochen rechnen.

Sie ....?

Vertreter Der Verkaufspreis beträgt momentan DM 3950.

Sie ....!

Vertreter Danke. Auf Wiedersehen!

STRUCTURES ▶

Eine gute Übersicht

Indirect object and dative case

Notice how the different cases can be used to show **who** (subject: *nominative*) does **what** (direct object: *accusative*) **to whom** (indirect object: *dative*) (see p 146):

> **Wir** (*nominative*) verkaufen **den Ausstellern** (*dative*) **die Quadratmeter** (*accusative*).
> *We sell the square metres to the exhibitors.*
> **Ich** (*nominative*) wünsche **Ihnen** (*dative*) **einen angenehmen Aufenthalt** (*accusative*).
> *I wish (to) you a good stay.*

In German, an indirect object (dative) usually comes before the direct object (accusative). The dative case is also used after some prepositions, eg **aus, bei, mit, nach, von, zu** (see p 142).

Werden

Werden is used in several different ways (see p 144):

1 As a main verb (*to become*)
Die Messe **wird** größer.

2 To form the future: **werden** + infinitive
Wie lange **werden** Sie in Hamburg **bleiben**?
Ich **werde** mich bei Ihnen **melden**.

3 To form the passive: **werden** + past participle
Die Schiffe **werden** in England **produziert**.

4 As an equivalent to the English *would*: **würde** + infinitive
Wieviel **würde** es ungefähr **kosten**?

Separable/inseparable verbs

Notice how a prefix can be added to a verb to create a new verb (see p 143):

> Es **kommen** immer mehr Besucher.
> Wo **bekommen** wir die Karten?
> Ich möchte **zurückkommen** am Freitag.

The points explained in **Nuts and Bolts** and **Structures** give you the basic patterns of the German language. Learning them will help you to communicate more efficiently.

The prefix **be-** is inseparable and always remains joined to the basic verb. Other inseparable prefixes are **ent-, er-, ge-, ver-**:

entwickeln, sich **er**kundigen, **ge**fallen, **ver**treiben

The prefix **zurück-** is separable and may go to the end of the sentence or clause:

Ich komme am Freitag **zurück**.

Other separable prefixes are **an-, auf-, aus-, ein-, her-, vor-**:

anbieten, **auf**bauen, **aus**stellen, **ein**tragen, **her**stellen, **vor**stellen

Past participles
Most verbs form past participles according to one of these patterns:

Infinitive	Past participle
machen	**ge**macht
fahren	**ge**fahr**en**

Verbs ending with **–ieren** in the infinitive and verbs with an inseparable prefix have no **ge-** at the beginning: polieren – polier**t**, verkaufen – verkauf**t**, versprechen – verspro**ch**en. Verbs with a separable prefix insert **-ge-** after the prefix: anreisen – an**ge**reist, aussehen – aus**ge**seh**en**, saubermachen – sauber**ge**mach**t** (see p 143).

Die Boote werden polier**t** und sauber**ge**mach**t**.

Bernd Aufderheide

die Eröffnung *opening*
die Pressekonferenz *press conference*
das Ereignis *event*
der Wassersport *water sports*
die Partnerschaft *partnership*
herzlich *sincere(ly), warm(ly)*
willkommen *welcome*
zunächst *first*
heute morgen *this morning*
begrüßen *to greet, to welcome*
repräsentieren *to represent*

HERZLICH WILLKOMMEN!

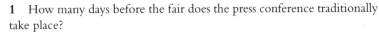

Listen to Bernd Aufderheide, head of the press office, welcoming participants to the opening press conference of Boot Düsseldorf 92.

1 How many days before the fair does the press conference traditionally take place?
2 How many people does Mr Aufderheide welcome?

A long-term view
Take a long-term view of the German market and expect to put in a lot of hard work to get orders. Exhibiting at the relevant trade fairs may not bring results immediately, but perseverance is essential to convince buyers of your commitment to the German market.

Old hands at trade fairs recommend that newcomers visit a fair a couple of times before committing resources to an exhibition stand.

FRAGE NUMMER EINS . . .

die Fachmesse   *specialist trade fair*
der Teilnehmer   *participant*
die Zukunft   *future*
die Lage   *position*
das Zentrum   *centre*
die Frage   *question*
die Antwort   *answer*
großartig   *splendid*
einzigartig   *unique*
bedeutend   *significant, important*
führend   *leading*
am liebsten   *best, most of all*
veranstalten   *to organize*
stattfinden   *to take place*
messen   *to measure*
bedeuten   *to mean, to signify*

Munich specializes in electronics, fashion and sportswear fairs. Peter Sahla talked to Ulrich Probst, press officer for the electronics fairs Systems and Productronica, to find out what makes Munich a **Messestadt**.

1   What four criteria does Ulrich Probst list for measuring the importance of a trade fair?
2   Which of his own questions does he answer?
3   How many fairs does Munich have over a period of three years?
4   What happens every two years?
5   What three reasons does Dr Probst give for the future of Munich as an exhibition centre?

ich . . . bin . . . beschäftigt als   *I . . . am employed . . . as*
am liebsten möcht' ich   *most of all I would like to*
die Zahl der Messen, die   *the number of trade fairs which*
finden Hoch-Technologie-Messen statt   *high-tech trade fairs take place*
aus einem ganz einfachen Grund   *for one very simple reason*
die man sich vorstellen kann   *which you can imagine*
bis hin zum   *through to the*

PRACTICE

Expand your vocabulary by making a note of compound nouns that include a noun you already know. For instance, how many compounds with the word **Messe** have you come across so far? Join it to the following to make compounds: *a* Gesellschaft; *b* Gelände; *c* Fach; *d* Boot; *e* Tag; *f* Stadt; *g* Hoch-Technologie; *h* Zeit.

SAMSTAG IST SYSTEMS-TAG

This advertisement is intended to attract visitors to the Systems fair.

1   How many exhibitors are there?
2   What advantages are given for the trade fair being open on Saturday?
3   How many types of product are mentioned?
4   What are they?

die Dienstleistung   *service*
das Angebot   *offer, range*
die Technik   *engineering, technology*
geöffnet   *open*
geschlossen   *closed*
nützlich   *useful*

Die SYSTEMS 91 ist auch am Samstag geöffnet. Mehr als 1.800 nationale und internationale Aussteller präsentieren ihre neuesten und attraktivsten Produkte. Computer- oder Kommunikationstechnik. Software, Dienstleistungen und das umfassende Angebot an Systemkomponenten, OEM-Produkten und modernster Netzwerktechnologie. Die SYSTEMS zeigt den Stand der Dinge. Auch am Samstag. Ein Tag mehr für ein Plus an Information. Für ein Plus an Kontakten. Für Messe + München. Nützliche Tips erhalten Sie über unser kostenloses SYSTEMS-Service-Telefon. Rufen Sie **01 30 / 85 51 51**.

(Anzeige, Süddeutsche Zeitung)

> **PRACTICE** ▶ German has 'borrowed' many words from other languages. Find the words used in the advertisement for the following indigenous words (if necessary, look up the words in the **Glossary**):   *a* der Rechner; *b* vorstellen;   *c* das Erzeugnis; *d* die Dienstleistung; *e* das Bauteil; *f* zeitgemäß;   *g* der Fernsprecher; *h* die Auskunft; *i* der Ratschlag.

BUSINESS FILE

das Messegelände   *trade fair complex, exhibition centre*
der Markt   *market*
das Schaufenster   *shop window*
ausstellen   *to exhibit*

Trade fairs are serious business in Germany, and presence at the relevant fair is essential for entry into the German market. The main centres are Berlin, Cologne, Düsseldorf, Frankfurt, Hanover and Munich, with Leipzig striking out to become the meeting point of east and west in the new order. The Frankfurter Messe and Hannover-Messe Industrie are exceptional in being broadly-based, since trade fair companies now concentrate on specialist exhibitions. Exhibitors view these fairs not only as an entry into the German market, but also as an international shop window.

As the German market for trade fairs becomes saturated, trade fair companies like the Messe Frankfurt GmbH are now exporting the German trade fair concept to the Far East.

Trade fairs range from the world's largest book fair in Frankfurt, through catering and pet supplies to electronics and printing equipment. The Confederation of German Trade Fair and Exhibition Industries publishes a handbook: AUMA Ausstellungs- und Messe-Ausschuß der Deutschen Wirtschaft e.V., Lindenstraße 8, D-50674 Köln. Tel: (0221) 2 09 07-0. Fax: (0221) 2 09 07-12.

Unser Schaufenster
„Wir machen hier unser Schaufenster. Wir verkaufen sehr viel hier am Stand. Wir verkaufen sehr viel übers Jahr. Wir verkaufen immer nur direkt. Das heißt, wir müssen auf den Messen sein!"
(Aussteller, *Boot Düsseldorf 92*)

4

Deutsche BP, Hamburg

SIE SEHEN HIER...

COMPANIES, PROFILES, TOURS

Peter Sahla visited oil company Deutsche BP and window manufacturer Kaiser Fenster to find out about the companies and their products.

WAS FÜR EINE FIRMA IST DAS?

▶ Give the following facts for BP and Kaiser: *a* location of head office; *b* product;   *c* annual turnover;   *d* number of employees.

Uwe Reif

Eine wichtige Frage

,,Umweltschutz ist für alle Unternehmen heute eine sehr wichtige Frage. BP hat sich frühzeitig ihrer Verantwortung gestellt und dieses Thema aufgegriffen. Die Herausforderungen, die sich daraus ergeben für das Unternehmen, sind immens – entsprechend auch hoch die Aufwendungen dafür."
(Uwe Reif, *Deutsche BP*)

DEUTSCHE BP AKTIENGESELLSCHAFT, HAMBURG

Herr Sahla   Was für eine Firma ist die Deutsche BP?
Herr Reif   Die Deutsche BP ist eine der führenden Mineralölgesellschaften in Deutschland.
Herr Sahla   Was für einen Jahresumsatz hat die Deutsche BP?
Herr Reif   Der Jahresumsatz bewegt sich in der Größenordnung von 13 Milliarden D-Mark.
Herr Sahla   Wieviel Angestellte hat die Deutsche BP, ungefähr?
Herr Reif   Die Deutsche BP hat derzeit rund 6200 Angestellte. Das beinhaltet auch die Mitarbeiter in den Chemie- und Kunststoff-Aktivitäten der Deutschen BP.
Herr Sahla   Der Hauptsitz der Deutschen BP ist hier in Hamburg. Wo haben Sie überall Niederlassungen?
Herr Reif   Die BP hat Niederlassungen ihrer verschiedenen Marketinggesellschaften im gesamten Bundesgebiet.

4 3

der Jahresumsatz *annual turnover*
der Sitz *head office*
die Tochtergesellschaft
  subsidiary
die Niederlassung *branch office*
die Filiale *branch*
das Holz *wood, timber*
das Fenster *window*
verschieden *various, different*
machen *to make, do*
sitzen *to sit, have the head office*
wissen *to know*
schwanken *to fluctuate*

Bruno Kaiser

Herr Sahla Wie heißen Sie?
Herr Kaiser Ich heiße Bruno Kaiser.
Herr Sahla Und was sind Sie von Beruf?
Herr Kaiser Von Beruf bin ich Diplom-Kaufmann.
Herr Sahla Und für welche Firma arbeiten Sie?
Herr Kaiser Ich bin als Geschäftsführer hier in der W. Kaiser GmbH & Co. KG beschäftigt, und wir fertigen Holzfenster und Türen aller Art.
Herr Sahla Und wieviel Mitarbeiter hat Ihre Firma?
Herr Kaiser Sechzehn.
Herr Sahla Und wissen Sie, was der Jahresumsatz ist?
Herr Kaiser Das ist etwas unterschiedlich. Je nach Jahr, er schwankt so zwischen 1,8 und 2,2 Millionen.
Herr Sahla Hat Ihre Firma Filialen?
Herr Kaiser Nein, wir haben nur dieses Einzelunternehmen.
Herr Sahla Wo sitzt Ihr Unternehmen?
Herr Kaiser Die Firma hat ihren Sitz in Köln-Zollstock, in der Brandstraße Nummer 4.

bewegt sich in der Größenordnung von *is roughly in the order of*
das beinhaltet *that includes*
ihrer verschiedenen Marketinggesellschaften *of its various marketing companies*
ich bin als ... beschäftigt *I work as ...*
das ist etwas unterschiedlich *that varies a little*
je nach Jahr *depending on the year*

NUTS AND BOLTS ▶

When talking about the present, remember the verb endings **-(e)t** for the *singular* form with **er/sie/es/man** and **-en** for the *plural* form with **wir/sie/Sie** (see p 145):

> Das beinhalt**et** die Mitarbeiter.
> Die Schott Gruppe entwickel**t**, fertig**t** und vertreib**t** rund 50.000 Artikel.
> Wir fertig**en** Holzfenster und Türen.

You may have noticed that some verbs are used with **sich** in the infinitive: **sich erkundigen, sich bewegen** (lit. *to move oneself*). **Sich** is used with **er, sie, es, man** and with **sie, Sie**. **Mich** is used with **ich**, and **uns** with **wir** (see p 140):

> Der Jahresumsatz **bewegt sich** in der Größenordnung von 13 Milliarden D-Mark.
> Der Wagen **befindet sich** im Parkhaus.
> Ich wollte **mich** bei Ihnen **erkundigen** ...
> Wir haben **uns überlegt**, was wir besser machen können.

To find out more about what you learn in *Nuts and bolts*, look up the page references to the *Grammar* section.

▶

1 **Haben**, **sich bewegen**, **sein**, **schwanken** are used in the interviews with Mr Reif and Mr Kaiser. Which one of the following are they used for? *a* product; *b* company; *c* turnover; *d* employees.

2 Find three ways of describing the location of a company's head office.

3 You need information about a company. Practise asking about:
a type of company; *b* annual turnover; *c* number of employees; *d* location of head office; *e* existence of branches.

4 You're talking to an employee at a large chemical company. Ask her about herself and the company.

Sie ....?

Dr. Wiemer Ich heiße Karin Wiemer.

Sie ....?

Dr. Wiemer Ich bin Apothekerin.

Sie ....?

Dr. Wiemer Ich arbeite für die Firma Stocker Chemie.

Sie ....?

Dr. Wiemer Die Firma Stocker Chemie ist ein führender Chemiekonzern.

Sie ....?

Dr. Wiemer Stocker Chemie hat weltweit 27.000 Angestellte.

Sie ....?

Dr. Wiemer Die Firma hat ihren Hauptsitz in Hamburg.

JETZT GEHEN WIR HIER DURCH

otto bosse.

Carl-Bernd Bosse is managing director of Otto Bosse GmbH & Co. KG, known as OBO. Founded in 1869, the company makes laminated wood products for use in furniture, model-making and environmental technology. Mr Bosse takes Peter Sahla on a tour of the plant.

▶ Find the order in which these are mentioned: *a* loading of presses with resinated logs; *b* stacks of logs; *c* press room; *d* role of heat; *e* filter systems; *f* steam vats; *g* finishing process; *h* source of heat.

Die Stämme werden entrindet

Der Presseraum

Strenge Fertigungskontrollen

die Verarbeitung *processing*
die Endbearbeitung *finishing*
die Anlage *system, installation*
die Fabrik *factory*
die Bestimmung *regulation*
streng *strict*
fertigen *to produce, make*
produzieren *to produce*
erzeugen *to produce*

Herr Bosse Ja, also dieses ist die ... unsere Kraftzentrale. Für die Herstellung von Lagenhölzern braucht man sehr viel Wärme, weil die Hölzer erst gedämpft, dann getrocknet und dann gepreßt werden. Für alle diese Dinge braucht man Wärme. Da sehr viel Holz bei der Verarbeitung als Brennholz anfällt, leben wir autark. Das heißt, unsere Wärme können wir erzeugen mit dem Abfallholz, was bei der Produktion anfällt.

Jetzt gehen wir hier einfach durch, nicht?

Dieses sind die Filteranlagen. Die Bestimmungen in Deutschland für die Abgase sind sehr streng, so daß wir zwei Filtertypen brauchen: einen Zyklonfilter und einen Elektrofilter.

Und jetzt gehen wir da hinten durch ...

Da im Hintergrund sehen wir den Holzvorrat. Da liegen die Stämme alle aufgestapelt und werden im Sommer mit Wasser berieselt, damit sie nicht leiden und nicht platzen. Hier vorne im Vordergrund sind die Dämpfgruben, wo die Stämme reingelegt werden und ein paar Tage gedämpft werden. Dann kommen sie auf diesen Polder, und hier werden sie der Länge nach abgeschnitten, je nach Plattenformat.

So, hier sind wir bei uns in unserem Presseraum, wo die schweren Pressen stehen. Diese schweren Pressen werden mit dem hochgeharzten, phenolgeharzten Material beschickt.

So, dieses ist unsere Endbearbeitung. Hier werden die Platten von allen Seiten besäumt und auch abgeschliffen und kalibriert auf genaue Stärke.

Lagenhölzer *laminated wood*
weil die Hölzer erst gedämpft ... werden *because the logs are first steamed ...*
da sehr viel Holz ... als Brennholz anfällt *as a lot of wood is obtained for firewood ...*
leben wir autark *we're self-sufficient*
daß heißt *that is*
gehen wir hier einfach durch *we'll just go through here*
so daß wir ... brauchen *so that we need ...*
da hinten durch *through over there*
alle aufgestapelt *all stacked up*
werden ... mit Wasser berieselt *are sprinkled with water ...*
wo die Stämme reingelegt werden *into which the logs are laid*
dann kommen sie auf diesen Polder *then they're placed on this platform*
der Länge nach *according to length*
je nach Plattenformat *depending on the size of the panel*
diese schweren Pressen werden ... beschickt *these heavy presses are loaded ...*
hier werden die Platten ... besäumt *here the panels are edged ...*
auf genaue Stärke *to precise thickness*

German and English belong to the same language family, which means many words are similar, eg the German for *water* is **Wasser**. So it's often worth guessing the meaning of a word – but do make sure you check with the **Glossary** or a dictionary.

Notice how Carl Bosse uses the passive (**werden** + past participle) to describe industrial processes (see p 145):

> Die Hölzer **werden** erst **ge**dämp**ft**, dann **ge**trockn**et**.

Some verbs have a vowel change in the past participle, eg **abschneiden** and **abschleifen**:

> Die Stämme werden ab**ge**schn**itt**en.
> Die Platten werden ab**ge**schl**iff**en.

The past participles of these *strong verbs* end in **–en** (see p 143).

1 Find the eleven different past participles which Mr Bosse uses.

2 Now, with the help of the past participles, identify in English the various processes involving   *a* the logs (**Stämme**): three processes; *b* the presses (**Pressen**): one process;   *c* the panels (**Platten**): three processes.   Use the *Glossary* for help.

3 Describe in German what happens to the logs and the panels. Use the passive: *a* Hölzer/dämpfen;   *b* Hölzer/trocknen; *c* Hölzer/pressen;   *d* Platten/besäumen;   *e* Platten/abschleifen; *f* Platten/kalibrieren.

4 How does Mr Bosse: *a* ask his visitor to come through;   *b* point out that something is in the background;   *c* point out that something is in the foreground?

5 Now give a short presentation in German on the manufacturing process at Otto Bosse, based on the key points *a–h* listed in the questions marked ▶ before the tour (in the right order).

EIN JUNGGEBLIEBENES UNTERNEHMEN

Joachim Esche

[3] Joachim Esche, a dispensing chemist by training, is director of international operations for Europe and Australasia with chemical company Schering.

▶ Find the following information about the company and its history: *a* sector;   *b* number of employees worldwide;   *c* annual turnover; *d* age of company;   *e* founder;   *f* location of original pharmacy.

SCHERING AG, CHEMIEKONZERN, BERLIN

Herr Sahla Wie heißen Sie, bitte?
Dr. Esche Ich heiße Joachim Esche.
Herr Sahla Und was sind Sie von Beruf?
Dr. Esche Von der Ausbildung her bin ich Apotheker.
Herr Sahla Und für welche Firma sind Sie jetzt tätig?
Dr. Esche Für die Firma Schering AG in Berlin.

die Branche	*sector*
das Erzeugnis	*product*
der Stoff	*material*
die Ausbildung	*training*
die Geschichte	*history*
der Gründer	*founder*
tätig	*active*
vertreiben	*to sell, market*
ausbilden	*to train*
gründen	*to found*
sich entwickeln	*to develop*

Schering AG, Berlin

Herr Sahla In welcher Branche ist diese Firma Schering tätig?

Dr. Esche Die Firma Schering ist tätig in der Branche Chemie, Pharmazie. Wir verstehen uns als Unternehmen, was Pharmazeutika herstellt und vertreibt, Pflanzenschutzmittel, galvanotechnische Erzeugnisse, Industriechemikalien und auch Naturstoffe.

Herr Sahla Und für welchen Bereich sind Sie zuständig?

Dr. Esche Für den Pharmabereich.

Herr Sahla Wie viele Mitarbeiter hat die Firma?

Dr. Esche Also, weltweit haben wir etwa 27.000 Mitarbeiter.

Herr Sahla Und was für einen Umsatz?

Dr. Esche Wir haben einen Umsatz etwa von 6,3 Milliarden Deutsche Mark.

Herr Sahla Können Sie mir ein ganz klein bißchen die Geschichte von Schering umreißen?

Dr. Esche Ja. Schering ist jetzt über 120 Jahre auf der Welt, aber ich hoffe, daß es trotzdem ein junggebliebenes Unternehmen ist. Es ist mal gegründet worden von einem Apotheker, Ernst Schering, der im Gebiete des heutigen Ostberlins die sogenannte Grüne Apotheke gegründet hat. Und aus dieser Apotheke heraus hat sich letztlich die ganze Firma Schering entwickelt.

wir verstehen uns als Unternehmen, was	*we see ourselves as a company which*
können Sie mir . . . umreißen?	*can you outline . . . for me?*
ein ganz klein bißchen	*very briefly*
über 120 Jahre	*more than 120 years*
auf der Welt	*in existence* (lit. *in the world*)
ich hoffe, daß	*I hope that*
es ist mal gegründet worden	*it was founded*
von einem Apotheker	*by a pharmacist*
der . . . gegründet hat	*who founded . . .*
hat sich . . . entwickelt	*. . . developed*

NUTS AND BOLTS ▶

Notice how **anfallen, betragen, geben, sehen** and **laufen** change the vowel in the **er, sie, es, man** form of the present tense (see p 143):

was bei der Produktion **anfällt**

Der Weltumsatz **beträgt** über 2 Milliarden D-Mark.

Wieviel Messen **gibt** es?

Wie **sieht**'s aus?

Wie **läuft** es?

Check the *Glossary* to see how the vowel changes of these verbs are indicated.

Notice the German conventions for writing decimals and thousands:

6,3 Milliarden (sechs Komma drei)

27.000 Mitarbeiter (siebenundzwanzigtausend)

The comma is used for decimals and the stop to indicate thousands.

Bürokratie und Ordnung

,,Aus meiner Erfahrung ist es so, daß gerade bei großen deutschen Firmen auf Bürokratie und Ordnung sehr viel Wert gelegt wird." (Matthias Hölscher, *Psion GmbH*)

der Besuch *visit*
der Besucherausweis *visitor's pass*
besuchen *to visit*
abgeben *to give up, surrender*

1 How would you say that a number is approximate? *a* Wir haben .... 27.000 Mitarbeiter; *b* Der Umsatz beträgt .... 6,3 Milliarden D-Mark.

2 Give a short profile of Dr Esche in German and include the following facts: *a* profession; *b* company; *c* area of responsibility.

3 Give a short presentation on Schering based on: *a* Sitz; *b* Branche; *c* Tätigkeit; *d* Mitarbeiterzahl; *e* Umsatz; *f* Gründer; *g* Ort der Gründung.

4 Look at the information requested for the visitor's pass at Schering. Work out how you'd fill in sections *a–f* if you had visited Mr Scheipl at Stahlgruber, arriving at 9.30 and leaving at 13.10.

5 What does the pass also ask you to do?

6 How long is the pass valid for?

Visitors take note
The receptionist at Schering gave Peter Sahla a visitor's pass. Some companies may ask you to surrender your ID card or passport during your visit.

Practise finding out about a company, giving information on your company, and taking a visitor on a company tour.

Type of company, head office, subsidiaries and sector
Was für eine Firma ist die Deutsche BP?
Wo ist der Hauptsitz der Firma?
Haben Sie Tochtergesellschaften/Niederlassungen/Filialen?
In welcher Branche ist diese Firma tätig?

Company turnover and number of employees
Was für einen Jahresumsatz hat/macht die Firma?
Was ist der Jahresumsatz der Firma?
Wie viele Angestellte/Mitarbeiter hat die Firma?

Location of head office and subsidiaries
Der Hauptsitz ist in Hamburg.
Die Firma hat ihren Sitz in Köln.
Wir haben zwei Niederlassungen/Tochtergesellschaften.

Say what kind of company you are
Wir verstehen uns als Unternehmen, was/das Pharmazeutika
    herstellt/vertreibt.

Annual turnover and number of employees
Wir haben einen Umsatz von etwa/über 500 Millionen.
Der Jahresumsatz bewegt sich in der Größenordnung von...
Die Firma hat 6200 Angestellte.

On a tour of the plant...
... point out something
Dies(es) ist/sind...
Da (im Vordergrund/Hintergrund) sehen wir...
Hier vorne ist/sind...

... lead someone through
Jetzt gehen wir hier durch.

... give a location
Hier sind wir im/in der...

... and describe a process
Das Holz wird gedämpft.
Die Stämme werden abgeschnitten.
Die Pressen werden beschickt.
Die Platten werden kalibriert.

Use the *Checklist* survival kit to take a visitor round your own company.

1 Complete these sentences with the past participles of the verbs given in brackets. Separable prefixes are in italics.

a Diese Produkte werden in Frankreich .... und .... (*her*stellen, verkaufen)

b Die Boote werden .... und .... (polieren, *sauber*machen)

c Diese Computer werden auf der Productronica .... (präsentieren)

d Das Holz wird ...., ... und dann .... (dämpfen, trocknen, pressen)

e Die Wärme wird mit dem Abfallholz .... (erzeugen)

f Bei der W. Kaiser GmbH werden Holzfenster .... (fertigen)

g Schering ist von einem Apotheker .... worden. (gründen)

h Schering hat sich aus dieser Apotheke heraus .... (entwickeln)

2 From the following verbs, form nouns ending with **–ung** and add the appropriate definite article: *a* ordnen; *b* leisten; *c* führen; *d* bearbeiten; *e* bilden.

3 Keeping to the same order, combine the nouns from *Review 2* with the following to make compound nouns. An **s** or **n** may be needed to join two words. In *d* you'll need to drop a letter. Remember that nouns begin with a capital, and give the gender of each compound:

a Größe; *b* Dienst; *c* Geschäft; *d* Ende; *e* aus.

4 Now give a visitor a short tour of the production facilities at Kaiser Fenster, based on the photos and the following points:

a Your name; W. Kaiser GmbH & Co. KG; fertigen, Holzfenster; gehen, durch.

b hier, Endbearbeitung; hier, Fenster, abgeschliffen.

c dieses, unsere Lackierhalle; hier, Fenster, lackiert.

d hier, Fenster, gelagert (*stored*).

a

b

c

d

Loan words

German has a large number of words 'borrowed' from other languages, especially English. Here are a few examples.

Masculine	Feminine	Neuter
der Moment	die Produktion	das Telefon
der Tourismus	die Technologie	das System
der Computer	die Software	das Management

Some Germans complain about the extensive use of English words in business and leisure, and by young people. But you can make the most of these words you already know!

Definite article

The definite article (**der**, **die**, **das**: see p 139) has several forms:

> Was ist **der** Jahresumsatz **der** Firma?
>
> im Gebiete **des** heutigen Ostberlins
>
> Da im Hintergrund sehen wir **den** Holzvorrat.

The form depends on whether a noun is *masculine*, *feminine* or *neuter*, whether it's *singular* or *plural*, but also on whether it's the *subject*, the *direct object* or the *indirect object* of the sentence (see p 146).

Don't worry too much if you get the form wrong when speaking; it'll probably still be perfectly clear what you're saying. When listening or reading, just remember that **der**, **die**, **das**, **den**, **des**, **dem** may mean *of the*, *to the*, or *from the*, rather than simply *the*.

On their own without a noun, **der**, **die**, **das**, **den**, **des**, **dem** may be acting as a pronoun, meaning (*of/to/from*) *it/this/that* (see p 140).

The past

You can talk about the past using either the *perfect* or the *past tense*. In spoken German, the *perfect* is more usual. Most verbs form the perfect with **haben**, but some common verbs use **sein**:

> Ich **habe** ein Zimmer **bestellt**.
>
> Diese Firma **ist** 1929 **entstanden**.

The past tense is used more in written German; you'll find some examples of it in the Stahlgruber brochure on p 54. For the forms see p 145.

Past participles

These can be used to form the perfect tense, or a passive construction with **werden** (see p 143):

> Ernst Schering **hat** die Grüne Apotheke **gegründet**.
>
> Die Hölzer **werden gedämpft**, **getrocknet** und **gepreßt**.

Peter Sahla visited the head office of automotive accessories chain Stahlgruber in Munich and was given a company tour by advertising manager Walter Scheipl.

1 List the departments and areas in the order in which they're visited:
a Ausbildung; *b* Empfang; *c* Buchhaltung; *d* Verkauf;
e Telefonzentrale; *f* Personalabteilung; *g* Konferenzraum;
h Geschäftsleitung; *i* Einkauf; *j* Rechtsabteilung;
k Datenverarbeitungszentrale; *l* Exportabteilung; *m* Hauptkasse.
2 Is the export department one of the *a* smallest; *b* most important; *c* largest departments in the company?
3 What's going on in the offices in the export department?
4 What kind of employee does the export department have a lot of?
5 How many countries does Stahlgruber have representatives in?
6 Why is Mr Scheipl unable to explain about data processing?
7 Which department shares the same floor as the personnel department?

die Verwaltung *administration*	
die Geschäftsleitung *(board of) management*	
die Abteilung *department*	
der Vertrieb *sales (department)*	
die Exportabteilung *export department*	
der Einkauf *purchasing department*	
der Verkauf *sales (department)*	
die Rechtsabteilung *legal department*	
die Datenverarbeitungszentrale *data-processing centre*	
die Buchhaltung *accounts department*	
die Personalabteilung *personnel department*	
der Empfang *reception*	
die Telefonzentrale *switchboard*	
der Konferenzraum *conference room*	

entsprechend der Bedeutung der   *in accordance with the importance of the*
in allen wird telefoniert   *people are phoning in all of them*
in der Sprache des betreffenden Landes   *in the language of the country concerned*
mit niedrigen Wänden abgetrennt   *divided by low partitions*
dieser Abteilung angeschlossen   *next to this department*
um ... zu halten   *in order to keep...*
ganz in der Nähe   *nearby*
auf keinen Fall verzichten kann   *can't do without under any circumstances*
die ... einnimmt   *which takes up...*
ich ... verstehe zu wenig von   *... I know too little about*
um Ihnen ... geben zu können   *to be able to give you...*
sowohl der ... als auch der   *both of the ... and of the*
wie es heute heißt   *as they're called nowadays*
schneiden in der Regel ... sehr gut ab   *generally do very well...*

The pronunciation of vowels and consonants varies widely between north and south and you'll need to get used to a Bavarian accent like that of Mr Scheipl. By tuning in to the different accents, you'll be prepared for the variety you'll meet in Germany.

NUTS AND BOLTS

In English, the subject of a sentence normally comes before the verb. If a German sentence starts with something other than the subject, the verb stays in second place and the subject comes after it (see p 147):

Sie **sehen** hier...
Hier **sehen** Sie...

German companies generally make a lot of their history and achievements. This brochure gives facts and figures on Stahlgruber.

Give the following facts about the company: *a* year of foundation; *b* original two activities; *c* present owners; *d* number of production facilities; *e* sales outlets in Germany and Austria; *f* number of subsidiaries; *g* number of countries where Stahlgruber is active; *h* annual turnover.

die Zentrale *head office*
das Werk *works, factory*
die Fabrik *factory*
das Verkaufshaus *sales outlet*
das Tochterunternehmen
   subsidiary
die Vertretung *agent,*
   representative, sales office
das Programm *programme,*
   product range
der Kunde *customer*
die Kundin *customer (f.)*
der Verbraucher *consumer*
beraten *to advise*
betreuen *to take care of*
beschäftigen *to employ*

Geschichtliches

Im Jahre 1923 wurde die Firma Otto Gruber & Co. gegründet, die neben Handelsaktivitäten auch in Eigenproduktion Hebebühnen und Kompressoren herstellte. Durch dieses Programm kam es zur Namensverbindung STAHLGRUBER.
Die Firmengründer vererbten die Firma 1969 einer Anzahl langjähriger, bewährter Mitarbeiter.

Was ist TIP TOP STAHLGRUBER heute?

Das Unternehmen wird heute in der Rechtsform einer GmbH & Co. KG geführt.
In der Zentrale München, in 8 Werken und in 32 Verkaufshäusern in Bayern, Sachsen, Thüringen und in Österreich werden zur Zeit rund 2.600 Mitarbeiter beschäftigt. Dazu kommen noch rund 1.000 Mitarbeiter, die in derzeit 16 ausländischen Tochterunternehmen die Kunden beraten und betreuen. Den weltweiten Erfolg des Unternehmens dokumentieren Vertretungen in über 140 Ländern der Welt und ein Jahres-Weltumsatz von über 800 Millionen DM.

(Stahlgruber 2000, Stahlgruber GmbH & Co.)

Don't be discouraged by words you don't understand immediately – you can't expect to get everything right first time round. Look back through any words and expressions that are explained, read **Nuts and bolts**, check the **Glossary**, and then go over the German again. If it's still not clear, leave it and move on. You'll find it will fall into place with time!

die ... herstellte *which produced ...*
durch dieses Programm kam es zur *this product range gave rise to the*
vererbten ... einer Anzahl *left ... to a number of*
in der Rechtsform einer *in the legal structure of a*
Mitarbeiter, die ... die Kunden beraten und betreuen *employees who advise and*
   look after the customers ...

A particular point can be placed in front of the verb for emphasis, and the subject of the sentence then follows the verb (see p 147):

> Den weltweiten Erfolg des Unternehmens **dokumentieren** Vertretungen in über 140 Ländern.
>
> *Agencies in more than 140 countries **demonstrate** the world-wide success of the company.*

The verb remains the second element. In German, cases show which is the subject (*nominative case*) and which the direct object (*accusative case*): here, **den weltweiten Erfolg (des Unternehmens)** is the direct object.

1 Name one of Stahlgruber's founders.
2 Why was the company called Stahlgruber?
3 What's the function of the foreign subsidiaries?
4 Give a short presentation on Stahlgruber, using the verbs **sein, es gibt, beschäftigen, haben, haben, machen**, in that order, and including the following information: *a* the location of head office; *b* the number of: *i* sales outlets in Bavaria, Saxony, Thuringia and Austria, *ii* employees there, *iii* foreign subsidiaries, *iv* countries with representatives; *c* the annual turnover worldwide.

„AUF DAS RADIO mag praktisch kein Autofahrer mehr verzichten. Das Sicherheits-Bremssystem ABS dagegen findet sich bislang noch erst in wenigen Autos."
(Süddeutsche Zeitung)

Beliebte Auto-Extras
Von je 100 Pkw haben als Sonderausstattung:

Radio 94

44	Metallic-Lack
35	Schiebedach
28	Servolenkung
26	Zentralverriegelung
26	Wärmedämmendes Glas
22	Breitreifen
21	Leichtmetallräder
12	Automatik
12	Anhängerkupplung
10	Elektrische Fensterheber
8	ABS

Quelle: DAT

© Globus 9133

? Which extra does virtually no driver want to do without?

die Aktiengesellschaft (AG)
  *public company, joint-stock
  company* (comparable with Plc)
die Gesellschaft mit beschränkter
  Haftung (GmbH) *private
  company* (comparable with Ltd)
die Aktie *share*
der Aufsichtsrat *supervisory board*
der Vorstand *board of management*
die Kommanditgesellschaft
  (KG) *limited partnership*
der Gesellschafter *shareholder,
  partner*
der Komplementär *general
  partner, personally liable
  partner*
der Kommanditist *limited
  partner*
der/die Angestellte *employee*
der Betriebsrat *works council*

Once you've got to the end of a unit, don't assume you've finished with it! Go over it again at a later stage to remind yourself of what you've learnt.

Shares in an **Aktiengesellschaft (AG)** have a stock-market listing, whereas shares in a **Gesellschaft mit beschränkter Haftung (GmbH)** are not available for purchase by outside investors. In an **AG**, the board of management is responsible for running the company and reports to the supervisory board, which is made up of representatives of shareholders and employees. A **GmbH** is headed by a managing director. **GmbH** may be represented as **mbH** if **Gesellschaft** is part of the company name, as in **Messegesellschaft mbH**.

The **Kommanditgesellschaft (KG)** is a partnership with limited liability. It has one or more personally liable partners and at least one partner whose liability is limited to the amount of capital invested. The **GmbH & Co. KG** is a type of limited partnership in which the limited liability company (**GmbH**) is the general partner, and one or more individuals are the limited partners (usually shareholders in the **GmbH**).

Employees in companies with a workforce of five or more full-time employees can set up a works council which is legally obliged to act in accordance with the company's well-being.

Company hierarchy in Germany tends to be vertically structured, with closely defined areas of responsibility. Management style has a reputation for being relatively risk-averse.

All companies are under a legal obligation to belong to their local chamber of commerce. These august institutions represent the interests of the local economy, advise businesses, and are charged with overseeing the country's training system. They also give advice free of charge to foreign companies wishing to import goods. The Federation of German Chambers of Industry and Commerce will put you in touch with the local chamber of the area you are interested in. Contact: Deutscher Industrie- und Handelstag, Adenauerallee 148, D-53113 Bonn. Tel.: (0228) 10 40.   Fax: (0228) 10 41 58.

Dresden

ZUM WOHL!

OPINIONS, HOBBIES, ENTERTAINING

Meeting people isn't just about business. You need to be able to talk about yourself, give opinions and entertain your contacts.

MEINE FREIZEIT

Claudia Birnbaum

Claudia Birnbaum and Thomas Barth are trainees at the Dresdner Bank. They talked to Kerstin Wachholz about their home town and leisure pursuits.

► Find the *a* age *b* home town *c* hobbies of the trainees interviewed.

die Heimat	*home country/town*
die Freizeit	*leisure*
das Hobby	*hobby*
das Kino	*cinema*
die Disko	*disco*
der Sport	*sport(s)*
der Fußball	*football*
die Kunst	*art*
die Musik	*music*
das Lesen	*reading*
lesen	*to read*
lieben	*to love*

DRESDNER BANK AG, DRESDEN

Frau Wachholz   Können Sie sich bitte einmal vorstellen?
Frau Birnbaum   Also, ich heiße Claudia Birnbaum, bin 18 Jahre alt und komm' hier aus Dresden.
Frau Wachholz   Was für Hobbys haben Sie?
Frau Birnbaum   Eh, die meiste Zeit – meine Freizeit – bin ich mit meinen Freunden zusammen ... gehen irgendwohin, ins Kino, zur Disko. Und ich bin 'ne absolute Leseratte, also ich lese sehr gern, ich mag Literatur.

DRESDNER BANK AG, DRESDEN

Herr Barth   Ich heiße Thomas Barth. Ich bin 16 Jahre alt und komme aus Dresden.
Frau Wachholz   Was für Hobbys haben Sie?

Thomas Barth

Herr Barth   Meine Hobbys sind Sport, Lesen – bei Sport speziell Handball und Fußball.

Frau Wachholz   Wie finden Sie die Stadt Dresden?

Herr Barth   Also, als Dresdner liebe ich natürlich meine Stadt aus verschiedenen Gründen. Natürlich, da sie auch eine Kunststadt ist: viele Bauwerke, viele berühmte Bauwerke. Aber ich liebe auch die Menschen in Dresden. Also, es ist meine Heimat, und ich fühle mich sehr zu Dresden hingezogen.

können Sie sich . . . einmal vorstellen?   *can you . . . introduce yourself?*
die meiste Zeit   *most of the time*
ich lese sehr gern   *I love reading*
aus verschiedenen Gründen   *for various reasons*
ich fühle mich . . . hingezogen   *I feel drawn . . .*

NUTS AND BOLTS ▶

If you need to think about how to express something, don't rush. Listen to the sounds or expressions Germans use when hesitating, and get used to saying **eh** or **hm** or **also** to give yourself time to think.

Notice how Claudia Birnbaum and Thomas Barth make a point and then explain it, or repeat it with more detail:

> Ich bin eine absolute Leseratte, also ich lese sehr gern, ich mag Literatur.
> die meiste Zeit – meine Freizeit
> viele Bauwerke, viele berühmte Bauwerke
> Meine Hobbys sind Sport, Lesen – bei Sport speziell Handball und Fußball.

Spoken language tends to have more 'redundancy' than written language – repeated words, ideas expressed more than once in different ways, filler words and hesitations.

PRACTICE ▶

1 You're attending a 'get to know' session before a seminar and have to introduce yourself. Give your: *a* name; *b* age; *c* home town; *d* job; *e* area of responsibility; *f* company; *g* hobbies.

2 Which hobbies do Claudia Birnbaum and Thomas Barth mention?

3 Which is the odd one out: *a* der Handball; *b* der Sport; *c* das Tennis; *d* der Fußball; *e* das Golf?

4 Find at least three ways in which the trainees say they like (doing) something.

5 How could you say you like: *a* reading; *b* working; *c* driving (**fahren**)?

6 Say you love: *a* your home town; *b* literature; *c* music.

Regional loyalty

Regional loyalties have contributed to a rather static population in Germany, although there has been considerable pressure from east Germans seeking to move to higher wages in the more affluent western part of the country.

ICH HÄTTE GERN EINEN FENSTERPLATZ

Alessandra Folco phones to book a restaurant table for Mr Harms.

Listen for the main points that the waiter needs to know:
a Datum; *b* Tag; *c* Zeit; *d* Personenzahl; *e* Sonderwünsche;
f auf den Namen von...

der Tisch *table*
die Ecke *corner*
die Woche *week*
der Geschäftsmann *businessman*
die Geschäftsfrau *businesswoman*
die Geschäftsleute (*pl.*) *business people*
ruhig *quiet*
laut *noisy, loud*

DEUTSCHE BP AKTIENGESELLSCHAFT, HAMBURG

Frau Folco Ja, Deutsche BP, Folco ist mein Name, schönen guten Tag! Ich hätte gern einen Tisch reserviert für nächste Woche Freitag, den dreizehnten zwölften.

Kellner Ja, wo möchten Sie bitte sitzen?

Frau Folco Also, ich hätte gern schon einen Fensterplatz. Das ist für vier Personen. Und das sind vier Geschäftsleute, und ich möchte sie gern in einer ruhigeren Ecke unterbringen.

Kellner Ja. Soll ich den Tisch auf Ihren Namen reservieren?

Frau Folco Nein, auf den Namen von Herrn Harms.

Kellner Herr Harms...

Frau Folco Ja? Und um 18 Uhr.

Kellner Für wie viele Personen?

Frau Folco Für vier Personen. Ja?

Kellner Das geht in Ordnung.

Frau Folco Gut. Vielen Dank. Auf Wiederhören!

Kellner Auf Wiederhören!

NUTS AND BOLTS

Notice how Ms Folco gives the date:
> für nächste Woche, d**en** dreizehnt**en** zwölft**en**

After the preposition **für** you always need the accusative ending (see p 142).

Remember that the 1st, 2nd, 3rd are represented in figures with a full stop: **1.**, **2.**, **3**.

The preposition **um** is used to specify a time (see p 148):
> Ich hätte gern einen Tisch reserviert, um 18 Uhr.
> Um wieviel Uhr...? *At what time...?*

PRACTICE

1 How would you ask *At what time is the appointment* (**der Termin**)?
2 Use **ich hätte gern** to say you'd like: *a* eine Karte; *b* einen Sitzplatz; *c* ein Zimmer; *d* einen Tisch.
3 Ring up a restaurant and make the following booking: *a* a table for six; *b* at seven o'clock; *c* in your name.
4 Say you'd like a table for: *a* Friday, 13.11, at 7 pm; *b* Wednesday, 30.6, at 8.30 pm; *c* Monday, 2.4, at 12 noon; *d* Saturday, 20.7, at 12.30 pm; *e* Tuesday, 4.3, at 7.45 pm; *f* Thursday, 18.5, at 8 pm.

Guten Appetit!

Gerrit Neuhaus has invited Peter Sahla and two business colleagues, Constanze and Christian Magunna, to lunch at the **Funk-Restaurant** in Munich.

DER APERITIF

▶ **1** How many different drinks are mentioned?

2 True or false? *a* Alle trinken Champagner als Aperitif; *b* Herr Neuhaus trinkt kein Mineralwasser.

 FUNK-RESTAURANT, MÜNCHEN

Herr Neuhaus	Tag!
Empfangsdame	Bitte?
Herr Neuhaus	Neuhaus. Ich habe einen Tisch bestellt . . . Danke.
Empfangsdame	(*Shows him to a table*) Ich hoffe, der sagt Ihnen zu.
Herr Neuhaus	Ja, wunderbar! Danke schön!

(*Menus are handed round*)

Herr Neuhaus	Danke schön! So. Möchte jemand einen Aperitif?
Herr Sahla	Ja, ich schon.
Frau Magunna	Ja.
Herr Magunna	Ja, gerne.
Herr Neuhaus	So, und was? (*Studies the list*) Also, da gibt es einen Port, einen Sherry, Cinzano, Campari, Pernod . . .
Herr Magunna	Oder wie wär's mit einem Glas Sekt?
Herr Neuhaus	(*To waitress*) Also, gibt es einen Champagner? Glas Champagner?
Kellnerin	Ja, Champagner, ja.
Herr Neuhaus	Gut. Ja? Eins, zwei, drei. Und ich hätte gern nur ein Mineralwasser, bitte.
Kellnerin	Ja, gern.

der Aperitif *aperitif*
das Glas *glass*
der Sekt *sparkling wine*
der Saft *juice*
das Mineralwasser *mineral water*
wunderbar *wonderful*

Remember, you don't have to say everything perfectly, understand every word or be a genius at languages in order to communicate. Just think about what you want to say first and then start talking!

der sagt Ihnen zu *you like it*
möchte jemand . . . ? *would anyone like . . . ?*
da gibt es *there's*
wie wär's mit . . . ? *what about . . . ?*

NUTS AND BOLTS ▶

The German equivalent for *there is* and *there are* is **es gibt**:
   Es gibt einen Port, einen Sherry . . .
   Gibt es einen Champagner?

DIE SPEISEKARTE

True or false? *a* Die Riesencrevetten sind ein Hauptgericht; *b* Herr und Frau Magunna bestellen Feldsalat und Kalbssteak.

FUNK-RESTAURANT, MÜNCHEN
(The waitress serves the drinks)

Herr Neuhaus Danke schön...
Kellnerin Zum Wohl!
Herr Neuhaus Danke.
Kellnerin Haben Sie schon etwas gewählt?
Herr Neuhaus So, dann wollen wir doch mal schauen. Wer nimmt jetzt was? Bitte?
Frau Magunna Dann möcht' ich bitte einmal den Feldsalat mit rohen Champignons und den Riesencrevetten. Und als Hauptgericht nehm' ich das Kalbssteak auf Basilikumsoße.
Herr Neuhaus So, und?
Herr Magunna Ich glaube, ich werd' mich dem anschließen, ich hätte auch gern den Feldsalat mit den Riesencrevetten und das Kalbssteak...
(And once they've finished ordering)
Herr Neuhaus Zum Wohl!
Herr Magunna Zum Wohl! Vielen Dank für die Einladung!
Herr Neuhaus Ja. Vielen Dank! Danke. Ich freue mich, daß Sie gekommen sind.

die Speisekarte *menu*
das Hauptgericht *main course*
die Einladung *invitation*
zum Wohl! *cheers!*
guten Appetit! *enjoy your meal!*
wählen *to choose*
nehmen *to take*
glauben *to think, believe*
sich anschließen *to follow, do/have the same*
sich freuen *to be pleased*

wollen wir *let's*
nehm' ich *I'll have*
ich werd' mich dem anschließen *I'll have the same*
ich freue mich, daß *I'm pleased that*

NUTS AND BOLTS

Daß (*that*) signals the start of a *subordinate clause*, in which the verb comes at the end (see p 147):

> Ich freue mich, **daß** Sie gekommen **sind**.
> *I am pleased **that** you **have** come.*

Notice also in that sentence that **kommen**, like some other verbs, forms the perfect with **sein** rather than **haben** (see p 144).

Eating patterns
Meal times in Germany tend to be early. Breakfast in a hotel is generally served from 6.30 am onwards. Many employees have a 'second breakfast' between 9 am and 10 am. Lunch starts at noon. The traditional German supper, generally cold with sausage and cheese, is around 6 pm, though eating patterns are now becoming more varied.

das Frühstück *breakfast*
das zweite Frühstück *second breakfast*
das Mittagessen *lunch*
Kaffee und Kuchen *coffee and cakes*
das Abendessen *supper*
Mahlzeit! *enjoy your meal!*

DIE GETRÄNKEKARTE

▶ Which is true?   Fendant ist ein   *a* Rotwein   *b* Weißwein   *c* Rosé.

FUNK–RESTAURANT, MÜNCHEN

Herr Neuhaus   Ja, was trinken wir zum Essen? Weiß oder rot oder überhaupt keinen Wein?
Herr Magunna   Zu den Crevetten vielleicht einen trocknen Weißwein.
Frau Magunna   Ja, würd' ich eigentlich sagen.
Herr Neuhaus   Deutschen, Schweizer, italienischen oder französischen? Trocken oder nicht so trocken?
Frau Magunna   Also, ich lieber trocken.
Herr Sahla   Wie wär's, wenn wir mal den Fendant probieren . . . ?
Herr Magunna   Ja, sehr gerne.
Herr Neuhaus   Ja, gut! Dann nehmen wir doch . . . einen 89er Fendant. Gut. (*To waitress*) Danke schön! Wir hätten gerne eine Flasche von dem Fendant.
Kellnerin   Gerne.
Herr Neuhaus   Danke.

das Essen	*meal, food*
das Getränk	*drink*
die Getränkekarte	*wine list*
der Wein	*wine*
das Bier	*beer, lager*
weiß	*white*
rot	*red*
trocken	*dry*
lieblich	*sweet (for wine)*
lieber	*preferably*
essen	*to eat*
trinken	*to drink*

NUTS AND BOLTS

▶ Notice how **kein** is used as a negative to say *not a* or *no*:
   Weiß oder rot oder überhaupt **keinen** Wein?
Kein has the same endings as **ein** (see p 139).

DIE RECHNUNG

▶ True or false?   Herr Neuhaus braucht keine Quittung.

FUNK–RESTAURANT, MÜNCHEN

Herr Neuhaus   So, darf's denn noch irgend etwas sein?
Frau Magunna   Nein.
Herr Neuhaus   Gut. In Ordnung.
Frau Magunna   Es war sehr lecker.
Herr Magunna   Köstlich.
Herr Neuhaus   (*To waitress*) Kann ich zahlen, bitte?
Kellnerin   Ja.
Herr Neuhaus   So. Sagen Sie, nehmen Sie Kreditkarten?
Kellnerin   Ja.
Herr Neuhaus   Danke. So, danke schön. Machen Sie mir dann bitte noch eine Quittung? Danke. (*He's given the receipt*) So, herzlichen Dank, danke schön. (*To his guests*) Ich danke herzlich.
Herr Magunna   Ja, vielen Dank!
Herr Neuhaus   Es war nett.

die Rechnung	*bill*
die Quittung	*receipt*
nett	*nice*
köstlich	*delicious*
lecker	*delicious*

| To attract someone's attention, simply say **Entschuldigen Sie, bitte!**

NUTS AND BOLTS ▶

Keine Kreditkarte

„Also, ich persönlich habe noch keine Kreditkarte, aber die Kreditkarte ist sicher eine sehr feine Angelegenheit. Ich hab's jetzt bemerkt, wie ich in England war, und Kollegen sich am Sonntag aus dem Bankautomaten die Pfunde haben auszahlen lassen. Das hat mich sehr beeindruckt. Ich werde mir demnächst eine zulegen." (Guntram Kraus, *Deutsche Telekom*)

PRACTICE ▶

die Vorspeise   *starter, hors-d'œuvre*
die Nachspeise   *dessert*
der Nachtisch   *dessert*
das Fleisch   *meat*
der Fisch   *fish*
die Beilage   *side dish*
das Gemüse   *vegetable(s)*
der Salat   *salad (also lettuce)*
der Pfeffer   *pepper*
das Salz   *salt*

Ein kleines Trinkgeld

„Es ist durchaus üblich, in Deutschland in Restaurants, aber auch beim Friseur zum Beispiel, ein kleines Trinkgeld zu geben." (Hartmut Schmidt, *Berliner Verkehrsbetriebe*)

An adjective used after the verb **sein** has no additional ending:
Es **war** sehr **lecker**.

But an ending is added when an adjective comes before a noun:
für nächst**e** Woche
schön**en** gut**en** Tag
unser kostenlos**es** Service-Telefon

The ending varies according to the gender, number and case of the noun described by the adjective (see p 141).

Notice the ending **–en** used in front of masculine nouns in the *accusative case*:
Ich möchte d**en** Feldsalat.
Ich hätte gern ein**en** Fensterplatz.
Wir trinken ein**en** trockn**en** Weißwein.
Wir trinken kein**en** Wein.

1   You have to host a dinner at a restaurant. Practise your role beforehand: *a* say you've ordered a table;   *b* offer your guests an aperitif;   *c* ask for the menu;   *d* ask who'd like what;   *e* ask about wine with the meal;   *f* suggest a German wine;   *g* order a **Vorspeise (Melone)**, **Hauptgericht (Schweinefilet)** and **Wein (Mosel, '91)**;   *h* say you'd like to pay;   *i* ask if credit cards are accepted;   *j* ask for a receipt;   *k* thank your guests for coming.
2   A colleague has invited you for an evening meal. Say it was enjoyable and thank him or her for the invitation.
3   Gerrit Neuhaus uses the modal verbs   *a* können;   *b* dürfen;   *c* wollen.   Look for the form of each and the verb that goes with it.
4   Say you don't want the following, using **Ich möchte . . . .** Depending on gender and whether it's singular or plural, use **keinen** (*m.*), **keine** (*f.* and *pl.*), or **kein** (*n.*):   *a* wine;   *b* an aperitif;   *c* a starter;   *d* a main course;   *e* a dessert;   *f* mushrooms;   *g* beer;   *h* prawns;   *i* vegetables.
5   You're outlining the wine list and menu to your guests. Say there is/are the following: *a* port;   *b* sherry;   *c* Cinzano;   *d* Campari;   *e* sparkling wine;   *f* mineral water;   *g* salad;   *h* mushrooms;   *i* steak.

Tipping

In a café it's common to round up your bill to the nearest mark, possibly adding 50 pfennigs or a mark on top. In restaurants, service is generally included and an extra 5% would be regarded as a reasonable tip. The tip is given to the waiter or waitress with the money for the meal rather than left on the table. In taxis, a tip of 10% would be normal.

The **Glossary** gives details of the gender and plurals of nouns and the different parts of verbs with translations relating to the contexts in which they appear in **German means Business**. If you look up a word in a dictionary, you may find a variety of meanings for any one word. Often the different meanings will be accompanied by some indication of context, so look for a translation which matches what you want to say.

Practise talking about yourself and your interests, ordering a meal and entertaining your guests.

Give your age
Ich bin 40 Jahre alt.

Say where you're from
Ich komme aus Washington.
Wir kommen aus Sydney.

Give your leisure pursuits
Mein Hobby ist Lesen.
Meine Hobbys sind Golf und Tennis.
In meiner Freizeit gehe ich (gern) ins Kino.

Say you like (doing) something
Ich lese sehr gern.
Ich mag Literatur/Sport/ Fußball/Musik.
Ich liebe Literatur/meine Stadt.

Ask about hobbies
Was für Hobbys haben Sie?

Ask how someone likes a place
Wie finden Sie die Stadt Dresden?

Book a table
Ich hätte gern einen Tisch reserviert.
Ich hätte gern einen Fensterplatz.
Für vier Personen.

Say the date
Für nächste Woche.
Für Freitag, den dreizehnten zwölften.

Say something will be fine
(Das geht) in Ordnung.

Say you've ordered a table
Ich habe einen Tisch bestellt.

Offer/suggest a drink/dish
Möchten Sie . . . ?
Was trinken wir zum Essen?
Wie wär's mit . . . ?

Accept a suggestion
Ja, gut.
Ja, gern(e).

Order drinks/food
Ich hätte gern(e) . . .
Wir hätten gern(e) . . .
Ich möchte/nehme . . .

Say you'd prefer something
Ich möchte lieber . . .

Ask for the bill
Kann ich zahlen, bitte?
Ich möchte bitte zahlen.

Ask for a receipt
Machen/Geben Sie mir bitte eine Quittung.

Thank someone for coming
Ich freue mich, daß Sie gekommen sind.

Say it was delicious/nice
Es war köstlich/lecker/sehr gut.
Es war nett.

Thank someone for the invitation
Vielen Dank für die Einladung!

Use the **Checklist** to describe your hobbies and entertain your guests.

Ein paar Blümchen
,,Es ist in Deutschland relativ üblich, daß, wenn eine Frau zu Hause ist, man ihr ein paar Blümchen mitbringt. Das wird immer gerne gesehen. Es ist natürlich auch üblich, daß man vielleicht etwas Trinkbares mitbringt. Eine Flasche Whisky oder eine Flasche Champagner.''
(Joachim Esche, *Schering AG*)

1   You return to your hotel in the evening and would like a number of things. Ask for the following: *a* meinen Schlüssel;   *b* eine Tasse Kaffee;   *c* ein Glas Wein;   *d* Frühstück um halb sieben.

2   You meet some delegates at a conference. Ask for the following information, using these question words: **Wie . . . ? Für welche . . . ? Was . . . ? Was für . . . ?**   *a* their name;   *b* their company;   *c* their profession;   *d* their leisure interests.

3   Don't confuse **das** (*it, this/that*) with **daß** (*that,* the signal of a **daß** clause). Fill in the gaps in the following sentences with **daß** or **das:**   *a* Wenn Sie sich vorstellen, ... die Boot bei Null angefangen hat.   *b* So, ... ist der Schlüssel.   *c* .... Auto befindet sich in dem Parkhaus.   *d* Wir versprechen, ... die Besucher in ausreichender Zahl kommen.   *e* Für zwei Nächte, ... habe ich noch frei.   *f* .... wäre .... Zimmer 462.   *g* Die Bestimmungen in Deutschland sind sehr streng, so .... wir zwei Filtertypen brauchen.   *h* .... ist eine relativ kleine Werft.   *i* Ich hoffe trotzdem, ... es ein junggebliebenes Unternehmen ist.

4   You're at a trade fair. Ask an exhibitor about: *a* the cost of a product;   *b* the company's turnover;   *c* the number of employees.

5   You're at the trade-fair press office. Ask about: *a* the number of visitors;   *b* the number of exhibitors.

6   You're in the bank. Use **ich möchte gern** to say you want to: *a* change some money;   *b* change $ 1500;   *c* cash a Eurocheque (**einen Euroscheck**);   *d* transfer DM 600;   *e* withdraw DM 1000 from your account;   *f* change £ 500;   *g* open an account.

7   Match the nouns to the verbs:
angenehmen Aufenthalt   Platzkarten   Geld   Umsatz   Euroscheck
wünschen   einlösen   wechseln   machen   reservieren.
Now try making up a sentence with each pair.

---

das Geld   *money*
die Mark   *mark*
der Dollar   *dollar*
das Pfund   *pound*
(ein Konto) aufmachen   *to open (an account)*
(Geld) abheben   *to withdraw (money)*
(Geld) überweisen   *to transfer (money)*
(Geld) wechseln   *to change (money)*
(einen Scheck) einlösen   *to cash (a cheque)*

Adjectives
Adjectives are used to describe nouns or pronouns.

> Die Bestimmungen sind **streng**.
> Es war **nett**.

Whenever they appear in front of a noun, they have an added ending, depending on the gender of the noun and its case:

> Ich bin eine absolut**e** Leseratte.
> Ich möchte den Feldsalat mit roh**en** Champignons.

As well as **-e** and **-en**, you'll also find the endings **-em**, **-er**, **-es** (see p 141).

Note that the comparative form of adjectives consists of the adjective plus **-er** plus the adjective ending:

> in einer ruhig**eren** Ecke

Subordinate clauses

As in English, the main clause of a sentence may be accompanied by a *subordinate clause,* which wouldn't make much sense on its own. Conjunctions such as **daß** (*that*), **so daß** (*so that*), **wenn** (*if*), **weil** (*because*) or **da** (*since, because*) signal a subordinate clause with the verb at the end:

> Wie wär's, **wenn** wir mal den Fendant **probieren**?
>
> Natürlich, **da** Dresden auch eine Kunststadt **ist**.

In written German, you'll find that subordinate clauses are always separated from the main clause by a comma (see p 147).

The nominative case

The main use of the nominative is to indicate the subject of a sentence, ie the noun or pronoun that's 'doing' the action of the verb. Because the subject is identified by its case in German, its position is flexible; it may come at the beginning of the sentence, or later on, after the verb (see p 146–147):

> **Ich** heiße Thomas Barth.
>
> Als Dresdner liebe **ich** natürlich meine Stadt.

With the verb **sein**, both the subject and the noun or pronoun that follow are in the nominative case:

> **Es** ist **meine Heimat**.
>
> **Ich** bin **eine Leseratte**.
>
> **Die Boot** ist **die größte Bootmesse** der Welt.

TREIBEN SIE SPORT?

Golf – ein elitärer Sport?

Although lunch is time for talking business, at some point the conversation inevitably turns to leisure activities. Discussion at the Funk-Restaurant turns to golf.

1 How many sports are mentioned and what are they?
2 Why does Mr Magunna not do much sport at present?
3 Why does Peter Sahla think that golf is elitist in Germany?
4 Does Mr Magunna agree that golf is elitist?

der Club/Klub *club*
das Mitglied *member*
das Golf *golf*
das Tennis *tennis*
der Pferdesport *riding*
das Segeln *sailing*
die Gebühr *fee, dues*
Sport treiben *to go in for sports*
ansonsten *otherwise*
spielen *to play*
reden *to talk, to speak*
sich unterhalten *to talk, to have a conversation*

was mal ganz anderes *something quite different*
weil die Möglichkeiten … relativ eingeschränkt sind *because the possibilities are relatively restricted …*
wenn ich so mir … anhöre *when I hear…*
in der Öffentlichkeit ist es *the public sees it as*
wenn man eigentlich mal das Ganze hinterfragt *but once you analyse the whole question*
dem Golf wird das … angehängt *it's … associated with golf*
elitär zu sein *of being elitist*
meines Erachtens *in my opinion*
überhaupt nicht *not at all*

Notice how Peter Sahla uses **mal**, **ja** and **eigentlich** when he changes the subject:

> Aber **mal** was ganz anderes, weil ... man kann **ja** nicht immer nur übers Geschäft reden: Treiben Sie **eigentlich** auch Sport?

These words add little definite meaning. Instead, they soften what might otherwise seem rather abrupt (**eigentlich**) or they invite agreement (**ja**), and generally give a statement a personal slant.

1 How many times does Mr Magunna explain a point with **weil** ...?

2 You'd like to change the subject. What might you say?

3 Practise emphasizing your opinion using **Meines Erachtens ist/sind** ... For example:

Herr Sahla   **Golf ist elitär.**

Sie   **Meines Erachtens ist Golf nicht elitär.**

a Herr Sahla   Tennisspielen ist teuer.   *Sie* ....

b Herr Sahla   Die Produkte sind teuer.   *Sie* ....

c Herr Sahla   Die Mitgliedsgebühren sind hoch.   *Sie* ....

d Herr Sahla   Die Organisation ist nicht gut.   *Sie* ....

e Herr Sahla   Das Meeting ist nicht wichtig.   *Sie* ....

f Herr Sahla   Der Service ist freundlich.   *Sie* ....

Innenstadt, Oschatz

die Kreisstadt   *district town*
die Innenstadt   *(town/city) centre*
der Einwohner   *inhabitant*
die Kirche   *church*
der Park   *park*
die Landschaft   *countryside*
der Urlaub   *holiday(s)*
berühmt   *famous*
niedlich   *pretty*
reizvoll   *attractive*
sich erholen   *to relax*
weggehen   *to go away/out*
wandern gehen   *to go walking/hiking*

EINE NIEDLICHE KREISSTADT

Listen to Heike Redmann talking about the attractions of her home town Oschatz, near Dresden.

Put these facts in the order in which they're mentioned: *a* restoration work;   *b* status of town;   *c* number of inhabitants;   *d* surrounding countryside;   *e* presence of church;   *f* going out in the evenings;   *g* location of town;   *h* park;   *i* type of tourist.

schön restauriert   *beautifully restored*
gut erhalten   *well preserved*
'ne Kirche, die ... restauriert worden ist   *a church which has been restored ...*
könnte man sich eventuell mal angucken   *it's perhaps worth having a look at*
wenn man jetzt Urlaub machen will   *if you want to spend a holiday here*
es ist mehr was   *it's more something*
die sich jetzt wirklich erholen wollen   *who really want to relax*

1 Give a short description of Oschatz in German with the following facts: *a* number of inhabitants;   *b* location;   *c* town centre;   *d* building of note;   *e* park;   *f* surrounding countryside.

2 Now give a short description of your own home town based on the points in **1**.

Select a starter, main course and dessert of your choice from a Funk-Restaurant menu, making sure the bill doesn't come to more than DM 50 in total. There's no key to this one!

FUNK-RESTAURANT

MÜNCHEN

SPEISEKARTE

Kalte Vorspeisen — DM

Matjesfilet „Hausfrauen Art" mit Salzkartoffeln	13,50
Melonenschiffchen mit Parmaschinken	14,50

Warme Vorspeisen

Königscrevetten am Spieß mit Dillschaum und Reistimbale	11,50

Suppen

Rinderkraftbrühe mit Mark, Ei oder Gemüse Julienne	4,80
Tomatensuppe mit Gin verfeinert, Sahnehaube und Basilikum	6,50

Salate

Gartenfrisch und bunt gemischt Kleiner gartenfrischer Beilagensalat	4,80
Großer gartenfrischer, gemischter Salat	7,80
Blattsalate der Saison in Rose-Island-Dressing, mit gebratener Hähnchenbrust und Speckscheiben	12,80
Grönländer Crevetten auf frischen Salaten, Cocktail-Dressing und exotischen Früchten	15,80

Fischgerichte

Filet vom Atlantikdorsch –auf Blattspinat, mit Sauce Hollandaise überbacken, dazu Salzkartoffeln	21,50
–auf Currysahne, mit Paprikastreifen und Früchten, dazu Butterreis	21,50
Riesencrevetten vom Grill, mit Café de Paris-Butter überbacken, dazu Gemüse und Reis	31,50

Fleischgerichte

Zürcher Geschnetzeltes in Weißweinsauce Champignons und Butterrösti	28,50
Kalbsleber „Berliner Art" mit Apfelscheiben und Röstzwiebeln, dazu Kartoffelschnee	26,50
Medaillons vom argentinischen Rinderfilet auf Morchel-Cognacsauce mit Gemüse umlegt und Kroketten	34,50
Schweinefilet im Netz mit Spinat gefüllt, auf Kräuterrahmsauce und Butterspätzle	25,–
Piccata von der Putenbrust auf Tomatenspaghetti dazu sautierte Champignons und Schinkenstreifen	22,–

Beilagen

Pommes frites	3,50
Spätzle	3,50
Reis	3,50
Rösti	4,20
Salzkartoffeln	3,50
Tagesgemüse	4,–

Nachspeisen

Mandelcreme mit Beeren	7,80
Frischer Obstsalat mit Maraschino	7,80
Käseauswahl	7,80

KREUZWORTRÄTSEL

Here's a culinary crossword to keep you busy. You'll need to refer to the menu and the rest of Unit 5.

ä = AE, ö = OE, ü = UE, ß = SS.
Omit endings on adjectives etc.

Across

1 They come as soup and with spaghetti. (7)
4 This European capital figures on the menu. (5)
8 They come with the calves' liver, fried, as the second part of a compound noun, and beginning with a Z. (8)
13 You may think this French drink is wasted in a sauce. (6)
17 An alternative word for **Nachtisch**. (10)
18 They vary from day to day and you can have them 'à la Julienne' in soup. (7)
19 The dish for you if you like poultry but can't stand salads. (10)
23 Your main reading matter in a restaurant. (11)
24 You'd need this to say you're going to the cinema and restaurant: **Wir gehen** .... **Kino und dann** .... **Restaurant**. (3)
25 The restaurant likes cooking with this type of fat. (6)
26 Preposition used with salad dressing and white wine sauce. (2)
27 Normally you'd get it with tonic rather than soup. (3)
28 For these, you'd have to have a look at the **Getränkekarte**. (9)
32 Delicious! (9)
33 'A la Hausfrau' – substitute a German word for 'style'. (3)
35 Starter. (9)
37 You can drink wine out of it. (4)
38 One of the options that come with beef consommé. (2)
39 You'd be unlikely to go to Munich without having some. (4)
40 Starters come **kalt** or like this. (4)
41 Vegetarians avoid it. (7)
44 **Riesencrevetten** are cooked on it. (5)
47 The German for 'bonnet' – here it consists of cream (**Sahne**) and adorns the tomato soup. (5)
48 The colour of wine you'd tend to drink with fish. (5)
50 To refer to **der Wein**, would you use the pronoun **er** or **es**? (2)
51 This is what you'd do with wine, beer, juice or water. (7)
53 The German word for 'pig' and 'pork'. (7)
54 You use this word when drinking to people's health, and it goes with **8 down**. (4)
55 You sit at this when eating. (5)
56 It's fresh from the garden and small or large. (5)
57 You can use this verb meaning 'to take' when you order. It's used by Gerrit Neuhaus and Constanze Magunna. (6)

Down

1 Constanze Magunna prefers her wine like this. (7)
2 It forms part of a creamy compound with **Haube** or **Curry**. (5)
3 This verb says you love something or someone. (6)
5 This piece of paper is the least pleasant part of the meal. (8)
6 **Soße** would be the indigenous German spelling of this saucy number. (5)
7 A choice of this would be an alternative to a sweet dessert. (5)
8 It goes with **54 across**. (3)
9 A non-alcoholic non-sweet aqueous beverage. (6)
10 Mr Harms will be sitting in a quiet one with his guests. (4)
11 It begins with a B, ends with a T, means 'colourful(ly)', and describes a mixed salad. (4)

12 Mr Neuhaus concludes a pleasant occasion with this adjective. (4)

14 A liquid starter. (5)

15 A mixed salad can be **klein** or like this. (5)

16 Main dish – Constanze Magunna orders veal as this. (12)

18 In a salad, chicken comes cooked like this. (8)

20 It means day and precedes vegetables. (3)

21 It costs under DM 5,- and there's a choice of six (omit ending). (7)

22 This type of red meat is mentioned twice on the menu. When it stands on its own, it ends with a D. (4)

29 This is what you do with the food. (5)

30 **Rose-Island-Dressing** is in this language. (8)

31 An alternative type of main course to **Fleisch**. (5)

34 Mr Neuhaus does this with a credit card. (6)

36 A salad you can have for dessert is made with this. (4)

41 Savoury and sweet salads are described with this adjective. (6)

42 You could be excused for thinking that this marrow served in beef consommé is a type of currency. (4)

43 German version of champagne. (4)

45 The size of a salad costing DM 4,80. (5)

46 An equally starchy alternative to **Kartoffeln**. (4)

48 It comes in bottles or by the glass. (4)

49 This preposition is used 14 times on the menu. (3)

52 The colour of wine you'd tend to drink with beef. (3)

BUSINESS FILE

Work in a factory starts between 6 and 7 am, and many offices have flexitime from 7 to 9 am. Offices tend to close promptly at 5 pm, and on Fridays it may be fruitless to try and contact anyone much after 1 pm.

There are a large number of public holidays, some of which are celebrated in different parts of the country – Catholic holidays in the Rhineland and the south, and Protestant holidays in the north.

FEIERTAGE	
Neujahr	1. Januar
Heilige Drei Könige (Baden-Württemberg und Bayern)	6. Januar
Rosenmontag, Fastnachts-/Faschingsdienstag (teilweise Rheinland, Bayern)	42/41 (Wochen-)Tage vor Ostern
Karfreitag	Ostern
Ostersonntag, Ostermontag	Ostern
Maifeiertag (Tag der Arbeit)	1. Mai
Christi Himmelfahrt (immer am Donnerstag)	40 Tage nach Ostern
Pfingstsonntag und Pfingstmontag	7. Sonntag nach Ostern
Fronleichnam (katholische Bundesländer)	2. Donnerstag nach Pfingsten
Mariä Himmelfahrt (Saarland und teilweise Bayern)	15. August
Tag der Deutschen Einheit	3. Oktober
Reformationstag (teilweise in den neuen Bundesländern)	31. Oktober
Allerheiligen (katholische Bundesländer)	1. November
Buß- und Bettag (in den neuen Bundesländern nur teilweise)	3. Mittwoch im November
Weihnachten	(24.), 25., 26. Dezember

If the holiday happens to fall at a weekend, tough luck – there's no day in lieu. On the other hand, many people take a day off if a working day falls between a holiday and a weekend.

Christmas is celebrated solemnly with presents and an obligatory **Tannenbaum** complete with candles on **Heiligabend** (*Christmas Eve*). **Silvester** (*New Year's Eve*) is the time for extravagant fireworks.

In the Rhineland and in Bavaria, the run-up to Lent (**Karneval**, **Fastnacht** or **Fasching**) officially starts in November, **am elften elften um elf Uhr elf**. It culminates in wild parties on **Rosenmontag** and **Faschingsdienstag**.

6

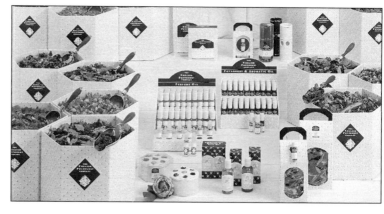

DIE PRODUKT-MERKMALE

PRODUCTS, PRESENTATIONS, LAUNCHES

German consumers like to know exactly what they're getting, and require detailed information on product features.

EINZIGARTIG

For the launch of their Series III pocket computer, Psion had an advertising budget of DM 1 000 000. Ms Rieger-Jäger of advertising agency Tradecom gives a presentation.

► How many different features are highlighted?

PSION GMBH, BAD HOMBURG

Frau Rieger-Jäger Ja, Sie haben uns beauftragt, für Ihr neues Produkt, Serie III, ein Konzept zu finden für das nächste Jahr. Wir haben uns erst mal die Produktmerkmale herausgegriffen: daß es ein Taschencomputer ist, daß es sich um ein Palm-Top-Gerät handelt. Es hat 'ne handliche Form, ist elegant und hat 'ne sehr hohe Kapazität. Es hat 'n Wordprocessor, dann Multi-Task-Funktion, ist sehr bedienungsfreundlich, kann an 'n Drucker angeschlossen werden, und das beste daran ist eben, daß es sehr klein ist und 'ne hohe Speicherkapazität hat, und das dürfte ja einzigartig sein im Moment.

wir haben uns ... herausgegriffen   ... *we have identified*
daß es sich um ... handelt   *that it is ...*
es ... kann ... angeschlossen werden   *it ... can be connected ...*
das dürfte ... sein   *that must be ...*

das Merkmal	*feature*
der Computer	*computer*
der Drucker	*printer*
der Speicher	*memory*
die Festplatte	*hard disk*
das Laufwerk	*disk drive*
die Funktion	*function*
die Tasche	*pocket, bag*
handlich	*convenient, compact*
bedienungsfreundlich	
	user-friendly
beauftragen	*to commission*
finden	*to find*

Notice how **da** can join a preposition to refer back to something:
(Das Produkt) Das beste **daran** ist, daß es sehr klein ist.
*The best thing **about it** is that it's very small.*

Look out for words like **dabei**, **dafür** and **dazu**. Others like **daran**, **darauf** or **darin** are often spoken and written **dran**, **drauf**, **drin**. These words are used a lot to link up sentences and ideas. Get used to recognizing them and seeing how they work.

At the Systems trade fair in Munich you want some information about a product. Base your enquiry on the following: *a* sich interessieren/ Computer; *b* Was für/Computer; *c* Wie hoch/Kapazität; *d* Was/ Produktmerkmale.

PIONIERARBEIT

Schering has been established in the German market for over a century and prides itself on its research record and pioneering products.

▶ List the areas Dr Esche mentions in which Schering has done pioneering work.

Anovlar® – die erste europäische „Pille"

SCHERING AG, BERLIN

Dr. Esche   Die Firma Schering ist tätig in der Branche Chemie, Pharmazie. Wir verstehen uns als Unternehmen, was Pharmazeutika herstellt und vertreibt, Pflanzenschutzmittel, galvanotechnische Erzeugnisse, Industriechemikalien und auch Naturstoffe.
Herr Sahla   Und für welchen Bereich sind Sie zuständig?
Dr. Esche   Für den Pharmabereich.
Herr Sahla   Was macht Schering so besonders in diesem Bereich, in dem Sie tätig sind?
Dr. Esche   Hauptbereiche sind Hormontherapie, insbesondere die orale Kontrazeption, umgangssprachlich schlicht „die Pille" genannt. Das ist eine Domäne von Schering, wo Schering auch Pionierarbeit geleistet hat. Die zweite Nische, in der wir uns sehr erfolgreich bewegen, sind Röntgenkontrastmittel. Und auch hier hat Schering Pionierarbeit geleistet. Und insofern, denke ich, kann ich hier ohne falsche Bescheidenheit sagen, da sind wir einfach wer.

die Industrie   *industry*
das Produkt   *product*
die (Markt)nische   *(market) niche*
die Pionierarbeit   *pioneering work*
die Pharmazeutika   *pharmaceuticals*
die Chemikalien (*pl.*)   *chemicals*
tätig sein   *to be active*
denken   *to think*
verstehen   *to understand*
sich verstehen (als)   *to see oneself (as)*
sich bewegen   *to move, operate*

in diesem Bereich, in dem   *in this area in which*
schlicht   *simply*
wo Schering . . . geleistet hat   *where Schering has carried out . . .*
in der wir uns . . . bewegen   *in which we operate . . .*
da sind wir einfach wer   *we're really someone*

NUTS AND BOLTS ▶

Notice how Dr Esche says:

Wir verstehen uns als Unternehmen, was...

Sich verstehen (*to see oneself*) is a reflexive verb. Some German verbs require a reflexive pronoun where the English equivalent doesn't:

Die zweite Nische, in der **wir uns** erfolgreich **bewegen**, ...

Ich interessiere mich für Ihre Schiffe.

The *Glossary* lists reflexive verbs with **sich** in front (see p 140 and 143).

PRACTICE ▶

Riesennachholbedarf

„Der Grad der Aufgeschlossenheit in den ehemaligen kommunistischen Ländern ist ungeheuer groß. Also Prospekte, Informationsmaterial und dergleichen wird uns geradezu aus der Hand gerissen." (Joachim Esche, *Schering AG*)

1   Give the following information about Schering, presented in complete German sentences: *a* sector;   *b* types of product;   *c* two success stories in the pharmaceuticals division.

2   Practise using reflexive verbs. Complete the following sentences with the appropriate reflexive pronoun – **mich**, **sich** or **uns**:   *a* In Mainz befindet .... der Sitz der Gruppenleitung;   *b* Ich interessiere .... für Ihre Schiffe;   *c* Die Firmen haben .... zusammengeschlossen;   *d* Wenn Sie .... vorstellen, daß die Boot bei Null angefangen hat;   *e* Der Jahresumsatz bewegt .... in der Größenordnung von 13 Milliarden D-Mark;   *f* Wir haben .... überlegt;   *g* Ich wollte .... erkundigen;   *h* Es handelt .... um ein Palm-Top-Gerät.

3   Look up the infinitives of the reflexive verbs in **2** and check their meanings.

EIN ABGERUNDETES SORTIMENT

Dieter Jung

der Vertreter   *agent, representative*
der Handelsvertreter   *agent*
die Provision   *commission*
der Vertrag   *contract*
in der Nähe von   *near*
handeln (mit)   *to trade / deal (in)*
vertreten   *to represent*
importieren   *to import*
exportieren   *to export*

Many companies opt to channel their products through an agent. Dieter Jung and Dieter Michael Putz, two agents in Munich, outlined their product ranges.

1   Give the sectors in which   *a* Dieter Jung and   *b* Dieter Putz operate.

2   List the products   *a* sold by Mr Jung and   *b* sold by Mr Putz.

JUNG HANDELSVERTRETUNG CDH, MÜNCHEN

Herr Sahla   Können Sie mir zunächst einmal sagen, wie Sie heißen?
Herr Jung   Ja, mein Name ist Dieter Jung.
Herr Sahla   Und was sind Sie von Beruf?
Herr Jung   Ich bin gelernter Industriekaufmann und übe den Beruf eines Handelsvertreters aus.
Herr Sahla   Und wo sitzt Ihr Unternehmen, Ihre Firma?
Herr Jung   In Bayern, in der Nähe von München, in Inning am Ammersee.
Herr Sahla   Könnten Sie mir sagen ... Also, Sie haben gesagt Vertreter. Genau was vertreten Sie?

die Kunstgewerbebranche *arts and crafts (sector)*
der Geschenkartikel *gift*
das Sortiment *product range*
die Herrenbekleidung *menswear*
der Anzug *suit*
das Sakko *jacket*
die Hose *trousers*
das Hemd *shirt*
die Strickwaren (*pl.*) *knitwear*
das Beispiel *example*
sich etablieren *to get established*
sich konzentrieren auf *to concentrate on*

Dieter Putz

Herr Jung Ich bin in der Glas-, Porzellan- und Kunstgewerbebranche tätig.

Herr Sahla Kunstgewerbebranche, was für Artikel sind das?

Herr Jung Das sind Geschenkartikel, die ich speziell aus England entweder als Vertretung oder selbst importiere. Zum Beispiel Potpourris, englische Potpourris, das ist ein sehr guter Artikel, seit '88 hier auf dem Markt. Momentan ein Trendartikel. Wird sich aber meines Erachtens fest im Markt etablieren.

DIETER M. PUTZ TEXTIL AGENTUR CDH, MÜNCHEN

Herr Sahla Könnten Sie mir erst einmal sagen, wie Sie heißen?

Herr Putz Mein Name ist Dieter Michael Putz.

Herr Sahla Und was sind Sie von Beruf?

Herr Putz Ich bin von Beruf Handelsvertreter CDH. Mit der Erklärung dazu, CDH ist die Abkürzung für Centralvereinigung Deutscher Handelsvertreter- und Handelsmakler-Verbände. Eine Berufsorganisation.

Herr Sahla Und in welcher Branche dieses Verbandes sind Sie spezifisch tätig?

Herr Putz Ich bin speziell tätig in der Bekleidung, und ganz genau in der Herrenbekleidung.

Herr Sahla Und konzentrieren Sie sich auf spezifische Artikel im Rahmen der Herrenbekleidung?

Herr Putz Konzentrieren nicht, weil eigentlich das Sortiment eines Handelsvertreters möglichst in sich abgerundet sein sollte. Und hier ist es also bei mir zutreffend, daß ich Anzüge, Sakkos, Hosen, Hemden und Herrenstrickwaren verkaufe.

(ich) übe den Beruf . . . aus *(I) am . . . (lit. practise the profession of)*
was für . . . sind das? *what type of . . . are they?*
wird sich . . . fest . . . etablieren *will . . . become firmly established . . .*
ich bin speziell tätig *in particular, I'm active*
ganz genau *to be precise*
weil . . . das Sortiment . . . in sich abgerundet sein sollte *because . . . the range . . . should be rounded*
hier ist es also bei mir zutreffend *in my case it's true*

NUTS AND BOLTS ▶

Notice how Dieter Putz says *my name is* and Dieter Jung says *in my opinion*:

> **mein** Name **meines** Erachtens

Mein (*my*), **sein** (*his, its*), **unser** (*our*), **ihr** (*her, their*), **Ihr** (formal *your*) have the same endings as **ein, eine, ein** (see p 139–140).

PRACTICE ▶

1 Give a short portrait of Dieter Jung and Dieter Putz: *a* profession; *b* sector; *c* location of business; *d* products.

2 Ask questions using **Was für ein . . . ist das?** to find out about: *a* product; *b* company; *c* boat; *d* trade fair; *e* stand.

Regional variations

The 16 German **Länder**, or states, are based on historical divisions, and there are at least as many regional variations in language and pronunciation. All over Germany, the standard is considered to be the type of German spoken around Hanover, **Hochdeutsch**. But people are generally proud of their local dialect and many will speak with a strong local accent, especially in the south.

Die Bundesrepublik Deutschland

Du and Sie

First names are not the norm in German companies, and close colleagues may still be on **Herr** and **Frau** terms after working together for 30 years. However, first names are often used among younger colleagues, and Germans who are familiar with Anglo-Saxon customs may make allowances and accept first-name terms. This is a complex area of social interaction, and it's best to take the lead from the people you're with.

The **Sie** form (formal *you*) is used for anyone you address by surname. If you're on first-name terms, it's the familiar **du** (see p 140).

ENGLISCHE WARE IM TREND

 Dieter Jung specializes in gifts and trinkets from all over Europe. Here he gives Peter Sahla an insight into how he started his business.

▶ 1 When did Mr Jung start up as an agent?
2 How did he select his products?
3 Are English goods popular?
4 Does Mr Jung make new contacts in Munich or on his travels?

<table>
<tr><td>die Ware</td><td>goods, wares</td></tr>
</table>

die Ware	*goods, wares*
das Kaufhaus	*department store*
der Fabrikant	*manufacturer*
der Händler	*dealer, buyer*
das Muster	*sample*
die Botschaft	*embassy*
im Trend	*fashionable*
ausländisch	*foreign*
beziehungsweise/bzw.	*or (rather)*
kontaktieren	*to contact*
sich umsehen	*to look around*

JUNG HANDELSVERTRETUNG CDH, MÜNCHEN

Herr Sahla Wie kommen Sie an Ihre Produkte heran? Tritt man an Sie heran, oder gehen Sie ... reisen Sie rum und suchen?
Herr Jung '88 fing ich an. Da war ich unbekannt auf 'm Markt als Händler mit ausländischen Waren und bin selbst nach England gefahren und habe mich dort in den großen Kaufhäusern umgesehen, weil ich mir gesagt habe, was da drin steht und gut ist, müßte eigentlich auch in Deutschland passen, und die englische Ware ist momentan hier im Trend. Und ich hatte damit recht. Und wenn man mal eine gute Firma bekommt, wird die Umwelt der Händler aufmerksam, beziehungsweise der Fabrikanten, und dann kriegt man automatisch Angebote.
Herr Sahla Das heißt, Sie werden kontaktiert direkt hier oder bei Messen?
Herr Jung Die Leute schreiben mich an, kriegen meine Adresse über die Botschaft heraus oder über den Handelsvertreterverband und kommen persönlich sogar hierher mit Mustern und so weiter. Oder eben während meiner Reisen, oder wenn Messen in England sind, knüpf' ich auch immer wieder Kontakte.

wie kommen Sie an ... heran? *how do you get ...?*
tritt man an Sie heran ...? *are you approached ...?*
(ich) bin ... gefahren *(I) went ...*
(ich) habe mich ... umgesehen *(I) looked around ...*
weil ich mir gesagt habe *because I said to myself*
müßte ... passen *ought to go ...*
ich hatte damit recht *I was right*
wird die Umwelt der Händler aufmerksam *other agents notice you*
beziehungsweise der Fabrikanten *or rather the manufacturers*
das heißt *that is*
kriegen ... über ... heraus *get ... through ...*
kommen ... hierher *come here ...*
und so weiter *and so on*
knüpf' ich auch immer wieder Kontakte *I also frequently make contacts*

Englische Potpourris

Remember that some verbs in German have a separable prefix which may be shunted to the end of the sentence or clause, eg **anschreiben**:

> Die Leute **schreiben** mich **an**.

The past participles of separable verbs, eg **sich umsehen, anschließen**, are formed by inserting **-ge-** between the prefix and the verb (see p 143):

> Ich habe mich in den Kaufhäusern **umgesehen**.
> Das Gerät kann an einen Drucker **angeschlossen** werden.

You may have noticed the abbreviated form of **dem** in **auf 'm Markt**. It's similar to the contractions **zum (zu dem)** and **im (in dem)**, but unlike these it's not used in writing.

1   Give a short introduction to Mr Jung's business: *a* date of start-up;   *b* initial position in market;   *c* initial method of selecting a product range;   *d* three ways of getting to know new products now;   *e* present status of English products.

2   To check that you've understood something correctly, you can repeat or paraphrase what's just been said. What two-word phrase could you use?

3   The following basic verbs appear in *Englische Ware im Trend* with a separable prefix: *a* kommen;   *b* tritt;   *c* reisen;   *d* fing;   *e* schreiben;   *f* kriegen;   *g* kommen.   Find the prefix for each one and work out the infinitive.

Noch schneller

„Die Schwierigkeiten sind die langen Lieferzeiten teilweise der englischen Firmen. Und wenn man das weiß, muß man sich darauf einstellen. In Deutschland kann man nur Geschäfte machen, wenn man den Auftrag heute bekommt, und man kann innerhalb von 10, 14 Tagen dann liefern, oder noch schneller."
(Dieter Jung, *Handelsvertretung*)

Delivery times and service

In order to do well in the German market, you must convince your potential customers of the quality of your products, your commitment to meeting delivery deadlines, and the effectiveness of your service network.

EINE RIESENNACHFRAGE

Munich is one of Germany's top fashion centres. Dieter Putz is chairman of the Munich Mode-Zentrum, a group of fashionwear agents offering wholesale facilities under one roof. He reviews cooperation with companies exporting to Germany.

1   What advice does he offer to foreign manufacturers?
2   What does he cite as a typical English product?
3   What is the demand for this product at present?

DIETER M. PUTZ TEXTIL AGENTUR CDH, MÜNCHEN
Herr Putz   Ich glaube, daß die ausländischen Hersteller am besten beraten wären, wenn Sie nicht versuchen würden, alles auf dem deutschen Markt zu verkaufen, sondern sich eben auf Dinge konzentrieren würden, die für ihr Land besonders typisch sind. Ein praktisches Beispiel: Ich habe seit

> der Artikel   *product*
> der Erfolg   *success*
> die Nachfrage   *demand*
> das Ding   *thing*
> versuchen   *to try, attempt*

Mode-Zentrum, München

wenigen Wochen die Vertretung von britischen Wachsjacken. Und das ist ein typischer Artikel, der gar nicht britisch genug sein kann, um hier Erfolg zu haben. Und das ist etwas, was mir also die letzten drei, vier Wochen wahnsinnig Freude macht, weil da eben einfach im Moment eine Riesennachfrage ist.

am besten beraten wären   *would be best advised*
alles ... zu verkaufen   *to sell everything ...*
die für ihr Land ... typisch sind   *which are ... typical of their country*
der gar nicht britisch genug sein kann   *which can't be British enough*
etwas, was mir ... Freude macht   *something which I've been enjoying ...*

NUTS AND BOLTS ▶

Notice how Mr Putz uses a **weil** (*because*) clause to explain why he's enjoying selling waxed jackets:

> Das ist etwas, was mir Freude macht, **weil** da im Moment eine Riesennachfrage **ist**.

Note the verb at the end of the clause. Mr Putz gives specific details about a noun in a *subordinate clause* starting with the equivalent of *which*:

> Dinge ..., **die** für Ihr Land besonders typisch **sind**.
> ein Artikel, **der** gar nicht britisch genug sein **kann**.

These *relative clauses* start with a form of **der**, **die** or **das**, and the verb goes to the end (see p 140 and 147).

PRACTICE ▶

1   Use the word **weil** to join up each pair of sentences (don't forget to use commas):
a Herr Putz verkauft Wachsjacken. Es gibt im Moment eine Riesennachfrage.
b Herr Putz ist Mitglied der CDH. Er ist Handelsvertreter.
c Herr Jung verkauft englische Potpourris. Sie sind ein Trendartikel.
d Herr Jung bekommt automatisch Angebote. Er ist auf dem Markt bekannt.

CHECKLIST ▶

Not entrepreneurial enough
'If one tells a German middle-manager to do something, he will do it superbly. And certainly the junior to middle-management we have – we have had and we have now – is in my opinion excellent. But the senior management is not entrepreneurial enough.' (David Elder, *Psion GmbH*)

Practise presenting a product.

Say which products are produced/sold
Die Firma X produziert/fertigt Fenster.
Wir stellen Pharmazeutika her.
Wir vertreiben Wachsjacken.
Ich verkaufe Herrenanzüge.

Say what type of product it is
Es ist ein Taschencomputer.
Es handelt sich um ein Palm-Top-Gerät.

High-quality goods

'I think you have to convince the Germans first of all that your products are of sufficient quality to make them become interested in the first place. They are quite sceptical, and quite rightly sceptical, of foreign products in particular industries – particularly in our industry of computing.' (David Elder, *Psion GmbH*)

Present product features

Das Gerät ist sehr bedienungsfreundlich.
Das beste daran ist, daß es sehr klein/handlich ist.
Der Computer hat eine sehr hohe Kapazität.
Das Gerät kann an einen Drucker angeschlossen werden.

Praise a product

Das ist ein sehr guter Artikel.
Das Produkt ist einzigartig.

Present important company features

Die Firma X ist tätig in der Branche ...
Wir sind in der Computerbranche tätig.
Die Firma X hat Pionierarbeit geleistet.

Use the *Checklist* survival kit to practise presenting your own products or services.

REVIEW ▶

1 Give the **er/sie/es/man** form in the present tense for the verbs: *a* gefallen; *b* laufen; *c* mögen; *d* können; *e* sich bewegen; *f* nehmen; *g* sehen; *h* werden; *i* dürfen.

2 You've encountered a number of different types of business, for example **eine Mineralölgesellschaft**. Name the types of business that operate in the area of: *a* film; *b* computers; *c* trade fairs; *d* travel; *e* banking; *f* glass; *g* accommodation; *h* car-hire; *i* ship-building.

3 Ask someone about their company's products using **was für** with each of the following verbs: *a* vertreiben; *b* verkaufen; *c* fertigen; *d* herstellen; *e* erzeugen.

4 **Ich bräuchte Ihre Privatadresse** ... Mr Tuebner, the Sixt car-hire assistant at Munich Airport (see p 17), uses **bräuchte**, the *subjunctive* form of the verb **brauchen** (*to need*) (see p 146). Now ask for someone's: *a* Telefonnummer; *b* Faxnummer; *c* Name; *d* Adresse; *e* Kontonummer; *f* Geburtsdatum. Use **Ihren** (*m.*), **Ihre** (*f.*) or **Ihr** (*n.*), depending on the gender of the noun. Then practise the same with **ich brauche** (*present tense*, p 145), which you'd be more likely to hear in North Germany.

5 From the following lists, match up a preposition and a verb to form ten separable verbs you've met in this unit:

herum heran her an heraus heraus heran aus an an
kriegen stellen üben kommen fangen schreiben schließen
treten greifen reisen

No less than 100%

'The image that a lot of Germans have, would be a British car stuck on an *Autobahn* somewhere. Which is completely the wrong one to have. And it's very difficult to regain one's reputation for quality products with that sort of image. The British will tend to expect 95% quality standards where the Germans would expect no less than 100%.' (David Elder, *Psion GmbH*)

6 You're giving a presentation. Use **es handelt sich um** to explain that the product is: *a* a palm-top; *b* a wordprocessor; *c* a computer; *d* potpourris; *e* waxed jackets.

7 A salesman's keen to sell you his product. Say that you'll contact him.

8 Put the following words in the correct order to produce sentences with a **daß** clause: *a* die kommen versprechen in Besucher Zahl daß ausreichender wir; *b* daß ein Unternehmen ich junggebliebenes es hoffe ist; *c* Sie freue ich sind daß mich gekommen; *d* ist daran sehr daß ist beste es das klein.

9 Complete the sentences with one of these forms of **mein**:

meinen meine mein meine meine mein mein meine meines meine

a .... Name ist Günther Gräter; *b* Ich arbeite für .... eigene Firma; *c* Golf ist .... Erachtens nicht elitär; *d* Ich kann Ihnen .... Visitenkarte geben; *e* Dresden ist .... Heimat; *f* Wagner ist .... Name; *g* .... Hobbys sind Lesen und Fußball; *h* .... Beruf ist Reisebürokauffrau; *i* Als Dresdner liebe ich .... Stadt; *j* Ich möchte .... Schlüssel, bitte.

10 If you like detail, try working out the reason for each form of **mein** in *Review* 9 by identifying gender, number and case of the noun it goes with. Compare your findings with the table of endings for **ein** on p 139.

STRUCTURES ►

Word order

Remember these general rules for word order in statements (see p 147):

The subject can come before or after the verb:
> **Ich fing** '88 an. **Ich war** da unbekannt auf dem Markt.
> '88 **fing ich** an. Da **war ich** unbekannt auf dem Markt.

The verb in a main clause is the second element:
> Das Gerät **hat** einen Wordprocessor.
> Und dann **kriegt** man automatisch Angebote.

But only the part of the verb with the ending related to the subject stays in second place. Infinitives, past participles or separable prefixes that form part of the verb normally go to the end of the clause:
> Es **kann** an einen Drucker angeschlossen **werden**.
> Da **habe** ich mich dort in den großen Kaufhäusern **umgesehen**.
> Die Leute **kriegen** meine Adresse über die Botschaft **heraus**.

The verb in a subordinate clause goes to the end:
> ..., **daß** ich Anzüge, Sakkos und Hosen **verkaufe**.
> ..., **weil** da im Moment eine Riesennachfrage **ist**.
> **Wenn** man mal eine gute Firma **bekommt**, ...
> ... Geschenkartikel, **die** ich aus England **importiere**.
> ... in diesem Bereich, in **dem** ich aus England **importiere**.

Sehr hohe Qualitätsstandards

„Britische Produkte haben in der Bundesrepublik den Ruf, sehr hohe Qualitätsstandards zu erreichen. Sie haben mit Sicherheit einen höheren Stellenwert als vergleichbare Produkte aus China oder aus Fernost oder aus Amerika." (Horst Dieter Grodtke, *Psion GmbH*)

Lists

Product presentations are often given in terms of lists:

> **daß es** ein Taschencomputer ist, **daß es** sich um ein Palm-Top-Gerät handelt.

> **Es hat** eine handliche Form, **ist** elegant und **hat** eine sehr hohe Kapazität. **Es hat** einen Wordprocessor, **dann** Multi-Task-Funktion, **ist** sehr bedienungsfreundlich.

> **Hauptbereiche** sind Hormontherapie..., wo Schering auch **Pionierarbeit geleistet hat. Die zweite Nische** sind Röntgenkontrastmittel. Und auch hier hat Schering **Pionierarbeit geleistet.**

When you listen to or read German, it will help you to understand what's going on if you can recognize that points are being enumerated. When speaking yourself, you can take a simple structure and keep repeating it with different points.

Harald Nickol

ES LIEGT GUT IN DER HAND

At the launch of Psion's Series III, Harald Nickol, head of sales and marketing, gave a presentation to retailers and the trade press in Saarbrücken.

Number these points in the order in which they're given:
a personalization of Series III; *b* Series III from the outside;
c password; *d* display, sensor field, keyboard; *e* good design; *f* data security; *g* customizing to German market; *h* pocket computer;
i introduction.

die Serie *series*
der/das Display *display*
die Tastatur *keyboard*
das Keyboard *keyboard*
die Datensicherheit *data security*
die Batterie *battery*
außen *outside*
innen *inside*
unten *below, at the bottom*
oben *above, at the top*
installieren *to install*
einbauen *to install*

ich möchte . . . anfangen, . . . vorzustellen *I'd . . . like to begin to introduce . . .*
man hat sich also auch viel Mühe gegeben *so a lot of effort has been put in*
er ist immerhin so handlich, daß *it's so compact that*
man hat weiterhin . . . eine Back-up-Batterie eingebaut *in addition a back-up battery has been installed . . .*
es bleibt also . . . stehen *it stays . . .*
unten drunter *underneath*
da offenbart sich gleich *there it's immediately obvious*
so weit es geht *as far as possible*
er ist also wirklich so gestaltet, daß *it really has been designed in such a way that*
nur man sollte es auch tun *and this should be done*
sonst ergeben sich *otherwise there are*
zum einen *first of all*
um . . . identifizieren zu können *in order to be able to identify . . .*

Notice how Harald Nickol uses **man**, the German equivalent of the impersonal pronoun *one*:

> **Man** hat alles rund gemacht.
>
> **Man** hat eine Back-up-Batterie eingebaut.

In German, **man** is often used where English would use *you, we,* or a passive construction such as *A back-up battery has been installed.*

1 Use the verb **sein** to describe these aspects of Psion's organizer: *a* type of computer; *b* size; *c* compactness; *d* convenience; *e* uniqueness.

2 Use the verb **haben** to present these features: *a* word processor; *b* multi-tasking function; *c* memory capacity; *d* back-up battery; *e* display; *f* keyboard.

3 You're giving a product presentation: *a* say you want to start; *b* say you'll go into detail; *c* say a lot of effort has been devoted to design; *d* say delivery times are guaranteed; *e* say you've tried to prepare the product for the German market.

4 Use **man** to say: *a* a lot of effort has been invested (**sich Mühe geben**); *b* a battery has been installed (**einbauen**); *c* one gets a good overview (**bekommen**); *d* you can't always talk about business (**reden**); and *e* to ask someone how their name is spelt (**buchstabieren**).

There are a lot of 'foreign' words in German, particularly in marketing and computing. Make a note of any you come across, together with their gender. If you're really stuck for a word, you could try using the English word with a German accent and stress!

? **1** What are the goods protected against?

2 What are you not allowed to do?

100 JAHRE PHARMA-FORSCHUNG

German companies are proud of their research record, and investment is a top priority. Schering has been investing in research for over a century.

die Forschung *research*	
der Forscher *researcher*	
die Entwicklung *development*	
die Innovation *innovation*	
die Markteinführung *launch*	
der Wettbewerb *competition*	

1 What are the three main points about research?
2 How long does it take to develop a new drug?
3 What percentage of Schering's workforce is engaged in research?
4 How many illnesses can't be treated properly?
5 What is the problem in developing countries?
6 What is the problem in industrialized countries?

Wenn wir heute über Pharma-Forschung reden, müssen wir in die Zukunft blicken: Unter welchen Bedingungen findet Forschung im nächsten Jahrhundert statt?

• Forschung wird immer aufwendiger:
Die Entwicklung eines neuen Arzneimittels dauert von der Suche nach dem Wirkstoff bis zur Markteinführung des Medikaments etwa zwölf Jahre und kostet rund 250 Millionen DM.

Über 2.500 Mitarbeiter – zehn Prozent der gesamten Belegschaft – sind heute weltweit bei Schering in der Pharma-Forschung tätig.

• Forschung wird immer schwieriger:
Der Zwang zur Innovation nimmt weiter zu, denn der Wettbewerb wird härter.

Die gesetzlichen Vorschriften werden umfangreicher, und die Pharma-Forscher bekommen zu spüren, daß in der Öffentlichkeit Forschung zunehmend kritisch gesehen und kontrovers diskutiert wird.

• Forschung wird dennoch immer wichtiger:
Drei von vier Krankheiten können heute immer noch nicht ursächlich behandelt werden. Dazu kommen neue Aufgaben: Das starke Bevölkerungswachstum in den Entwicklungsländern erfordert neue Methoden der Familienplanung. Mit steigender Lebenserwartung der Menschen in den hochzivilisierten Ländern treten vermehrt altersbedingte Krankheiten auf.

(Das aktuelle Thema, Schering AG)

aufwendig *expensive, complex*	über ... reden *talk about*
teuer *expensive*	unter welchen Bedingungen *under what conditions*
billig *cheap*	findet ... statt *will ... take place*
blicken *to look*	von der Suche nach ... bis zur ... *from the search for ... to the ...*
forschen *to (do) research*	nimmt weiter zu *continues to increase*
auftreten *(sep.)* *to occur*	bekommen zu spüren, daß *are being affected by the fact that*
	treten vermehrt auf *are increasingly occurring*

To help when you're reading corporate literature in German, look for the way it's been crafted: parallel paragraphs, parallel examples, several verbs relating back to one noun given earlier. An introduction that focuses on the main point may help you to find your way through a complex document.

1 Which question does *100 Jahre Pharma-Forschung* seek to answer?

2 Which word in the headline of each of the three main paragraphs indicates what the paragraph is about?

3 What concrete examples are given in each paragraph?

4 Which is the odd one out? *a* teuer; aufwendig; billig; viel Geld kosten. *b* Mitarbeiter; Vorschrift; Forscher; Menschen. *c* Forschung; Entwicklung; Zwang; Innovation. *d* weiter; Wettbewerb; steigend; vermehrt. *e* Medikament; Öffentlichkeit; Pharmazeutika; Arzneimittel.

5 Spot two words in *100 Jahre Pharma-Forschung* meaning *approximately*.

6 The verb **werden** appears seven times. How many times is it used: *a* meaning *to become*; *b* to form the passive; *c* to form the future?

BUSINESS FILE

German consumers have the wealth to buy costly products, but they're not easy to please. Companies like to deal with a German entity, which could be in the form of an agent or GmbH, and long-term commitment to the market is essential. Because of Germany's cultural history, regional preferences play an important role in marketing a product. One agent is unlikely to cover the whole country, and it may well be necessary to have several. For information on agents in the area and sector you are interested in, you can contact the Centralvereinigung Deutscher Handelsvertreter- und Handelsmakler-Verbände (CDH), Geleniusstr. 1 (CDH-Haus), D-50931 Köln. Tel.: (0221) 51 40 43.   Fax: (0221) 52 57 67.

The ethos of the DIN standard runs right through German industry and commerce. In the past, Germany has been accused of using high standards to erect non-tariff barriers. The Deutsches Institut für Normung (DIN) has written more than 25 000 standards. For information on the GS safety-tested seal of approval (**geprüfte Sicherheit**) contact the German Technical Inspectorate: Verband der Technischen Über-wachungs-Vereine e.V., Kurfürstenstr. 56, D-45138 Essen. Tel.: (0201) 89 87-0.   Fax: (0201) 89 87-120.

Products have to be delivered on time and with documentation in German. Representatives will be expected to have a high level of technical knowledge about the product and should be familiar with the local market, regional differences and competition.

As a powerful export nation, Germany is committed to free trade, and the biggest nation in western Europe, with a pent-up demand in eastern Germany, offers exciting opportunities. There is a trade information office for providing information to foreign exporters wishing to sell in the Federal Republic: Bundesstelle für Außenhandelsinformation, Blaubach 13, D-50676 Köln. Tel.: (0221) 20 57-1.   Fax: (0221) 20 57-212.

Fernsehturm am Alexanderplatz, Berlin

BITTE WARTEN...

CALLS, CONNECTIONS, APPOINTMENTS

Getting through to the right person on the phone can be a challenge in a foreign language. Listen to German business people dealing with common situations which you might encounter.

KÖNNTE ICH BITTE HERRN NEUHAUS SPRECHEN?

Listen to the phone calls several times, then work out, in German, how to: *a* ask to speak to someone; *b* check someone's name; *c* ask if you have the right connection; *d* ask to be put through to someone; *e* say you'll ring back later; *f* ask for someone to call you back.

PSION GMBH, BAD HOMBURG

Frau Fabricius Fabricius.
Herr Grodtke Guten Tag, hier ist Grodtke, Firma Psion. Ich würde gern Herrn Sazinski sprechen.
Frau Fabricius Ja. Wie war der Name noch?
Herr Grodtke Grodtke mein Name, Firma Psion.
Frau Fabricius Moment, bitte mal...
Herr Grodtke Danke.

MÜNCHENER MESSE- UND AUSSTELLUNGSGESELLSCHAFT MBH

Frau Schwamm Pressestelle, Schwamm, grüß Gott!
Anrufer Grüß Gott! Bin ich bei der Pressestelle Systems?
Frau Schwamm Sie sind richtig, Pressestelle Systems.
Anrufer Könnten Sie mich bitte mit Dr. Probst verbinden?
Frau Schwamm Der spricht grad auf der anderen Leitung.
Anrufer Okay, dann ruf' ich nachher nochmal an.
Frau Schwamm Ja, danke!... Pressestelle, Schwamm, grüß Gott!...

NEUHAUS & NEUHAUS GMBH, MÜNCHEN

Frau Wagner Firma Neuhaus & Neuhaus, Wagner, guten Tag.
Frau Müller Guten Tag! Hier Müller, Firma Atelier GmbH.
Frau Wagner Ach, die Frau Müller. Guten Tag!
Frau Müller Könnt' ich bitte Herrn Neuhaus sprechen?
Frau Wagner Nein, der Herr Neuhaus ist heute leider nicht da, Frau Müller. Aber der ist nächste Woche Montag wieder im Hause.
Frau Müller Könnten Sie ihn bitten, mich zurückzurufen?
Frau Wagner Ja.

das Telefon	*telephone*
der Fernsprecher	*telephone*
(officialese)	
die Leitung	*line*
die Durchwahl	*direct line*
der Apparat	*phone, extension*
gerade/grad	*at the moment, just*
zurückrufen	*to ring back*

Frau Müller	Meine Nummer ist null, acht, neun ...
Frau Wagner	Null, acht, neun ...
Frau Müller	Eins, zwo, drei ...
Frau Wagner	Eins, zwo, drei ...
Frau Müller	Drei, acht, zwo, sechs.
Frau Wagner	Drei, acht, zwo, sechs. Okay, Frau Müller. Und er wird Sie dann am Montag umgehend zurückrufen.
Frau Müller	Vielen Dank! Auf Wiederhören!
Frau Wagner	Wiederschauen!

wie war der Name noch?	*what was the name again?*
Moment, bitte mal	*just a moment, please*
auf der anderen Leitung	*on the other line*
leider nicht da	*unfortunately not here/there*
wieder im Hause	*back in the office*

> **NUTS AND BOLTS** ▶

When asking for someone, it sounds more polite to use the form **könnte/könnten** (*could*) rather than **kann/können** (*can*). And remember that the associated infinitive goes to the end of the clause or sentence (see p 144):

> **Könnte** ich bitte Herrn Neuhaus **sprechen**?
> **Könnten** Sie mich mit Dr. Probst **verbinden**?

> **PRACTICE** ▶

1 Work out how to say: *a* a colleague isn't in today; *b* she'll be back in the office next Monday; *c* your colleague is on the other line.
2 Now look at the following situations and practise your replies: *a* A colleague is out. What do you say? *b* The secretary answers your call. Say you want to speak to Mr Grodtke. *c* Dr Hahn isn't in today. Ask if she could ring you back. *d* You answer the phone. Ask the caller to wait a moment. *e* Ask if you're connected to the Productronica press office. *f* Give your name and company and say you'd like to speak to Mr Schmidt.

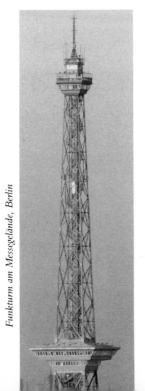

Funkturm am Messegelände, Berlin

ANTON, ÄRGER, BERTA...

There's a standard phone alphabet that you can use when you need to spell your name, company or town on the phone:

Anton, **Ä**rger, **B**erta, **C**äsar, **CH**arlotte, **D**ora, **E**mil, **F**riedrich, **G**ustav, **H**einrich, **I**da, **J**ulius, **K**aufmann, **L**udwig, **M**artha, **N**ordpol, **O**tto, **Ö**konom, **P**aula, **Q**uelle, **R**ichard, **S**iegfried/**S**amuel, **SCH**ule, **T**heodor, **U**lrich, **Ü**bermut, **V**iktor, **W**ilhelm, **X**anthippe, **Y**psilon, **Z**eppelin/**Z**acharias.

DEUTSCHE BP AG, HAMBURG

Empfang   Queens Hotel, guten Tag!

Frau Folco   Ja, Folco ist mein Name, von der Deutschen BP. Schönen guten Tag! Ich hätte gern zwei Zimmer bei Ihnen reserviert. Und zwar vom 13. auf den 14. Dezember...

Empfang   Ja, auf welchen Namen?

Frau Folco   Das ist einmal für Herrn David Simon...

Empfang   Können Sie das bitte buchstabieren?

Frau Folco   Ja. Dora Anton Viktor Ida Dora. Und Simon, Siegfried Ida Martha Otto Nordpol...

Empfang   Simon. Ja, und...?

Frau Folco   Und für Herrn Robert Horten: Heinrich Otto Richard Theodor Emil Nordpol...

Empfang   Robert Horten. Für eine Nacht?

Frau Folco   Ja, für eine Nacht...

DANN RUFE ICH NACHHER NOCHMAL AN

Horst Dieter Grodtke at Psion is trying to catch up on some sales calls.

▶ 1   Where is Mr Johannsen and when will Mr Grodtke ring again?
2   Where is Mr Sazinski and when will Mr Grodtke ring again?
3   Where is Mr Röding and when will Mr Grodtke ring again?

PSION GMBH, BAD HOMBURG

Herr Stotter   Bitte, Stotter.

Herr Grodtke   Guten Tag, hier ist Grodtke, Firma Psion. Herrn Johannsen hätt' ich gern gesprochen.

Herr Stotter   Sie, der ist grad beim Essen; der ist grad weg.

Herr Grodtke   Okay, ruf' ich nachher nochmal an.

Herr Stotter   Ja, so gute Viertelstunde, ja, 20 Minuten, ja.

Herr Grodtke   Danke. Alles klar. Danke. Wiederhören.

Herr Stotter   Ja, Wiederhören.

Herr Grodtke   Tschüs.

PSION GMBH, BAD HOMBURG

Frau Fabricius   Fabricius.

Herr Grodtke   Guten Tag, hier ist Grodtke, Firma Psion. Ich würde gern Herrn Sazinski sprechen.

Frau Fabricius   Ja. Wie war der Name noch?

Herr Grodtke   Grodtke mein Name, Firma Psion.

Frau Fabricius   Moment, bitte mal.

Herr Grodtke   Danke.

Horst Grodtke

das Meeting   *meeting*
die Geschäftsreise   *business trip*
gestern   *yesterday*
morgen   *tomorrow*
nochmal   *again*
wieder   *again*
weg   *away, out*
probieren   *to try*
erreichen   *to reach, achieve*

die Sekunde	second
die Minute	minute
die Stunde	hour
der Tag	day
der Monat	month
das Jahr	year
das Jahrzehnt	decade
das Jahrhundert	century
das Jahrtausend	millennium

Frau Fabricius   Hören Sie! Der Herr Sazinski ist im Moment in einem Meeting. Kann er Sie zurückrufen?
Herr Grodtke   Ich probier's glaub' ich besser morgen nochmal dann.
Frau Fabricius   Okay, danke. Wiederhören.
Herr Grodtke   Danke schön. Wiederhören!

PSION GMBH, BAD HOMBURG

Frau Siegel   Firma Interdata, Siegel, guten Tag!
Herr Grodtke   Guten Tag, hier ist Grodtke, Firma Psion. Ich hätte gern Herrn Röding gesprochen.
Frau Siegel   Hmm, der ist zu 'ner Geschäftsreise. Ist morgen erst wieder zu erreichen.
Herr Grodtke   Der ist morgen wieder da? Gut, ruf' ich morgen nochmal an. Danke. Wiederhören!

so gute Viertelstunde	*a good quarter of an hour*
hören Sie!	*hello? (lit. listen!)*
im Moment	*at the moment*
kann er Sie zurückrufen?	*can he call you back?*
zu 'ner Geschäftsreise	*away on business*
ist morgen erst wieder zu erreichen	*can't be reached till tomorrow*
wieder da	*back (again)*

NUTS AND BOLTS ▶

Immer alles sofort

„Ich glaube, daß wir Deutschen der Meinung sind, wir müssen immer alles sofort haben: Punkt A. Und Punkt B: daß wir bestimmte Sachen zu irgendwelchen genauen Zeiten haben müssen. Wenn ich diese Sache morgen haben möchte, dann möchte ich sie beispielsweise morgen um 10 Uhr 15 haben, und nicht um 10 Uhr 16!" (Harald Nickol, *Psion GmbH*)

When asking for people on the phone, you'll need to know the personal pronouns (*I/me, he/him, she/her*, etc.) (see p 140):

Kann **er Sie** zurückrufen?   *Can **he** call **you** back?*
Könnten **Sie ihn** bitten, **mich** zurückzurufen?
*Could **you** ask **him** to call **me** back?*

Mein (*my*), **sein** (*his/its*), **ihr** (*her/their*), **unser** (*our*), **Ihr** (formal *your*) indicate possession (see p 140):

Grodtke **mein** Name.   **unser** mobiles Datenerfassungsgerät

And remember that **der/die/das** is often used instead of **er/sie/es**, especially in conversation (see p 140):

Ich hätte gern **Herrn Röding** gesprochen. – **Der** ist auf Geschäftsreise.

PRACTICE ▶

1   A caller rings several times to speak to Ms Schuster. Unfortunately she's doing something each time.
Frage   Ich hätte gern Frau Schuster gesprochen.
Antwort   Die ist leider .... *a* at lunch;   *b* out;   *c* away on business;   *d* in a meeting.
2   This time: *a* tell the caller Ms Schuster is on the other line;   *b* say you'll connect him/her to Mr Hauser;   *c* ask if Ms Schuster can phone the caller back in 10 minutes.
3   See if you can find out how to say you'll ring again tomorrow.
4   The sales manager isn't in when you phone. Say you'll try later.

Horst Grodtke is following up a previous call to Miko Data. He wants to speak to Mr Mischke.

▶ **1** How does Mr Grodtke say *How are you?*
2 What is Mr Mischke's response?

PSION DEUTSCHLAND GMBH, BAD HOMBURG

Frau Weidemann	Miko Data, Weidemann, guten Tag!
Herr Grodtke	Guten Tag, Frau Weidemann! Grodtke, Firma Psion.

Ich hätte gerne Herrn Mischke gesprochen.
Frau Weidemann Ich konnte Ihren Namen leider nicht verstehen.
Herr Grodtke Grodtke ist mein Name, Firma Psion.
Frau Weidemann Grodtke. Einen kleinen Moment.
Herr Grodtke Danke schön!
(*She puts him through*)
Herr Mischke Mischke.
Herr Grodtke Guten Tag, Herr Mischke! Grodtke, Firma Psion.
Herr Mischke Ja!
Herr Grodtke Ich grüße Sie. Wie geht es Ihnen?
Herr Mischke Ah, danke vielmals. Ich bin sehr knapp mit Zeit im Moment.
Herr Grodtke Okay, Herr Mischke, machen wir's relativ kurz. Wir hatten uns über den HC unterhalten, unseren neuen Hand-held Computer. Haben Sie die Unterlagen bekommen? . . .

ich hätte gerne . . . gesprochen   *I'd like to speak to . . .*
ich konnte . . . leider nicht verstehen   *unfortunately I couldn't understand . . .*
wie geht es Ihnen?   *how are you?*
sehr knapp mit Zeit   *very pushed for time*
machen wir's . . . kurz   *let's make it . . . brief*
wir hatten uns über . . . unterhalten   *we spoke about . . .*

---

kurz   *short, briefly*
knapp   *scarce, short (of time)*
relativ   *relative(ly)*
vielmals   *many times*
grüßen   *to greet*

When learning nouns, make sure you learn the gender and plural. You can always check with the **Glossary**. When learning a new verb that isn't regular, learn the infinitive, the past tense and the past participle. The forms are in the **Glossary**.

NUTS AND BOLTS ▶

Remember that in German the subject is not necessarily the first element in the sentence (see p 147). Horst Grodtke asks for Mr Mischke like this:

subject	*verb*	*object*
Ich	hätte gerne	Herrn Mischke gesprochen.

In another phone call he changes the emphasis and starts with the person he wants to talk to:

object	*verb*	*subject*	
Herrn Johannsen	hätte	ich	gerne gesprochen.

When **Herr** is the direct object, it has an added **-n**. Professional titles are often used as well as **Herr** or **Frau**: **Herr(n) Doktor Probst, Frau Doktor Martin.**

1 Practise your best telephone manner by completing the following phone calls. There's more than one way of asking to speak to someone.

a Sie Ich .... Herrn Haller gesprochen.

Telefonistin Wie ist Ihr Name, bitte?

Sie (*your name*)

b Sie Ich .... Frau Kopp sprechen.

Telefonistin Ihr Name, bitte?

Sie .... (*your name*).

c Sie .... Frau Becker ....

Telefonistin Wie .... noch?

Sie (*your name*)

2 You're put through to Mr Althof. Greet him and ask how he is.

Herr Althof Althof.

Sie .... Herr Althof! (*your name*), ... (*your company*). .... Ihnen?

Herr Althof Danke, gut!

Pushed for time

When Mr Mischke answers Horst Grodtke's phone call, he cuts off the polite enquiries, saying he's pushed for time. Be prepared to get your message across right away.

SPRECHEN SIE NACH DEM PIEPTON

Don't be put off by recorded messages when you're phoning Germany.

Listen to the following and identify which: *a* asks you to wait; *b* asks you to speak after the signal; *c* tells you that you have got the wrong number; *d* tells you that you're talking to an answering machine.

i Kein Anschluß unter dieser Nummer!

ii Bitte warten! Bitte warten! Bitte warten!

iii Wir bemühen uns um Ihre Verbindung.

iv Bitte sprechen Sie nach dem Piepton.

v Sprechen Sie jetzt!

vi Hier ist der automatische Anrufbeantworter . . .

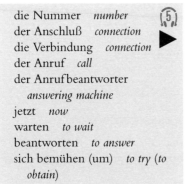

die Nummer *number*
der Anschluß *connection*
die Verbindung *connection*
der Anruf *call*
der Anrufbeantworter
  answering machine
jetzt *now*
warten *to wait*
beantworten *to answer*
sich bemühen (um) *to try (to obtain)*

NUTS AND BOLTS ▶

Notice how the recorded message instructs the caller to speak:
  Bitte **sprechen Sie** nach dem Piepton.
In the same way, a command like *listen!* includes **Sie** after the verb:
  Hören Sie!
This is the imperative verb form (see p 147).

By the way, if you ask for someone on the phone and they reply **Am Apparat!**, this means you're talking to them.

EINE GUTE ZEIT

 Horst Grodtke follows up a call he made the previous week to fix a meeting with a prospective client.

 At what time will Mr Grodtke be meeting Mr Biegner?

möglich *possible*
zwischen *between*
(so) gegen *around*
annehmen *to assume*
vorführen *to demonstrate*
sich treffen *to meet*

PSION GMBH, BAD HOMBURG

Herr Timm ... Timm, guten Tag!

Herr Grodtke Guten Tag, hier ist Grodtke, Firma Psion. Ich hätte gern Herrn Biegner gesprochen.

Herr Timm Einen kleinen Moment.

Herr Grodtke Danke.

Herr Biegner Biegner.

Herr Grodtke Guten Tag, Herr Biegner! Grodtke, Firma Psion, ich grüße Sie!

Herr Biegner Hallo, Herr Grodtke!

Herr Grodtke Herr Biegner, eine Frage. Ich hatte angenommen oder anberaumt, daß wir uns heute mal kurz treffen können, daß ich Ihnen unsere Produkte nochmal vorführen kann. Ist es möglich, daß wir uns so gegen halb vier treffen?

Herr Biegner Halb vier ist schlecht. Wäre vier Uhr möglich?

Herr Grodtke So zwischen halb vier und vier.

Herr Biegner Ja, okay. Das wär' 'ne gute Zeit.

Herr Grodtke Alles klar. In Mainz ist das?

Herr Biegner In Mainz, ja.

Herr Grodtke Okay. Danke schön! Wiederhören!

Herr Biegner Wiederhören!

ich hatte angenommen oder anberaumt *I had assumed or planned*
daß wir uns ... treffen können *that we could meet ...*
daß ich Ihnen ... vorführen kann *so that I can demonstrate to you ...*

Horst Grodtke

NUTS AND BOLTS Notice how Mr Grodtke and Mr Biegner use special forms of the verbs **haben** and **sein**:

Ich **hätte** gern Herrn Biegner gesprochen.

Das **wäre** eine gute Zeit.

This is the subjunctive form, which you met earlier: **könnte/könnten** (from **können**). It's often used with these common verbs to soften requests and statements. You'll also often find the forms **würde/würden** (from **werden**) (see p 144 and 146).

Practise getting information in German by ringing a German tourist office, railway station or hotel. Start off with **Guten Tag!** and your name, company and country. Then introduce your request: **Ich hätte gern eine Information**...

A contact rings you. Fill in your replies:

Herr Schmidt   Guten Tag, Schmidt, Firma Comitel.
Sie   ...., ...
Herr Schmidt   Ist es möglich, daß wir uns morgen gegen 15.00 Uhr treffen?
Sie   .... schlecht. ....?
Herr Schmidt   Ja, okay, so gegen 16.00 Uhr.
Sie   .... klar. .... Feldkirchen ....?
Herr Schmidt   Ja, um 16.00 Uhr in Feldkirchen.
Sie   ....! ....!
Herr Schmidt   Wiederhören!

You should now be able to phone contacts and colleagues.

Give your name and company
Guten Tag, hier ist König, Firma Computron.
Mein Name ist König, Firma Computron.

Check your connection and ask to speak to a person
Bin ich bei der Firma Fischer?
Ich hätte gern(e) Herrn/Frau (Doktor) Meyer gesprochen.
Ich würde gern(e) Herrn/Frau Meyer sprechen.
Könnte ich bitte Herrn/Frau Meyer sprechen?

Say you will ring back later
Ich rufe nachher nochmal an.
Ich probiere es morgen nochmal.

Ask for and check a caller's name
Wie ist Ihr Name, bitte?
Wie war der Name noch?
Ich konnte Ihren Namen leider nicht verstehen.

Ask a caller to hold the line
(Einen kleinen) Moment, bitte.

Say a colleague is away
Er/Sie ist leider weg / heute nicht da.
Er/Sie ist gerade beim Essen / im Moment in einem Meeting.

Ask a caller to ring back later
Könnten Sie nachher nochmal anrufen?

Ask how someone is
Wie geht es Ihnen?

Use *Checklist* when phoning your own business contacts.

1 Complete the sentences with the correct form (present tense) of the verbs in brackets: *a* Der Zwang zur Innovation .... (nehmen) weiter zu. *b* Insgesamt .... (sehen) es gut aus. *c* Er .... (sprechen) auf der anderen Leitung. *d* Der Weltumsatz .... (betragen) über 2 Milliarden D-Mark. *e* Wie .... (laufen) es?

2 Fill the gaps with the correct preposition: bei für an von im in in

a Das Zimmer ist .... dritten Stock. *b* Wir verteilen Broschüren und Kataloge .... unsere Kunden. *c* .... erster Linie. *d* Er arbeitet .... der Deutschen BP. *e* Die Firma macht einen Umsatz .... zirka sechs Millionen Mark. *f* Ich arbeite .... meine eigene Firma. *g* Der Sitz befindet sich .... Mainz.

3 Practise the following: *a* introduce yourself on the phone; *b* say you'll ring back later; *c* ask to speak to Mr Grodtke; *d* say Mr Sazinski is away; *e* ask someone to hold the line; *f* say someone is on the other line; *g* ask someone to repeat their name.

When making a phone call, think out what you want to say in German first, make sure you know the name of the person you want to speak to, then start your call.

Personal pronouns

The personal pronouns (eg **ich** *I*, **er** *he/it*) change their form depending on their case (see p 140). In fact, the same is true of English. Compare:

Ich rufe **ihn** an.   **Er** ruft **mich** an.
*I phone **him**.*   *He phones **me**.*

Nominative	Accusative	Dative
ich	Er ruft **mich** an.	Sie schickt **mir** die Unterlagen.
er	**ihn**	**ihm**
sie	**sie**	**ihr**
es	**es**	**ihm**
wir	**uns**	**uns**
sie	**sie**	**ihnen**
Sie	**Sie**	**Ihnen**

Possessives

Possessives show who or what something belongs to or is associated with. The formal form for *your* (**Ihr**) always begins with a capital letter.

my	**mein**	*our*	**unser**	
his/its	**sein**	*their*	**ihr**	
her/its	**ihr**	*your (formal)*	**Ihr**	

The endings vary according to the case of the noun (see p 139–140).

Ich bin mit **meinen** Freunden zusammen.
Wir bemühen uns um **Ihre** Verbindung.

ES GING DARUM, DASS...

Mr Schröder has promised to ring Mr Grodtke about Psion's hand-held computer. Mr Grodtke now tries to get hold of him – without success.

Listen to the phone call and find out what happens. *a* What had Mr Grodtke described? *b* What did Mr Grodtke want to do? *c* Who does the receptionist suggest putting him through to first? *d* Who is he transferred to? *e* When did Mr Schröder want to meet? *f* What did he want to discuss?

Die Serie III – ein Taschencomputer

PSION

um was geht's denn? *what is it about?*
es ging darum, daß *it was about the fact that*
HC *hand-held computer*
Datenerfassungsgerät *data-acquisition unit, hand-held computer*
Unterlagen *documentation*
bleiben Sie mal ... dran *just hold the line ...*
etwas davon *something about it*
das ist möglich *that's possible*
mehrfach *several times*
ganz dringend *quite urgently*
um ins Detail zu gehen *in order to go into details*

NUTS AND BOLTS ▶

Sometimes the definite article is used with the name of a person:
> Vielleicht weiß **der** Herr Nohr etwas davon.
> **Der** Herr Sazinski ist in einem Meeting.

This is only usual in speech, not in written German.

PRACTICE ▶

1 The phone rings and the caller asks for a colleague who is out. What do you say?
2 Ask someone what they want to discuss.
3 Ask a caller to wait a moment.
4 What's the German for *I'll transfer you*?
5 You're making a cold call to introduce yourself and your company on the phone. Include the following points: *a* your name and company; *b* your job and area of responsibility; *c* type of company; *d* location of head office; *e* existence and location of branches/sales offices/subsidiaries. You may need to use an English–German dictionary for this exercise.

EINE HERKULESARBEIT

Peter Sahla interviewed Guntram Kraus at the state-owned Deutsche Bundespost Telekom in Munich to find out about deregulation.

Listen to the interview a few times and answer these questions:
a When was the postal service restructured?
b What happened to the telephone network?
c Where can customers buy telephones, fax machines, etc.?
d Where is there competition in the German telephone network?
e Who are the two competitors?

die Deregulierung *deregulation*
das Monopol *monopoly*
das Netz *network*
die Einrichtung *installation, equipment*
das Faxgerät *fax machine*
das Telex *telex*
das Datenendgerät *data terminal*
der Mobilfunk *mobile phone network*
der Anbieter *supplier*
anschließen *to connect*
managen *to manage*
erwerben *to buy*
achten (auf) *to pay attention (to)*

Telekom-Laden

Get used to understanding different speakers and types of language. Horst Grodtke deals with corporate sales and aims to get across a straight-forward message in short, fast sentences. Guntram Kraus is an administrator explaining an abstract structure in complex sentences and a measured tone. Bear in mind the context, and concentrate on the stressed words.

die Rede ist von *there's talk about*
auf diesem Gebiet *in this area*
auf Grund der *because of the*
die ... stattgefunden hat *which took place ...*
zur Verfügung stellt *makes available*
die ... angeschlossen werden können *which can be connected ...*
sei es *whether they are*
die kann der Kunde ... kaufen *the customer can buy these ...*
oder aber auch *or else*
von jedem beliebigen *from any*
wo es ... gibt *where there are ...*
nicht in Aussicht gestellt *not on the cards*
was ... anbelangt *as far as ... is concerned*
über ... hinweg *right across ...*

PRACTICE

Try filling in the gaps in the following sentences: *a* Die Telekom .... das Netz zur .... *b* Das ist hier nicht in .... *c* Die Telekom .... das D1-Netz ....

TELEFONNUMMER UND VORWAHL

This is Telekom's advice on how to leave a message on an answering machine.

Guntram Kraus

deutlich *clear(ly)*
achten (auf) *to pay attention (to)*
genau *carefully*
möglichst *if possible*
ggf. = gegebenenfalls *where relevant*
ebenfalls *also*

1 Achten Sie genau auf den Startton.

2 Nennen Sie möglichst zweimal Ihren Namen.
Sprechen Sie dabei langsam und deutlich.

3 Geben Sie Datum, Uhrzeit sowie ggf. den Grund Ihres Anrufes an.

4 Formulieren Sie die Bitte um Rückruf ebenfalls zweimal.
Und nicht vergessen: Ihre Telefonnummer und Vorwahl angeben!

(Übers Telefonieren, Telekom)

NUTS AND BOLTS ▶

Notice how you can say *once, twice, three times* with the number followed by **-mal**, eg ein**mal**, drei**mal**, hundert**mal**:
Formulieren Sie die Bitte um Rückruf **zweimal**.

PRACTICE ▶

1 Read through Telekom's instructions and then answer the following questions in English: *a* What do you have to listen for before giving your message? *b* How many times should you give your name?
c How should you speak? *d* What should you give apart from the date and time of your call? *e* What should you not forget?
2 You want to talk to Mr Liebermann, but he's out. Leave a message on his answerphone asking him to call you back.
3 You're returning a call from Mrs Schumann but you get a recorded message. Say you called, leave your name, company and phone number, and give times when you'll be available.
4 Ask someone to speak after the beep.

EIN NEUES OVERLAYNETZ

Eine neue Telefonzelle

The following report stresses Telekom's improvements to telecommunications between east and west in the year after reunification.

▶ Look for the following information: *a* the method of improving communication between east and west; *b* the number of lines between east and west at the end of the year; *c* the number of phones in the east at the end of the year.

> *Wir haben 1991 neue Verbindungen für den wirtschaftlichen Aufschwung im Osten Deutschlands geschaffen.*

Telekom hatte sich schon für das erste Jahr sehr viel vorgenommen. Und die Erwartungen der Öffentlichkeit, der Wirtschaft, der Politik waren nicht geringer. Mit einem neuen Overlaynetz haben wir in kürzester Zeit die schlechten Verbindungen zwischen alten und neuen Bundesländern spürbar verbessert.

Die Zahl der Ost–Westverbindungen wurde von rund 1450 vor der Wende auf 50 000 Ende 1991 gesteigert.

Im Osten wurde die Zahl der Telefonanschlüsse pro Jahr annähernd verzehnfacht – auf 500 000. Wir haben damit ein wichtiges Ziel für 1991 erreicht.

(Ein Jahr Deutschland, Telekom)

die Politik *policy, politics*
die Wirtschaft *economy*
die Betriebswirtschaft *business administration, management*
die Volkswirtschaft *(macro)economics*
die Erwartung *expectation*
das Ziel *aim, objective*
das Bundesland *federal state, Land*
die Mauer *the Wall*
die Wende *the breaching of the Berlin Wall*
spürbar *discernible*
annähernd *almost*
wirtschaftlich *economic(ally)*
verbessern *to improve*
steigern *to increase*

hatte sich ... vorgenommen *had planned ...*
in kürzester Zeit *in a very short space of time*
zwischen alten und neuen Bundesländern *between old and new Länder*
von rund ... auf *from about ... to*
wurde ... annähernd verzehnfacht – auf *... was increased almost tenfold – to*
wir haben damit ... erreicht *this means that we have reached ...*

PRACTICE ▶

Read the report again and put the following points in the order in which they occur: *a* the number of east–west connections; *b* expectations of public, economy and politics; *c* number of phones in the east; *d* plans for the first year; *e* important target for 1991; *f* new connections for economic upturn.

die Konkurrenz	*competition*
das Autotelefon	*carphone*
das schnurlose Telefon	*cordless phone*
die Telefonzelle	*phone box*
die Telefonkarte	*phonecard*
die Münze	*coin*
die Vermittlung	*operator*
die Verbindung	*connection*
das Telefonbuch	*phone book*
die gelben Seiten	*Yellow Pages*
die Auskunft	*directory enquiries*
die Vorwahl	*dialling code*
national	*national(ly)*
international	*international(ly)*

Mr Kraus mentions that competition now exists in the German carphone market with two digital mobile cellular systems. The **D1-Netz** is operated by Telekom and the **D2-Netz** by Düsseldorf-based Mannesmann Mobilfunk. Mobile systems have played an important part in the move to jump-start the east German economy. Cordless phones are so far only officially available when licensed by Telekom, but unlicensed, cheaper models are also being sold in the shops.

Public phone boxes are traditionally yellow, but a new design is being introduced with the pink Telekom logo. Phonecards are now widely available and it's a good idea to get one from a post office. Make sure you have a phonecard or 30 pfennigs ready if you need to ring directory enquiries from a phone box. If you need a phone or fax number in Germany, ring international directory enquiries. The number for directory enquiries within Germany is 0 11 88.

Many companies in Germany are family businesses that like to stress cooperation and partnership with their business partners. Remember that phone calls, letters and faxes in German will increase your prestige and bring you closer to your customers.

☏ T·e·l·e·k·o·m·Telefax
Oberpostdirektion Hannover/Braunschweig

Deutsche Bundespost Telekom, Oberpostdirektion Hannover/Braunschweig

i   Empfänger

ii   Bitte weiterleiten an

iii   Ihre Telefaxnummer

iv   Sie erhalten Anzahl Seiten (inkl. Deckblatt)

v   zum Thema

? **1** Which heading refers to   *a* your fax number;   *b* subject of the fax;   *c* recipient;   *d* number of pages;   *e* other recipients?

2 In what circumstances should you contact the sender?

Haben Sie alle Seiten gut erhalten? Wenn nicht, nehmen Sie bitte mit uns Kontakt auf.

ES GEHT UM . . .

MEETINGS, ANALYSES, REPORTS

Gear up for meetings in German. By mastering ways of presenting your point, interjecting and contradicting, you can achieve your objectives.

PRIMA!

 Horst Grodtke has made an appointment to visit Mr Biegner at E.Y.E. Identifikationssysteme in Mainz, where he wants to demonstrate Psion's products. Kerstin Wachholz talks to him in the car on the way to the meeting.

▶ 1 What does E.Y.E. Identifikationssysteme specialize in?
2 What is Horst Grodtke's aim?
3 How did Mr Biegner find out about Psion?
4 What is he looking for?
5 Is Mr Grodtke satisfied with the outcome of the meeting?

PSION GMBH, BAD HOMBURG

Frau Wachholz   Was erwarten Sie sich von dem Gespräch jetzt in Mainz?
Herr Grodtke   Wir fahren jetzt zu der Firma E.Y.E. Identifikationssysteme. Diese Firma beschäftigt sich ausschließlich mit mobiler Datenerfassung. Und ich möchte dem Herrn Biegner unsere Produkte demonstrieren und möchte erreichen, daß Herr Biegner unsere Produkte und seine Software dem Kunden anbietet.

(At the meeting)
Herr Biegner   Ja, Herr Grodtke, wir haben ja zusammen telefoniert. Ich hatte also mehrere Anzeigen in Fachzeitschriften gesehen über Psion-

---

das Gespräch *conversation, meeting*
die Anzeige *advertisement*
die Fachzeitschrift *trade journal*
die Zusammenarbeit *cooperation*
zukunftsweisend *future-oriented*
fruchtbar *fruitful*
sich spezialisieren (auf) *to specialize (in)*
(sich) erwarten *to expect*
telefonieren *to phone*
vorstellen *to present*

Das Gespräch

Geräte. Und wir sind also 'n Systemhaus, das sich auf mobile Daten-erfassungsgeräte spezialisiert hat. Und wir sind auf der Suche nach einem zukunftsweisenden Gerät. Vielleicht zeigen Sie mir mal 'n bißchen was.

Herr Grodtke   Hm, prima! Vielleicht darf ich Ihnen ganz kurz Psion in zwei Sätzen vorstellen, und dann gehen wir kurz auf die Produkte ein.

Herr Biegner   Okay, selbstverständlich . . .

Herr Grodtke   Psion wurde . . .

(And following the meeting)

Frau Wachholz   War das Gespräch eben erfolgreich?

Herr Grodtke   Ich würde schon sagen, daß es erfolgreich war. Ich glaube, es wird eine sehr fruchtbare Zusammenarbeit zwischen Herrn Biegner und uns geben.

diese Firma beschäftigt sich . . . mit   *this company deals . . . with*
ich . . . möchte erreichen, daß   *I . . . would like to reach the position that*
das sich auf . . . spezialisiert hat   *which has specialized in . . .*
wir sind auf der Suche nach   *we're looking for*
'n bißchen was   *a little bit, something*
dann gehen wir kurz auf . . . ein   *then we can briefly talk about . . .*
ich würde schon sagen   *yes, I would say*
ich glaube, es wird . . . geben   *I think there will be . . .*

NUTS AND BOLTS

Before going on a trip to Germany, give yourself some intensive language training. Make a list of the things you have to do, work out what you'll have to say, and then practise hard. Remember that a little German can go a long way!

Some German verbs and nouns are associated with a specific preposition:

das **sich auf** mobile Datenerfassungsgeräte **spezialisiert** hat

auf der **Suche nach** einem zukunftsweisenden Gerät

Diese Firma **beschäftigt sich mit** mobiler Datenerfassung.

In the *Glossary* you'll find these prepositions given after the verbs and nouns they're used with. It helps to learn verbs or nouns with any associated prepositions.

Notice how **ja** and **also** are used when summarizing what the other person already knows:

Wir haben **ja** zusammen telefoniert.

Ich hatte **also** mehrere Anzeigen gesehen.

Wir sind **also** ein Systemhaus . . .

These words help to establish a common basis for communication by emphasizing uncontroversial points known to both parties.

PRACTICE

1   Ask a representative to show you a product.

2   Say that company X specializes in: *a* computers; *b* pharmaceutical products; *c* clothing; *d* manufacturing windows; *e* chemicals.

3   Give a presentation of your product based on the following:
a reference to phone call; *b* introduction to company; *c* type of product; *d* product features; *e* details; *f* price; *g* delivery times.

100

DARF ICH UNTERBRECHEN?

Klaus Harms chaired a meeting of the PR team at BP to discuss cost-cutting measures. He started by welcoming the participants, Hans-Jürgen Buchhorn, Elke Heuck and Stefanie Baasner. He then called on Mr Buchhorn for comments. Listen to the discussion and then answer the questions.

1   What time does the meeting begin?
2   How many topics are there on the agenda and what are they?
3   What does Mr Buchhorn have to give suggestions on?
4   What is every journalist convinced about?
5   Why is the order of the agenda changed?
6   What document does Ms Heuck pass round?

die Geschäftsordnung   *agenda*
das Thema   *subject, topic*
die Unterlage   *document(ation)*
der Vorschlag   *suggestion*
die Bemerkung   *remark*
das Verständnis   *understanding*
generell   *generally*
diskutieren   *to discuss*
überzeugen   *to convince*
unterbrechen   *to interrupt*

DEUTSCHE BP AG, HAMBURG

Herr Harms   So, guten Morgen...
Alle   Morgen... Morgen... Guten Morgen.
Herr Harms   Es freut mich, daß Sie alle gekommen sind. Vielen Dank, daß Sie es ermöglicht haben, heute, wie vereinbart, um 10 Uhr hier im 5K13 zu erscheinen. Über das Thema haben wir ja letztes Mal schon gesprochen. Es geht also um die Leistungsvereinbarung zwischen dem Bereich PR und den Service-Einheiten sowie den einzelnen Tochtergesellschaften. Zum zweiten geht es darum, Einsparmöglichkeiten zu finden, um auch von daher in der Lage zu sein, beim Budget einen Ausgleich zwischen Einnahmen und Ausgaben zu erzielen und generell die Kosteneinsparungen, die uns angedient wurden, auch zu realisieren. Kann ich mal Sie, Herr Buchhorn, fragen, ob Sie zu den Leistungsvereinbarungen einen Kommentar abgeben möchten, oder wo Sie eine Chance sehen, noch Einsparungen vorzunehmen, sagen wir beim Rechnungswesen, beispielsweise?
Herr Buchhorn   Also, generell eine Vorbemerkung: Jeder Zeitungsmann ist traurig, wenn ihm die Mittel gekürzt werden, denn er ist davon überzeugt, ein wichtiges Produkt dem Leser anzubieten, und um ein gutes Produkt herzustellen, benötigt man Geld. Okay, wir müssen das zur Kenntnis nehmen, daß diese Mittel in dem bisherigen Maße nicht mehr vorhanden sind, und müssen uns auf die neue Situation einstellen. Mein Vorschlag...
Herr Harms   Darf ich Sie mal kurz unterbrechen? Wir waren eigentlich jetzt bei den Leistungsvereinbarungen... Aber da Sie jetzt etwas in Zeitdruck auch sind und es Ihren Bereich betrifft, können wir auch die Geschäftsordnung umdrehen, daß wir erst die Einsparungen bei der Werkzeitung diskutieren und uns dann später mit den Leistungsvereinbarungen auseinandersetzen.

das Budget *budget*
die Mittel (*pl.*) *means, resources*
das Rechnungswesen *accountancy, accounting, book-keeping*
die Zahl *number*
die Kosteneinsparung *cost saving*
die Einsparmöglichkeit *possibility for cost-cutting*
die Leistung *service*
die Vereinbarung *agreement*
der Ausgleich *balance*
berechnen *to calculate*
einsparen *to save*
erzielen *to achieve*

Herr Buchhorn Okay, herzlichen Dank für das Verständnis, Herr Harms . . .

Frau Heuck Darf ich noch kurz unterbrechen, hierzu hab' ich eine Unterlage vorbereitet, die ich jetzt mal verteile. Das ist eine Kostenaufstellung von Januar bis September dieses Jahres. Und das ist vielleicht ganz gut, wenn wir darüber reden, daß wir hier einige Zahlen vorliegen haben.

daß Sie es ermöglicht haben, . . . zu erscheinen *that you've made it possible to come . . .*
es geht also um *it's about*
geht es darum, . . . zu finden *it's about finding . . .*
um auch von daher in der Lage zu sein *in order to be in a position, from that point of view, too*
beim Budget einen Ausgleich . . . zu erzielen *to achieve a balance . . . in the budget*
die uns angedient wurden *which have been forced upon us*
ob Sie zu . . . einen Kommentar abgeben möchten *whether you'd like to comment on . . .*
wenn ihm die Mittel gekürzt werden *when his resources are cut*
er ist davon überzeugt, . . . anzubieten *he's convinced that he's offering . . .*
zur Kenntnis nehmen *accept, take on board*
in dem bisherigen Maße *to the same extent as before*
müssen uns auf . . . einstellen *have to adjust to . . .*
wir waren eigentlich jetzt bei *really we were now dealing with*
da . . . und es Ihren Bereich betrifft *because . . . and it affects your area*
(daß wir) uns . . . mit den Leistungsvereinbarungen auseinandersetzen *(that we) discuss the service agreements . . .*

NUTS AND BOLTS ▶

Notice how Mr Harms thanks his colleagues for having *made it possible to come*, using a clause that ends with **zu** and an infinitive:

daß Sie es ermöglicht haben, heute um 10 Uhr hier im 5K13 **zu erscheinen**.

If the verb has a separable prefix, eg **vornehmen**, **anbieten**, **herstellen**, **zu** goes between the prefix and the main verb, eg **vorzunehmen**, **anzubieten**, **herzustellen** (see p 147).

Notice the vowel change in the present tense of this *strong verb* (see p 143):

betreffen: er/sie/es betrifft

Similarly, the vowel changes in the present tense of these verbs:

nehmen: er/sie/es/man nimmt
sprechen: er/sie/es/man spricht

PRACTICE ▶

1 You're preparing for a meeting. Say that you've done the following:
a prepared/document; *b* phoned/clients; *c* ordered/coffee;
d prepared/agenda; *e* distributed/documentation.
2 Open a meeting by welcoming the participants.

8

80 Prozent der Leute

„Mit den Fachzeitschriften und den Tageszeitungen *FAZ* und *Süddeutsche* deck' ich 80 Prozent der Leute, die wir ansprechen wollen, ab. Das heißt, Leute aus dem Management, aus dem Middle-Management, Entscheidungsträger, sowohl in Deutschland-Süd, -Mitte, -Nord, -Ost und -West." (Claude Heinz, *Mach Eins Werbeagentur*)

Hierarchie nicht so dominant

„Ich glaube, im Vergleich zu einer deutschen Firma ist die Hierarchie bei Psion vielleicht nicht ganz so dominant ausgeprägt. Wir besprechen alle Dinge mehr im Team als bei einer anderen vergleichbaren deutschen Firma." (Horst Dieter Grodtke, *Psion GmbH*)

3 Es geht um ... Say that the meeting is about the following (don't forget to use the *accusative*): *a* solutions to the problems; *b* the sales network; *c* the subsidiaries; *d* the new head office; *e* the purchase price; *f* the new exhibition; *g* the price list; *h* the turnover; *i* the delivery times.

4 Try strengthening your arguments by saying why something is necessary, using **um ... zu**: *a* Man benötigt qualifizierte Mitarbeiter/ein gutes Produkt/herstellen; *b* Man braucht Geld/eine Firma/aufbauen; *c* Wir benötigen Auslandsvertretungen/weltweit Erfolg/haben; *d* Man benötigt gute Exponate/eine erfolgreiche Messe/veranstalten.

5 Say that the following things are available: *a* good employees; *b* the resources; *c* money; *d* good exhibits.

6 You're going to chair a meeting to decide on the venue, time and date of an important sales conference. Practise the following: *a* thank colleagues for coming; *b* give the main subject of the meeting; *c* introduce a second subject of the meeting; *d* suggest changing the agenda; *e* say you have prepared a document.

7 Practise getting your message across and maintaining good relations: *a* say you're convinced; *b* say that in your view ...; *c* interrupt someone; *d* introduce a suggestion; *e* ask a colleague if she wants to comment; *f* thank someone for their consideration; *g* say it's necessary to accept something.

KEIN PROBLEM!

At the meeting, Mr Harms suggests a coffee break.

1 Who arranges for coffee to be brought?
2 Who is to bring the coffee?
3 What should not be forgotten?

DEUTSCHE BP AG, HAMBURG

der Kaffee	*coffee*
der Tee	*tea*
die Milch	*milk*
das Kännchen	*pot*
der Zucker	*sugar*
der/das Keks	*biscuit*

Herr Harms Sie möchten sicher einen Kaffee trinken. Kann ich Ihnen einen Kaffee besorgen? Frau Baasner, könnten Sie vielleicht mal ...
Frau Baasner Ja, gern. Ich geh' ...
Herr Harms ... dem Sekretariat Bescheid sagen, daß wir ...
Frau Heuck Ich hätte gerne Tee.
Frau Baasner Ja.
Herr Harms Und ich hätte gern ein Kännchen Kaffee.
Frau Baasner Mmhm.
Herr Buchhorn Und bitte die Kekse nicht vergessen!
Frau Baasner Kein Problem!

If you're stuck for a word, don't panic! Just ask, eg **Wie sagt man 'juice' auf deutsch?** You'll find people are always willing to help. Also carry a pocket dictionary in case you need to look something up in a hurry.

die Strukturierung   *structure*
die Finanzierung   *finance*
der Laden   *shop*
die Privatisierung   *privatization*
das Recht   *law*
die Steuer   *tax*
das Besichtigen   *tour*
die Verbesserung   *improvement*
der Schritt   *step*
der Punkt   *point*
untersuchen   *to examine*
sich anschauen   *to look at*

1   How would you say 'no problem'?
2   How would you remind a colleague not to forget something?
3   Ask a visitor if you can get them the following: *a* tea;   *b* coffee;   *c* mineral water;   *d* juice.

DER SCHRITT IN DIE PRIVATISIERUNG

Before reunification, Orthopädie- und Rehatechnik Dresden GmbH supplied artificial limbs and bandages to the local medical academy. Dieter Sackmann, an accountant and consultant with Price Waterhouse in Dresden, has been carrying out an analysis of the company's position and prospects in the market economy. He reports on his findings to the joint managing directors of the company, Klaus Oschatz and Rolf Herzog.

1   What did Mr Sackmann notice in particular when looking round?
2   Which two aspects did he single out for change?

ORTHOPÄDIE– UND REHATECHNIK DRESDEN GMBH, DRESDEN

Herr Sackmann   Herr Oschatz, Herr Herzog! Ich hatte mir kurz Ihren Betrieb angeschaut und einige Bereiche im Detail untersucht. Zunächst hatten wir uns die Entstehungsgeschichte angeschaut, dann die Übernahme der PGH, insbesondere hier die rechtliche Strukturierung, auch unter steuerlichen Aspekten. Ein weiterer Punkt war die Finanzierung der GmbH.

Beim Besichtigen der Betriebe, des Ladens, habe ich auch gesehen die Mitarbeiter, die Sie haben, und da ist insbesondere mir aufgefallen, daß Sie doch sehr viel ältere Mitarbeiter haben. Ich glaube, diesen Punkt sollten wir später nochmal im Detail diskutieren. Auch den Bereich des Rechnungswesens, denn da sind, glaube ich, doch noch einige Verbesserungsmöglichkeiten vorhanden. Ansonsten glaube ich, daß Sie den Schritt sehr gut geschafft haben, den Schritt in die Privatisierung ...

ich hatte mir kurz ... angeschaut   *I briefly looked (lit. had looked) at* ...
zunächst   *first of all*
PGH=Produktionsgenossenschaft des Handwerks   *(former GDR) trade/craft collective*
unter steuerlichen Aspekten   *from the point of view of tax*
die Mitarbeiter, die Sie haben   *the employees you have*
denn da sind ... vorhanden   *because there are* ...
ansonsten   *otherwise*
den Schritt ... geschafft haben   *have accomplished the move*

Remember that **haben** can be used on its own:

..., daß Sie doch sehr viel ältere Mitarbeiter **haben**.

It is also used with another verb to talk about the past:

Beim Besichtigen **habe** ich auch die Mitarbeiter **gesehen**, ...

To form the perfect tense of another verb, you use the present tense of **haben**. For the pluperfect, you use **haben** in the past tense (see p 144):

Ich **hatte** mir kurz Ihren Betrieb **angeschaut**.

Notice that Mr Sackmann doesn't invariably put the second part of the verb at the end of the clause, as would be normal in written German:

... **habe** ich auch **gesehen** die Mitarbeiter, ...

Word order is flexible in speech, but to make sure you're understood, it's best if you keep to the standard order (see p 147).

PRACTICE ▶

die Krankenkasse *health-insurance company/scheme*
freiberuflich *self-employed, freelance*
der Krankenschein *health-insurance voucher*

1 Report back to your boss on a company you've just visited: *a* ich/besichtigen/Firma X; *b* Geschäftsführer/zeigen/mir/ Firma; *c* Firma/gründen/1930; *d* Firma/beschäftigen/heute/120 Mitarbeiter; *e* Umsatz/2,5 Millionen Mark; *f* Sitz/sich befinden/ Hamburg; *g* Firma/herstellen/Fenster; *h* ich/anschauen/einige Bereiche/im Detail; *i* ich/sehen/Lackierhalle; *j* ich/sehen/Mitarbeiter.
2 Write a report, in German, on Dieter Sackmann's findings at Reha-technik. Give: *a* three aspects of the company he looked at; *b* two aspects of the PGH takeover he paid particular attention to; *c* particular impression when looking round the business; *d* area where improvements can be made; *e* overall opinion on the privatization.

Healthcare

Reha's main customer is the national health-insurance scheme. Unless you're self-employed or a high-earner, you're legally obliged to belong to one of the state-supervised **Krankenkassen**. Healthcare is obtained by handing in an insurance voucher to a doctor or hospital.

Dr. med.
Detlef Friedewald
Arzt und Psychotherapeut
Naturheilverfahren

Dr. Inge Kalischer

Zahnärztin

Sprechzeiten
Mo. u. Do. 8 - 15 Uhr
Di. u. Fr. 11 - 18 Uhr

MORALISCH VERPFLICHTET

Klaus Oschatz is a master craftsman (**Meister**) in orthopaedic prostheses. He's responsible for the technical side of the business and PR. He feels a conflict between his sense of responsibility towards fellow employees and the economic realities of the new system.

▶ **1** Which of the options are true? Klaus Oschatz thinks *a* Mr Sackmann's advice is: *i* unwichtig; *ii* hilfreich; *iii* moralisch; *b* the past is: *i* unglücklich; *ii* ökonomisch; *iii* relevant; *iv* sicher.
2 Why does Mr Oschatz feel a moral obligation towards his employees?

Klaus Oschatz

ORTHOPÄDIE- UND REHATECHNIK DRESDEN GMBH, DRESDEN

Frau Wachholz   Herr Oschatz, was halten Sie von der Analyse von Herrn Sackmann? Werden Sie einige seiner Ratschläge befolgen?

Herr Oschatz   Ich hielt die Ratschläge von Herrn Sackmann sehr interessant. Sicher sieht er vieles rein aus der Sicht des Altbundesländlers. Aber Zahlreiches hat mir auch doch manchen Hinweis gegeben, den wir berücksichtigen werden. Aber manches sah er eben auch zu ökonomisch, da spielt eben auch unsere Vergangenheit noch eine Rolle. Es ist eben so: Wenn man 40 Jahre Planwirtschaft und Mangel gemeinsam durchgestanden hat, dann kann man sich – wenn der glückliche Umstand des Neubeginns nun gegeben ist – sich nicht auf einmal von denen, die diesen Weg auch mit uns gegangen sind, wie Ballast trennen. Da fühl' ich mich auch moralisch gegenüber diesen verpflichtet, wohlwissend, daß sie ökonomisch hemmend wirken könnten.

die Analyse *analysis*	
der Ratschlag *advice*	
der Hinweis *pointer, advice*	
die Planwirtschaft *planned economy*	
der Mangel *shortage*	
die Vergangenheit *past*	
ökonomisch *economic(ally)*	
glücklich *happy, happily*	
verpflichtet *obliged, responsible*	
berücksichtigen *to take account of*	

was halten Sie von . . . ?   *what is your view on . . . ?*
ich hielt . . . sehr interessant (more usual: hielt . . . für sehr interessant)   *I found . . . very interesting*
rein aus der Sicht   *purely from the point of view*
den wir berücksichtigen werden   *which we'll take into account*
zu ökonomisch   *too much from the economic standpoint*
spielt . . . eine Rolle   *. . . plays a role*
es ist eben so   *it's like this*
kann man sich . . . nicht auf einmal von denen . . . trennen   *you can't just suddenly . . . jettison those people . . .*
die diesen Weg . . . gegangen sind   *who have been along this path . . .*
hemmend wirken könnten   *could prove restrictive*

NUTS AND BOLTS ▶

Notice how **dies**, **viel** and **manch** can be used either in front of a noun,
  diesen Weg   **viel(e)** ältere Mitarbeiter   **manchen** Hinweis
or as a pronoun that takes the place of a noun (see p 139–140):
  Ich fühle mich gegenüber **diesen** (*these people*) verpflichtet.
  Er sieht **vieles** (*many things*) rein aus der Sicht des Altbundesländlers.
  Aber **manches** (*many things*) sah er zu ökonomisch.

PRACTICE ▶

1   Say you thought a colleague's advice was important.
2   How did Mr Sackmann say *I think . . .?*
3   Mr Oschatz uses two verbs in the past tense: **hielt** and **sah**. How could he have made these points in the present tense?   *a* Ich .... die Ratschläge für sehr interessant.   *b* Manches .... er zu ökonomisch. (The clues are in the interview.)
4   Give a brief summary, in German, of Klaus Oschatz' assessment of Dieter Sackmann's report. Include the following points: *a* Oschatz' opinion on the advice;   *b* Sackmann's perceived perspective;   *c* Oschatz' criticism;   *d* Oschatz' intention with regard to the advice;   *e* Oschatz' approach to the workforce;   *f* disadvantage of this approach.

8

Keine eigenen Immobilien

„Probleme gibt es für Betriebe dieser Größe sicherlich. Unser Problem ist, daß wir keine eigenen Immobilien haben. Wir sind also hier zur Miete. Und dieses Mietverhältnis ist zur Zeit etwas auf wackligen Beinen, weil es Rückforderungsansprüche früherer Eigner gibt. Das ist ein Unsicherheitsfaktor, der mich manche schlaflose Nacht kostet." (Rolf Herzog, *Orthopädie- und Rehatechnik Dresden GmbH*)

Der Markt ist offen

„Ich glaube, daß gerade ausländische Unternehmen in der ehemaligen DDR eine sehr gute Möglichkeit haben zu investieren. Genau wie in der Bundesrepublik. Es ist rechtlich kein anderer Staat, und es sind größere Chancen, sich dort zu siedeln und zu setteln. Der Markt ist natürlich total für ausländische Investoren offen." (Gerrit Neuhaus, *Neuhaus & Neuhaus GmbH*)

Practise getting your message across and presenting an analysis.

Welcome the participants
Es freut mich, daß Sie (alle) gekommen sind.

Give the subject
Es geht um die Leistungsvereinbarung.
Es geht darum, Einsparmöglichkeiten zu finden.

Say you think/you're convinced that . . .
Ich glaube . . .
Ich würde sagen, daß . . .
Ich bin davon überzeugt, daß . . .
Ich halte/hielt es für interessant/wichtig.

Say you ought to discuss a point (later)
Diesen Punkt sollten wir (später nochmal) im Detail diskutieren.

Say you have to accept something
Wir müssen das zur Kenntnis nehmen.

Introduce a suggestion
Mein Vorschlag wäre . . .

Interrupt someone or change the agenda
Darf ich Sie (mal kurz) unterbrechen?
Wir können die Geschäftsordnung umdrehen.

Thank someone for their consideration
Herzlichen Dank für das Verständnis, Herr/Frau . . .

Say you've prepared documentation
Ich habe eine Unterlage vorbereitet.

Present a company's speciality
Die Firma X ist ein Systemhaus, das sich auf . . . spezialisiert hat.
Die Firma X beschäftigt sich mit . . .

Say you've looked at something
Ich habe mir den Betrieb angeschaut.
Ich habe einige Bereiche im Detail untersucht.

Say you've noticed something
Mir ist aufgefallen, daß . . .

Give an evaluation
Ich glaube, daß Sie den Schritt sehr gut geschafft haben.
Da sind noch einige Verbesserungsmöglichkeiten vorhanden.

Use *Checklist* to practise presenting your own company and products.

Remember that it's very easy to expand your vocabulary in German. You can make compound nouns, form nouns from verbs and verbs from nouns, and use foreign words. Make the most of all the avenues open to you when talking to people.

1 Find (in this unit) the other members of these word families.

Verb	Noun	Adjective
a mobilisieren	die Mobilität	....
b	die Sicht	sichtbar
c kürzen	die Kürzung	....
d verstehen	....	verständnisvoll
e sich interessieren	das Interesse	....

2 You want the name of a person you wish to contact. Ask the receptionist for the name of the: *a* marketing manager; *b* project manager; *c* secretary; *d* press spokesman; *e* film producer; *f* colleague; *g* managing director.

3 The run-up to a trade fair is always the busiest time for the press office. Unscramble sentences *i–v* and use them to take the part of callers trying to get through to Dr Probst:

i Dr. Probst verbinden Sie könnten mich bitte mit

ii Gott ich Herrn gern gesprochen grüß Dr. Probst hätte

iii morgen ich es nochmal probiere okay

iv Systems Pressestelle ich bei guten der bin Tag

v Dr. möchte Herrn Probst sprechen gern ich

a Frau Schwamm   Pressestelle, Schwamm, grüß Gott!
Anrufer   .... ! ....
Frau Schwamm   Der spricht gerade auf der anderen Leitung.
Anrufer   .... , ...
Frau Schwamm   Okay, bitte. Tschüs!

b Frau Schwamm   Pressestelle, Schwamm, grüß Gott!
Anrufer   .... ! .... ?
Frau Schwamm   Sie sind richtig, Pressestelle Systems.
Anrufer   ....
Frau Schwamm   Ja . . .

c Frau Knöpfler   Presseabteilung, Knöpfler.
Anrufer   .... ?
Frau Knöpfler   Ja, einen Moment, bitte. *(to Frau Schwamm)* Kann ich den zu Herrn Probst durchstellen?
Frau Schwamm   Nee, der spricht auf der anderen Leitung. Muß warten.

4 To say where something is located, you can use the reflexive verb **sich befinden**, eg **Der Wagen befindet sich im Parkhaus**. Practise giving locations using the words *a–f*, without worrying about the form of the articles and endings. Then try and work out the correct forms. The prepositions **auf**, **bei** and **in** are here followed by the dative case. *a* Auto (*n.*)/auf/Parkplatz (*m.*); *b* Hauptsitz (*m.*)/in/Mainz; *c* Tür (*f.*)/bei/Aufzug (*m.*); *d* Restaurant (*n.*)/in/Zentrum (*n.*); *e* Büro (*n.*)/in/zweite Etage (*f.*); *f* Kasse (*f.*)/bei/Eingang (*m.*).

Sehr gute Chancen
„Ich halte die ehemalige DDR für ein schlechtes Investmentland, wenn jemand ganz schnell sehr hohen Gewinn machen möchte. Das halte ich für nicht möglich. Ich glaube, daß es ein Investmentland ist mit sehr, sehr guten Chancen, aber auf die Dauer von Gewinnzonen ab sieben bis zehn Jahren." (Gerrit Neuhaus, *Neuhaus & Neuhaus GmbH*)

5 Try deriving verbs from the following nouns and check them in the *Glossary*: *a* Besuch; *b* Übernahme; *c* Strukturierung; *d* Finanzierung; *e* Mitarbeiter; *f* Verbesserung; *g* Privatisierung; *h* Untersuchung; *i* Diskussion; *j* Rechnung; *k* Lösung; *l* Besichtigen.

STRUCTURES ▶

um . . . zu

This is equivalent to *in order to . . .* and is used to talk about how to achieve objectives (see p 147):

> **um** in der Lage **zu** sein, beim Budget einen Ausgleich zu erzielen
> *in order to be in a position to achieve a balance in the budget*

Notice the position of **zu** plus infinitive at the end of the clause.

Infinitive clauses

A clause ending with **zu** + infinitive often gives additional information about the preceding clause (see p 147):

> Es geht darum, Einsparmöglichkeiten **zu finden.**
> Vielen Dank, daß Sie es ermöglicht haben, heute **zu erscheinen.**

The more German you hear, the more you'll understand what's going on. Try tuning in to German radio to get used to the sound of spoken German. Relax as you listen, without worrying about how much or how little you understand. If you have access to German TV, that's even better, because the pictures will help your understanding.

Notice the use of **da(r)** + **um** in the first example: **es geht** needs the preposition **um** + object (**es geht um** . . . *it's about* . . .). **Da** acts as a dummy object in the main clause and points forward to an infinitive clause (see p 142). This construction occurs when the verb in the main clause requires a preposition + object to complete the meaning, eg **überzeugen von** (*to convince of*):

> Jeder Zeitungsmann ist **davon überzeugt**, ein wichtiges Produkt **anzubieten.**

In case you're confused – don't worry! There's no need to use a complex construction like this, but it's useful to be able to recognize it.

ORT UND ZEITPUNKT

The PR team at BP needed a brief meeting to fix a time for the meeting to discuss the PR budget! Listen to the discussion about place and time.

der Zeitpunkt	*time*	▶
letzte Woche	*last week*	
nächste Woche	*next week*	
nächsten Dienstag	*next Tuesday*	
verlegen	*to postpone*	
bekanntgeben	*to make known, inform*	

1 What are the details of time and place which are agreed on?
2 Who has to make the arrangements?
3 What does Mr Buchhorn agree to do?

damit wir uns über . . . verständigen   *so that we can agree on . . .*
den Ort . . . festzulegen   *to establish the place . . .*
wann es uns . . . allen paßt   *when it suits us all . . .*
wie sieht das . . . aus   *how does it look . . .*
zur Verfügung haben   *have available*

denen wir ... andienen   *for whom we provide ...*
am kommenden Dienstag   *this Tuesday*
wir sehen uns   *we'll see each other*
... wird allen noch bekanntgegeben   *everyone will be informed of ...*

NUTS AND BOLTS ▶

Wann and **damit** are like **wenn** and **weil**. They introduce a subordinate clause in which the main verb is shunted to the end (see p 147):

    ..., **wann** es uns am besten allen **paßt**.
    ..., **damit** wir uns über einen Termin **verständigen**.

PRACTICE ▶

1   Ask someone to inform the following people: *a* managing director;   *b* secretary;   *c* project manager;   *d* engineer;
e representatives.
2   Say the following would suit you: *a* 10.00;   *b* next Wednesday;
c tomorrow;   *d* the location;   *e* the time.
3   Say you have an appointment: *a* at 8.15/with a colleague;
b today/at the factory;   *c* at 12.30/in the PR department;   *d* at
14.00/with a customer;   *e* at 15.30/with the press office;   *f* next
Friday/with the trade-fair company.
4   Say you'll postpone the appointment until: *a* Wednesday;   *b* 12.30;
c next week;   *d* next month;   *e* tomorrow.
5   Say you'll see everybody: *a* on Thursday;   *b* in May;   *c* next
year;   *d* on Monday;   *e* in March.
6   Say people will be informed of the following: *a* date;   *b* time;
c room;   *d* location;   *e* appointment.

E. Heuck, J. Buchhorn, S. Baasner, K. P. Harms

Rolf Herzog

MODERNSTE HILFSMITTEL

This article from the tabloid *Bild* gives a short overview of Rehatechnik. Rolf Herzog is a computer engineer and joint managing director. He's in charge of the company's accounts and administration.

1 What type of company is REHA and what does it produce?
2 How many employees does the company have?

die Zeitung *newspaper*
die Boulevardzeitung *tabloid*
das Hilfsmittel *aid*
die Erleichterung *relief*
die Anpassung *fitting*
die Investition *investment*
technisch *technical(ly)*
körperbehindert *disabled*
investieren *to invest*
tun *to do*

Dresden – **Ein neues Geschäft bringt körperbehinderten Dresdnern Erleichterung: die Orthopädie- und Rehatechnik Dresden GmbH in der Antonstraße 23. Die Firma fertigt Prothesen und bietet eine breite Auswahl modernster Hilfsmittel – vom Rollstuhl bis zum Kompressionsstrumpf.**

Das Unternehmen wurde von vier Mitarbeitern der Abteilung technische Orthopädie der *MedAk* gegründet. Sie investierten eine Million Mark in das 1000 Quadratmeter große Unternehmen mit angeschlossener Werkstatt. 41 Angestellte sind in der Firma beschäftigt.

„Unser Spezialgebiet sind Brustprothesen", sagt Geschäftsführer Rolf Herzog (46). In der Ex-DDR wurde für diese Frauen fast nichts getan. Die Rehatechnik ließ sich deshalb etwas Besonderes einfallen: Eine Psychotherapeutin betreut die Frauen bei der Prothesen-Anpassung.

(Bild-Zeitung)

bringt . . . Erleichterung *brings relief to . . .*
ließ sich deshalb . . . einfallen *therefore thought of . . .*

1 Put the following points in the order in which they're mentioned:
a Gründungsland; *b* Zahl der Mitarbeiter; *c* Gründer; *d* Kunden; *e* Adresse; *f* Leiter; *g* Größe der Firma (m²); *h* Name des Unternehmens; *i* besonderer Service; *j* Gründungskapital; *k* Produktspektrum; *l* Werkstatt; *m* Spezialgebiet.
2 Give a short presentation including the following points, in German: *a* products; *b* founders; *c* investment capital; *d* size of premises; *e* number of employees; *f* specialist area; *g* special service offered.

ICH WÜRDE MICH FREUEN

BP is committed to providing information and know-how to the new *Länder*. This letter is about an energy seminar being held in Magdeburg.

1 Is this letter informing, inviting and/or thanking the addressee?
2 How do you know there's an enclosure?
3 Find the German in the letter for the following: *a* letter; *b* Dear; *c* to organize; *d* Yours sincerely; *e* to enclose; *f* to be pleased.

Deutsche BP Aktiengesellschaft
BP Medien
Überseering 2
Postfach 60 03 40
2000 Hamburg 60

Herrn
Werner Lambrecht
Vorsitzender des Vorstandes
Brennstoffhandelsverband
Sachsen-Anhalt
Thomas-Münzer-Straße 168 a
O-4254 Hergisdorf

16.09.91

Sehr geehrter Herr Lambrecht,

die Deutsche BP AG veranstaltet am Mittwoch, dem 9. Oktober 1991, ein
Energie-Seminar in Magdeburg. Ich möchte Sie hierzu herzlich einladen
und füge meinem Schreiben das vorgesehene Programm sowie die
Einladung des Vorstandes unserer Gesellschaft bei.

Ich würde mich freuen, wenn Sie unserer Einladung folgen könnten und
bin

mit freundlichen Grüßen

Anlage

BUSINESS FILE

Meetings are generally scheduled well in advance and may begin with a round of hand-shaking. You're likely to be offered coffee and biscuits at some point, and mineral water and soft drinks may also be provided.

Take the lead from your host. If your host offers to speak English, it would be churlish to refuse, unless your German is of an exceptionally high standard. Remember to gauge the standard of your partner's English correctly and don't use language which is too complex if this would create embarrassment – particularly in front of junior colleagues.

Meetings are taken seriously and may go into considerable detail, so it pays to be well prepared. Make sure you arrive punctually, and dress up rather than down for the occasion! The formality of a meeting may make it difficult to assess how things are going, but a lengthy examination of a proposal will indicate serious intent.

As a rule, important documentation for a meeting should be in German, as should product literature and press releases for the German market.

Useful information can be found in the directory *Verbände, Behörden, Organisationen der Wirtschaft*. It gives addresses and phone numbers of associations, public bodies and organizations in trade and industry, and can be obtained from Verlag Hoppenstedt & Co., Havelstraße 9, D-64295 Darmstadt. Tel.: (06151) 38 01. Fax: (06151) 3 80–3 60.

9 DER KUNDE IST KÖNIG

AIMS, ASSESSMENTS, REACTIONS

After years of exile in West Germany, the Dresdner Bank has re-established itself in its home town, Dresden. Kerstin Wachholz talked to people at the bank to find out how east German trainees were faring in the west German apprenticeship system.

MASSGEBEND FÜR DIE AUSWAHL

Although the bank sets its own aptitude test, the head of training and further education in Dresden, Peter Teschner, stresses the importance of school qualifications in the selection procedure.

▶ 1 What kind of school result is expected?
 2 What's the next step after a successful aptitude test?
 3 What's the candidate offered after a successful outcome?

Dresdner Bank, Hauptverwaltung, Frankfurt am Main

die Ausbildung *education, training*
der Abschluß *qualification*
das Zeugnis *certificate*
die Lehre *apprenticeship, training (scheme)*
der Lehrling *trainee, apprentice*
der/die Auszubildende (*abbreviated* Azubi) *trainee, apprentice*
die Auswahl *selection*
der Bewerber *applicant*
maßgebend *decisive*
auswählen *to select*

DRESDNER BANK AG, DRESDEN

Frau Wachholz Sie haben sich in den letzten Monaten mit der Auswahl der neuen Lehrlinge befaßt. Nach welchen Kriterien wurden diese ausgewählt?

Herr Teschner Maßgebend für die Auswahl sind in erster Linie die uns eingereichten Schulzeugnisse. Wir erwarten einen ordentlichen Schulabschluß, der in etwa der Mittleren Reife bzw. dem Abitur in den alten Bundesländern entspricht. Danach führen wir für diese Bewerber einen schriftlichen Eignungstest durch, der im übrigen identisch ist mit dem in den alten Bundesländern. Läuft das auch zufriedenstellend, führen wir anschließend noch ein persönliches Gespräch, in dem wir uns ein Bild machen über den Bewerber, über seine Persönlichkeit, sein Auftreten, seine Kontaktfähigkeit zum Beispiel. Und wenn das positiv am Ende abgelaufen ist, unterbreiten wir ein Vertragsangebot.

Sie haben sich ...... befaßt   *... you have been concerned with ...*
die uns eingereichten Schulzeugnisse   *the school certificates sent in to us*
einen ordentlichen Schulabschluß   *a respectable school qualification*
der in etwa ... entspricht   *which approximately corresponds to ...*
führen wir ... durch   *we carry out ...*
läuft das auch zufriedenstellend   *if that is also satisfactory*
wenn das positiv ... abgelaufen ist   *if that has ... been positive*
unterbreiten wir ein Vertragsangebot   *we offer a contract*

If you're in Germany and have a few moments to spare, practise your German. Go into a newsagent and ask for a particular paper, buy some stationery, buy a souvenir, or simply ask for directions.

1 Find two words for *then/afterwards*.
2 List the following in the sequence in which Peter Teschner talks about them: *a* personal interview; *b* offer of a contract; *c* aptitude test; *d* building up a picture of the candidate; *e* school qualifications.
3 What three qualities does he look for in an applicant?

GEWINNORIENTIERT

Customer service is a particularly important part of the training process for east German trainees, and Axel Kreimeier runs a seminar on the ethos of banking in the market economy.

1 Why is the customer the most important factor for the bank?
2 What is the mechanism by which the bank makes a profit?
3 What does the bank sell?
4 What other types of product does Mr Kreimeier mention?
5 What does the bank have to pay for out of its profits?

DRESDNER BANK AG, DRESDEN

Herr Kreimeier Meine Damen und Herren, wir kommen jetzt zum wichtigsten Teil des Seminars – nämlich zu dem Teil, der sich mit dem Kunden beschäftigt. Der Kunde ist tatsächlich das Wichtigste für unsere Bank, denn letztendlich bringt uns der Kunde das Geld, mit dem wir arbeiten können, mit dem wir Kredite rausgeben können, um über den Zinsgewinn, den wir dabei machen, dann auch als Unternehmen Gewinn zu machen. Sie wissen, wir verkaufen kein Produkt wie 'n Auto oder 'n Tennisschläger oder irgend etwas Ähnliches. Wir verkaufen Dienstleistungsprodukte. Das ist ein klein wenig komplizierter. Wir haben also kein Auto, keinen PKW, der schön glänzt, schön poliert ist und von sich aus schon überzeugt, sondern wir haben ein Produkt, was auf 'm Blatt Papier steht und was dem Kunden begreiflich gemacht werden soll und begreiflich gemacht werden muß. Denn der Kunde soll dies Produkt kaufen am Ende. Und das kauft er nur dann, wenn Sie ihn davon überzeugt haben, daß es für ihn das Richtige ist. Kaufen muß er es deswegen, weil wir Gewinn machen müssen, um letztendlich Ihre Ausbildungsvergütung und auch letztendlich mein Gehalt zahlen zu können. Wir sind 'n Unternehmen, was gewinnorientiert arbeitet, das muß man so ganz deutlich mal sagen, und wir können nur dann Gewinn machen, wenn wir unsere Produkte auch verkaufen.

Das Seminar

das Dienstleistungsprodukt *service product*
der Gewinn *profit*
die Gewinn- und Verlustrechnung *profit and loss account*
der Zins *interest*
der Kredit *loan, credit*
der Teil *part*
das Wichtigste *the most important thing*
letztendlich *in the final analysis*
deutlich *significant(ly)*
bringen *to bring*

irgend etwas Ähnliches *anything similar*
von sich aus schon überzeugt *impresses in itself*
was auf 'm Blatt Papier steht *which is on a piece of paper*
was ... begreiflich gemacht werden soll *which should be conveyed (to)* ...
kaufen muß er es deswegen, weil *he has to buy it because*
um ... zahlen zu können *in order to be able to pay* ...

9

NUTS AND BOLTS ▶

Notice how both Peter Teschner and Axel Kreimeier use the equivalent of *which* or *that*:

> Wir erwarten **einen ordentlichen Schulabschluß, der** der Mittleren Reife bzw. dem Abitur in den alten Bundesländern **entspricht.**

> Der Kunde bringt uns **das Geld,** mit **dem** wir arbeiten **können.**

These *relative pronouns* introduce a *relative clause* that gives additional detail about a preceding noun. Their gender and number (*sing.* or *pl.*) are the same as those of the noun they refer back to. As well as **der/die/das**, you'll also find **was** used as a relative pronoun:

> Wir haben **ein Produkt, was** auf einem Blatt Papier **steht.**

Remember, a relative clause is always preceded by a comma, and the verb normally comes at the end (see p 140 and 147).

PRACTICE ▶

die Hauptschule   *intermediate school (age 10–15)*

der Hauptschulabschluß   *basic school-leaving certificate (age 15/16)*

die Realschule   *vocational school (age 10–16)*

die Mittlere Reife   *vocational qualification (age 16/17)*

das Gymnasium   *grammar school*

das Abitur   *university-entrance qualification (age 19/20)*

die Berufsschule   *vocational college*

der Lehrbrief   *apprenticeship certificate*

die Universität   *university*

das Diplom   *diploma, degree*

1   What answers would Axel Kreimeier expect his trainees to give to these questions: *a* Was verkaufen Sie?   *b* Was ist das Wichtigste für die Dresdner Bank?   *c* Was ist das Ziel der Dresdner Bank?

2   Complete the sentences by filling in the gaps with one of the relative pronouns listed: der   der   dem   dem   das   der
a Wir führen ein Gespräch, in .... wir uns ein Bild machen über
...   *b* Wir erwarten einen Schulabschluß, ... dem Abitur entspricht.   *c* Wir führen einen Eignungstest durch, ... identisch ist mit dem in den alten Bundesländern.   *d* Wir sind ein Unternehmen, ... gewinnorientiert arbeitet.   *e* Wir kommen zu dem Teil, ... sich mit dem Kunden beschäftigt.   *f* Der Kunde bringt uns das Geld, mit .... wir Kredite rausgeben können.

3   Work out the gender and number of each relative pronoun in **2** and the noun it refers back to. The case of a relative pronoun depends on its role in the relative clause. Try working it out for each one.

Qualifications

There are three types of school-leaving certificate: the basic **Hauptschulabschluß** (age 15/16), the vocational **Mittlere Reife** (age 16/17) and the academic **Abitur** (age 19/20). School-leavers who choose a vocational training continue their studies at a vocational college and work towards qualification in a registered trade.

?   You'll see a similar sign in many German banks. Why should you wait at this sign until the person in front of you has finished his or her transaction?

> **Bitte
> treten Sie wegen
> der Diskretion
> einzeln
> an den Schalter**

DIE LEHRE ALS BANKKAUFMANN

Thomas Barth

Trainee Thomas Barth talked to Kerstin Wachholz about the training.

1 Work out: *a* his feelings at the interview; *b* how he heard about the training scheme; *c* his reaction on being accepted.
2 How much will he earn in the first year? Gross or net?
3 How long will the apprenticeship last?
4 Find the German for: *a* above all; *b* by chance; *c* actually.

DRESDNER BANK AG, DRESDEN

Frau Wachholz	Können Sie sich bitte vorstellen?
Herr Barth	Ich heiße Thomas Barth. Ich bin 16 Jahre alt und komme aus Dresden.
Frau Wachholz	Was für eine Schulausbildung haben Sie?
Herr Barth	Ich habe die Mittlere Reife.
Frau Wachholz	Wie lief Ihre Bewerbung ab? Waren Sie nervös?
Herr Barth	Ich war sehr nervös, vor allem bei dem Vorstellungs-gespräch. Die Bewerbung lief ab: Ich habe durch Zufall eigentlich von der Lehre als Bankkaufmann gehört und habe dann meine Unterlagen eingeschickt. Ich war sogar sehr überrascht, als ich dann eine Zusage bekommen hatte. Ich hatte eigentlich nicht damit gerechnet.
Frau Wachholz	Wieviel werden Sie im ersten Lehrjahr verdienen?
Herr Barth	Im ersten Lehrjahr verdiene ich 500 Mark – 500 D-Mark brutto.
Frau Wachholz	Wie lange dauert die Lehrzeit?
Herr Barth	Also, meine Lehrzeit dauert jetzt zweieinhalb Jahre.

---

die Lehrzeit   *(period of) apprenticeship, training*
die Bewerbung   *application*
die Zusage   *acceptance*
der Zufall   *chance*
brutto   *gross*
netto   *net*
kommen (aus)   *to come (from)*
ablaufen   *to proceed*
hören (von)   *to hear (from)*
einschicken   *to send in*
verdienen   *to earn*
dauern   *to last*

NUTS AND BOLTS

Germans often use the present tense to talk about the future, if the time referred to is clear (see p 145). Notice how Kerstin Wachholz asks a question using the future, whereas Thomas Barth answers in the present:
Wieviel **werden** Sie im ersten Lehrjahr **verdienen**?
Im ersten Lehrjahr **verdiene** ich 500 Mark.

PRACTICE

---

die Berufsausbildung   *vocational training*
das Studium   *(university) course of studies*
die Promotion   *doctorate, PhD*
der Facharbeiter   *skilled worker*
der Meister   *master craftsman*

---

1 Expand your vocabulary by separating these compound nouns. Use the *Glossary* to check the article for the separate nouns. Then predict the article for each compound.   *a* Schulausbildung;
b Vorstellungsgespräch;   *c* Bankkaufmann;   *d* Berufsschule;   *e* Lehrjahr.
2 You have received some news. Give your reaction and say: *a* you were surprised;   *b* you were nervous;   *c* you hadn't expected it.
3 Words like **eigentlich** (*actually*) and **vor allem** (*above all*) are useful for modifying your statements. Practise saying you were *actually/above all*:   *a* surprised;   *b* nervous.
4 The German for *heard* is **gehört**, from **hören**. Can you work out the German for *sent*, from **schicken**, and *reckoned*, from **rechnen**?

EINS DER FÜHRENDEN UNTERNEHMEN

Ramona Krause

Ramona Krause talked about her interests and aspirations.

Give: *a* three reasons why she's interested in banking; *b* two reasons why she opted for Dresdner Bank; *c* two aspects she's looking forward to; *d* her dream.

DRESDNER BANK AG, DRESDEN

Frau Wachholz Können Sie sich bitte einmal vorstellen?

Frau Krause Mein Name ist Ramona Krause, ich bin 16 Jahre alt und komme aus einer Stadt in der Nähe von Dresden.

Frau Wachholz Was interessiert Sie besonders am Bankwesen?

Frau Krause Ja, der Umgang mit den Kunden am Schalter, privat – also im Privatkundengeschäft –, der Umgang mit dem Geld, das Anlegen des Geldes, einfach alles. Es dreht sich ums Geld!

Frau Wachholz Und warum haben Sie sich für die Dresdner Bank entschieden?

Frau Krause Weil die Dresdner Bank eins der führenden Unternehmen in Deutschland ist. Ich hab' mich an vielen Instituten beworben zum Beruf der Bankkauffrau, und sie war halt einfach schneller.

Frau Wachholz Und was für Erwartungen haben Sie in Bezug auf die Lehrzeit?

Frau Krause Also, ich stell' mir eine vielseitige, interessante Ausbildung vor, in der viel Praxis vorherrschen wird. Also in der Bank direkt am Schalter arbeiten. Und dann ja eben die Schule, die Berufsschule wird auch sehr interessant werden. Ich werd' viel Neues kennenlernen in Bereichen, die wir bis jetzt noch nicht gekannt hatten; Wertpapiergeschäft zum Beispiel interessiert mich sehr. Also, im großen und ganzen freue ich mich.

Frau Wachholz Was, glauben Sie, werden Sie in drei Jahren machen?

Frau Krause Ich weiß es noch nicht so genau. Natürlich hat jeder 'n Wunsch am Anfang, 'n Traum – von 'ner eigenen Filiale vielleicht. Es wird sich zeigen in drei Jahren oder später.

am Bankwesen *in banking*
der Umgang mit dem Geld *dealing with money*
eins der führenden *one of the leading*

---

der Schalter *counter*
das Wertpapier *security*
das Wertpapiergeschäft *securities business/trading*
das Anlegen *investment*
die Praxis *practice*
die Theorie *theory*
der Wunsch *wish*
der Traum *dream*
der Anfang *start*
vielseitig *many-sided*
besonders *particularly*
genau *precise(ly), right(ly)*
vorherrschen *to predominate*
kennenlernen *to get to know*
sich entscheiden (für) *to decide (on)*
sich zeigen *to emerge*
sich bewerben *to apply*

NUTS AND BOLTS ▶ Notice how certain prepositions are used with particular verbs and nouns:
Ich **komme aus** einer Stadt in der Nähe von Dresden.
Es **dreht sich ums** (um das) Geld.
Natürlich hat jeder einen Wunsch **am** (an dem) **Anfang**.
in Bezug auf die Lehrzeit

1 **Das Bankwesen interessiert mich**. Say you're interested in: *a* investing money; *b* training; *c* trading in securities.
2 **Die Dresdner Bank war schneller**. Practise saying that your company was: *a* better; *b* slower; *c* cheaper; *d* more expensive; *e* more interesting; *f* more important. If you need help, see p 141.
3 Ramona Krause comes from a town **in der Nähe von** Dresden. Say that the head office (**der Sitz**) of a company is based near: *a* Berlin; *b* Hamburg; *c* Munich; *d* Bremen; *e* Essen; *f* Cologne.
4 Ms Krause uses relative clauses (see p 115) to give extra information about two nouns. Pick them out from the following:
Stadt Umgang Ausbildung Schalter Bereiche Anfang.
5 Ms Krause doesn't yet know what she'll be doing in three years' time. If asked about something you don't know, what could you say?

VIEL PRAXIS

Claudia Birnbaum

Listen to what Claudia Birnbaum expects from her training and then say whether the following are true or false: *a* she expects practical experience; *b* she likes theory; *c* she doesn't anticipate many seminars; *d* she likes practice in customer relations.

DRESDNER BANK AG, DRESDEN
Frau Wachholz Können Sie sich bitte einmal vorstellen?
Frau Birnbaum Also, ich heiße Claudia Birnbaum, bin 18 Jahre alt und komm' hier aus Dresden.
Frau Wachholz Und was für Erwartungen haben Sie an Ihre drei Jahre Lehrzeit?
Frau Birnbaum Nun, das erste ist, daß wir viel Praxis haben, daß wir viel in der Bank selbst arbeiten, das gefällt mir. Und auch, daß viel mit uns gearbeitet wird – auch in Seminaren usw.; daß wir da schon Übung haben für Kundengespräche und Ähnliches. Und das find' ich gut.

die Übung *practice*
das Kundengespräch *contact with customers, presentation*
viel *much, many*
wenig *little*
ähnlich *similar*
usw. (und so weiter) *etc.*

Claudia Birnbaum uses a series of *that* clauses, with the verb at the end:
..., **daß** wir viel in der Bank selbst **arbeiten**.
..., **daß** viel mit uns gearbeitet **wird**.
And compare her use of the *active* construction **daß wir arbeiten** with her use of the *passive* **daß viel mit uns gearbeitet wird**. The *agent* (training staff) is left implicit in her passive sentence (see p 145).

1 Ms Birnbaum says she likes something in two ways. What are they?
2 Say you like/dislike: *a* Angeln; *b* Musik; *c* Theater; *d* Kino; *e* Lesen; *f* Fotografieren; *g* Reisen; *h* Autofahren; *i* Sport.

Get a feel for Germany and what's going on by buying the occasional magazine. Don't read it to understand every word, but select articles on topics you're interested in. Go for quantity and skim-read a number of articles rather than concentrating on one. Gradually you'll recognize words and phrases you've learnt.

Practise stating your views and objectives.

Say you like or don't like something
Das gefällt mir (nicht).
Das finde ich gut/schlecht.

Say you're pleased/surprised
Ich freue mich.
Ich war (sehr) überrascht.

Say you don't know
Ich weiß es nicht (so genau).

Say you expect, or hadn't expected, something
Wir erwarten...
Ich hatte eigentlich nicht damit gerechnet.

Say something will become clear with time
Es wird sich zeigen.

Say you find something interesting
Ich finde den Umgang mit Geld besonders interessant.
Das Wertpapiergeschäft interessiert mich sehr/besonders.

Say X is a leading company/product
X ist ein führendes Unternehmen/Produkt.

Say something is important
Der Kunde ist wichtig.
Der Kunde ist das Wichtigste für unsere Bank.
Die Schulzeugnisse sind maßgebend.

State your objective and emphasize your opinion
Das Ziel der Firma ist...
Wir arbeiten gewinnorientiert.
Das muß man ganz deutlich sagen.

Use *Checklist* to express your opinions on your own products, company and aims.

1   Listen to the interviews in this unit again and identify how Kerstin Wachholz asks about: *a* interviewees' education;   *b* length of the apprenticeship;   *c* selection criteria;   *d* reasons for a decision.
2   Practise gathering information related to time. Use **Wie lange dauert...?** to ask a colleague for the length of the: *a* apprenticeship;   *b* school education.

Offensives Verkaufsverhalten

„Nach unseren Erfahrungen bisher haben die Lehrlinge aus dem Osten Schwierigkeiten, wenn es um Themen geht wie offensives Verkaufsverhalten. Das ist ja ein ganz wesentlicher Punkt im Bankgeschäft, Produkte zu verkaufen. Früher war das ja auf dem Gebiet der ehemaligen DDR etwas völlig Ungewöhnliches und auch gar nicht Erwünschtes." (Peter Teschner, *Dresdner Bank*)

3 Complete the questions to ask someone about their background and education. You'll find the clues in the answers.

a Wo ....?   Ich wohne in Dresden.

b Woher ....?   Ich komme aus München.

c Wie ....?   Ich bin dreißig Jahre alt.

d Was für ....?   Ich habe Abitur.

e Wie lange ....?   Die Lehrzeit dauert zweieinhalb Jahre.

4 Build up a profile of the trainees selected by Peter Teschner using the following headings: *a* name; *b* age; *c* city of origin.   Now practise the questions which would obtain this information.

5 You're presenting your reasons for selecting a particular candidate for a job. Practise giving the decisive reasons for your selection: **Maßgebend für meine Auswahl ist/sind...**   *a* die Schulzeugnisse; *b* die Schulausbildung; *c* sein/ihr Alter.

6 A new contact asks you about your responsibilities. Give your main responsibility: **Ich bin in erster Linie für .... zuständig**   *a* die Pressestelle; *b* die Produktion; *c* das Büro; *d* die Ausbildung; *e* die Lehrlinge.

7 Give a short introduction to your company including the following information: *a* Sitz; *b* Produkte; *c* Jahresumsatz; *d* Tochtergesellschaften/Niederlassungen/Filialen; *e* Mitarbeiter.

8 Talk about yourself, your hobbies and your home town (you may want to use an English–German dictionary): *a* give your name; *b* say where you go in your leisure time; *c* say you like doing two activities; *d* give your hobbies; *e* say where you come from; *f* say you like your home town.

? Identify the following in this Eurocheque: *a* amount; *b* currency; *c* amount in letters; *d* place; *e* date; *f* signature; *g* payee; *h* account number; *i* cheque number.

Axel Kreimeier

Feminine nouns

Nouns referring to abstract concepts tend to be feminine. You'll also find it helpful to remember the following endings (see p 139):

–heit/–keit	Einheit, Persönlichkeit
–in	Schaltermitarbeiterin, Sekretärin
–schaft	Wirtschaft, Gesellschaft
–tion	Produktion, Information
–tät	Aktivität, Kapazität, Qualität
–ung	Ausbildung, Erwartung

Relative pronouns

The various forms of the relative pronoun **der**, **die**, **das**, and the invariable **was**, are all equivalent to the English *who*, *which* or *that*. They're used to give further information about nouns which have already been mentioned (see p 140):

> Ich werde viel Neues kennenlernen in **Bereichen**, **die** wir bis jetzt noch nicht gekannt **hatten**.
> Wir sind ein **Unternehmen**, **was** gewinnorientiert **arbeitet**.

The gender and number of the relative pronoun depend on the noun it refers back to. Its case depends on its role in the relative clause.
Remember that the relative pronoun shunts the main verb to the end of the clause (see p 147).

Loyalty

Company loyalty is fostered in German companies, and a skilled worker who has trained in a particular company will think twice about moving firms. This makes cost-intensive training a worthwhile investment.

AKTIVES VERKAUFSVERHALTEN

Axel Kreimeier gives a rundown on the trainees interviewed and then outlines an area they still need to work on.

1 What characteristics does Mr Kreimeier use to describe: *a* Claudia Birnbaum; *b* Ramona Krause; *c* Thomas Barth?
2 Where has the bank had problems with trainees?
3 What kind of company does Dresdner Bank consider itself?

die ... sich ... engagiert   *who ... is involved/committed ...*
die ich mir vorstelle   *that I envisage*
sie fängt ... positiv ein   *she captivates ... positively*
der Bereich ist, an dem   *is the area in which*
um Anträge zu stellen   *in order to place applications*
das ist nicht das, was   *that is not what*

---

das Dienstleistungsunternehmen
   service company
die Laune   *mood*
der Berater   *adviser*
die Beraterin   *adviser* (f.)
das Verhalten   *behaviour*
die Art und Weise   *manner*
trotz   *despite*
stark   *strong(ly)* ▶
reif   *mature*
souverän   *confident*
sich engagieren   *to be committed*
sich präsentieren   *to present oneself*
genehmigen   *to approve*
ablehnen   *to reject*
bestehen   *to exist*

Notice how these verbs are used with a **reflexive pronoun** (see p 140):

die **sich** sehr stark **engagiert**

Sie kann **sich** sehr sehr gut **präsentieren**.

And remember that **sie** is the personal pronoun both for *she* and for 'feminine' things:

(Ramona Krause) **Sie** fängt Menschen positiv ein.

(Die Dresdner Bank) Und **sie** war schneller.

ADMINISTRIERUNG DER BERUFLICHEN BILDUNG

Peter Sahla interviewed Helgo Alberts, Deputy Secretary General at Munich's **Industrie- und Handelskammer**, on Germany's vocational training system.

▶ **1** What are the educational functions of the **Industrie- und Handelskammer**?

2 What example of training does Mr Alberts give?

angehender   *prospective, trainee*
erteilt bekommt   *receives*
ob sie ... geeignet sind   *whether they're suitable ...*

Gesamtinteresse der Wirtschaft
„Wir vertreten das Gesamtinteresse der oberbayerischen Wirtschaft gegenüber der bayerischen Staatsregierung. Gleichzeitig haben wir die Beratungsfunktion gegenüber den Unternehmen. Und als dritte große Säule unserer Tätigkeit ist zu nennen die Administrierung der beruflichen Bildung. Wir haben in der Bundesrepublik insgesamt 87 Industrie- und Handelskammern." (Helgo Alberts, *Industrie- und Handelskammer, München*)

Mark Twain once complained: 'Whenever the literary German dives into a sentence, that is the last you are going to see of him till he emerges on the other side of his Atlantic with his verb in his mouth'. This tendency isn't confined to written German:

In der beruflichen Ausbildung, wo zum Beispiel [ein] angehender Bankkaufmann zwei oder drei Jahre Lehrling ist bei einer Bank und gleichzeitig im Dualsystem in einer Berufsschule einmal in der Woche Unterricht erteilt bekommt, **organisieren die Industrie- und Handelskammern den gesamten Prüfungsverlauf.**

Notice how the main clause (in bold type) is interrupted by a long subordinate clause with a verb at the end. Fortunately, such sentences are becoming unfashionable even in writing and there's no need for you to use them, but it's worth learning to keep track of a construction for longer than is customary in English.

Put the following points in the order in which Helgo Alberts talks about them: *a* issuing a certificate;   *b* organization of examination process;   *c* teaching at the vocational college;   *d* a trainee bank clerk;   *e* recognition of certificates;   *f* the twin-track system;   *g* examining;   *h* inspection of the company.

Find out about the practicalities of getting 24-hour cash in a society where credit cards are by no means universally accepted.

 1 Can you withdraw 4000 marks in: *a* a day; *b* a week, or *c* a month with the DresdnerCard?
2 Does this service: *a* cost money, or *b* is it free of charge?
3 Is DresdnerCard accepted at 9.4 million outlets in: *a* Germany; *b* Europe, or *c* the world?

AB SOFORT: BARGELD-SERVICE.
KOSTENLOS.

Rund um die Uhr.

Ab sofort bieten wir allen Dresdner-Card-Besitzern einen kostenlosen Bargeld-Service: In allen unseren Geschäftsstellen erhalten Sie nun ebenso problemlos wie kostenfrei bis zu 4.000 Mark pro Woche. Direkt von Ihrem laufenden Konto. Gleichgültig, ob es sich dabei um ein Dresdner-Bank-Konto handelt oder nicht. Zusätzlich können Sie diesen Service rund um die Uhr an unseren Geldautomaten nutzen, die mit dem EUROCARD/Master Card-Zeichen gekennzeichnet sind: mit Ihrer DresdnerCard und der dazugehörigen Geheimzahl.

Alle bekannten Vorteile der EUROCARD gelten selbstverständlich auch weiterhin: An weltweit rund 9,4 Millionen Akzeptanzstellen sind Sie mit Ihrer DresdnerCard ein gerngesehener Kunde oder Gast. Dafür sorgt die reibungslose Zusammenarbeit mit MasterCard und Access. Und in fast jedem Staat der Erde können Sie sich problemlos mit Landeswährung versorgen. Auch die Reservierung von Hotels oder Mietwagen ist bargeldlos und ohne Kaution möglich. Mit der DresdnerCard Gold haben Sie zusätzlich ganz automatisch einen umfangreichen Versicherungsschutz für sich und Ihre Familie.

Alle diese Vorzüge haben natürlich ihren Preis. Allerdings einen, wie wir meinen, erfreulich geringen: jährlich 40 Mark für die Dresdner-Card und 130 Mark für die DresdnerCard Gold.

Entscheiden Sie sich für DresdnerCard sofort, und senden Sie uns bitte den nebenstehenden Antrag ausgefüllt und unterschrieben zurück. Sie erhalten dann in Kürze Ihre DresdnerCard Gold oder DresdnerCard.

Mit den DresdnerCards – den EUROCARDs der Dresdner Bank.
Kostenloser Bargeld-Service. In allen unseren
Geschäftsstellen und an unseren Geldautomaten.

(Bargeld-Service, Dresdner Bank)

der Besitzer   *holder, owner*
das Bargeld   *cash*
die Geschäftsstelle   *branch*
der Antrag   *application form*
das laufende Konto   *current / cheque account*
die Geheimzahl   *PIN number*
die Landeswährung   *local currency*
der Versicherungsschutz   *insurance protection*
in Kürze   *shortly*
rund um die Uhr   *24-hour, round the clock*
ab sofort   *from now*
erhalten   *to receive, obtain*
unterschreiben   *to sign*
meinen   *to think, consider*

ebenso ... wie *both ... and*
ob es sich dabei um ... handelt *whether it is ...*
können Sie diesen Service ... nutzen *you can use this service ...*
die mit ... gekennzeichnet sind *which are identified with ...*
gelten ... weiterhin *... continue to apply*
dafür sorgt die ... Zusammenarbeit ... *the ... cooperation ... ensures this*
können Sie sich ... mit ... versorgen *you can obtain ... ...*
allerdings einen ... erfreulich geringen *albeit, ..., a pleasingly low one (ie price)*

NUTS AND BOLTS ▶

In contrast to traditional written German with its long sequences of subordinate clauses, modern advertising tends to go in for short main clauses or even sentences with no subject or verb:

Direkt von Ihrem laufenden Konto.

This makes advertisements sound colloquial and dynamic, and draws them closer to the customer.

PRACTICE ▶

1 Find the German for the following in the advertisement: *a* free of charge (two ways of saying it); *b* cheque account; *c* 24 hours; *d* cash dispenser; *e* PIN number; *f* cashless; *g* deposit.

2 Order these points as in the advertisement: *a* facility for booking hotels and hiring cars; *b* cash limit; *c* method of application; *d* additional insurance facility; *e* availability of cash abroad; *f* type of account; *g* annual charge; *h* 24-hour cash-dispensing service; *i* cooperation with other financial institutions; *j* number of places accepting DresdnerCard worldwide.

BUSINESS FILE

Education and training are given a high priority in Germany. Many business people in the upper echelons of companies have a doctorate. Registered trades and vocations have their own training schemes, and skilled workers are proud of their training. Master craftsmen with their own businesses have considerable status in the community.

Training in Germany is highly developed – although recently it has been criticized for being inflexible. It is based on a twin-track system of on-the-job training and theoretical training at vocational colleges where trainees receive specialist tuition and study general subjects.

Vocational education is run by the chambers of industry and commerce to which all companies belong. The chambers set the exams and ensure that companies can provide adequate training with qualified instructors.

Germans who have followed an academic path are often in their late twenties by the time they apply for their first job. They may be 20 or even 21 when they finish school, men have to do military or community service, and university courses last around five years.

10

EIN MITTELSTÄNDISCHES UNTERNEHMEN

PROFILES, PRODUCTS, PRESENTATIONS

Ein mittelständisches Unternehmen is a case study of Herbert Walter GmbH, a medium-sized engineering company. It follows the company through from its beginnings in a rural workshop to cooperation with a leading Japanese machine-tool company, and launch of the company's latest product.

Herbert Walter GmbH is known the world over for its high-precision machine tools. It's a subsidiary of Exeron Erodiertechnologie GmbH and specializes in spark-erosion machines, which use an electrical discharge for shaping metal (EDM = electrical discharge machining). The company's latest machine is the EDEM (Electrical Discharge and Electrode Milling) machine which can produce complex metal shapes continuously in a single operation.

ICH BIN HIER GEBOREN

Herbert Walter

Herbert Walter obtained a bank loan to help start his machine-tool business in the Swabian village of Fluorn-Winzeln, where he was born.

► 1 How long was he away from Fluorn?
2 Who did he work for before coming back?
3 Why did he decide to set up his own company?
4 How much was the bank loan?

das Elternhaus *family home*
die Umgebung *surrounding area*
das Kapital *capital*
die Bürgschaft *surety*
das Drittel *third*
adäquat *suitable*
geboren *born*
versuchen *to try*
bürgen *to stand surety*
ausnutzen *to use*
sich entschließen *to decide*

Nach wie vor das SIE

„Die ältere Generation – so sagen wir mal über vierzig – wird nach wie vor beim SIE bleiben, aber die jüngere Generation – so um die zwanzig rum – hat auf jeden Fall unter den Kolleginnen und Kollegen das DU. Im Verhältnis zum Vorgesetzten oder zu einem außenstehenden Mitarbeiter ist nach wie vor das SIE angebracht." (Guntram Kraus, *Deutsche Telekom*)

NUTS AND BOLTS ▶

PRACTICE ▶

Qualifizierte Mitarbeiter

„Grundsätzlich ist es für uns kein Problem, qualifizierte Mitarbeiter zu finden – hier aus der Gegend. Unsere Firma ist bekannt für gutes Betriebsklima. Man weiß auch rund rum, daß man, wenn man beim ‚Walter' ist, die Welt kennenlernt." (Herbert Walter, *Herbert Walter GmbH*)

Frau Wachholz Herr Walter, warum haben Sie Ihre Firma gerade hier in Fluorn-Winzeln aufgebaut?
Herr Walter Ja, ich bin hier geboren, und das ist mein Elternhaus. Und mich hat es nach 13 Jahren Fremde einfach wieder in meine Heimat zurückgezogen.
Frau Wachholz Und warum haben Sie sich entschlossen, Ihre eigene Firma zu gründen? Was haben Sie vorher gemacht?
Herr Walter Ich war zuletzt als Entwickler bei der AEG und habe, nachdem ich mich entschlossen hatte, wieder hierher zurück in den schönen Schwarzwald zu ziehen, versucht, eine adäquate Stelle zu finden. Die gab's nicht hier in der Umgebung. Und dann hab' ich mir gesagt, warum sollst du es nicht für dich selber probieren. So hab' ich meine Firma gegründet.
Frau Wachholz Und woher hatten Sie das nötige Kapital dazu?
Herr Walter Mmm ... Von der Bank! Wie ich hierherkam, hatte ich 2001 Mark Schulden. Mein Vater hat für mich gebürgt bei der hiesigen Bank, und ich habe ungefähr zwei Drittel dieses Hauses als Bürgschaft ausgenutzt. Das waren 70.000 Mark, die ich bekommen habe.

mich hat es ... zurückgezogen *I felt drawn back ...*
die gab's nicht *there wasn't one (a suitable position)*
es ... für dich selber probieren *... try it on your own*

Notice how Herbert Walter refers to the past using the pluperfect:
   ich **habe**, nachdem ich mich **entschlossen hatte**, in den
      Schwarzwald zu ziehen, **versucht** ...
Ich habe versucht (*I tried*) refers to the past, while **ich hatte mich entschlossen** (*I had decided*) refers even further back (see p 145).

Mr Walter uses the familiar form, **du** and **dich**, to address himself:
   Warum sollst **du** es nicht für **dich** selber probieren?
The familiar possessive is **dein** (see p 140).

1 Give a run-down on Mr Walter, using the verbs in brackets: *a* home village (**kommen**); *b* location of village (**sich befinden**); *c* place of birth (**geboren**); *d* position at AEG (**beschäftigt sein**); *e* return to home village (**zurückziehen: ist ... zurückgezogen**); *f* no job in locality (**geben**); *g* foundation of company (**gründen**); *h* capital (**bekommen**); *i* surety (**bürgen**).
2 Now give a run-down on your own life and company: *a* Name; *b* Geburtsdatum; *c* Geburtsort; *d* Alter; *e* Ausbildung (Lehre/Studium); *f* Beruf/Arbeit; *g* Firma; *h* Stelle; *i* zuständig für; *j* Sitz der Firma; *k* Produkte/Dienstleistungen; *l* Zahl der Mitarbeiter; *m* Jahresumsatz; *n* Tochtergesellschaften/Vertriebsnetz/Produktionsstätten; *o* Hobbys; *p* Adresse/Telefonnummer.

Herbert Walter trod the path of many German company owners and managers in the engineering sector. First he worked as an apprentice, then he studied engineering at university. In 1966 he founded his own company and began developing his own machines.

▶ Read Herbert Walter's CV and underline any information in the CV that you've already gathered from the interview on page 126.

Das Elternhaus

die Mechanikerlehre
apprenticeship as a machinist
das Fernstudium *distance-learning degree course*
der Werkzeugmacher *toolmaker*
der Entwickler *design engineer*
der Maschinenbau *mechanical engineering*
der Ingenieur *engineer*
der Maschinenbauingenieur
mechanical engineer

Herbert Walter	
1935	In Fluorn geboren.
1941–49	Volksschule in Fluorn.
1949–52	Mechanikerlehre in Oberndorf. Fernstudium in Mathematik.
1954–56	Werkzeugmacher in der Schweiz. Erster Kontakt mit Funkenerosion.
1956	Zurück nach Deutschland. Abendstudium in Stuttgart (Maschinenbau). Tagsüber Arbeit bei Bosch.
1958–66	Bei AEG in Remscheid (Abteilung Funkenerosionsentwicklung).
1960	Abschluß Maschinenbauingenieur.
1961	Heirat.
1966	Zurück nach Fluorn. Gründet in Scheune des elterlichen Hauses ersten Lohnerodierbetrieb in BRD.
Ab 1975	Entwicklung von Erodiermaschinen und Zubehör.
Ab 1978	Vertrieb eigener Produkte. 60 Mitarbeiter.
1982	Umwandlung von KG in GmbH.
1988–90	Eintritt von Götz Klusmann als Gesellschafter und kaufmännischer Geschäftsführer.
1.1.90	50% Beteiligung von Okuma.

PRACTICE ▶

Use the information in the CV and interview to present Herbert Walter's career and his company's development: *a* date and place of birth; *b* education; *c* first job; *d* marriage; *e* return to village; *f* foundation of company; *g* development of spark-erosion machines; *h* sales development; *i* Götz Klusmann; *j* partnership with Okuma.

Heimat

Herbert Walter's career is in many ways typical. He did his apprenticeship close to Fluorn, where he was born, then travelled further afield to develop his skills. Having gained the necessary theoretical knowledge in a degree course, he returned home to set up his own company specializing in innovative technology. In the Black Forest, traditional home of clock-making, he has no difficulty finding skilled labour.

In jeder Scheune eine Uhrenwerkstatt

„Hier war früher die Uhrenindustrie sehr stark zu Hause. Vor 100 Jahren, da war in jeder Scheune eine Uhrenwerkstatt. Auch daraus haben sich so viele kleine mittelständische Betriebe entwickelt heute." (Herbert Walter, *Herbert Walter GmbH*)

Die neue EDEM-Maschine

die Reise *journey*
das Fischen *fishing*
die Fähre *ferry*
die Zwischenzeit *meantime,*
interim

PRACTICE ▶

DIE ZÜNDENDE IDEE

Herbert Walter has a reputation for being innovative. The idea for his new EDEM machine came to him while he was on holiday with his son.

▶ **1** Where was he when the idea first occurred to him?
2 When did he make a patent application?

HERBERT WALTER GMBH, FLUORN–WINZELN

Frau Wachholz Wie und in welchem Zeitraum wurde diese neue Maschine entwickelt?
Herr Walter Die Idee zu einer solchen Maschine kam bei einer Reise nach Irland. Zum Fischen mit meinem Sohn bin ich da gefahren. Ich hab' nach der zündenden Idee gesucht, und bevor ich in Frankreich an der Fähre war, war die Idee geboren. Das war vor drei Jahren. Ich habe dann nach meiner Rückkehr direkt 'ne Patentanmeldung gemacht, und in der Zwischenzeit haben wir die Entwicklung betrieben.

Explain the origin of Herbert Walter's idea for the EDEM machine with these words: *a* Irland/fahren; *b* Idee/suchen; *c* Frankreich/fahren; *d* Idee/haben; *e* Patentanmeldung/machen; *f* Maschine/entwickeln.

COMPUTERGESTEUERT

Herbert Walter shows how complex metal shapes are produced by a conventional spark-erosion machine as compared with the new EDEM machine.

1 How many processes does the old method involve?
2 How are the processes handled by the new machine?

HERBERT WALTER GMBH, FLUORN–WINZELN

Herr Walter Das ist die bisherige Methode. Die Elektrode wird hier auf einer Drehbank hergestellt und dann in der Erodiermaschine eingespannt, manuell. Je nach der Form, die hergestellt werden muß, werden die Elektroden entweder gedreht oder gefräst oder geschliffen. In diesem Falle wird gefräst. Bei der neuen Maschine ist es so, daß diese ganze Arbeit, die hier der Mann manuell gemacht hat, vollautomatisch computergesteuert gemacht wird und somit die Maschine rund um die Uhr, bei Tag und bei Nacht und sonntags und feiertags arbeiten kann.

Note the passive construction with no subject:
In diesem Falle **wird gefräst**.
It places the emphasis on the operation being carried out. The context makes it clear that in this case it's the electrode that's being milled.

die Werkzeugmaschine
machine tool
die Drehbank *lathe*
manuell *manual(ly)*
automatisch *automatic(ally)*
computergesteuert *computer-*
controlled
entweder ... oder *either ... or*
bearbeiten *to machine*
drehen *to turn*
fräsen *to mill*
schleifen *to grind*

NUTS AND BOLTS ▶

Ein Geben und Nehmen

„Wir haben in Deutschland die Philosophie, daß eine Exportnation wie die
deutsche zugleich auch importieren
muß. Hier wird ganz bewußt Importförderung betrieben. Das heißt, wir versuchen, ausländische Firmen zu beraten,
wie sie in Deutschland absetzen können
oder wie sie in Deutschland Lieferfirmen
finden für bestimmte Produkte. Das ist
ein Geben und Nehmen." (Helgo
Alberts, *Industrie- und Handelskammer,
München*)

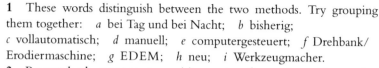

1 These words distinguish between the two methods. Try grouping
them together: *a* bei Tag und bei Nacht; *b* bisherig;
c vollautomatisch; *d* manuell; *e* computergesteuert; *f* Drehbank/
Erodiermaschine; *g* EDEM; *h* neu; *i* Werkzeugmacher.
2 Present both processes to a visitor, using the passive with **werden**
where appropriate: *a* bisherige Methode/sein; *b* Arbeit/
Werkzeugmacher/machen; *c* Elektrode/Drehbank/herstellen;
d Elektrode/Erodiermaschine/einspannen; *e* Elektrode/
Erodiermaschine/fräsen, drehen, schleifen; *f* neue Methode/sein;
g Arbeit/vollautomatisch/machen; *h* Elektrode/EDEM-
Maschine/herstellen; *i* Elektroden/rund um die Uhr/fertigen.

EINE GROSSE FAMILIE

Herbert Walter prides himself on a friendly working atmosphere.

1 What two sections of the company does Mr Walter mention?
2 How long has Mrs Krapfl worked for Exeron GmbH?
3 What's the main reason why she likes working for Exeron?

HERBERT WALTER GMBH, FLUORN–WINZELN

Herr Walter   Sowohl in unserem Betrieb, wo die Maschinen hergestellt
werden, als auch hier in der Entwicklung haben wir ein fantastisches
Betriebsklima. Es könnte eigentlich nicht besser sein! Daran arbeite ich
immer. Und ich geh' mit meinen Leuten auch übers Wochenende
beispielsweise in die Berge. Wir sind eine große Familie.

EXERON GMBH, FLUORN–WINZELN

Frau Wachholz   Also, seit wann arbeiten Sie hier?
Frau Krapfl   Ich arbeit' jetzt seit sieben Jahren hier, und seit fünf
Jahren halbtags.
Frau Wachholz   Und was für eine berufliche Qualifikation haben Sie?
Frau Krapfl   Ich hab' 'ne Ausbildung zur technischen Zeichnerin, und
das dauert dreieinhalb Jahre.
Frau Wachholz   Warum arbeiten Sie gern hier bei Exeron?
Frau Krapfl   Weil ich hier die Möglichkeit hab', halbtags zu arbeiten.
Ich hab' 'n Kind mit fünf, das bring' ich morgens vor der Arbeit in 'n
Kindergarten und hol's dann eben nachher wieder ab. Außerdem haben
wir 'n sehr gutes Betriebsklima hier. Es sind nur wenige, bißchen 'ne
familiäre Atmosphäre. Kommt auch privat mal was zustande.

das Betriebsklima   *atmosphere at work*
die Atmosphäre   *atmosphere*
das Wochenende   *weekend*
am/übers Wochenende   *at/over the weekend*
familiär   *family, friendly*
privat   *private(ly)*
fantastisch   *fantastic(ally)*
halbtags   *part-time*
sowohl … als auch   *both … and*

wo … hergestellt werden   *where … are manufactured*
daran arbeite ich immer   *I'm always working on it*
hol's dann eben nachher wieder ab   *then collect it again afterwards*
kommt auch privat mal was zustande   *we sometimes get together privately*

1 Say that you do the following at the weekend: *a* play golf; *b* go to the mountains; *c* go walking; *d* play tennis; *e* like going sailing; *f* go to the cinema; *g* take part in a sport; *h* like reading.
2 Say you've worked for your company for: *a* a year; *b* 2 years; *c* 10 years; *d* 14 years; *e* 25 years.
3 **Ich habe eine Ausbildung zum** (*m.*)/**zur** (*f.*) . . . Say you've been trained as a: *a* salesman; *b* toolmaker; *c* bank clerk; *d* secretary; *e* accountant; *f* engineer; *g* technician; *h* tax adviser.
4 Say you work: *a* weekends; *b* Saturdays; *c* part-time.
5 Describe *a* Mrs Krapfl, *b* yourself, and *c* a colleague, giving the following details: profession, time at company, training, family, reasons for liking the workplace.

KOPF UND HERZ

Götz Klusmann

Götz Klusmann, joint managing director of Herbert Walter GmbH, sees Herbert Walter as the company's heart and himself as the head.

1 What areas are Götz Klusmann and Herbert Walter responsible for?
2 When is it difficult for a company to operate properly?

HERBERT WALTER GMBH, FLUORN-WINZELN
Frau Wachholz Was ist Ihre Rolle in diesem Unternehmen?
Herr Klusmann Ich bin in dem Unternehmen der Herbert Walter GmbH – so versteh' ich mich zumindestens – der Kopf. Herr Walter ist das Herz. Meine Funktionen liegen im Bereich Marketing und Finanzen. Herr Walter macht Produktion, Technik und Technologie. Und diese Symbiose in einem Unternehmen halt' ich für ideal, weil wenn ein Unternehmen zwei Köpfe hat oder zwei Herzen, dann kann das in der Regel nicht lange gut funktionieren.

die Rolle *role*
der Kopf *head*
das Herz *heart*
die Technologie *technology*
die Symbiose *symbiosis*
die Regel *rule*
ideal *ideal*
funktionieren *to function*

so versteh' ich mich zumindestens *at least that's how I see myself*
liegen im Bereich *are in the area of*
halt' ich für ideal *I consider to be ideal*
weil wenn *because if*
in der Regel *as a rule*

1 **Wie finden Sie die Lösung?** Say you think the solution is ideal.
2 Use **zuständig für** to say you're responsible for: *a* planning; *b* organization; *c* public relations; *d* advertising; *e* training.
3 Use **liegen** to give your functions in: *a* marketing; *b* advertising; *c* production; *d* sales; *e* purchasing; *f* management.
4 Give a short profile of *a* yourself, and *b* a colleague, including name, profession/trade, company, role in the company, functions.

The Japanese company Okuma decided against developing its own electrical discharge machines. Under licence from Herbert Walter, it now manufactures and markets the machines in Asia and the USA. Götz Klusmann explains how cooperation started and gives an outline of Okuma.

1 How does Okuma rank in the world?
2 What was Okuma looking for?

HERBERT WALTER GMBH, FLUORN–WINZELN

Herr Klusmann Okuma ist einer der weltgrößten Hersteller von Werkzeugmaschinen, und zwar von gesteuerten, also High-Tech-Werkzeugmaschinen, und ist führend auf dem Gebiet Drehmaschinen, Fräsmaschinen und Schleifmaschinen.
Frau Wachholz Wie kam es zur Zusammenarbeit mit Okuma?
Herr Klusmann Die Zusammenarbeit mit Okuma begann eigentlich seitens Okuma, ohne daß wir das merkten, weil Okuma auf dem europäischen Markt einen leistungsfähigen High-Tech-Partner auf dem Gebiet der Senkerosion suchte. Und die Recherchen von Okuma führten dann zu uns.

wie kam es zur...? *how did ... come about?*
ohne daß wir das merkten *without our noticing it*
weil Okuma ... suchte *because Okuma was looking for...*

---

die Senkerosion *spark erosion, EDM, diesinking*
die Drahterosion *spark erosion, EDM, wire cutting*
die Funkenerosion *spark erosion, EDM*
die Recherchen (*pl.*) *investigations*
seitens *on the part of*
leistungsfähig *competitive*
merken *to notice*
führen *to lead*

NUTS AND BOLTS ▶

Remember how to form the past tense? Notice Mr Klusmann's use of the past tense of **merken, suchen** and **führen** (*weak verbs*) (see p 143):
    ohne daß wir das **merkten**
    weil Okuma einen High-Tech-Partner **suchte**
    Die Recherchen von Okuma **führten** dann zu uns.
Kommen and **beginnen** are *strong verbs,* which change the vowel in the past tense (see p 143):
    Wie **kam** es zur Zusammenarbeit mit Okuma?
    Die Zusammenarbeit **begann** seitens Okuma, ...

Also and **und zwar** introduce more detailed or precise explanations:
    Okuma ist einer der weltgrößten Hersteller von Werkzeugmaschinen, **und zwar** von gesteuerten, **also** High-Tech-Werkzeugmaschinen.

Okuma Europe GmbH, Krefeld

PRACTICE ▶

1 Say a company is a market leader in the following areas: *a* machine tools; *b* film-making; *c* hormone therapy; *d* chemicals; *e* securities.
2 Combine **–fähig** with the nouns in brackets to say a company is:
a competitive (**Leistung**); *b* solvent (**Zahlung**); *c* competitive (**Wettbewerb**); *d* competitive (**Konkurrenz**).

Dipl. Ing. Cornelius Hertling
Architekt BDA

Titles

Considerable emphasis is placed on qualifications in Germany, and this is reflected in the seriousness with which people use titles when addressing each other. On notepaper the name of an engineer will be accompanied by **Dipl.-Ing. Frau Doktor** and **Herr Professor** are common forms of spoken address. But if two people with doctorates get together, they simply address each other as **Herr** or **Frau** with the surname!

CHECKLIST ▶

If you're unsure what a person has said, just say you haven't quite understood: **Moment bitte, ich habe Sie nicht ganz verstanden**. The person will repeat what he/she has said, probably phrasing it slightly differently. If a particular word has thrown you, say **Was bedeutet . . . ?**

Practise talking about your role, your company and its products:

State your qualification
Ich bin von der Ausbildung her Apotheker(in).
Ich habe eine Ausbildung zum Bankkaufmann/zur Bankkauffrau.

Say how long you've been working in the company
Ich arbeite seit drei Jahren bei der Firma X.

Give your role in the company
Ich bin in diesem Unternehmen Exportleiter(in).
Ich mache Produktion.
Meine Funktionen liegen im Bereich Marketing.

Say you have done/are able to do something
Ich habe eine Patentanmeldung gemacht.
Ich habe die Möglichkeit, halbtags zu arbeiten.

Say you've tried/decided to do something
Ich habe versucht, eine adäquate Stelle zu finden.
Ich habe mich entschlossen, eine Firma zu gründen.

Say a company is a leading manufacturer
Firma X ist der (welt)größte Hersteller von Chemikalien.
Firma X ist führend auf dem Gebiet Pharmazeutika.

Say how a product is manufactured, and describe a process
Die Elektrode wird auf einer Drehbank hergestellt.
Diese Arbeit wird vollautomatisch gemacht.
Die Elektrode wird eingespannt.
Die Elektroden werden gedreht.

Say (you think) something is ideal
Diese Symbiose ist ideal.
Ich halte diese Symbiose für ideal.

Say you are/were impressed by something
Ich bin/war von der Firma beeindruckt.

Go back over all the *Checklists* and use them to build up a profile of yourself, your company and its products.

1   Ich werde mich bei Ihnen melden. Practise talking about the future, saying you will: *a* contact someone next Friday;   *b* ring someone tomorrow;   *c* arrange an appointment next month;   *d* fax someone on Monday;   *e* visit someone on 6th April.

2   Complete each sentence with the perfect tense of the verb in brackets: *a* Ich .... eine Patentanmeldung .... (machen); *b* Ich .... mehrere Anzeigen .... (sehen); *c* Man .... sich viel Mühe .... (geben);   *d* Ich .... nach England .... (fahren)

3   Practise using reflexive verbs. Fill in the gaps with the correct reflexive pronouns (**mich**, **sich** or **uns**):   *a* Das Auto befindet .... im Parkhaus gegenüber.   *b* Wir verstehen .... als Unternehmen, was Pharmazeutika herstellt.   *c* Können Sie .... bitte vorstellen? *d* Ich habe .... dort umgesehen.   *e* Es ist was für ältere Leute, die .... erholen wollen.   *f* Ich werde .... bei Ihnen melden.

4   Select words from the list below to: *a* ask someone to help you; *b* ask the time;   *c* ask the way.

bitte   können   Sie   sagen   helfen   die Uhrzeit   sagen   mir   den Weg

Nouns from verbs

You can turn verbs into nouns by simply starting the word with an upper case letter. Verbal nouns are always neuter:

entwickeln – das Entwickeln	fischen – das Fischen
herstellen – das Herstellen	arbeiten – das Arbeiten
erodieren – das Erodieren	reisen – das Reisen

In fact, a whole family of words can often be generated from one verb: **entwickeln**, **sich entwickeln**, **entwickelt**, **entwickelnd**, das **Entwickeln**, die **Entwicklung**, der **Entwickler**.

Past participles can be used as adjectives, eg **das entwickelte Produkt**, or as nouns: **das Entwickelte** (*the developed thing*) (see p 141 and 143).

INNOVATIONSFREUDIG

der Inhaber   *proprietor*
der Wettbewerber   *competitor*
der Mittelstand   *small and medium-sized companies*
die Erfahrung   *experience*
die Konstruktion   *design*
mittelständisch   *medium-sized*
praxisnah   *practical*
sich auszeichnen (durch)   *to be characterized (by)*

Karl-Heinz Möller, a journalist with trade journal *Der Stahlformenbauer*, gives an appraisal of Herbert Walter GmbH.

1   What kind of company is Herbert Walter GmbH?
2   What is a particular characteristic of the company?
3   Where are Exeron machines well known?

ein Unternehmen, das sich durch . . . auszeichnet   *a company which is characterized by . . .*
es liegt . . . daran, weil   *it is . . . because*
eine riesige Erfahrung . . ., die er . . . einbringt   *massive experience . . . which he applies . . .*

Prof. Karl Schekulin

die Ausführung   *model*
die Aufmerksamkeit
   attention
außerhalb   *outside*
innerhalb   *inside*
nämlich   *that is*
etwa   *approximately*

Welt-Maschinist Deutschland

„Die Bundesrepublik Deutschland – alte Bundesländer – ist der wichtigste Maschinenlieferant der Welt. Von deutschen Maschinenbau-Firmen stammten 1990 schätzungsweise 21,8 Prozent der Maschinenausfuhr westlicher Industrieländer; die nächstfolgenden wichtigen Maschinenexporteure, Japan und die USA, brachten es nur auf 17,1 und 17 Prozent Anteil." (*Süddeutsche Zeitung*)

? What do the black sections of the circles in the chart refer to?

1 Put the following points in the right order: *a* advantage of Exeron machines; *b* example of an innovative product; *c* comparison with other German companies; *d* perspective of managing director(s); *e* capacity for innovative products; *f* Herbert Walter's advantages; *g* medium-sized company; *h* deployment of their advantages.

2 Give a presentation on Herbert Walter GmbH based on the points in **1** (in the correct order) using the following verbs in this order: *a* sein; *b* sein; *c* sich auszeichnen; *d* sein; *e* sein; *f* sein; *g* kommen; *h* einbringen.

WIR ZEIGEN IHNEN …

In 1991, Herbert Walter GmbH celebrated its 25th anniversary with the launch of the new EDEM machine. Professor Karl Schekulin invited guests to see the technology for themselves.

1 Where's the Exeron minicenter and what is it used for?
2 Where are the conventional spark-erosion machines?
3 Which machine is not located inside the hall?

Professor Schekulin talks about three machines and makes the transition with the expressions **ferner … schließlich … last, not least** … Signals like these structure lists of items and they can help you get your bearings.

1 You're about to make an announcement at a conference. What do you say to attract the delegates' attention?
2 Thank members of a conference for their attention. What do you say?

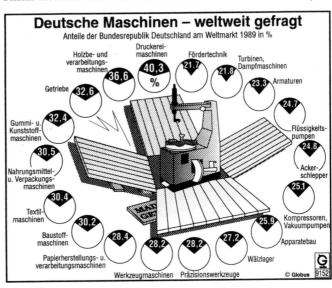

Deutsche Maschinen – weltweit gefragt
Anteile der Bundesrepublik Deutschland am Weltmarkt 1989 in %

Druckereimaschinen **40,3 %**
Holzbe- und verarbeitungsmaschinen **36,6**
Fördertechnik **21,7**
Turbinen, Dampfmaschinen **21,8**
Getriebe **32,6**
Armaturen **23,3**
24,7
Gummi- u. Kunststoffmaschinen **32,4**
Flüssigkeitspumpen **24,8**
Nahrungsmittel- u. Verpackungsmaschinen **30,5**
Ackerschlepper **25,1**
Textilmaschinen **30,4**
Kompressoren, Vakuumpumpen **25,9**
Baustoffmaschinen **30,2**
Apparatebau
Papierherstellungs- u. verarbeitungsmaschinen **28,4**
Werkzeugmaschinen **28,2**
Präzisionswerkzeuge **28,2**
Wälzlager **27,2**
© Globus 9152

134

This press release explains the advantages of the link-up between Herbert Walter and Okuma. Read it and then answer the following questions.

▶ 1 How will Okuma manufacture products from Walter?
2 What are the three advantages to Okuma of this partnership?
3 What is the advantage to Herbert Walter GmbH?
4 How many employees are there at Walter?
5 What's the size of Okuma's shareholding?

Mineo Nakamura

„Als wir uns in der Welt nach Hochtechnologie umgesehen haben, waren wir sofort von Deutschlands hochentwickelter Infrastruktur beeindruckt sowie vom Ausbildungsniveau der deutschen Arbeitskräfte. Das sind die Hauptgründe für unsere Wahl eines deutschen Unternehmens." (Mineo Nakamura, Geschäftsführer, *Okuma Europe GmbH*)

---

der Produktionsstandort
   production facility
der Abnehmer *customer*
der Abnehmerkreis *customers*
das Wachstum *growth*
die Erweiterung *expansion*
der Beschäftigte *employee*
die Kooperation *cooperation*
in Lizenz *under licence*
erweitern *to expand*
gewinnen *to gain*
zählen zu *to belong to, be among*

Okuma und Herbert Walter vereinbaren Partnerschaft

Der mittelständische schwäbische Erodiermaschinenhersteller Herbert Walter und die führende japanische Werkzeugmaschinengruppe Okuma haben eine enge Kooperation vereinbart. Im Rahmen der Zusammenarbeit zwischen Okuma und Walter wird Okuma die technologisch zu den Spitzenprodukten zählenden Senkerodierzentren von Walter in Lizenz fertigen und in Japan und anderen Märkten vertreiben.

Für Okuma bedeutet diese Kooperation eine Erweiterung der Werkzeugmaschinenpalette – High-Tech Fräs-, Dreh- und Schleifmaschinen – um technisch anspruchsvolle Erodiermaschinen. Okuma erweitert damit auch seinen Abnehmerkreis um den Werkzeug- und Formenbau und sichert sich nicht zuletzt einen Produktionsstandort im Herzen der EG. Okuma Japan gilt als weltweit führender Hersteller von zerspanenden Werkzeugmaschinen mit einem Umsatzvolumen in Japan von rund 1,4 Milliarden DM.

Die Walter-Gruppe gewinnt mit dieser Zusammenarbeit einen High-Tech-Partner mit weltweitem Vertrieb. Die Walter-Gruppe hat 100 Beschäftigte und erreichte 1990 bei einem 25%-igen Wachstum einen Jahresumsatz von fast 30 Mio. DM. Walter vertreibt Senk- und Drahterodiermaschinen sowie Ultraschall-Bearbeitungsmaschinen. Alleiniger Gesellschafter der Herbert Walter GmbH ist exeron Erodiertechnologie GmbH. Im Zuge der vereinbarten Zusammenarbeit hat Okuma 50 Prozent des Kapitals an der exeron Erodiertechnologie GmbH.

(Presse-Information, Herbert Walter GmbH)

im Rahmen der Zusammenarbeit *within the framework of cooperation*
wird Okuma … in Lizenz fertigen *Okuma will manufacture … under licence*
die technologisch zu den Spitzenprodukten zählenden Senkerodierzentren *the spark-erosion centres, which are technologically at the leading edge*
technisch anspruchsvolle Erodiermaschinen *technically sophisticated spark-erosion machines*
nicht zuletzt *last but not least*
im Zuge der *as a result of the*

In written German, you may find a lot of information packed in between the article and noun:

der mittelständische schwäbische **Erodiermaschinenhersteller**

die technologisch zu den Spitzenprodukten zählenden **Senkerodier-zentren**

You may have noticed that Exeron spells itself with a lower-case initial as does the trade fair Boot. This is a popular German advertising practice, as it sets off the name from other nouns, which are normally written with a capital.

1 Put the main points of the article in the order in which they're given: *a* relationship between Walter and Exeron; *b* advantages to Okuma; *c* machines sold by Walter; *d* Okuma's manufacture and sale of Herbert Walter's machine; *e* advantage to Herbert Walter; *f* Okuma's stake in the company; *g* cooperation between the two companies; *h* position and turnover of Okuma; *i* company data on Herbert Walter.

2 Give a short presentation in German on the link-up between Herbert Walter GmbH and Okuma: *a* sector of companies; *b* Walter – number of employees, growth, turnover; *c* status of Okuma Japan; *d* significance of cooperation for Okuma; *e* advantage to the Walter group; *f* nature of the cooperation between Okuma and Walter.

BUSINESS FILE

The **Mittelstand** (medium-sized companies employing 50 to 5000 people) has been the foundation of Germany's economic success. Herbert Walter GmbH is a family engineering company known the world over for producing **deutsche Wertarbeit** (German craftsmanship).

Germany has a social market economy based on the strength of the deutschmark, which is vested in the custody of the **Bundesbank**. Consensus has played a large role in Germany's economic growth, with government, unions and employers working together to create favourable economic conditions. The banks are important in providing money to German industry, and they hold considerable stakes in companies. It is typical that Herbert Walter borrowed his start-up capital from the bank.

Many German companies are family businesses and would like to remain so, as it avoids conflict of interest with outside shareholders. Control of large publicly-quoted companies may still be in family hands, and hostile takeovers are often regarded as a foreign concept. This tends to exclude investors from abroad and generates a more patriarchal approach than in a company with non-family management. However, as the postwar generation of entrepreneurs retires, there are sometimes problems of succession.

If you have a couple of hours to spare while in Germany, make the most of it and sample some German culture. Visit a museum and read the descriptions of the exhibits; go to a concert and see if you can figure out the programme; then have a meal at a restaurant and work your way through the menu!

PRONUNCIATION AND SPELLING

To help you acquire German pronunciation, listen to the recordings (**Hören Sie bitte zu!**) and imitate the speakers. See how much you can understand, repeat when asked (**Wiederholen Sie, bitte!**) and answer the questions (**Beantworten Sie die Fragen!**). But don't stop there. Play the recordings over again without looking at the book, until you feel you could speak along with the speakers. At first, you may find some sounds unfamiliar, and difficult to reproduce, but as long as you listen, and listen again, you'll soon master them.

The written form of a German word gives you a good idea of how it's pronounced. This section offers you some guidance.

VOWELS

Different vowels are distinguished from each other by the position of the lips, the position of the tongue, and by their length.

Short vowels

a	as in *luck*	Bank, das, Land, Fax, am
e, ä	as in *neck*	denn, englisch, hätte
i	as in *pick*	ist, in, bin, Film, mit
o	as in *stock*	Bonn, kosten, Gott
u	as in *put*	und, plus, zum, Null, uns
unstressed e	as in *begin*	Name, heiße, Reise, Beginn
unstressed er	as in *matter*	oder, aber, hier
ö	like short German **e**, but lips are rounded as for **o**	können, geöffnet, Köln
ü	like short German **i**, but lips are rounded as for **u**	müssen, fünf, zurück

In writing, a double consonant after a vowel shows that the vowel is short, eg Pre**ss**e, a**ll**es.

Long vowels

Long German vowels are more like the 'pure' Scottish vowels than the diphthongized vowels of southern English. If a vowel is doubled in writing, or followed by an **h**, it's pronounced long, eg B**oo**t, fa**h**ren.

a, aa, ah	as in *bath*	Tag, mal, Staat, zahlen
e, ee, eh	as in Scottish *bake*	Meter, Kaffee, nehmen
ä, äh	(like **e, ee, eh**)	wären, Aktivität, ungefähr
i, ie, ih	as in *bee*	Termin, wieviel, Ihnen
o, oo, oh	as in Scottish *boat*	Montag, oder, Boot, froh
u, uh	as in Scottish *boom*	gut, Beruf, zu, Uhr, Huhn
ö, öh	like long German **e** but lips are pursed as if for a kiss	schön, ungewöhnlich
ü, üh	like long German **i**, but lips are pursed as if for a kiss	über, natürlich, früh

Diphthongs

German diphthongs are always written as two letters (but note that **ie** is pronounced like *ee* in the English word *bee*).

au	as in *power*	Kauffrau, schauen, aus
ei, ai	as in *mine*	mein, bei, Reise, Mainz
eu, äu	as in *coil*	Europa, neu, Fräulein

CONSONANTS

Pronounce consonants strongly when speaking German. The following list only gives the consonants that differ markedly from English. The pronunciation of foreign words usually roughly corresponds to that of the original word, eg **Manager, Chip**.

c	before **a, l, o, r, u** like English *k*; otherwise like English *ts*	Café, Computer Cäsar
ch	after **a, o, u** (but not **eu, äu**) as in Scottish *Loch*; before **s** usually like *k*; otherwise usually like exaggerated *h* in *huge*	gesprochen, acht wechseln, sechs Chemie, sprechen
h	at start of words and parts of compounds as in English; not pronounced if part of long vowel	hier, abheben zahlen, nehmen
j	like *y* in *yes*	ja, Projekt
l	like English initial *l* in *life*, with tongue flat against roof of mouth (not rounded as in *all*)	Geld, wollen
p	as in English, but also pronounced before **n** and **s** at start of word	Psychotherapeutin
qu	like English *kv*	Qualität
r	at back of throat, like **ch**, though with less force; endings **-er** and **-r** of words and parts of compounds like very short unstressed German **a**	Presse, Beruf Leiter, für, mir
s	like English *z* if before a vowel; like English *sh* before **p** or **t**; otherwise, and if doubled, like English *s*	sagen, Reise Sport, zuständig ist, es, Messe
sch	like English *sh*	schön, deutsch
ß	identical to **ss**, ie like English *s*	grüßen, heißen
v	like English *f*; but in loan words like *v*	von, Vertrieb variabel
w	like English *v*	wie, überweisen
z	like English *ts*	Zeit, zwei, ganz

STRESS

Most German words have the main stress at the beginning:

Name, **Fir**ma, **sa**gen, **Pres**sestelle, **zu**ständig, **her**stellen

But words starting with one of the following (unstressed) syllables normally have the main stress second:

be-, **emp-**, **ent-**, **er-**, **ge-**, **ver-**, **zer-**
Be**reich**, ent**wick**eln, Ge**sell**schaft, Ver**sich**erung

Words of foreign origin are often stressed as in the source language, eg Comp**u**ter (English), Produ**zent** (Latin).

THE ALPHABET

This is roughly how German letters are pronounced:

a	ah	**h**	ha	**o**	oh	**u**	uh
b	beh	**i**	ih	**p**	peh	**v**	fau
c	tseh	**j**	jott	**q**	kuh	**w**	weh
d	deh	**k**	kah	**r**	err	**x**	iks
e	eh	**l**	ell	**s**	ess	**y**	üpsilon
f	eff	**m**	emm	**t**	teh	**z**	tsett
g	geh	**n**	enn				

ä	ah Umlaut
ö	oh Umlaut
ü	uh Umlaut
ß	ess tsett
A	groß(es) ah
b	klein(es) beh

On the telephone, use the standard phone alphabet (**see p 86**).

GRAMMAR

It has been estimated that by the time an average child is five years old, it will have spent over 9000 hours learning its first language. Many more hours are needed to reach adult competence. You're unlikely to have that amount of time, so you'll want to take short cuts. By spending some effort on getting to grips with the structure of the German language, you'll go a long way in a fraction of those hours!

This **Grammar** is specifically designed to help you with the language used in **German means Business**.

THE GERMAN WORD

German words tend to come in families (**see p 133**). Their elements are often called *prefix – **root** – suffix* (the same principle applies in English, eg *disagreement*).

sprechen (*to speak*)
be**sprech**en (*to speak about*), ver**sprech**en (*to promise*)
an**sprech**en (*to address*), ent**sprech**en (*to correspond*)
Sprechen (*speaking*), Ver**sprech**en (*promise*)
Sprecher (*speaker*), Be**sprech**ung (*meeting*)
Sprache (*language*), An**sprach**e (*speech, address*)
sprachlos (*speechless*)

German is also notorious for joining up words to form compounds (**see p 10**):

Fremd**sprach**e (*foreign language*), Presse**sprech**er (*press officer*)
Fern**sprech**er (*telephone*), **Sprech**zeiten (*consultation times*)

Words may be joined up using their base form, or the first one may change its ending, usually adding either **s** or **n**:

Film + Gesellschaft = Filmgesellschaft
Ausstellung + Gesellschaft = Ausstellung**s**gesellschaft
Aktie + Gesellschaft = Aktie**n**gesellschaft

THE GERMAN SENTENCE

Think of a sentence as basically having three parts:

subject + **verb** + *direct object*
Die Firma **fertigt** ein Produkt.

You may also find additional elements that give more detail:

Die Schott Gruppe **entwickelt, fertigt und vertreibt**
weltweit mit ca. 18.000 Mitarbeitern rund 50.000 Artikel.

Sometimes you may find only two basic parts, or more than three:

subject + **verb**
Die Besucher **kommen**.

subject + **verb** + *indirect object* + *direct object*
Wir **verkaufen** den Ausstellern die Quadratmeter.

The form of the words gives information about their role in a particular sentence. This variation is called *case*:

subject:	nominative case	**who/what does**
direct object:	accusative case	**what**
indirect object:	dative case	**to whom**

Wir (*nom.*) **verkaufen** den Ausstellern (*dat.*)
die Quadratmeter (*acc.*).
Ich (*nom.*) **wünsche** Ihnen (*dat.*) einen angenehmen
Aufenthalt (*acc.*).

There's a fourth case, which is usually equivalent to the English *of*. This is the *genitive case*:

die Planung **Ihres Seminars** *the planning **of your** seminar*

Because the case of a word indicates its role in the sentence, German word order is relatively flexible (**see p 55 and 89**).

NOUNS

Nouns are the words for people or animate creatures, things and concepts, eg **Manager**, **Computer**, **Marketing**. In German, they're written with a capital, and in spoken German they tend to be stressed. The form of a noun and any associated words may vary depending on its *case*. See table with *Determiners*.

Gender

German nouns are either *masculine*, *feminine* or *neuter*, and this affects the form of associated words, eg articles or adjectives. Grammatical gender normally has little to do with sex, though job names have 'natural' gender (*see p 7 and 10*):

masculine	feminine
der Leiter	die Leiter**in**
der Sachbearbeiter	die Sachbearbeiter**in**
der Kauf**mann**	die Kauf**frau**

About 20% of German nouns are neuter, 35% feminine and 45% masculine. Abstract nouns tend to be feminine, as are nouns with the following endings (*see p 121*):

-enz	Konfer**enz**, Konkurr**enz**, Liz**enz**
-heit/keit	Sicher**heit**, Öffentlich**keit**
-ik	Techn**ik**, Elektron**ik**, Polit**ik**
-in	Telefonist**in**, Sekretär**in**, Manager**in**
	(*except chemical terms, eg das Benz**in***)
-schaft	Gesell**schaft**, Gemein**schaft**, Mann**schaft**
-sion/-tion	Ero**sion**, Pen**sion**, Funk**tion**, Informa**tion**
-tät	Identi**tät**, Quali**tät**, Universi**tät**
-ung	Plan**ung**, Herstell**ung**, Niederlass**ung**
-ur	Strukt**ur**, Kult**ur**, Nat**ur**

Compound nouns take the gender of the last noun (*see p 10*):

die Welt + der Umsatz = **der** Welt**umsatz**

das Wasser + der Sport + die Saison = **die** Wassersport**saison**

Most masculine and neuter nouns add -(**e**)**s** in the *genitive singular*:

das Wasser (*nom.*)	des Wasser**s** (*gen.*)
der Umsatz (*nom.*)	des Umsatz**es** (*gen.*)

Plural nouns

Nouns vary in the way they form the plural. This is how plural forms are indicated in the **Glossary** and in dictionaries (*see p 24*):

singular	plural	
Leiter, Hersteller	-	Leiter, Hersteller
Flughafen, Garten	⸚	Flughäfen, Gärten
		(*umlaut on stressed vowel*)
Gerät, Beruf	-e	Geräte, Berufe
Auftrag, Paß	⸚e	Aufträge, Pässe
Messe, Vertretung	-(e)n	Messen, Vertretung**en**
Geld, Land	⸚er	Gelder, Länder
		(*umlaut on a, o or u*)
Büro, Auto, Hotel	-s	Büros, Autos, Hotels

Nouns ending in -**in** or -**nis** double the final consonant, eg Sekretärin – Sekretärin**nen**. A few nouns of Latin origin have yet other plurals, eg Firm**a** – Firm**en**, Material – Material**ien**.

Here are some useful rules of thumb:

-	Most nouns ending in -**el**, -**en**, -**er** don't change.
-**e** or ⸚**e**	Added to most masculine nouns.
-(**e**)**n**	Added to over 90% of feminine nouns and all masculine nouns ending in -**e**.
-**s**	Added to many loan words from English or French.

If a plural noun is in the *dative case*, -**n** is added unless the ending is -**n** or -**s**:

den Leiter**n**, **den** Berufen, **den** Messen, **den** Büros.

DETERMINERS AND PRONOUNS

A noun is usually preceded by an *article* (the or a in English) or some other word that fulfils a similar function (eg *this*, *that*, *my*). These *determiners* help to indicate the noun's role in the sentence. Their forms vary according to the gender, number and case of the noun they're associated with (*see p 8 and 52*).

Forms of the definite article **der, die, das** (*the*):

	masculine	feminine	neuter	plural
nom.	der Mann	die Frau	das Boot	die Männer
acc.	den Mann	die Frau	das Boot	die Frauen
gen.	des Mann(e)s	der Frau	des Boot(e)s	der Boote
dat.	dem Mann	der Frau	dem Boot	den Männern/ Frauen/Booten

You'll find similar endings with these determiners:

dieser (*this*), **jeder** (*every*), **welcher** (*which*)

	masculine	feminine	neuter	plural
nom.	dieser	diese	dies(es)	diese
acc.	diesen	diese	dies(es)	diese
gen.	dieses	dieser	dieses	dieser
dat.	diesem	dieser	diesem	diesen

Forms of the indefinite article **ein** (*a*) and the negative article **kein** (*not a/no*) (*see p 21 and 62*):

	masculine	feminine	neuter	plural
nom.	(k)ein	(k)eine	(k)ein	keine
acc.	(k)einen	(k)eine	(k)ein	keine
gen.	(k)eines	(k)einer	(k)eines	keiner
dat.	(k)einem	(k)einer	(k)einem	keinen

In speech, the indefinite article is often shortened (*see p 34*):

'n (**ein** or **einen**)	**'ne** (**eine**)
'ner (**einer**)	**'nem** (**einem**)

Demonstratives

For *this/these*, you can use **dieser, diese, dies(es)** or **der, die, das**. For *that/those*, use **der, die, das**.

Der, die, das and **dieser, diese, dies(es)** can stand on their own, as *pronouns* 'in place of a noun'. Their gender depends on what they refer to – though sometimes **das** is used for masculine or feminine nouns or a general idea (*see p 18, 36, 88 and 106*):

> **Das/Dies(es)** (Boot) würde mich interessieren.
> **Die/Diese** (Firma) würde mich interessieren.

For the forms of **der, die, das** as pronouns, see *Relative pronouns*. The *dative plural* differs from the definite article: **denen**. The genitive is hardly ever used as a demonstrative pronoun.

Relative pronouns

The relative pronouns **der, die, das** are equivalent to the English *who* or *which* or *that*. They refer back to a noun (or occasionally a pronoun), giving more detail. The form is the same as for the definite article, except in the *genitive*, and in the *dative plural*.

	masculine	*feminine*	*neuter*	*plural*
nom.	der	die	das	die
acc.	den	die	das	die
gen.	dessen	deren	dessen	deren
dat.	dem	der	dem	denen

The gender and number of the relative pronoun is the same as that of the noun it refers to. The case depends on the role of the pronoun in the *relative clause* (*see p 115, 121 and 147*):

> … mit freundlichem **Service, der** einen erfolgreichen Tagungsverlauf garantiert.

Personal pronouns

	person	*nom.*	*acc.*	*dat.*
singular	*I*	ich	mich	mir
	you (familiar)	du	dich	dir
	you (formal)	Sie	Sie	Ihnen
	he/it	er	ihn	ihm
	she/it	sie	sie	ihr
	it	es	es	ihm
	one	man	einen	einem
plural	*we*	wir	uns	uns
	you (familiar)	ihr	euch	euch
	you (formal)	Sie	Sie	Ihnen
	they	sie	sie	ihnen

The form depends on person, number and case (*see p 82, 88 and 93*). Note the equivalents of *you*: the familiar **du** (*sing.*) and **ihr** (*pl.*), and the formal **Sie** (*sing./pl.*) (*see p 75 and 126*). Formal **Sie** has the same pronoun and verb forms as the 3rd person plural **sie** (*they*). Personal pronouns are rarely in the genitive.

The gender of the pronoun matches the gender of the person, thing or concept it refers to (*see p 122*):

> **der Jahresumsatz** (*m.*)… **Er** schwankt…

After a preposition, you refer to a thing with **da-** or **dar-** plus preposition, eg **dafür** (*for it/them*), **darin** (*in it/them*) (*see p 142*):

> …wenn wir **darüber** reden… **Daran** arbeite ich immer.

Possessives

Possessives show who or what somebody or something belongs to or is associated with (*see p 88 and 93*).

singular		*plural*	
my	mein	*our*	unser
your (familiar)	dein	*your (familiar)*	euer
your (formal)	Ihr	*your (formal)*	Ihr
his/its (m./n.)	sein	*their*	ihr
her/its (f.)	ihr		

These are the base forms. Their endings depend on the gender, number and case of the noun that follows, and are the same as those of the indefinite article **ein, eine, ein** (*see p 74*):

> unsere Firma macht einen Umsatz… (*f. sing. nom.*)
> in unserem Parkhaus (*n. sing. dat.*)
> Ich möchte unsere Gäste vorstellen. (*pl. acc.*)

Possession can also be expressed in other ways. With proper names, you add **-s**, and you can link two nouns with **von** or the *genitive case*:

> Europas größter Spezialglas-Hersteller
> die Aktivitäten **von** 40 Produktionsstätten
> bei der Planung (*f. dat.*) **Ihres** Seminars (*n. gen.*)

Reflexive pronouns

Similar to English verbs like *to wash yourself*, a number of German verbs – more than in English – are used with a *reflexive pronoun*, which means that subject and object are the same person or thing (*see p 44, 73 and 122*). In the **Glossary** these are preceded by **sich**, eg **sich interessieren** (*to be interested*):

> ich interessiere **mich**
> du interessierst **dich**
> er/sie/es/man interessiert **sich**
>
> wir interessieren **uns**
> ihr interessiert **euch**
> sie/Sie interessieren **sich**

Ich (*subject*) **interessiere mich** (*object*) für Ihr Schiff.

Usually, the object is in the accusative. A few verbs (eg **sich anschauen**) have a dative object. This only affects the **ich** and **du** forms, where the dative reflexive pronouns are **mir** and **dir**:

> Ich (*subject*) **hatte mir** (*object*) Ihren Betrieb **angeschaut**.

ADJECTIVES

Adjectives describe or modify nouns. If an adjective follows a noun, it retains its base form:

Die Exponate sind **gut**.   Die Pressen sind **schwer**.

But before a noun, the ending varies according to the gender, number and case of that noun, and according to the determiner it follows (*see p 63, 65 and 141*). The simplest pattern is that used after **der, die, das** and **dieser**..., **jeder**..., **welcher**...:

	masculine	feminine	neuter	plural
nom.	der gute Umsatz	die gute Presse	das gute Exponat	die guten Umsätze/Pressen/Exponate
acc.	den guten Umsatz	die gute Presse	das gute Exponat	die guten Umsätze/Pressen/Exponate
gen.	des guten Umsatzes	der guten Presse	des guten Exponats	der guten Umsätze/Pressen/Exponate
dat.	dem guten Umsatz	der guten Presse	dem guten Exponat	den guten Umsätzen/Pressen/Exponaten

When the determiner is **ein, eine, ein, kein**... or a *possessive* (eg **mein, Ihr**) three of the forms differ:

Masc. sing. nom.   ein gut**er** Umsatz
Neuter sing. nom./acc.   ein gut**es** Exponat

If there's no determiner, the adjective indicates the case:

	masculine	feminine	neuter	plural
nom.	guter	gute	gutes	gute
acc.	guten	gute	gutes	gute
gen.	guten	guter	guten	guter
dat.	gutem	guter	gutem	guten

(Ich wünsche Ihnen) schön**en** gut**en** Morgen (*m. sing. acc.*)!
Mit zeitgemäß**er** Konferenztechnik (*f. sing. dat.*) und
freundlich**em** Service (*m. sing. dat.*).

Adjectives used as nouns

Adjectives and participles (*see p 143*) can be used as nouns. If the noun is masculine or feminine, it refers to a particular quality of a person or persons. If it's neuter, it means *that which is*...:

der/die Fremde *stranger*, der/die Angestellte *employee*
etwas Ähnliches *something similar*

An adjectival noun ends like an adjective before a noun.

ADVERBS

Adverbs modify verbs, adjectives or other adverbs, and usually give information of *when, where, how, how much* something is. They have no variations of form.

heute (*today*)   größtenteils (*largely*)   sehr (*very*)

Most adjectives can be used as adverbs, without an ending:

Adjective: mit **modernen** Konferenzräumen
Adverb: mit **modern** ausgestatteten Konferenzräumen

Here are the adjective endings after **der, die, das** in schematic form:

	m.	*f.*	*n.*	*pl.*
nom.	-e	-e	-e	-en
acc.	-en	-e	-e	-en
gen.	-en	-en	-en	-en
dat.	-en	-en	-en	-en

COMPARISONS

Many adjectives are gradable, as in the English *dry – drier – driest* (*see p 32 and 33*):

	comparative		superlative
international	international**er**		international**ste**
wichtig	wichtig**er**	der	wichtig**ste**
trocken	trocken**er**	die	trocken**ste**
groß	größ**er**	das	größ**te**
gut	**besser**		**beste**
viel	**mehr**		**meiste**

Some common adjectives require an umlaut when they're graded (eg **groß**), and a few are completely irregular (eg **gut, viel**). Comparative and superlative forms of adjectives have the usual adjective endings if they precede a noun (*see p 65*):

Die Dresdner Bank war schnell**er**.
Sie haben viele ält**ere** Mitarbeiter (*pl. acc.*).
Was sind die wichtig**sten** Messen (*pl. nom.*)?
Es gibt keine wichtig**ste** (*f. sing. acc.*)!

The comparative form of adverbs is the same as the basic comparative form of adjectives:

Ich probiere es **besser** morgen.

The superlative form has **am** in front and the ending **-en**:

am international**sten**   **am** wichtig**sten**   **am besten**

Es geht darum, den Zeitpunkt festzulegen, wann es uns **am besten** paßt.

And note the irregular adverb **gern – lieber – am liebsten** (*gladly – preferably – best of all*):

Ich **lieber** trocken. *I'd prefer dry.*
Für mich **am liebsten** trocken. *I'd like dry best.*

PREPOSITIONS

A preposition normally precedes a noun (and associated words) or a pronoun. It often answers the questions *where?*, *when?*, or *how?* Some common prepositions are frequently fused with the following article (*see p 26*):

am	(an dem)	im	(in dem)	unterm	(unter dem)
ans	(an das)	ins	(in das)	vom	(von dem)
beim	(bei dem)	übers	(über das)	zum	(zu dem)
fürs	(für das)	ums	(um das)	zur	(zu der)

Each preposition requires a following noun or pronoun to be in a particular case, normally accusative or dative (*see p 8 and 59*).

Prepositions used with the accusative

bis	von Januar **bis September**
durch	**Durch dieses Programm** kam es zur Namensverbindung Stahlgruber.
für	Ich arbeite **für die Firma** Pan Imperial Reisen.
gegen	Wir treffen uns so **gegen halb vier**.
ohne	Das kann ich **ohne falsche Bescheidenheit** sagen.
um	Es dreht sich **ums Geld**!

Prepositions used with the dative

aus	Wenn Sie bitte **aus der Tür** rausgehen . . .
bei	Ich arbeite **bei der Deutschen BP**.
gegenüber	Ich fühle mich **gegenüber diesen** verpflichtet.
mit	**mit modernen Konferenzräumen**
nach	die Suche **nach dem Wirkstoff**
seit	Ich habe **seit wenigen Wochen** die Vertretung.
von	Folco ist mein Name, **von der Deutschen BP**.
zu	**Zu den Crevetten** einen trocknen Weißwein.

Prepositions used with the accusative or dative

In principle, the following are used with the *accusative* if there's movement from one place to another (*where to?*). They're used with the *dative* if there is no movement, or the movement is not directional (*where?*).

an	Wir verteilen sie **an die Öffentlichkeit** (*acc.*).
	Ich habe mich **an vielen Instituten** (*dat.*) beworben.
auf	Wir sind **auf einen Bazillus** (*acc.*) gestoßen.
	Ist die Adresse aktuell **auf dem Führerschein** (*dat.*)?
in	bis **ins kleinste Detail** (*acc.*)
	Soll es **im Raucher** (*dat.*) sein?
neben	**Neben Handelsaktivitäten** (*dat.*) stellte die Firma Hebebühnen und Kompressoren her.
über	**Über das Thema** (*acc.*) haben wir gesprochen.
unter	Kein Anschluß **unter dieser Nummer** (*dat.*)!
vor	die Ost-Westverbindungen **vor der Wende** (*dat.*).
zwischen	die Vereinbarung **zwischen dem Bereich PR und den Service-Einheiten** (*dat.*).

Prepositions are often combined with other words, eg:

Ausstellung, **Mit**arbeiter, **Unter**nehmen, **Zwischen**ergebnis **an**rufen, **auf**bauen, **durch**gehen, **über**weisen, **vor**stellen

Some verbs, nouns and adjectives are followed by a particular preposition (*see p 100 and 117*):

Wir **handeln mit** Versprechen.
Wir **bemühen uns um** Ihre Verbindung.
Dann **gehen** wir kurz **auf** die Produkte **ein**.
Ich bin **zuständig für** den Individualtourismus.
Wir sind auf der **Suche nach** einem zukunftsweisenden Gerät.

da(r) + preposition

This is roughly equivalent to a preposition plus the pronoun *it* in English: da**mit**, da**zu**, da**ran** (*see p 72*).

Ich bin **dafür** zuständig. *I am responsible **for it**.*
Ich hatte **damit** recht. *I was right **about it**.*
Riesencrevetten, **dazu** Reis *prawns, **with** (them) rice*

It's also sometimes used to refer forward or back to detail elsewhere in the sentence (*see p 109*):

Vielleicht soll ich jetzt **drauf** eingehen, was wichtig ist.
Perhaps I should now go into that which is important.
Es ging **darum**, daß ich ihm den HC beschrieben habe.
*It was **about the fact** that I had described the hand-held computer to him.*

VERBS

In the *Glossary* and in dictionaries, verbs are given in their *infinitive* form, which consists of the *root* and the ending **-en**, or, with a few verbs, **-n**, eg:

sag**en**, könn**en**, herstell**en**, heiß**en**, entwickel**n**, wechsel**n**

The infinitive is also used to form the *future tense* (*see p 145*), and in *infinitive clauses*, which depend on another verb (*see p 147*).

Normal sentences have a verb that corresponds in form to the *subject*, ie the person, thing or concept 'doing' the action of the verb. The verb may have several parts, including a *prefix*, *past participle* or *infinitive*:

Die Firma *produziert* 450 Boote.
Die Firma *stellt* 450 Boote **her**.
Die Firma *hat* 450 Boote **hergestellt**.
Die Firma *will* 450 Boote **herstellen**.

The form of a verb in a sentence depends on the *subject* of the sentence and the *tense* of the verb, eg:

Present tense	*Past tense*
Ich arbeite für die Firma.	**Ich** arbeitete . . .
Wir arbeiten für die Firma.	**Wir** arbeiteten . . .

Weak, strong and irregular verbs

Most German verbs are *weak*, which means their form in the various tenses and in the *past participle* (see below) changes according to a pattern that leaves the root unaltered:

Infinitive	-(e)n	sag**en**	arbeit**en**
Present (er/sie/es/man)	-(e)t	sag**t**	arbeit**et**
Past (er/sie/es/man)	-(e)te	sag**te**	arbeit**ete**
Past participle	**ge**---(e)t	**ge**sag**t**	**ge**arbeit**et**

But some common verbs are *strong*, with changes in the vowel of the root, and the past participle ending -(e)n (*see p 48 and 102*):

Infinitive	-(e)n	fahr**en**	sprech**en**
Present (er/sie/es/man)	-(e)t		
often vowel change		f**ä**hr**t**	spri**ch**t
Past (er/sie/es/man)			
vowel change		f**u**hr	spr**a**ch
Past participle	**ge**---(e)n		
often vowel change		**ge**f**a**hr**en**	**ge**spr**o**ch**en**

A few verbs double the consonant after the vowel (*see p 47*):

> schneiden (schneidet), schn**itt**, **ge**schn**itt**en

The *Glossary* lists vowel changes like this:

> fahren (ä), u, a   sprechen (i), a, o

The present tense is omitted if it remains unchanged. You'll find similar indications of vowel changes in any dictionary.

Irregular verbs follow neither pattern. Their forms are given in full in the *Glossary* (omitting any unchanged present tense), eg:

> **denken**, dachte, gedacht   **sein** (ist), war, gewesen
> **essen** (ißt), aß, gegessen   **tun** (tut), tat, getan
> **gehen**, ging, gegangen   **wissen** (weiß), wußte, gewußt

Separable and inseparable verbs

Many German verbs consist of a simple verb with a prefix, which either remains joined to the root in all forms (*inseparable verbs*) or separates off in some forms (*separable verbs*) (*see p 39*).

Inseparable prefixes

There is a limited number of these:

> **be-, emp-, ent-, er-, ge-, ver-, zer-**
> **be**arbeiten, **emp**fehlen, **ent**wickeln, **er**halten, **ge**winnen, **ver**treiben, **zer**spanen

And a few prefixes may be inseparable or separable:

überweisen (*insep.*)	**über**ordnen (*sep.*)
umfassen (*insep.*)	**um**drehen (*sep.*)
unternehmen (*insep.*)	**unter**bringen (*sep.*)

Inseparable prefixes are not stressed. The stress (indicated by underlining above) falls on the root of the verb. Inseparable verbs have no **ge-** in the past participle, eg bearbeit**et** (compare: **ge**arbeit**et**).

Separable prefixes

These usually also exist as words in their own right – eg as prepositions or adverbs, which tend to retain their basic meaning when they combine with a verb. In the *Glossary*, separable verbs are listed (*sep.*). Here are some examples:

> **auf**bauen, **ein**bauen, **an**bieten, **aus**bilden, **vor**stellen, **her**stellen, **zurück**kommen, **raus**gehen

In simple sentences and main clauses, the prefix separates off and goes to the end (*see p 30*):

> Dann **rufe** ich nachher nochmal **an**. (anrufen)
> Jetzt **gehen** wir hier einfach **durch**. (durchgehen)
> Ich **übe** den Beruf eines Handelsvertreters **aus**. (ausüben)

The past participle has the prefix before the past participle of the simple verb, so **ge-** comes *after* the prefix (*see p 77*):

> auf**ge**baut, ein**ge**baut, an**ge**boten, aus**ge**bildet, vor**ge**stellt, her**ge**stellt, zurück**ge**kommen, raus**ge**gangen

Reflexive verbs

These verbs are used with a *reflexive pronoun* (*see p 44, 73, 122 and 140*) that refers to the same person or thing as the subject:

> Der Jahresumsatz bewegt **sich** in der Größenordnung von 13 Milliarden D-Mark.
> **Wir verstehen uns** als Unternehmen, was Pharmazeutika herstellt.

Past participles

Past participles are formed according to the following patterns (*see p 40*):

	Infinitive	Past participle
Weak verbs		
ge---(e)t	machen	**ge**macht
	arbeiten	**ge**arbeitet
Infinitive -ieren		
omit **ge-**	produzieren	produziert
	interessieren	interessiert
Strong verbs		
ge---**en**	fahren	**ge**fahren
	sprechen	**ge**sprochen
(+ vowel change)	bleiben	**ge**blieben
Inseparable prefix		
omit **ge-**	bestellen	bestellt
	versprechen	versprochen
Separable prefix		
-**ge**-	herstellen	her**ge**stellt
	abschneiden	ab**ge**schnitten

Past participles are used to form the *perfect* and *pluperfect* tenses and the *passive* (*see p 52 and 145*). They can also be used as adjectives (with the usual adjective endings) to describe things or people (*see p 141*):

> mit **gebraten**er Hähnchenbrust
> mit modern **ausgestattet**en Konferenzräumen
> Ich bin **gelernt**er Industriekaufmann.

Auxiliary verbs: *haben, sein, werden*

infinitive		haben	sein	werden
present tense	ich	habe	bin	werde
	du	hast	bist	wirst
	er/sie/es/man	hat	ist	wird
	wir	haben	sind	werden
	ihr	habt	seid	werdet
	sie/Sie	haben	sind	werden
past tense	ich	hatte	war	wurde
	du	hattest	warst	wurdest
	er/sie/es/man	hatte	war	wurde
	wir	hatten	waren	wurden
	ihr	hattet	wart	wurdet
	sie/Sie	hatten	waren	wurden
subjunctive II	ich	hätte	wäre	würde
	du	hättest	wärst	würdest
	er/sie/es/man	hätte	wäre	würde
	wir	hätten	wären	würden
	ihr	hättet	wärt	würdet
	sie/Sie	hätten	wären	würden
past participle **used for the passive:**		gehabt	gewesen	geworden worden

These verbs can be used as full verbs (*see p 2, 32 and 36*):

Wir **haben** eine Zweigstelle. *We **have** a branch office.*
Ich **bin** Pressesprecher. *I **am** a press officer.*
Die Messe **wird** größer. *The fair **is becoming** bigger.*

As *auxiliary verbs* they help form compound tenses.

Haben is used to form the perfect and pluperfect of most verbs (*see p 36, 105 and 145*):

Aus dieser Apotheke heraus **hat** sich die Firma **entwickelt**.
Wir **hatten** uns über den HC **unterhalten**.

The *subjunctive II* form is often used with **gern(e)**:

Ich **hätte** gerne Herrn Mischke **gesprochen**.
Ich **hätte** gern zwei Zimmer **reserviert**.

Sein is used to form the perfect and pluperfect mainly of verbs of movement without an accusative object, eg **gehen, kommen** (*see p 52 and 61*). In the *Glossary*, such verbs are listed with **sein** in brackets.

... die Mitarbeiter, die diesen Weg mit uns **gegangen sind** ...
Ich freue mich, daß Sie **gekommen sind**.

Sein is also used to form the perfect and pluperfect passive forms:

Das Unternehmen **ist** von einem Apotheker **gegründet worden**.

Werden is used for the future (present tense of **werden** plus infinitive) and passive (**werden** plus past participle) (*see p 39 and 145*):

Der Artikel **wird** sich fest im Markt **etablieren**.
Die Schiffe **werden** in England **produziert**.

The *subjunctive II* form is used as an equivalent to English *would*:

Ich **würde** gern Herrn Sazinski **sprechen**.
Würden Sie sich schon mal **eintragen**?

Modal verbs: *dürfen, können, mögen, müssen, sollen, wollen*

infinitive		dürfen	können	mögen	müssen	wollen
present tense	ich	darf	kann	mag	muß	will
	du	darfst	kannst	magst	mußt	willst
	er/sie/es/man	darf	kann	mag	muß	will
	wir	dürfen	können	mögen	müssen	wollen
	ihr	dürft	könnt	mögt	müßt	wollt
	sie/Sie	dürfen	können	mögen	müssen	wollen
past tense	ich	durfte	konnte	mochte	mußte	wollte
	du	durftest	konntest	mochtest	mußtest	wolltest
	er/sie/es/man	durfte	konnte	mochte	mußte	wollte
	wir	durften	konnten	mochten	mußten	wollten
	ihr	durftet	konntet	mochtet	mußtet	wolltet
	sie/Sie	durften	konnten	mochten	mußten	wollten
subjunctive II	ich	dürfte	könnte	möchte	müßte	wollte
	du	dürftest	könntest	möchtest	müßtest	wolltest
	er/sie/es/man	dürfte	könnte	möchte	müßte	wollte
	wir	dürften	könnten	möchten	müßten	wollten
	ihr	dürftet	könntet	möchtet	müßtet	wolltet
	sie/Sie	dürften	könnten	möchten	müßten	wollten

Sollen has no vowel change, and the same endings as **wollen**.

These verbs can be used as full verbs, but normally they are followed by another verb in the infinitive, which says what someone (or something) *may, can, would like, must, should* or *wants* to do (*see p 19 and 34*):

Ich **konnte** Ihren Namen leider nicht **verstehen**.
Dann **muß** ich mal **schauen**.

Modal verbs often occur in the *subjunctive II* form, usually with the sense of *would*, eg *would be able to, would have to* (*see p 86*):

Könnten Sie mir bitte **sagen**, wie Sie heißen?
Sie **müßten** mit einer Lieferzeit von 11 Monaten **rechnen**.
Ich **möchte** gern 250 Mark **überweisen**.

Present

	weak verbs		strong verbs	
	parken	**mieten**	**fahren**	**sprechen**
ich	park**e**	miet**e**	fahr**e**	sprech**e**
du	park**st**	miet**est**	f**ä**hr**st**	spr**i**ch**st**
er/sie/es/man	park**t**	miet**et**	f**ä**hr**t**	spr**i**ch**t**
wir	park**en**	miet**en**	fahr**en**	sprech**en**
ihr	park**t**	miet**et**	fahr**t**	sprech**t**
sie/Sie	park**en**	miet**en**	fahr**en**	sprech**en**

These are the basic patterns (*see p 3, 10 and 44*).

Uses of the present tense

- present states, actions, events, and habitual or timeless occurrences. There are no continuous tenses in German (the English *I am working* would simply be **ich arbeite**):

Ich **heiße** Alessandra Folco.
Die Schott Gruppe **entwickelt** rund 50.000 Artikel.
Wenn Messen sind, **knüpfe** ich immer wieder Kontakte.

- the past continuing into the present:

Ich **arbeite** jetzt seit sieben Jahren hier.

- future actions or events, so long as the context makes it clear that the future is being referred to (*see p 116*):

Was **trinken** wir zum Essen?
Unter welchen Bedingungen **findet** Forschung im nächsten Jahrhundert **statt**?

Past

	weak verbs		strong verbs	
	parken	**mieten**	**fahren**	**sprechen**
ich	park**te**	miet**ete**	f**uhr**	spr**a**ch
du	park**test**	miet**etest**	f**uhr**st	spr**a**chst
er/sie/es/man	park**te**	miet**ete**	f**uhr**	spr**a**ch
wir	park**ten**	miet**eten**	f**uhr**en	spr**a**chen
ihr	park**tet**	miet**etet**	f**uhr**t	spr**a**cht
sie/Sie	park**ten**	miet**eten**	f**uhr**en	spr**a**chen

Weak verbs add **-(e)t** to the root plus personal endings. *Strong verbs* have a vowel change plus endings (*see p 52 and 131*).

Use of the past tense

It relates actions, events or facts completed in the past:

Die Firma **stellte** Kompressoren **her**.
Die Firmengründer **vererbten** die Firma.
1988 **fing** ich **an**.

Especially in spoken German, the *perfect tense* is often used where English would have the past tense.

Perfect

This is formed with the auxiliary **haben** and the past participle of the verb. Some verbs form the perfect with **sein** (*see p 144*). The perfect is the tense normally used to refer to the past in spoken German (*see p 52 and 105*), though speakers will sometimes switch freely between the past and perfect tenses:

Das ist eine Domäne, wo Schering Pionierarbeit **geleistet hat**.
Die Idee kam bei einer Reise nach Irland. Zum Fischen **bin** ich da **gefahren**. Ich **habe** nach der zündenden Idee **gesucht**.

Remember that the two parts of the verb may be a long way apart:

Man **hat** weiterhin in die Serie Drei unter diesen Klappen, in die Speichermedien reinsollen, eine Back-up-Batterie **eingebaut**, ...

Pluperfect

This is formed and used like the English pluperfect (eg *he had requested*). It's formed with the past tense of **haben** (or **sein**, *see p 144*) and the past participle of another verb (*see p 143*). It's normally used in the context of referring to the past, when the speaker or writer is looking even further back (*see p 126*):

Es ging um mobile Datenerfassung. Herr Schröder **hatte** mich **gebeten**, ihm Unterlagen zu schicken.

Future

The *future tense* is formed with the present tense of **werden** and the infinitive of another verb (*see p 34 and 39*). It's used to refer to a future action or event, and for predictions:

Ich **werde** mich bei Ihnen **melden**.
Der Artikel **wird** sich meines Erachtens fest **etablieren**.
Die Berufsschule **wird** sehr interessant **werden**.

Often, the present tense will be used instead, so long as it's clear that it points to the future (*see p 116*).

You'll need to bear in mind that the passive can seem very similar to the future.

Passive

The passive describes what someone or something is subjected to. It is formed with **werden** and the past participle of another verb (*see p 29, 39, 47, 118 and 128*). When forming the passive in compound tenses, the past participle of **werden** is **worden**:

Die Elektroden **werden geschliffen**.
*The electrodes **are** ground.*
Das Unternehmen **ist** von einem Apotheker **gegründet worden**.
*The company **was** founded by a pharmacist.*

Note that **von** used with the passive indicates the 'doer' of the action, equivalent to *by* in English.

Subjunctive

There are two forms, the more usual nowadays being *subjunctive II* (sometimes rather misleadingly called the *past subjunctive*). In *weak* verbs it's identical to the past tense, except that an umlaut is added to **a**, **o** or **u** in the stem. In most *strong* verbs, the stem is as in the past tense, with an added umlaut on any **a**, **o** or **u**, and the personal endings of the past tense of weak verbs, eg:

	past tense	*subjunctive II*	
er/sie/es/man	brauchte	br**äu**chte	*(weak)*
	fuhr	f**üh**re	*(strong)*
	sprach	spr**äch**e	*(strong)*
	fing	fing**e**	*(strong)*
	kam	k**äm**e	*(strong)*

The subjunctive is common as a means of expressing 'reported' speech, eg in newspaper articles. In spoken German it's rare, except with auxiliary and modal verbs and some other common verbs like **gehen**, **kommen** and **brauchen**. It frequently softens statements and requests (*see p 86 and 91*):

Ich **hätte** gern einen Wagen.
Um sechs Uhr **wäre** mir ganz recht.
Könnten Sie mich bitte mit Dr. Probst **verbinden**?
Das **käme** dann auf 852 Mark.
Ihre Privatadresse **bräuchte** ich noch.
Das **ginge** gut.

It's also used to say what *would be* or *would have been if . . .*, eg:

Wenn wir uns über Ihre Wünsche im Klaren **wären**, dann **könnten** wir eigentlich anfangen zu bauen.

SENTENCE PATTERNS AND THE USE OF THE CASES

If you're listening to, or reading German, you need to be able to distinguish the elements that convey the basic meaning. For example, the verbs **kommen** and **fahren** need a *subject* (*nominative case*) to complete their meaning, but any other elements are optional. The verbs **finden**, **produzieren**, **haben** and **präsentieren** need a *subject* and a *direct object* (*accusative case*). And the verb **geben** needs a *subject*, *indirect object* (*dative case*) and *direct object*:

subject +	*verb* +	*ind. obj.* +	*direct object*
(nominative)		*(dative)*	*(accusative)*
Die Besucher	**kommen**.		
Der Intercity	**fährt**.		
Die Besucher	**finden**		gute Exponate.
Wir	**produzieren**		Boote.
Die Firma	**hat**		6200 Angestellte.
Die Aussteller	**präsentieren**		ihre Produkte.
Ich	**gebe**	Ihnen	meine Visitenkarte.

Some verbs have a *prepositional object*, ie they demand a preposition plus a noun, often in addition to a direct or indirect object:

Es	**geht**	**um** die Leistungsvereinbarung.
Ich	**suche**	**nach** der zündenden Idee.

A few common verbs, notably **sein**, **werden** and **heißen**, require a *complement* which may consist of an adjective or adverb, or a noun in the nominative case:

subject +	*verb* +	*complement*
Das	**ist**	ein typischer Artikel.
Forschung	**wird**	aufwendiger.
Ich	**heiße**	Bruno Kaiser.

Main uses of the cases

Nominative

- The neutral form of a noun/pronoun, used when giving words out of context, eg in a dictionary.

- In a sentence, this case marks the *subject*, ie the 'doer' of the 'action' of the verb. The *number* (*sing.* or *pl.*) of the subject corresponds with that of the verb. Every normal German sentence has a noun or pronoun in the nominative (*see p 24*):

  Ich demonstriere dem Herrn Biegner unsere Produkte.
  Schicken **Sie** uns ein Fax.

- Used after a few verbs, notably **sein**, **werden**, **heißen** (*see p 66*):
  Die drei Bereiche sind **der Display, ein Sensorfeld** und **Tastatur**.

Accusative

- Marks the *direct object* of a verb, ie the person or thing directly affected by the action; the majority of verbs demand a direct object (*see p 24 and 55*):

  Schicken Sie uns **ein Fax**.
  Ich demonstriere dem Herrn Biegner **unsere Produkte**.

- Used after many prepositions (*see p 142*).

Genitive

- Links nouns/pronouns much like the English *of* or the German **von** (*see p 25*). A sentence remains grammatical even if any nouns/pronouns in the genitive are omitted:

  Die Entwicklung **eines neuen Arzneimittels** dauert von der Suche nach dem Wirkstoff bis zur Markteinführung **des Medikaments** etwa zwölf Jahre.

Dative

- Marks the *indirect object* of the verb, ie the person or thing *to whom* the action is done (*see p 39*):

  Schicken Sie **uns** ein Fax.
  Ich demonstriere **dem Herrn Biegner** unsere Produkte.

- Used after many prepositions (*see p 142*).

WORD ORDER

Clauses and sentences

A German sentence may consist of just one simple *main clause*:

Ich heiße Rüdiger Linde.
Die Deutsche BP ist eine der führenden Mineralölgesellschaften in Deutschland.

Or it may consist of two or more parallel main clauses linked by
und, oder, aber or **denn**. Each of these main clauses could stand
on its own:

Ich bin in einem Zweier-Sekretariat als Zweit-Sekretärin
angestellt, **und** das ist das Berufsbild Büro-Assistentin.
Der Kunde ist das Wichtigste für unsere Bank, **denn**
letztendlich bringt uns der Kunde das Geld.

Or it may have one main clause and one or more *subordinate
clauses*. A subordinate clause can't stand on its own, and is separated
from the main clause (in bold) by punctuation:

Das ist etwas, was mir wahnsinnig Freude macht.
Die zweite Nische, in der wir uns sehr erfolgreich bewegen,
sind Röntgenkontrastmittel.
Da sehr viel Holz als Brennholz anfällt, **leben wir autark.**

Main clause: position of subject and verb

The *verb* is the second element. The first element may consist of
many words, though, and it may be the subject, an object, an
adverb or even a clause (*see p 18, 53, 55, 80 and 89*):

Die Schott Gruppe **entwickelt** rund 50.000 Artikel.
Die Stimmung beim Team – aber auch bei unseren Partnern
in den Hallen und bei den Besuchern – **scheint** gut zu sein.
Gute Fahrt **wünsche** ich Ihnen!
In Mainz **befindet** sich auch der Sitz der Gruppenleitung.

The *subject* (underlined) is often the first element, but it may
come after the verb, though not always immediately after it.

Verbs consisting of two or more parts normally have one part with a
personal ending in second place, and any *past participle, infinitive*
or *separable prefix* at the end of the clause (*see p 80 and 105*):

Ich **habe** ein Zimmer **bestellt.**
Drei von vier Krankheiten **können** heute immer noch nicht
ursächlich **behandelt werden.**
Zur Zeit **reisen** noch die Kleinaussteller intensiv **an.**

Subordinate clauses

A subordinate clause always depends on another clause, and has
the verb at the end. If the verb has more than one part, the part
with the personal ending comes at the very end (*see p 80*).
Subordinate clauses normally start with a *subordinating conjunction*
or a *relative pronoun* (*see p 140*). Clauses introduced by *question
words* or ending with **zu** + *infinitive* also have the verb at the end.

**Subordinating conjunctions: als, da, damit, daß,
nachdem, so daß, während, wenn, weil** (*see p 61, 66, 78,
110 and 118*):

Das Produkt kauft er nur dann, **wenn** Sie ihn davon **überzeugt
haben, daß** es für ihn das Richtige **ist.**
Er muß es kaufen, **weil** wir Gewinn **machen müssen.**

Relative clauses (*see p 78, 115 and 140*)

Wir erwarten einen Schulabschluß, **der** in etwa der Mittleren
Reife **entspricht.**
Die zweite Nische, in **der** wir uns erfolgreich **bewegen**, sind
Röntgenkontrastmittel.
Wir sind ein Unternehmen, **was** gewinnorientiert **arbeitet.**

Question words (*see p 3 and below*)

Hier sind die Dämpfgruben, **wo** die Stämme **reingelegt
werden.**
Es geht darum, den Ort und den Zeitpunkt festzulegen, **wann**
es uns am besten allen **paßt.**

zu + infinitive (*see p 102 and 109*). Note that in separable verbs,
zu is inserted after the prefix.

Die Zwischenergebnisse geben mir Anlaß, wirklich positiv in
die kommende Wassersportsaison **zu schauen.**
Könnten Sie ihn bitten, mich **zurückzurufen?**

um...zu + infinitive (*in order to* + *infinitive*) (*see p 109*)

Das ist ein typischer Artikel, der gar nicht britisch genug sein
kann, **um** hier Erfolg **zu haben.**
Um ein gutes Produkt **herzustellen**, benötigt man Geld.

QUESTIONS AND COMMANDS

Questions asking for yes/no information consist of a statement
with the *subject* and *verb* reversed (*see p 7 and 16*):

Kann ich Ihnen helfen?   **Nehmen Sie** auch Kreditkarten?

Questions asking for more detail start with a **W**-question word
such as **wo, warum, was (für), wie, wann, wieviel, wie viele,
welche**, followed by the verb and then its subject (*see p 3*):

Wie kann ich Ihnen helfen?   **Was** sind Sie von Beruf?
Wo bekommen wir die Karten?   **Wieviel** kostet das?

You'll also find speakers asking questions using normal statements
but with a rising intonation:

Alles klar?   Bitte schön?   Frühstück ist ab halb sieben?

Commands are more commonly used in German than in English,
with the *imperative* form. If you're addressing one or more people
with the formal **Sie**, you simply use the same form as the infinitive,
followed by **Sie** (*see p 27 and 90*). The word order is as in a
yes/no question, but in speech, the intonation does not rise:

Achten Sie auf den Startton!   **Geben Sie** den Grund **an!**

NUMBERS

The -teens end with **-zehn** and most tens end with **-zig**.

0–9	10–19	20–29
null	zehn	zwanzig
eins	elf	einundzwanzig
zwei	zwölf	zweiundzwanzig
drei	dreizehn	dreiundzwanzig
vier	vierzehn	vierundzwanzig
fünf	fünfzehn	fünfundzwanzig
sechs	sechzehn	sechsundzwanzig
sieben	siebzehn	siebenundzwanzig
acht	achtzehn	achtundzwanzig
neun	neunzehn	neunundzwanzig

10, 20...	100, 200...	1000, 2000...
zehn	(ein)hundert	(ein)tausend
zwanzig	zweihundert	zweitausend
dreißig	dreihundert	dreitausend
vierzig	vierhundert	...
fünfzig	fünfhundert	zehntausend
sechzig	sechshundert	hunderttausend
siebzig	siebenhundert	eine Million
achtzig	achthundert	eine Milliarde (1 000 000 000)
neunzig	neunhundert	eine Billion (1000 000 000 000)

In numbers like **vierundzwanzig**, the unit (**vier**) comes before **zwanzig**, as in the nursery rhyme *four and twenty blackbirds*.

852: achthundertzweiundfünfzig
8523: achttausendfünfhundert(und)dreiundzwanzig
Years, eg **1995**: neunzehnhundertfünfundneunzig

the first...	firstly...	once...	half, a third...
der/die/das ers**te**	ers**tens**	ein**mal**	
der/die/das zwei**te**	zwei**tens**	zwei**mal**	die Hälfte
der/die/das drit**te**	drit**tens**	drei**mal**	ein Drit**tel**
der/die/das vier**te**	vier**tens**	vier**mal**	ein Vier**tel**
der/die/das fünf**te**	fünf**tens**	fünf**mal**	ein Fünf**tel**
der/die/das sechs**te**	sechs**tens**	sechs**mal**	ein Sechs**tel**
der/die/das sieb**te**	sieb**tens**	sieben**mal**	ein Sieb**tel**
der/die/das ach**te**	ach**tens**	acht**mal**	ein Ach**tel**
der/die/das neun**te**	neun**tens**	neun**mal**	ein Neun**tel**
der/die/das zehn**te**	zehn**tens**	zehn**mal**	ein Zehn**tel**

Stops and commas

In German, the 'decimal point' is represented by a *comma* and the thousands are separated by a *stop* or a *space* (*see p 48*):

50.000 = fünfzigtausend   *50,000 = fifty thousand*
17,1 = siebzehn Komma eins   *17.1 = seventeen point one*

1st, 2nd, 3rd is indicated by a stop: **1. 2. 3.**

DAYS, MONTHS, SEASONS, TIME

Tage	**Monate**
Montag	Januar
Dienstag	Februar
Mittwoch	März
Donnerstag	April
Freitag	Mai
Samstag/Sonnabend	Juni/Juno (*on phone*)
Sonntag	Juli/Julei (*on phone*)
	August
am Montag/Dienstag	September
montags/dienstags	Oktober
im Januar/Februar	November
	Dezember

Jahreszeiten
der Frühling/das Frühjahr   der Herbst
der Sommer   der Winter

Zeit
die Sekunde	der Tag	das Jahr
die Minute	die Woche	das Jahrzehnt
die Stunde	der Monat	das Jahrhundert

Wieviel Uhr ist es?   Es ist dreizehn Uhr zehn (13.10).
Es ist zwanzig **vor** acht (7.40).
Es ist zwanzig **nach** acht (8.20).
Es ist halb zehn (9.30).

Um wieviel Uhr?   Der Intercity fährt um 5.45 Uhr.

Remember that the 24-hour clock is standard in German, so get used to thinking of 4 pm as **sechzehn Uhr**, etc.

COUNTRIES AND CONTINENTS

Amerika	Griechenland	Österreich
Afrika	Großbritannien	Polen
Asien	Irland	Portugal
Australien	Island	Rumänien
Belgien	Italien	Rußland
Bulgarien	Japan	Schottland
China	Kanada	Schweden
Dänemark	Lettland	die Schweiz
Deutschland	Liechtenstein	die Slowakische Republik
England	Litauen	Spanien
Estland	Luxemburg	die Tschechische Republik
Europa	die Niederlande	die Ukraine
Finnland	Nordirland	Ungarn
Frankreich	Norwegen	die Vereinigten Staaten

die Bundesrepublik Deutschland (BRD)
die alten/neuen Bundesländer
die (ehemalige) Deutsche Demokratische Republik (DDR)

Himmelsrichtungen: Nord(en), Süd(en), Ost(en), West(en)

ANSWERS

The **Answers** section gives answers to ▶, **Practice, Review** and **?**. To help you find the information necessary for answering the questions, the relevant German is given in italics, in brackets. It has sometimes been modified slightly to highlight the main point. The English answers relate to the question and may not be a direct translation of the German in brackets. This means that if you haven't quite got the hang of the German, you can go back to the recording or article and use the German in brackets to help you understand what's going on. The **Answers** also contain transcripts for the listening comprehensions 🎧 at the end of each unit.

Key

Pr = Practice	*m.* = masculine	*nom.* = nominative
Re = Review	*f.* = feminine	*acc.* = accusative
T = True	*sing.* = singular	*gen.* = genitive
F = False	*pl.* = plural	*dat.* = dative

UNIT 1: MEIN NAME IST . . .

P 2 **Pr** *a* Guten Tag, Herr Grodtke! *b* Guten Tag, Herr Teufel! *c* Guten Morgen, Frau Wagner! *d* Guten Abend, Herr Gräter! *e* Grüß Gott, Frau von Asen!

P 4 **Pr 1** *a* Name; *b* heißen; *c* ist; *d* wie, heißen. **2** *Sie* Mein Name ist (*student's name*). *Frau Wagner* (*student's name*). *Sie* Darf ich vorstellen? Das ist Herr Linde. **3** *a* Ich wollte mich bei Ihnen erkundigen . . . *b* Ich möchte gern 250 Mark überweisen. *c* Ich möchte gern 400 Mark wechseln.

P 5 ▶ **1** *a* Gerrit Neuhaus; *b* film director and television producer (*Filmregisseur, Fernsehregisseur und Fernsehproduzent*); *c* Neuhaus & Neuhaus GmbH. **2** *a* Uwe Reif; *b* press officer (*Pressesprecher*); *c* Deutsche BP AG. **3** *a* Alessandra Folco; *b* assistant secretary (*Zweit-Sekretärin*); *c* Deutsche BP AG. **4** *a* Michaela Josefa von Asen; *b* travel agent (*Reisebürokauffrau*); *c* Pan Imperial GmbH.

P 7–8 **Pr 1** *a* Kundendienst-Techniker/in, Diplom-Ingenieur/in, Produktmanager/in, Marketing-Leiter(in), Sachbearbeiter/in, Vertriebs-Assistent/in, Buchhalter/in, Techniker(in), Industriekaufmann/frau, Bürokauffrau/-mann, Diplom-Kaufleute, Ingenieur(in); *b* Telefonistin, Vorstandsassistentin, Vorstandssekretärin, Telefon-/Empfangssekretär; *c* Bankkaufmann, Verkaufsprofi, Steuerberater, Wirtschaftsprüfer; *d i* Telefonistin, Vorstandsassistentin, Vorstandssekretärin, Telefon-/Empfangssekretärin; *ii* Sachbearbeiter/in, Vertriebs-Assistent/in, Industriekaufmann/frau, Bürokauffrau/-mann, Verkaufsprofi, Diplom-Kaufleute; *iii* Produktmanager/in, Marketing-Leiter(in); *iv* Kundendienst-Techniker/in; *v* Buchhalter/in, Steuerberater, Wirtschaftsprüfer; *vi* Bankkaufmann; *vii* Diplom-Ingenieur/in, Techniker(in), Ingenieur(in). **2** *a* Ich bin Pressereferent(in); *b* . . . Sekretärin (*the male form is not used*); *c* . . . Manager(in); *d* . . . Geschäftsführer(in); *e* . . . Sachbearbeiter(in); *f* . . . Werbeleiter(in); *g* . . . Vertreter(in); *h* . . . Vertriebsassistent(in). **3** *a* Mein Beruf ist Pressereferent(in); *b* . . . Sekretärin; *c* . . . Manager(in); *d* . . . Geschäftsführer(in); *e* . . . Sachbearbeiter(in); *f* . . . Werbeleiter(in); *g* . . . Vertreter(in); *h* . . . Vertriebsassistent(in). **4** *a* Ich arbeite für die Firma Psion GmbH. *b* Ich arbeite für die Firma Neuhaus & Neuhaus GmbH. *c* Ich arbeite für die Firma Price Waterhouse. *d* Ich arbeite für die Firma Telekom. **5** Für welche Firma arbeiten Sie? **6** *a* Mein Name ist/Ich heiße Carl-Bernd Bosse. Ich bin Technischer Geschäftsführer. Ich arbeite für die Firma Otto Bosse GmbH. *b* Mein Name ist/Ich heiße Elke Heuck. Ich bin Sachbearbeiterin. Ich arbeite für die (Firma) Deutsche BP AG. *c* Mein Name ist/Ich heiße Dieter Sackmann. Ich bin Wirtschaftsprüfer und Steuerberater. Ich arbeite für die Firma Price Waterhouse GmbH. *d* Mein Name ist/Ich heiße Ulrich Probst. Ich bin Pressereferent. Ich arbeite für die Firma Münchener Messe- und Ausstellungsgesellschaft mbH.

P 7 **?** *ii* (*Sachbearbeiter/in*)

P 9 **Re 1** *a* Ich bin Vertreter(in). *b* Ich bin Geschäftsführer(in). *c* Ich bin Sachbearbeiter(in). *d* Ich bin Ingenieur(in). **2** *a* Wie ist Ihr; *b* Wie heißen, bitte; *c* Wie ist, Name. **3** *a* Wie ist Ihr Name, bitte? Mein Name ist (*student's name*). *b* Wie heißen Sie, bitte? Ich heiße (*student's name*). *c* Könnten Sie mir bitte sagen, wie Sie heißen? Ich heiße (*student's name*). **4** *a* Darf ich vorstellen? Das ist Herr Wolf. *b* Wie buchstabiert man das? *c* Ich arbeite für die Firma (*name of student's company*). *d* Ich bin zuständig für Marketing. **5** *a* Wie heißen Sie, bitte? *b* Wie ist Ihr Name, bitte? *c* Wie buchstabiert man das? *d* Was sind Sie von Beruf? *e* Für welche Firma arbeiten Sie?

P 10 **?** **1** project manager (*Projektleiter*). **2** (030) 30 38 31 (*Durchwahl*).

P 11 ▶ **1** production of brochures (*zuständig für die Herstellung, Produktion von Broschüren.*). **2** schools and the public (*die wir verteilen an Schulen und an die Öffentlichkeit.*)

P 11 🎧 DEUTSCHE BP AKTIENGESELLSCHAFT, HAMBURG

Herr Sahla   Könnten Sie bitte mal sagen, wie Sie heißen?

Frau Heuck   Mein Name ist Elke Heuck.

Herr Sahla   Wie buchstabiert man das?

Frau Heuck   Heuck? Den Nachnamen? H - E - U - C - K.

Herr Sahla   Und was sind Sie von Beruf?

Frau Heuck   Ich bin Sachbearbeiterin bei der Deutschen BP AG.

Herr Sahla   Was heißt in diesem Fall Sachbearbeiterin?

Frau Heuck   Also, ich hab' ein eigenes Aufgabengebiet und bin dafür auch zuständig.

Herr Sahla   Und darf man fragen, was für ein Aufgabengebiet das ist?

Frau Heuck   Ja. Ich bin im Bereich Medien und dort zuständig für die Herstellung, Produktion von Broschüren.

Herr Sahla   Nur die deutschen oder auch internationale Broschüren?

Frau Heuck Nur die deutschen Broschüren. Also Informationsbroschüren, die wir dann verteilen an Schulen und an die Öffentlichkeit.

P 11   Pr 1 Wie buchstabiert man das? **2** Darf man fragen . . .?

P 12   Ein Jahresumsatz . . . ▸ 1 *d* (*Wie ist Ihr Name?*); *b* (*Was sind Sie von Beruf?*); *e* (*Für welchen Bereich sind Sie . . . zuständig?*); *a* (*. . . was für einen Umsatz Ihre Firma macht?*); *f* (*Wo ist der Hauptsitz der Firma?*); *c* (*Haben Sie irgendwelche Niederlassungen?*). **2** (NN) Neuhaus & Neuhaus GmbH. **3** broadcasting stations like the Bayerische Rundfunk (*Und ich arbeite auch für Sendeanstalten wie hier den Bayerischen Rundfunk.*). **4** managing director and all the executive duties of a producer (*Ich bin Geschäftsführer und darüber hinaus zuständig für alles, was im Bereich einer Tätigkeit eines Producers ist.*). **5** about 2.5 million marks (*Unsere Firma macht einen Jahresumsatz von zirka zweieinhalb Millionen Mark.*). **6** Forst, Lausitz (*Wir haben eine Zweigstelle in Forst, Lausitz – das ist in den neuen Bundesländern.*).

P 12   NEUHAUS & NEUHAUS GMBH, MÜNCHEN

Herr Sahla   Wie ist Ihr Name?

Herr Neuhaus   Mein Name ist Gerrit Neuhaus.

Herr Sahla   Und was sind Sie von Beruf?

Herr Neuhaus   Ich bin von Beruf Filmregisseur, Fernsehregisseur und Fernsehproduzent.

Herr Sahla   Und für welche Firma arbeiten Sie?

Herr Neuhaus   Ich arbeite in erster Linie für meine eigene Firma. Das ist die NN Neuhaus & Neuhaus GmbH, die selbst Fernsehfilme herstellt. Und ich arbeite auch für Sendeanstalten wie hier den Bayerischen Rundfunk zum Beispiel.

Herr Sahla   Für welchen Bereich sind Sie denn in Ihrer Firma zuständig?

Herr Neuhaus   Ich bin in erster Linie Geschäftsführer der Firma und darüber hinaus zuständig für alles, was im Bereich einer Tätigkeit eines Producers ist.

Herr Sahla   Können Sie mir sagen, was für einen Umsatz Ihre Firma macht?

Herr Neuhaus   Unsere Firma macht einen Jahresumsatz von zirka zweieinhalb Millionen Mark.

Herr Sahla   Wo ist der Hauptsitz der Firma?

Herr Neuhaus   Der Hauptsitz der Firma ist in München.

Herr Sahla   Und haben Sie irgendwelche Niederlassungen?

Herr Neuhaus   Wir haben eine Zweigstelle in Forst, Lausitz – das ist in den neuen Bundesländern.

P 12   Europas größter . . . ▸ *a* electronics manufacture (*Elektronik-Fertigung*); *b* 9 am to 6 pm (*Geöffnet 9.00–18.00 h*); *c* 9 am to 4 pm (*Samstag 9.00–16.00 h*); *d* 12–16 November 1991; *e* Munich exhibition centre (*München Messegelände*); *f* hall 5, stand B 01 (*Halle 5, Stand B 01*).

P 13   Pr 1 *b* (*Die Schott Gruppe fertigt rund 50.000 Artikel. Das Angebot umfaßt Spezialglas und Glaskeramiken.*); *c* (*Drei Sparten . . . – Das Vertriebsnetz . . .*); *a* (*Schott ist Europas größter Spezialglas-Hersteller. Schott Glaswerke, Mainz, Bundesrepublik Deutschland, sind das Hauptwerk.*). **2** *a* around 18,000 (*mit ca. 18.000 Mitarbeitern*); *b* around 50,000 (*rund 50.000 Artikel*); *c* special types of glass and glass ceramics (*Spezialgläser und Glaskeramiken*); *d* over two thousand million marks (*Der Weltumsatz beträgt über 2 Milliarden D-Mark.*); *e* over 40 (*über 40 Produktionsstätten*); *f* more than 20 (*mehr als 20 eigene Vertriebsgesellschaften*); *g* about

280 (*rund 280 Vertretungen*); *h* more than 100 (*Das Vertriebsnetz umfaßt Vertriebsgesellschaften und Vertretungen in mehr als 100 Ländern.*); *i* Mainz (*Schott Glaswerke, Mainz, sind das Hauptwerk.*); *j* Mainz (*In Mainz befindet sich auch der Sitz der Gruppenleitung.*). **3** *e* (*ca. 18.000 Mitarbeiter, rund 50.000 Artikel*); *a* (*als Komponenten für Spitzentechnologien, Apparate und elektronische Geräte*); *f* (*Drei Sparten koordinieren die unternehmerischen Aktivitäten von über 40 Produktionsstätten.*); *d* (*Das Vertriebsnetz umfaßt mehr als 20 eigene Vertriebsgesellschaften und rund 280 Vertretungen in mehr als 100 Ländern.*); *c* (*Schott ist Europas größter Spezialglas-Hersteller.*); *b* (*In Mainz befindet sich auch der Sitz der Gruppenleitung.*).

UNIT 2: GUTE FAHRT!

P 15   ▸ *a* Hamburg (*nach Hamburg*); *b* two (*zwei Karten*); *c* Monday (*Montag*); *d* 6th April (*der sechste April*); *e* early in the morning (*sehr früh; um fünf Uhr fünfundvierzig*); *f* seat reservation (*Möchten Sie Platzkarten reservieren? – Ja, bitte.*); *g* no smoking (*Nichtraucher, bitte.*); *h* Friday (*Ich möchte zurückkommen am Freitag.*); *i* depart 5.45 am, arrive 11.46 am (*Der erste Intercity wäre um fünf Uhr fünfundvierzig und wäre um elf Uhr sechsundvierzig in Hamburg.*).

P 16   Pr 1 *a* Der Bus fährt um fünf Uhr zwanzig/neun Uhr fünfundvierzig/dreizehn Uhr zwanzig/sechs Uhr/sechzehn Uhr fünfzehn/sieben Uhr. *b* Der Zug fährt um . . . *c* Der Intercity fährt um . . . **2** Ich hätte gern zwei Karten nach München/Berlin/ Hamburg/Dresden/London. **3** *a* Ich möchte (gerne) eine Fahrkarte nach Berlin. *b* Ich möchte (gerne) einen Sitzplatz reservieren. *c* Ich möchte (gerne) einen Wagen mieten. *d* Ich möchte (gerne) ein Taxi.

P 17   ▸ 1 an Opel Vectra. **2** *h* (*Personalausweis*), *b* (*Führerschein*), *f* (*Kreditkarte*), *d* (*Ihre Privatadresse bräuchte ich noch.*). **3** black (*ein schwarzer Opel Vectra*), Munich registration number (*Münchner Kennzeichen*), multistorey car park opposite (*in unserem Parkhaus gegenüber*), third storey (*im dritten Stock*), parking space 45 (*auf der Parkplatz-Nummer 45*).

P 18   Pr 1 Kein Problem. **2** *a* auf; *b* in; *c* im, auf; *d* mit; *e* nach; *f* in; *g* am. **3** *a* die; *b* der; *c* das; *d* der; *e* das; *f* der; *g* die; *h* der; *i* die.

P 18   ?   *c* (*Einbahnstraße*)

P 19   ▸ 1 Two rooms (*Ich hätte gern zwei Zimmer reserviert.*) for the night of 13 December (*Und zwar vom 13. auf den 14. Dezember.*). **2** *a* (*Ein Einzelzimmer, bitte.*), *c* (*Lieber Bad*), *f* (*Haben Sie noch ein Zimmer für zwei Nächte?*).

P 19   Pr 1 (*Schönen*) guten Tag! Kann ich Ihnen helfen? **2** *a* Möchten Sie ein Zimmer? *b* . . . ein Einzelzimmer? *c* . . . ein Doppelzimmer? *d* . . . Bad? *e* . . . WC? *f* . . . Dusche? **3** *a* Wieviel kostet ein Doppelzimmer? *b* . . . ein Zimmer mit Bad? *c* . . . ein Zimmer mit Dusche?

P 20   ▸ 1 the fourth (*in der vierten Etage*). **2** his key (*Ich möchte meinen Schlüssel.*). **3** at 6 am (*Möchten Sie sich wecken lassen? – Oh ja. Um sechs Uhr.*). **4** 6.30 to 10 am (*Frühstück ist ab halb sieben, bis zehn Uhr.*). **5** by credit card (*Nehmen Sie auch Kreditkarten?*).

P 21   Pr 1 Wieviel Uhr ist es, bitte? **2** *a* Es ist sieben Uhr. *b* Es ist zehn Uhr. *c* Es ist halb sieben. / Es ist sechs Uhr dreißig. *d* Es ist sechs Uhr. *e* Es ist halb elf. / Es ist zehn Uhr dreißig. **3** Ich habe ein Zimmer bestellt. **4** Kleinen Moment. **5** *a* Wie finde ich das Zimmer? *b* ...die Toilette? *c* ...das Reisebüro? *d* ...die Ausstellung? *e* ...das Telefon? **6** der Tag, das Zimmer, der Name, der Moment, die Etage, der Aufzug, der Aufenthalt, der Abend, der Schlüssel, die Uhr, das Frühstück, der Morgen, die Frage, die Kreditkarte, die Art, die Eurocard, das Problem, *you may have identified an eighteenth:* der Herr. **7** *a* Ich habe ein Zimmer bestellt/reserviert. *b* Ich habe zwei Karten bestellt/reserviert. *c* Ich habe ein Auto bestellt/reserviert.

P 22–23 **Re 1** Wieviel kostet das? **2** *a* Gute Fahrt wünsche ich Ihnen. / Ich wünsche Ihnen (eine) gute Fahrt. *b* Ich wünsche Ihnen (einen) angenehmen Aufenthalt. / (Einen) angenehmen Aufenthalt wünsche ich Ihnen. **3** *a* kann; *b* fährt; *c* macht; *d* ist. **4** *These are sentences you have already met: a* Kann ich Ihnen helfen? *b* Der Zug fährt um siebzehn Uhr. *c* Das Reisebüro macht einen Umsatz von zwei Millionen. *d* Mein Name ist Müller. **5** *a* ausstellen; *b* reservieren; *c* herstellen; *d* leiten. **6** *a* bei; *b* auf; *c* von; *d* in; *e* für; *f* für; *g* bei; *h* innerhalb.

P 23 **?** room rates, single room, double room, buffet breakfast per person, dog, hotel underground car park, prices subject to change, prices include VAT, prices valid during fairs and exhibitions.

P 24 **?** It's for purchasing a parking ticket (*Parkschein lösen*).

P 25 ▶ **1** engineer (*Ich bin von Beruf Diplom-Ingenieur.*). **2** construction and transport (*spezialisiert auf dem Sektor Bau- und Verkehrswesen*). **3** Berlin public transport system (*Berliner Verkehrsbetriebe*). **4** 1929 (*Dieses Unternehmen ist entstanden 1929.*). **5** Berliner Verkehrsgesellschaft **6** 1938 (*Die Berliner Verkehrsgesellschaft wurde dann umbenannt in Berliner Verkehrsbetriebe 1938.*).

P 25 🔊 BERLINER VERKEHRSBETRIEBE

Herr Sahla   Wenn Sie mir zunächst einmal sagen könnten, wie Sie heißen.

Herr Schmidt   Mein Name ist Hartmut Schmidt.

Herr Sahla   Und was sind Sie von Beruf?

Herr Schmidt   Ich bin von Beruf Diplom-Ingenieur, spezialisiert auf dem Sektor Bau- und Verkehrswesen.

Herr Sahla   Und für welche Firma beziehungsweise welches Unternehmen arbeiten Sie?

Herr Schmidt   Ich arbeite für die Berliner Verkehrsbetriebe und dort als Leiter der Direktionsabteilung Betriebs- und Haushaltsplanung. Dieses Unternehmen ist entstanden 1929. Der Omnibusbetrieb, der Straßenbahnbetrieb und das U-Bahn-Unternehmen, Hochbahn, haben sich zusammengeschlossen zu einem großen Verkehrsunternehmen. Und sie nannten sich damals Berliner Verkehrsgesellschaft und wurden dann umbenannt in Berliner Verkehrsbetriebe 1938, in der Zeit der Nazis.

P 25 **Pr 1** *a* Hartmut Schmidt ist Ingenieur. *b* Er arbeitet für die Berliner Verkehrsbetriebe. *c* Er ist Leiter der Direktionsabteilung Betriebs- und Haushaltsplanung. *d* Das Unternehmen ist 1929 entstanden. *e* Der Omnibusbetrieb, der Straßenbahnbetrieb, das U-Bahn-Unternehmen und die Hochbahn haben sich zusammengeschlossen. *f* Das Unternehmen wurde umbenannt. **2** *a* Das Unternehmen heißt Berliner Verkehrsbetriebe. *b* Es/das Unternehmen entstand 1929. *c* Es/das Unternehmen nannte sich damals

Berliner Verkehrsgesellschaft. *d* Es/das Unternehmen umfaßte den Omnibusbetrieb, den Straßenbahnbetrieb, das U-Bahn-Unternehmen und die Hochbahn. *e* Es/das Unternehmen wurde 1938 (in Berliner Verkehrsbetriebe) umbenannt.

P 26 ▶ *a* engineer (*Diplom-Ingenieur*); *b* the biggest automobile club in Europe (*Der ADAC ist der größte europäische Verband von Kraftfahrern.*); *c* Munich (*Der Hauptsitz des ADAC ist in München.*); *d* 18 (*Wir haben darüber hinaus 18 regionale Büros in den wichtigsten Städten von Deutschland.*).

P 26 🔊 ALLGEMEINER DEUTSCHER AUTOMOBIL-CLUB, MÜNCHEN

Herr Sahla   Wie heißen Sie, bitte?

Herr Linde   Ich heiße Rüdiger Linde.

Herr Sahla   Und was sind Sie von Beruf?

Herr Linde   Ich bin Diplom-Ingenieur für Bau- und Verkehrswesen.

Herr Sahla   Und für welche Firma arbeiten Sie, oder welches Unternehmen?

Herr Linde   Ich arbeite beim ADAC, das heißt lang gesprochen Allgemeiner Deutscher Automobil-Club und ist der größte europäische Verband von Kraftfahrern.

Herr Sahla   Wo ist Ihr Hauptsitz?

Herr Linde   Der Hauptsitz des ADAC ist in München. Wir haben darüber hinaus 18 regionale Büros in den wichtigsten Städten von Deutschland. Und wir haben einige Nebenbüros an typischen Urlaubsorten, wo deutsche Touristen im Sommer oder im Winter gerne sind. Zum Beispiel in Spanien, in Italien, in Griechenland, auch in Frankreich. In England bisher nicht.

P 26 **Pr 1** Ich bin Diplom-Ingenieur. **2** *a* Spanien; *b* Frankreich; *c* England; *d* Deutschland; *e* Italien; *f* Griechenland. **3** *a* Canada; *b* Poland; *c* Brazil; *d* Australia; *e* Argentina; *f* China; *g* Ireland; *h* Scotland; *i* Switzerland; *j* Belgium; *k* Denmark; *l* Norway; *m* Russia; *n* Austria; *o* the United States.

P 27 ▶ assistance in planning and organizing conferences, meetings and seminars (*IBIS unterstützt Sie bei der Planung und Organisation von Konferenzen, Tagungen und Seminaren.*), with modern conference rooms (*Mit modern ausgestatteten Konferenzräumen*), up-to-date conference technology (*mit zeitgemäßer Konferenztechnik*), friendly service (*mit freundlichem Service*).

P 27 **Pr 1** the first sentence, subject: IBIS; main verb: unterstützt. **2** verb: sind; subject: wir. **3** *a* die Straße; *b* das Dorf; *c* der Zoo(logische Garten); *d* der Platz; *e* das Rathaus; *f* der See; *g* Ost; *h* die Richtung; *i* der Garten; *j* schön; *k* das Haus; *l* Bhf.

UNIT 3: EINE GUTE ÜBERSICHT

P 29 ▶ **1** in the exhibition halls (*Die meisten Boote sind schon in den Hallen.*) **2** they are being polished and cleaned (*Sie werden poliert und saubergemacht.*); the small exhibitors (*Zur Zeit reisen noch die Kleinaussteller an.*).

P 30 **Pr** *a* Die Boote werden saubergemacht. *b* Die Boote werden poliert. *c* Die Boote werden in England gebaut. *d* Die Boote werden in Großbritannien produziert. *e* Die Boote werden auf der Messe präsentiert.

P 30 ▶ out of the door, turn right, ten metres along (*Wenn Sie aus der Tür rausgehen, nach rechts zehn Meter, da ist die Kasse.*).

P 30 ? **1** considered what could be done new and better for this year (*Wir haben uns überlegt, was wir für dieses Jahr neu und besser machen können.*). **2** Virus Nauticus. **3** every year in January at Boot Düsseldorf (*Taucht jedes Jahr im Januar zur boot Düsseldorf auf.*). **4** by means of the sticker, displayed by anyone who has caught the virus, ie been to the fair (*Wer vom boot-Bazillus erwischt wird, sollte ihn mit diesem Aufkleber weiter verbreiten.*).

P 31 **Pr 1** Wo ist die Kasse? **2** *a* 2; *b* 1; *c* 3; *d* 8; *e* 5; *f* 4; *g* 6; *h* 9; *i* 7. **3** *a* Wo ist die Informationsstelle, bitte? *b* Wo befindet sich der Meeting-Point, bitte? *c* Wo bekomme ich Information, bitte? *d* Wo sind die Behinderten-Einrichtungen, bitte? *e* Wo befindet sich die Garderobe, bitte? *f* Wo finde ich ein Restaurant, bitte? *g* Wo ist die Erste Hilfe, bitte? *h* Wo bekomme ich einen Katalog, bitte? *i* Wo sind die Toiletten, bitte? **4** *a* Geradeaus (zehn Meter), (dann) nach rechts, da ist die Informationsstelle. *b* Geradeaus, da ist der Meeting-Point. *c* Geradeaus, da ist das Restaurant. *d* Geradeaus, (dann) nach links, da sind die Behinderten-Einrichtungen. *e* Geradeaus, (dann) nach links, da ist die Garderobe. *f* Geradeaus, (dann) nach rechts, da sind die Telefone. *g* Geradeaus, (dann) nach links, da ist die Gepäckaufbewahrung. *h* Geradeaus, (dann) nach rechts, da sind die Toiletten.

P 31 ▶ **1** visitor: at least 4 or 5 times (*mindestens das vierte oder fünfte Mal*); exhibitor: about 20 times (*zirka das zwanzigste Mal*). **2** visitor: because you get a good overview (*weil man eine sehr gute Übersicht bekommt.*); exhibitor: because it has more and more visitors, is getting more and more international and bigger, and the organization is getting better (*Kommen immer mehr Besucher, wird immer internationaler, Messe wird größer, Organisation wird besser.*).

P 32 **Pr 1** *a* Sie sind als Aussteller(in) hier. *b* Sie sind als Besucher(in) hier. *c* Sie sind als Hersteller(in) hier. *d* Sie sind als Sekretärin hier. *e* Sie sind als Ingenieur(in) hier. *f* Sie sind als Geschäftsführer(in) hier. **2** Sind Sie als . . . hier? **3** Wie gefällt es Ihnen? *a* Wie gefällt Ihnen die Messe? *b* . . . Düsseldorf? *c* . . . das Boot? *d* . . . die Ausstellung? *e* . . . München? **4** *a* Ich bin das fünfte Mal auf der Boot. *b* Ich bin das vierte Mal auf der Systems. *c* Ich bin das zehnte Mal auf der Productronica. *d* Ich bin das achte Mal auf der Analytika. *e* Ich bin das dritte Mal hier. **5** *a* Die Messe wird größer. *b* Die Boote werden schneller. *c* Die Besucher werden internationaler. **6** *a* Das Produkt wird immer moderner. *b* . . . immer exklusiver. *c* . . . immer schöner; *d* . . . immer besser.

P 33 ▶ **1** 20 years ago, 50 exhibitors (*Die Boot hat mit 50 Ausstellern vor 20 Jahren angefangen.*). **2** floor space by the square metre (*Wir verkaufen den Ausstellern die Quadratmeter.*). **3** that there will be sufficient visitors and good exhibits (*Wir versprechen, daß die Besucher in ausreichender Zahl kommen und die Besucher dann auch gute Exponate finden.*)

P 33 **Pr 1** Wir handeln mit. . . **2** *a* Was sind die wichtigsten Messen? *b* Was sind die wichtigsten Städte? *c* Was sind die wichtigsten Hersteller? *d* Was sind die wichtigsten Firmen? *e* Was sind die wichtigsten Aussteller? **3** *a* kleinsten; *b* schnellsten; *c* schönsten; *d* größten; *e* besten; *f* neu(e)sten.

P 34 ▶ **1** about 11 months (*Sie müßten mit einer Lieferzeit von ungefähr 11 Monaten rechnen.*); 3.8 million marks (*Wir gehen von einem Verkaufspreis von 3,8 Millionen D-Mark aus.*). **2** by fax or phone (*Schicken Sie uns ein Fax oder rufen Sie an.*).

P 35 **Pr 1** *a* Schicken Sie ein Fax. *b* Rufen Sie an. **2** *a* Kann ich Ihnen meine Visitenkarte geben? *b* Kann ich Sie anrufen? *c* Kann ich Ihnen ein Fax schicken? *d* Kann ich Ihnen meine Telefonnummer geben?

P 35 ▶ **1** Italian boats (*Ich habe bis jetzt Italiener gefahren.*). **2** 400 to 450 (*Wir produzieren 400 bis 450 Boote.*). **3** diesel or petrol (*Wir können Ihnen das Boot mit diversen Motorisierungsmöglichkeiten anbieten – Diesel- oder Benzinmotorisierung.*).

P 36 **Pr 1** Wie kann ich Ihnen helfen? **2** Wieviel würde das kosten? / Wieviel kostet das? **3** Ich interessiere mich für diese *a* Produkte *b* Schiffe *c* Messe *d* Exponate *e* Broschüren *f* Maschinen *g* Computer. **4** Ich finde diese/die *a* Produkte *b* Schiffe *c* Messen *d* Exponate *e* Broschüren *f* Maschinen *g* Computer interessant. **5** *a* Die Schiffe werden in England produziert. *b* Die Maschinen werden in Frankreich produziert. *c* Die Computer werden in Deutschland produziert. *d* Die Autos werden in Italien produziert. *e* Die Broschüren werden in Kanada produziert. **6** Sie Guten Tag! Sie (*student's name*) ist mein Name. Sie Ich interessiere mich für diese Maschine. Sie Haben Sie vielleicht eine Broschüre? Sie Danke schön.

P 37 ▶ **1** very happy and impressed (*Ich bin persönlich sehr froh und beeindruckt von dem, was sich in diesen Tagen in den Hallen getan hat.*). **2** it seems to be good (*Die Stimmung scheint gut zu sein.*). **3** good (*Die Zwischenergebnisse, Auswertungen – persönliche Befragungen aus den Hallen geben mir Anlaß, wirklich positiv in die kommende Wassersportsaison zu schauen.*).

P 37 **Pr 1** Wie läuft es? **2** *a* Ich bin froh. *b* Ich bin beeindruckt. *c* Ich bin interessiert. *d* Ich bin optimistisch. *e* Ich bin zufrieden.

P 38–39 **Re 1** *a* Wieviel würde das kosten? / Wieviel kostet das? *b* Wie ist Ihr Name? / Wie heißen Sie? *c* Wie buchstabiert man das? *d* Für welche Firma arbeiten Sie? *e* Was für einen Umsatz macht Ihre Firma? **2** *a* forschen; *b* vertreten; *c* lösen; *d* vermieten. **3** *a* das Versprechen; *b* der Aussteller/die Ausstellerin, die Ausstellung; *c* der Beginn; *d* die Vorbereitung; *e* der Stand. **4** *a* Wie sieht es aus? *b* Was ist so der neueste Stand? *c* Wie läuft es? **5** Sie Wie lange wäre die Lieferzeit? Sie Wieviel würde das kosten? / Wieviel kostet das? Sie Danke (schön). Auf Wiedersehen!

P 38 ? stand (*rechts stehen*); keep moving (*links gehen*).

P 40 ▶ **1** one day (*unsere Eröffnungspressekonferenz Boot '92, traditionell einen Tag vor dem Wassersportmesseereignis des Jahres.*) **2** 4 (*Alan Hunt, Peter Gregory, Dieter Burmann, Erich Münzer*).

P 40 (8) BOOT DÜSSELDORF
Herr Aufderheide Liebe Kolleginnen und Kollegen, guten Tag und herzlich willkommen zu unserer Eröffnungspressekonferenz Boot '92, traditionell einen Tag vor dem Wassersportmesseereignis des Jahres. Ich möchte Ihnen zunächst kurz unsere Gäste und Gesprächspartner heute morgen vorstellen. Und zwar begrüße ich als Repräsentanten des Partnerlandes Großbritannien ganz herzlich den britischen Generalkonsul, Alan C. Hunt, der hier in Düsseldorf das Vereinigte Königreich repräsentiert. Ein

ganz herzliches Willkommen geht an Peter Gregory von der British Marine Industries Federation, der als Chairman des Partnerlandes Großbritannien sehr intensiv für das Zustandekommen der Partnerschaft gesorgt hat. Ich begrüße Herrn Dieter Burmann, Handelsreferent am britischen Generalkonsulat in Hamburg, und natürlich den Präsidenten der Boot 1992, Dr. Erich Münzer ...

P 41 Frage Nummer eins... ▶ 1 the number of fairs, the turnover, the number of visitors, the number of additional conference participants (*Wieviel Messen gibt es? Wieviel Umsatz wird gemacht? Wieviel Besucher kommen? Wieviel Kongreßteilnehmer kommen zusätzlich?*). 2 the first: *Wieviel Messen gibt es?* (*Am liebsten möchte ich die Frage beantworten durch die Zahl der Messen, die in München veranstaltet werden.*). 3 28 (*Wir haben innerhalb von drei Jahren 28 Messen.*). 4 high-tech trade fairs (*Alle zwei Jahre finden Hoch-Technologie-Messen statt.*). 5 *1:* it hosts leading European fairs (*Erstens mal haben wir mit unseren 28 Messen alle führenden Messen im europäischen Raum auf unserer Seite.*); *2:* the biggest high-tech fairs in electronics, mechanical engineering etc. through to construction machinery (*Zweitens haben wir die größten Hoch-Technologie-Messen, die man sich vorstellen kann, im Bereich Elektronik, im Bereich Maschinenbau etc. bis hin zum Baumaschinenbereich.*); *3:* Munich's unique position (*Die dritte Antwort würde ich auch gerne geben. Münchens Lage ist einzigartig.*).

P 41 🔊 MÜNCHENER MESSE- UND AUSSTELLUNGSGESELLSCHAFT MBH
Herr Sahla Könnten Sie mir bitte mal Ihren Namen sagen?
Dr. Probst Ja, ich heiße Ulrich Probst und bin bei der Messe München beschäftigt als Pressereferent für die elektronischen Fachmessen.
Herr Sahla Wie bedeutend ist München als Messestadt?
Dr. Probst Wir können diese Frage natürlich an unterschiedlichen Dingen messen und beantworten. Frage Nummer eins: Wieviel Messen gibt es? Frage Nummer zwei: Wieviel Umsatz wird gemacht? Frage Nummer drei: Wieviel Besucher kommen? Frage Nummer vier: Wieviel Kongreßteilnehmer kommen auch zusätzlich?
Herr Sahla Möchten Sie die Fragen selbst beantworten?
Dr. Probst Am liebsten möcht' ich die Frage beantworten durch die Zahl der Messen, die in München veranstaltet werden. Wir haben innerhalb von drei Jahren 28 Messen, und alle zwei Jahre finden Hoch-Technologie-Messen statt.
Herr Sahla Wie sehen Sie die Zukunft Münchens als Messestadt?
Dr. Probst Die Zukunft Münchens als Messestadt ist großartig, und zwar aus einem ganz einfachen Grund: Erstens mal haben wir mit unseren 28 Messen alle führenden Messen im europäischen Raum auf unserer Seite. Zweitens haben wir die größten Hoch-Technologie-Messen, die man sich vorstellen kann, im Bereich Elektronik, im Bereich Maschinenbau etc. bis hin zum Baumaschinenbereich. Und die dritte Antwort würde ich auch gerne geben. Münchens Lage ist einzigartig. Wir sind im süddeutschen Raum im Zentrum zwischen der Schweiz, Österreich, aber auch natürlich der südost-europäischen Länder.

P 41 Pr *a* Messegesellschaft; *b* Messegelände; *c* Fachmesse; *d* Bootmesse; *e* Messetag; *f* Messestadt; *g* Hoch-Technologie-Messe; *h* Messezeit.

P 41 Samstag... ▶ 1 more than 1800 (*Mehr als 1.800 nationale und internationale Aussteller*). 2 more information, more contacts (*Auch am Samstag. Ein Tag mehr für ein Plus an Information. Für ein Plus an Kontakten.*). 3 5. 4 software, services, system components, OEM products, network technology (*Software, Dienstleistungen und das umfassende Angebot an Systemkomponenten, OEM-Produkten und modernster Netzwerktechnologie.*).

P 42 Pr *a* der Computer; *b* präsentieren; *c* das Produkt; *d* der Service; *e* die Komponente; *f* modern; *g* das Telefon; *h* die Information; *i* der Tip.

UNIT 4: SIE SEHEN HIER ...

P 43 ▶ **BP:** *a* Hamburg (*Der Hauptsitz ist in Hamburg.*); *b* oil (*Mineralölgesellschaft*); *c* around 13 thousand million marks (*Der Jahresumsatz bewegt sich in der Größenordnung von 13 Milliarden D-Mark.*); *d* 6200 (*rund 6200 Angestellte*). **Kaiser:** *a* Cologne-Zollstock (*Die Firma hat ihren Sitz in Köln-Zollstock.*); *b* wooden windows and doors (*Wir fertigen Holzfenster und Türen.*); *c* between 1.8 and 2.2 million marks (*Er schwankt zwischen 1,8 und 2,2 Millionen.*); *d* 16 (*sechzehn*).

P 45 Pr 1 *c* turnover (*Was für einen Jahresumsatz hat die Deutsche BP? Der Jahresumsatz bewegt sich...; Was ist der Jahresumsatz? Er (der Jahresumsatz) schwankt...* 2 Der Hauptsitz (der Firma) ist in... Das Unternehmen/die Firma sitzt in... (*Wo sitzt Ihr Unternehmen?*). Die Firma hat ihren Sitz in... 3 *a* Was für eine Firma ist das?/(*or: name of company*)? *b* Was ist der Jahresumsatz? / Was für einen Jahresumsatz hat die Firma? *c* Wieviel Angestellte/Mitarbeiter hat die/Ihre Firma? *d* Wo sitzt die Firma/Ihr Unternehmen? / Wo ist der Hauptsitz Ihres Unternehmens? *e* Haben Sie Niederlassungen? / Hat Ihre Firma Filialen? 4 *Sie* Wie heißen Sie? *Sie* Was sind Sie von Beruf? *Sie* Für welche Firma arbeiten Sie? *Sie* Was für eine Firma ist die (Firma) Stocker Chemie / ist das? *Sie* Wieviel Angestellte/Mitarbeiter hat Stocker? *Sie* Wo sitzt die Firma / Ihr Unternehmen? / Wo hat die Firma ihren Sitz? / Wo ist der Hauptsitz des Unternehmens?

P 45 ▶ *d* (*Für die Herstellung von Lagenhölzern braucht man sehr viel Wärme, weil die Hölzer erst gedämpft, dann getrocknet und dann gepreßt werden.*); *h* (*Unsere Wärme erzeugen wir mit dem Abfallholz, das bei der Produktion anfällt.*); *e* (*Dieses sind die Filteranlagen.*); *b* (*Da liegen die Stämme alle aufgestapelt.*); *f* (*Dämpfgruben*); *c* (*Presseraum*); *a* (*Diese Pressen werden mit dem hochgeharzten, phenolgeharzten Material beschickt.*); *g* (*Endbearbeitung*).

P 47 Pr 1 gedämpft, getrocknet, gepreßt, aufgestapelt, berieselt, reingelegt, abgeschnitten, beschickt, besäumt, abgeschliffen, kalibriert. 2 *a* sprinkled with water (*werden ... berieselt*), steamed (*gedämpft werden*), cut to size (*werden der Länge nach abgeschnitten*); you may also have included the following: lie stacked (*liegen aufgestapelt*), placed in steam vats (*Dämpfgruben, wo die Stämme reingelegt werden*), placed on the platform (*dann kommen sie auf diesen Polder.*); *b* loaded with the resinated material (*Diese schweren Pressen werden mit dem hochgeharzten, phenolgeharzten Material beschickt.*); *c* edged (*besäumt*), sanded down (*abgeschliffen*), calibrated (*kalibriert*). 3 *a* Die Hölzer werden gedämpft. *b* Die Hölzer werden getrocknet. *c* Die Hölzer werden gepreßt. *d* Die Platten werden besäumt. *e* Die Platten werden abgeschliffen. *f* Die Platten werden kalibriert. 4 *a* Jetzt gehen wir hier einfach durch, nicht? Jetzt gehen wir da hinten durch. *b* Da im Hintergrund sehen wir ... *c* Hier vorne im Vordergrund sind ... **5** *This is an example of a short presentation you could give on the process:* *i* Man braucht sehr viel Wärme für die Herstellung von Lagenhölzern, weil die Hölzer erst gedämpft, dann getrocknet und dann gepreßt werden. *ii* Unsere Wärme können wir erzeugen mit dem Abfallholz, was bei der Produktion anfällt. *iii* Die Firma Otto Bosse hat zwei Filteranlagen: einen Zyklonfilter und einen Elektrofilter. *iv* Die Stämme liegen alle aufgestapelt. *v* Die Stämme werden in die Dämpfgruben reingelegt und ein paar Tage gedämpft. *vi* Die Firma hat einen Presseraum, wo die schweren Pressen stehen. *vii* Diese schweren Pressen werden mit dem hochgeharzten, phenolgeharzten Material beschickt. *viii* In der Endbearbeitung werden die Platten besäumt, abgeschliffen und kalibriert.

P 47 ▸ *a* chemicals, pharmaceuticals (*Die Firma Schering ist tätig in der Branche Chemie, Pharmazie.*); *b* about 27 000 (*Weltweit ·haben wir etwa 27.000 Mitarbeiter.*); *c* 6.3 thousand million marks (*Wir haben einen Umsatz etwa von 6,3 Milliarden Deutsche Mark.*); *d* 120 years (*Schering ist jetzt über 120 Jahre auf der Welt.*); *e* Ernst Schering (*Das Unternehmen ist gegründet worden von einem Apotheker, Ernst Schering.*); *f* East Berlin (*Ernst Schering hat im Gebiete des heutigen Ostberlins die Grüne Apotheke gegründet.*).

P 49 **Pr 1** *a* etwa/rund/zirka; *b* etwa/rund/zirka. **2** *a* Dr. Joachim Esche ist Apotheker. *b* Er arbeitet für die Firma Schering. / Er ist für die Firma Schering tätig. *c* Er ist für den Pharmabereich zuständig. **3** *This is an example of a short presentation:* *a* Die Firma Schering hat ihren Hauptsitz / sitzt in Berlin. *b* Schering ist tätig in der Branche Chemie, Pharmazie. *c* Schering stellt Pharmazeutika, Pflanzenschutzmittel, galvanotechnische Erzeugnisse, Industriechemikalien und Naturstoffe her und vertreibt (auch) diese Produkte. (*herstellen* is a separable verb.) / Schering ist ein Unternehmen, was Pharmazeutika herstellt und vertreibt, Pflanzenschutzmittel ... *d* Die Firma hat weltweit etwa 27.000 Mitarbeiter. *e* Schering hat einen Umsatz von etwa (*or* etwa von) 6,3 Milliarden Mark. *f* Ernst Schering hat die Firma Schering gegründet. *g* Er hat im Gebiete des heutigen Ostberlins die Grüne Apotheke gegründet. Aus dieser Apotheke heraus hat sich die Firma Schering entwickelt. **4** *a* (*student's name*); *b* (*student's company*); *c* Besucher; *d* Herr Scheipl; *e* 9.30, (*student's signature*); *f* 13.10, (*Walter Scheipl's signature*). **5** please read note overleaf (*Bitte Rückseite beachten!*). **6** one day (*Tagesausweis*).

P 51 **Re 1** *a* hergestellt, verkauft; *b* poliert, saubergemacht; *c* präsentiert; *d* gedämpft, getrocknet, gepreßt; *e* erzeugt; *f* gefertigt; *g* gegründet; *h* entwickelt. **2** *a* die Ordnung; *b* die Leistung; *c* die Führung; *d* die Bearbeitung; *e* die Bildung. **3** *a* die Größenordnung; *b* die Dienstleistung; *c* die Geschäftsführung; *d* die Endbearbeitung; *e* die Ausbildung. **4** *a* Mein Name ist (*student's name*). Die Firma heißt W. Kaiser GmbH & Co. KG. Wir fertigen/Die Firma fertigt Holzfenster. *b* Hier gehen wir durch. Hier ist unsere Endbearbeitung. / Hier sind wir in der Endbearbeitung. Hier werden die Fenster abgeschliffen. *c* Dieses ist unsere Lackierhalle. Hier werden die Fenster lackiert. *d* Hier werden die Fenster gelagert.

P 53 ▸ **1** *l, i, d, e, m, b, h, g, j, k, c, f, a.* **2** *c.* **3** people are telephoning (*In allen (Büros) wird telefoniert.*). **4** foreign employees

(*Wir haben sehr viele ausländische Mitarbeiter hier.*). **5** 140 (*140 Auslandsvertretungen*). **6** because he doesn't have enough technical know-how (*Ich verstehe zu wenig von den technischen Abwicklungen in dieser Abteilung.*). **7** training department (*Ebenfalls in diesem Stockwerk, angeschlossen an die Personalabteilung, ist eine Abteilung für die Ausbildung.*).

P 53 🔊 STAHLGRUBER, OTTO GRUBER GMBH & CO., MÜNCHEN
Herr Scheipl Sie sehen hier den Vertrieb, Export, das ist eine der größten Abteilungen bei uns im Haus, entsprechend der Bedeutung der 140 Auslandsvertretungen. Sie sehen auf beiden Seiten Büros. In allen wird telefoniert, zum Teil in der Sprache des betreffenden Landes. Wir haben also sehr viele ausländische Mitarbeiter hier. ... Hier sind die Büros der Leiter der Exportabteilung.
Sie sehen hier mit niedrigen Wänden abgetrennt den Einkauf. Dieser Abteilung angeschlossen ist der Verkauf, um die Wege möglichst kurz zu halten.
Hier sehen Sie unsere Telefonzentrale. Angeschlossen sind Räume der allgemeinen Verwaltung, wie die Hauptkasse, der Empfang für die Besucher.
Und jetzt kommen wir zu den Büros der Geschäftsleitung. Angeschlossen ist ein großer Konferenzraum für hausinterne Besprechungen und auch naturgemäß – ganz in der Nähe – die Rechtsabteilung, auf die ein Unternehmen in dieser Größe auf keinen Fall verzichten kann.
Hier ist jetzt die Datenverarbeitungszentrale, die zusammen mit der Buchhaltung ein ganzes Stockwerk einnimmt. Ich persönlich verstehe zu wenig von den technischen Abwicklungen in dieser Abteilung, um Ihnen hier nähere Auskünfte geben zu können.
In diesem Stockwerk hier ist die Personalabteilung. Das ist die zentrale Personalverwaltung sowohl der Werke, als auch der Zentrale, als auch der Verkaufshäuser.
Dann ebenfalls in diesem Stockwerk, angeschlossen an die Personalabteilung, ist eine umfangreiche Abteilung für die Ausbildung. Unsere Lehrlinge – oder, wie es heute heißt, Auszubildende, Azubis – schneiden in der Regel bei den Prüfungen sehr, sehr gut ab, weil eben eine entsprechende Lehrkraft vorhanden ist.

P 54 ▸ *a* 1923 (*1923 gegründet*); *b* trading, and production of lifting platforms and compressors (*die neben Handelsaktivitäten auch in Eigenproduktion Hebebühnen und Kompressoren herstellte*); *c* a number of long-serving, trusted employees (*Die Firmengründer vererbten die Firma einer Anzahl langjähriger, bewährter Mitarbeiter.*); *d* 8 (*in 8 Werken*); *e* 32 (*in 32 Verkaufshäusern in Bayern, Sachsen, Thüringen und in Österreich*); *f* 16 (*16 ausländische Tochterunternehmen*); *g* over 140 (*Vertretungen in über 140 Ländern der Welt*); *h* more than 800 million marks (*ein Jahres-Weltumsatz von über 800 Millionen DM*).

P 55 **Pr 1** Otto Gruber (*Im Jahre 1923 wurde die Firma Otto Gruber & Co. gegründet.*). **2** from the product range combined with the name (*Durch dieses Programm kam es zur Namensverbindung STAHLGRUBER.*). **3** advising and dealing with customers (*Mitarbeiter, die in derzeit 16 ausländischen Tochterunternehmen die Kunden beraten und betreuen.*). **4** *a* Die Zentrale der Firma Stahlgruber ist in München. *b* *i* Es gibt in Bayern, Sachsen, Thüringen und in Österreich 32 Verkaufshäuser. *ii* Die Firma beschäftigt dort 2.600 Mitarbeiter. / In den Verkaufshäusern werden rund 2.600 Mitarbeiter beschäftigt. *iii* Stahlgruber hat 16 ausländische Tochterunternehmen. *iv* Stahlgruber hat Vertretungen in über 140 Ländern (der Welt). *c* Die Firma macht einen Jahres-Weltumsatz von über 800 Millionen D-Mark.

P 55 **?** A radio.

UNIT 5: ZUM WOHL!

P 57 ▶ **Claudia Birnbaum: *a*** 18 (*Ich bin 18 Jahre alt.*); *b* Dresden (*Ich komme hier aus Dresden.*); *c* cinema, disco, reading (*Kino, Disko, Literatur*). **Thomas Barth: *a*** 16 (*Ich bin 16 Jahre alt.*); *b* Dresden (*Ich komme aus Dresden.*); *c* sport – handball and football – reading (*Meine Hobbys sind Sport, Lesen – bei Sport speziell Handball und Fußball.*).

P 58 **Pr 1** *a* Ich heiße/Mein Name ist (*student's name*). *b* Ich bin (*student's age*) Jahre alt. *c* Ich komme aus (*student's home town*). *d* Ich bin (*student's job*) von Beruf. *e* Ich bin zuständig für (*student's area of responsibility*). *f* Ich arbeite bei (der Firma)/für (die Firma) (*name of student's company*). *g* Meine Hobbys sind (*student's hobbies*). **2** cinema (*Kino*), disco (*Disko*), reading (*Ich lese gern. / Meine Hobbys sind Sport, Lesen.*), sport (*Meine Hobbys sind Sport, Lesen.*), handball (*Handball*), football (*Fußball*). **3** *b*, Sport is the umbrella term, *Handball, Tennis, Fußball, Golf* are all individual sports. **4** Ich lese sehr gern. Ich mag Literatur. Ich liebe meine Stadt. Ich fühle mich sehr zu Dresden hingezogen. **5** *a* Ich lese (sehr) gern. *b* Ich arbeite (sehr) gern. *c* Ich fahre (sehr) gern. **6** *a* Ich liebe meine Stadt. *b* Ich liebe Literatur. *c* Ich liebe Musik.

P 59 ▶ *a* 13 December (*für den dreizehnten zwölften*); *b* Friday (*Freitag*); *c* 6 pm (*18 Uhr*); *d* four (*Das sind vier Geschäftsleute.*); *e* a table by the window in a quiet corner (*Ich hätte gern einen Fensterplatz. Ich möchte sie gern in einer ruhigeren Ecke unterbringen.*); *f* Harms (*auf den Namen von Herrn Harms*).

P 59 **Pr 1** Um wieviel Uhr ist der Termin? **2** *a* Ich hätte gern eine Karte. *b* . . . einen Sitzplatz. *c* . . . ein Zimmer. *d* . . . einen Tisch. **3** *a* Ich hätte gern einen Tisch reserviert für sechs Personen *b* um neunzehn Uhr *c* auf den Namen von (*student's name*). **4** *a* Ich hätte gern einen Tisch reserviert für Freitag, den dreizehnten elften, um neunzehn Uhr. *b* . . . für Mittwoch, den dreißigsten sechsten, um zwanzig Uhr dreißig/halb neun. *c* . . . für Montag, den zweiten vierten, um zwölf Uhr (mittags). *d* . . . für Samstag, den zwanzigsten siebten, um zwölf Uhr dreißig/halb eins. *e* . . . für Dienstag, den vierten dritten, um neunzehn Uhr fünfundvierzig. *f* . . . für Donnerstag, den achtzehnten fünften, um zwanzig Uhr.

P 60 ▶ **1** 8 (*Port, Sherry, Cinzano, Campari, Pernod, Sekt, Champagner, Mineralwasser*). **2** *a* F (*Glas Champagner? . . . Eins, zwei, drei.*); *b* F (*Ich hätte gern nur ein Mineralwasser.*).

P 61 ▶ *a* F (*Ich möchte den Feldsalat mit rohen Champignons und den Riesencrevetten. Und als Hauptgericht nehme ich das Kalbssteak auf Basilikumsoße.*); *b* T (*Ich werde mich dem anschließen, ich hätte auch gern den Feldsalat mit den Riesencrevetten und das Kalbssteak.*).

P 62 **Die Getränkekarte** ▶ *b* (*Zu den Crevetten einen trocknen Weißwein.*).

P 62 **Die Rechnung** ▶ F (*Machen Sie mir bitte eine Quittung?*).

P 63 **Pr 1** *a* Ich habe einen Tisch bestellt/reserviert. *b* Möchte jemand/Möchten Sie einen Aperitif? *c* Ich hätte gern die (Speise)karte. *d* Wer nimmt jetzt was? *e* Was trinken wir zum Essen? *f* Vielleicht einen deutschen Wein? / Wie wäre es, wenn wir (mal) einen deutschen probieren? *g* Ich möchte bitte (einmal) die Melone. / Als Vorspeise nehme ich die Melone. Als Hauptgericht nehme ich das Schweinefilet. Und wir hätten gerne einen 91er Mosel/eine Flasche von dem 91er Mosel. *h* Kann ich zahlen, bitte? / Ich möchte bitte zahlen. *i* Nehmen Sie Kreditkarten? *j* Machen Sie mir bitte eine Quittung?/Ich hätte gern eine Quittung. *k* Ich freue mich, daß Sie gekommen sind. / So, ich danke herzlich. **2** Es war (sehr) nett. Vielen Dank für die Einladung! **3** *a* kann, zahlen; *b* darf, sein; *c* wollen, schauen. **4** *a* Ich möchte keinen Wein. *b* . . . keinen Aperitif. *c* . . . keine Vorspeise. *d* . . . kein Hauptgericht. *e* . . . keine Nachspeise/keinen Nachtisch. *f* . . . keine Champignons. *g* . . . kein Bier. *h* . . . keine Crevetten (*pl.*). *i* . . . kein Gemüse. **5** *a* Es gibt (einen) Port. *b* . . . (einen) Sherry. *c* . . . (einen) Cinzano. *d* . . . (einen) Campari. *e* . . . (einen) Sekt. *f* . . . (ein) Mineralwasser. *g* . . . (einen) Salat. *h* . . . Champignons. *i* . . . (ein) Steak.

P 65 **Re 1** *a* Ich möchte (bitte) meinen Schlüssel. *b* . . . eine Tasse Kaffee. *c* . . . ein Glas Wein. *d* . . . Frühstück um halb sieben. **2** *a* Wie ist Ihr Name, bitte? / Wie heißen Sie? *b* Für welche Firma arbeiten Sie? *c* Was sind Sie von Beruf? *d* Was für Hobbys haben Sie? **3** *a* daß; *b* das; *c* Das; *d* daß; *e* das; *f* Das, das; *g* daß; *h* Das; *i* daß. **4** *a* Wieviel kostet das? / Wieviel würde das kosten? *b* Was für einen Umsatz macht/hat Ihre Firma? / Was ist der Jahresumsatz der Firma? *c* Wieviel Angestellte/Mitarbeiter hat Ihre Firma? **5** *a* Wieviel Besucher kommen? *b* Wieviel Aussteller gibt es? **6** *a* Ich möchte gern(e) Geld wechseln. *b* . . . $ 1500 wechseln. *c* . . . einen Euroscheck einlösen. *d* . . . DM 600 überweisen. *e* . . . DM 1000 von meinem Konto abheben. *f* . . . £500 wechseln. *g* . . . ein Konto aufmachen. **7** angenehmen Aufenthalt – wünschen; Platzkarten – reservieren; Geld – wechseln; Umsatz – machen; Euroscheck – einlösen. Ich wünsche Ihnen einen angenehmen Aufenthalt! Ich möchte Platzkarten reservieren. Ich möchte Geld wechseln. Wir machen 2 Millionen Mark Umsatz. Ich möchte einen Euroscheck einlösen.

P 66 ▶ **1** 4 (*Golf, Pferdesport, Segeln, Tennisspielen*). **2** because he's too busy (*Weil die Möglichkeiten, wenn man sehr viel arbeiten muß, relativ eingeschränkt sind.*) **3** because of the cost (*Wenn ich mir die Zahlen anhöre, Mitgliedschaftsgebühr und so.*) **4** no (*Es hat diese Fama, elitär zu sein, ist es aber meines Erachtens überhaupt nicht.*).

P 66 🎧 FUNK-RESTAURANT, MÜNCHEN
Herr Sahla Aber was mal ganz anderes, weil . . . man kann ja nicht immer nur übers Geschäft reden. Treiben Sie eigentlich auch Sport?
Herr Magunna Im Moment leider zu wenig. Weil die Möglichkeiten, wenn man sehr viel arbeiten muß, relativ eingeschränkt sind. Ansonsten bin ich begeisterter Golfspieler.
Herr Neuhaus Ah ja?
Herr Magunna Auch Mitglied eines Golfclubs in Hamburg.
Herr Sahla Aber das ist in Deutschland etwas sehr Elitäres, Golf, nicht wahr? Also wenn ich so mir die Zahlen anhöre, was Sie bei Mitgliedschaftsgebühr und so . . .

Herr Magunna In der Öffentlichkeit ist es eine elitäre Angelegenheit. Wenn man eigentlich mal das Ganze hinterfragt, dann ist auch der Pferdesport, dann ist auch das Segeln eigentlich, müßte man dann auch ...
Frau Magunna Tennisspielen.
Herr Magunna ... oder Tennisspielen müßte man auch als elitär einstufen, nur dem Golf wird das immer so angehängt, weil es halt diese Fama hat, elitär zu sein, ist es aber meines Erachtens überhaupt nicht.

P 67 **Treiben Sie Sport?** **Pr 1** twice. **2** Aber mal etwas ganz anderes! (in fact, Peter Sahla says *Aber was mal ganz anderes.*) **3** *a* Meines Erachtens ist Tennisspielen nicht teuer. *b* ... sind die Produkte nicht teuer. *c* ... sind die Mitgliedsgebühren nicht hoch. *d* ... ist die Organisation gut. *e* ... ist das Meeting wichtig. *f* ... ist der Service nicht freundlich.

P 67 ▶ *b* (*Kreisstadt*); *c* (*zirka 20.000 Einwohner*); *g* (*liegt zwischen Leipzig und Dresden*); *a* (*schön restauriert*); *e* (*hat eine Kirche*); *h* (*hat einen schönen Park*); *d* (*liegt in einer reizvollen Landschaft*); *f* (*wenn man abends weggehen will, dann ist es nicht so gut*); *i* (*Es ist mehr was für ältere Leute.*).

P 67 🔊 DRESDNER BANK AG, DRESDEN
Frau Redmann Oschatz ist eine niedliche Kreisstadt mit zirka 20.000 Einwohnern, liegt zwischen Leipzig und Dresden und hat eine tolle Innenstadt, also ist schön restauriert, eigentlich gut erhalten. Und hat 'ne Kirche, die jetzt wieder restauriert worden ist. Also, könnte man sich eventuell mal angucken, hat auch 'n schönen Park und liegt in einer reizvollen Landschaft. Jedoch, wenn man jetzt Urlaub machen will und auch mal abends weggehen will, dann ist es nicht so gut! Es ist mehr was für ältere Leute, die sich jetzt wirklich erholen wollen und zum Beispiel wandern gehen wollen oder so.

P 67 **Eine niedliche Kreisstadt** **Pr 1** *a* Oschatz hat zirka 20.000 Einwohner. *b* Es/Oschatz liegt zwischen Leipzig und Dresden. *c* ... hat eine schöne/tolle Innenstadt. *d* ... hat eine Kirche. *e* ... hat einen schönen Park. *f* ... liegt in einer reizvollen Landschaft. **2** *Try following the format of* **1**.

P 69–70
Across: **1** Tomaten. **4** Paris. **8** Zwiebeln. **13** Cognac. **17** Nachspeise. **18** Gemuese (Gemüse). **19** Putenbrust. **23** Speisekarte. **24** ins. **25** Butter. **26** in. **27** Gin. **28** Getraenke (Getränke). **32** koestlich (köstlich). **33** Art. **35** Vorspeise. **37** Glas. **38** Ei. **39** Bier. **40** warm. **41** Fleisch. **44** Grill. **47** Haube. **48** weiss (weiß). **50** er. **51** trinken. **53** Service. **54** Wohl. **55** Tisch. **56** Salat. **57** nehmen.
Down: **1** trocken. **2** Sahne. **3** lieben. **5** Rechnung. **6** Sauce. **7** Kaese (Käse). **8** zum. **9** Wasser. **10** Ecke. **11** bunt. **12** nett. **14** Suppe. **15** gross (groß). **16** Hauptgericht. **18** gebraten. **20** Tag. **21** Beilage. **22** Rind. **29** essen. **30** Englisch. **31** Fisch. **34** zahlen. **36** Obst. **41** frisch. **42** Mark. **43** Sekt. **45** klein. **46** Reis. **48** Wein. **49** mit. **52** rot.

UNIT 6: DIE PRODUKTMERKMALE

P 71 ▶ 8 (*Taschencomputer/Palm-Top-Gerät/sehr klein, handliche Form, elegant, sehr hohe Kapazität/hohe Speicherkapazität, Wordprocessor, Multi-Task-Funktion, sehr bedienungsfreundlich, kann an einen Drucker angeschlossen werden*).

P 72 **Pr** *a* Ich interessiere mich für Ihren Computer. *b* Was für ein Computer ist das? *c* Wie hoch ist die Kapazität? *d* Was sind die Produktmerkmale?

P 72 ▶ .hormone therapy, in particular oral contraception/ the pill, X-ray contrast media (*Hormontherapie, Röntgenkontrastmittel.*).

P 73 **Pr 1** *a* Die Firma Schering ist tätig in der Branche Chemie, Pharmazie. *b* Schering stellt Pharmazeutika, Pflanzenschutzmittel, galvanotechnische Erzeugnisse, Industriechemikalien, Naturstoffe, Hormone (die Pille) und Röntgenkontrastmittel her und vertreibt (auch) diese Produkte. (*herstellen* is a separable verb.) / Schering ist ein Unternehmen, was Pharmazeutika, Pflanzenschutzmittel... herstellt und vertreibt. *c* Die Pille ist eine Domäne, wo Schering Pionierarbeit geleistet hat. Röntgenkontrastmittel sind die zweite Nische, wo Schering Pionierarbeit geleistet hat. / Die orale Kontrazeption und Röntgenkontrastmittel sind Bereiche, wo Schering Pionierarbeit geleistet hat. **2** *a* sich; *b* mich; *c* sich; *d* sich; *e* sich; *f* uns; *g* mich; *h* sich. **3** *a* sich befinden *to be located*; *b* sich interessieren *to be interested*; *c* sich zusammenschließen *to amalgamate, merge*; *d* sich vorstellen *to imagine*; *e* sich bewegen *to range, move*; *f* sich überlegen *to consider*; *g* sich erkundigen *to enquire*; *h* sich handeln (um) *to concern*.

P 73 ▶ **1** *a* glass, china, arts and crafts (*Ich bin in der Glas-, Porzellan- und Kunstgewerbebranche tätig.*); *b* clothing, specifically menswear (*Ich bin speziell tätig in der Bekleidung, und ganz genau in Herrenbekleidung.*). **2** *a* gifts: eg English potpourris (*Geschenkartikel. Zum Beispiel Potpourris.*); *b* suits, jackets, trousers, shirts and men's knitwear (*Ich verkaufe Anzüge, Sakkos, Hosen, Hemden und Herrenstrickwaren.*).

P 74 **Pr 1 Dieter Jung:** *a* Dieter Jung ist gelernter Industriekaufmann. Er ist von Beruf Handelsvertreter. / Er übt den Beruf eines Handelsvertreters. *b* Er ist in der Glas-, Porzellan- und Kunstgewerbebranche tätig. *c* Seine Firma sitzt/hat ihren Sitz in Inning am Ammersee. Das ist in Bayern, in der Nähe von München. *d* Er importiert und verkauft Geschenkartikel aus England, zum Beispiel Potpourris. **Dieter Putz:** *a* Dieter Putz ist von Beruf Handelsvertreter. *b* Er ist in der Bekleidung/ Bekleidungsbranche tätig, ganz genau in Herrenbekleidung. *c* Seine Firma sitzt/hat ihren Sitz in München. *d* Er verkauft Anzüge, Sakkos, Hosen, Hemden und Herrenstrickwaren. **2** *a* Was für ein Produkt ist das? *b* Was für eine Firma ist das? *c* Was für ein Boot ist das? *d* Was für eine (Fach)messe ist das? *e* Was für ein Stand ist das?

P 76 ▶ **1** 1988 (*'88 fing ich an.*). **2** he went to England and looked round big department stores (*Ich bin selbst nach England gefahren und habe mich in den großen Kaufhäusern umgesehen.*). **3** yes (*Die englische Ware ist momentan hier im Trend.*). **4** both (*Die Leute schreiben mich an und kommen persönlich hierher. Während meiner Reisen, oder wenn Messen in England sind, knüpfe ich immer wieder Kontakte.*).

P 77 **Pr 1** *a* Herr Jung fing '88 an. *b* Er war (damals noch) unbekannt auf dem Markt als Händler mit ausländischen Waren. *c* Er ist (dann) selbst nach England gefahren und hat sich dort in den großen Kaufhäusern umgesehen. *d* Er bekommt automatisch Angebote: Die Leute schreiben Herrn Jung an, sie kommen persönlich mit Mustern, und er knüpft während seiner Reisen Kontakte. *e* Die englische Ware ist momentan (in Deutschland) im Trend. **2** Das heißt. **3** *a* herankommen; *b* herantreten; *c* herumreisen (rumreisen); *d* anfangen; *e* anschreiben; *f* herauskriegen; *g* hierherkommen.

P 77 ▶ **1** not to attempt to sell their entire product range but to concentrate on products typical of their country (*Ich glaube, daß die ausländischen Hersteller am besten beraten wären, wenn Sie nicht versuchen würden, alles auf dem deutschen Markt zu verkaufen, sondern sich auf Dinge konzentrieren würden, die für ihr Land besonders typisch sind.*). **2** waxed jackets (*britische Wachsjacken – das ist ein typischer Artikel*). **3** very large (*eine Riesennachfrage*).

P 78 **Pr 1** *a* Herr Putz verkauft Wachsjacken, weil es im Moment eine Riesennachfrage gibt. *b* Herr Putz ist Mitglied der CDH, weil er Handelsvertreter ist. *c* Herr Jung verkauft englische Potpourris, weil sie ein Trendartikel sind. *d* Herr Jung bekommt automatisch Angebote, weil er auf dem Markt bekannt ist.

P 79–80 **Re 1** *a* gefällt; *b* läuft; *c* mag; *d* kann; *e* bewegt sich; *f* nimmt; *g* sieht; *h* wird; *i* darf. **2** *a* die Filmgesellschaft; *b* der Hand-held-Computerhersteller; *c* die Messegesellschaft; *d* das Reisebüro; *e* die Bank; *f* der Spezialglas-Hersteller; *g* das Hotel; *h* die Autovermietung; *i* die Werft. **3** *a* Was für Produkte vertreiben Sie? *b* . . . verkaufen Sie? *c* . . . fertigen Sie? *d* . . . stellen Sie her? *e* . . . erzeugen Sie? **4** *a* Ich bräuchte/brauche Ihre Telefonnummer. *b* . . . Ihre Faxnummer. *c* . . . Ihren Namen. *d* . . . Ihre Adresse. *e* . . . Ihre Kontonummer. *f* . . . Ihr Geburtsdatum. **5** herumreisen (*reisen rum*), herankommen, herstellen, anfangen (*fing an*), herauskriegen, herausgreifen (*herausgegriffen*), herantreten (*tritt heran*), ausüben, anschließen (*angeschlossen*), anschreiben. **6** *a* Es handelt sich um ein Palm-Top-Gerät. *b* . . . einen Wordprocessor. *c* . . . einen Computer. *d* . . . Potpourris. *e* . . . Wachsjacken. (you need the accusative endings of **ein**, see p 139) **7** Ich werde mich (nochmal) bei Ihnen melden. **8** *a* Wir versprechen, daß die Besucher in ausreichender Zahl kommen. *b* Ich hoffe, daß es ein junggebliebenes Unternehmen ist. *c* Ich freue mich, daß Sie gekommen sind. *d* Das beste daran ist, daß es sehr klein ist. **9** *a* Mein; *b* meine; *c* meines; *d* meine; *e* meine; *f* mein; *g* Meine; *h* Mein; *i* meine; *j* meinen. **10** *a* m., sing., nom.; *b* f., sing., acc.; *c* n., sing., gen.; *d* f., sing., acc.; *e* f., sing., nom.; *f* m., sing., nom.; *g* n., pl., nom.; *h* m., sing., nom.; *i* f., sing., acc.; *j* m., sing., acc.

P 81 ▶ *i, b, e, h, f, d, g, a, c.*

P 81 🔊 PSION GMBH, BAD HOMBURG

Herr Nickol Ich möchte einfach mal anfangen, die Serie Drei ganz kurz von außen nach innen mal vorzustellen, und möchte daher einfach mal mit dem geschlossenen Gerät anfangen. Es liegt wirklich gut in der Hand. Man hat sich also auch viel Mühe gegeben mit dem Design. Man hat alles rund gemacht, und dieser kleine Computer erscheint doch wesentlich kleiner und wesentlich handlicher, als er ist. Er ist immerhin so handlich, daß er in 'ne Hemdtasche paßt oder auch in die Innentasche des Jacketts.

Man hat weiterhin die Serie Drei unter diesen Klappen, in die Speichermedien rein sollen, eine Back-up-Batterie eingebaut, so daß im höchsten Maß die Datensicherheit garantiert ist.

Wenn man dann das Gerät aufklappt, es bleibt also in dieser Einstellung stehen. Unterteilt ist es in drei Bereiche. Die drei Bereiche sind der Display, dann kommt unten drunter ein Sensorfeld, wo Sie direkten Zugriff auf die acht eingebauten Applikationen haben, und unten drunter die Tastatur, und da offenbart sich gleich, daß es also ein deutsches Keyboard ist. Wir haben also versucht, so weit es geht, alles einzudeutschen.

Vielleicht soll ich jetzt mal drauf eingehen, was wichtig ist für die Kunden, wenn sie die Serie Drei zum ersten Mal in die Hand nehmen. Er ist also wirklich so gestaltet, daß man an vielen Stellen die Serie Drei für sich ganz persönlich machen kann, nur man sollte es auch tun, sonst ergeben sich ein paar Nachteile. Wichtig ist zum einen, daß wir eingeben die Uhrzeit, die richtige, damit auch unser Wecker so funktioniert, daß wir den Heimatort wählen, sonst stimmt die Zeit wieder nicht, und daß wir die Benutzerdaten eingeben können, um unsere Maschine jederzeit wieder identifizieren zu können, und als letztes ein Paßwort.

P 82 **Pr 1** *a* Die Serie III ist ein Taschencomputer. *b* Das Gerät ist sehr klein. *c* Es ist handlich. *d* Es ist sehr bedienungsfreundlich. *e* Es ist (im Moment) einzigartig. **2** *a* Die Serie III hat einen Wordprocessor. *b* Das Gerät hat Multi-Task-Funktion. *c* Es hat eine hohe Speicherkapazität. *d* Es hat eine Back-up-Batterie. *e* Es hat einen Display. *f* Es hat eine deutsche Tastatur/ein deutsches Keyboard. **3** *a* Ich möchte (mal) anfangen. *b* Vielleicht soll ich jetzt drauf eingehen, was wichtig ist. / Ich gehe jetzt drauf ein, was wichtig ist. *c* Man hat sich viel Mühe gegeben mit dem Design. *d* (Die) Lieferzeiten sind garantiert. *e* Wir haben versucht, so weit es geht, alles einzudeutschen. **4** *a* Man hat sich viel Mühe gegeben. *b* Man hat eine Batterie eingebaut. *c* Man bekommt eine gute Übersicht. *d* Man kann nicht immer über das Geschäft reden. *e* Wie buchstabiert man Ihren Namen?

P 82 ❓ **1** shoplifting (*gegen Diebstahl*). **2** smoke (*Rauchen verboten*).

P 83 ▶ **1** more and more expensive (*immer aufwendiger*), more and more difficult (*immer schwieriger*), more and more important (*immer wichtiger*). **2** about 12 years (*Die Entwicklung eines neuen Arzneimittels dauert etwa zwölf Jahre.*). **3** 10 per cent (*Zehn Prozent der gesamten Belegschaft sind in der Pharma-Forschung tätig.*). **4** 3 out of 4 (*Drei von vier Krankheiten werden heute immer noch nicht ursächlich behandelt werden.*). **5** strong population growth (*Neue Aufgaben: Das starke Bevölkerungswachstum in den Entwicklungsländern.*). **6** age-related diseases (*Mit steigender Lebenserwartung der Menschen in den hochzivilisierten Ländern treten vermehrt altersbedingte Krankheiten auf.*).

P 84 **Pr 1** under what conditions research will take place in the next century (*Unter welchen Bedingungen findet Forschung im nächsten Jahrhundert statt?*). **2** aufwendiger, schwieriger, wichtiger. **3 aufwendiger:** length of development time and cost (*Die Entwicklung eines neuen Arzneimittels dauert etwa zwölf Jahre und kostet rund 250 Millionen DM.*), percentage of employees in research (*Über 2.500 Mitarbeiter – zehn Prozent der gesamten Belegschaft – sind in der Pharma-Forschung tätig.*); **schwieriger:** need for innovation (*Der Zwang zur Innovation nimmt weiter zu.*), effect of competition (*Der Wettbewerb wird härter.*), legal regulations are becoming more comprehensive (*Die gesetzlichen Vorschriften werden* *umfangreicher.*), public opinion is becoming more critical (*Forschung wird in der Öffentlichkeit zunehmend kritisch gesehen und kontrovers diskutiert.*); **wichtiger:** the causes of three out of four illnesses still cannot be treated (*Drei von vier Krankheiten können heute immer noch nicht ursächlich behandelt werden.*), population growth requires new methods of family planning (*Das Bevölkerungswachstum erfordert neue Methoden der Familienplanung.*), more age-related diseases (*Mit steigender Lebenserwartung treten vermehrt altersbedingte Krankheiten auf.*). 4 *a* billig; *b* Vorschrift; *c* Zwang; *d* Wettbewerb; *e* Öffentlichkeit. 5 etwa, rund. 6 *a* five (*wird aufwendiger, wird schwieriger, wird härter, werden umfangreicher, wird wichtiger*); *b* two (*. . ., daß Forschung kritisch gesehen und kontrovers diskutiert wird. Krankheiten können nicht ursächlich behandelt werden.*); *c* none.

UNIT 7: BITTE WARTEN . . .

P 85 ▶ *a* Ich würde gern Herrn/Frau/Dr. (*name*) sprechen. / Könnte ich bitte Herrn/Frau/Dr. (*name*) sprechen? *b* Wie war der Name noch? *c* Bin ich bei (*name of company*)? *d* Könnten Sie mich bitte mit Herrn/Frau/Dr. (*name*) verbinden? *e* Dann rufe ich nachher nochmal an. *f* Könnten Sie ihn/sie bitten, mich zurückzurufen?

P 86 **Pr 1** *a* Herr/Frau/Dr. (*name*) ist (heute) leider nicht da. *b* Sie ist nächsten/am Montag wieder im Hause. *c* Der/Die/Er/Sie spricht gerade/grad auf der anderen Leitung. **2** *a* Herr/Frau/Dr. (*name*)/Er/Sie ist leider nicht da. *b* Ich würde gern Herrn Grodtke sprechen. / Könnte ich bitte Herrn Grodtke sprechen? *c* Könnten Sie sie bitten, mich zurückzurufen? *d* Moment, bitte (mal). / Einen Moment, bitte. *e* Bin ich bei der Pressestelle Productronica? *f* Guten Tag, hier ist (*student's name and company*). Ich würde gern Herrn Schmidt sprechen. / Könnte ich bitte Herrn Schmidt sprechen?

P 87 ▶ **1** at lunch (*Der ist grad beim Essen.*), in 20 minutes (*20 Minuten*). **2** in a meeting (*Herr Sazinski ist in einem Meeting.*), tomorrow (*Ich probiere es morgen nochmal.*). **3** on a business trip (*Der ist zu einer Geschäftsreise.*), tomorrow (*Gut, rufe ich morgen nochmal an.*).

P 88 **Pr 1** *a* Die ist leider beim Essen. *b* Die ist leider nicht da / grad/gerade weg. *c* Die ist leider auf/zu einer Geschäftsreise. *d* Die ist leider in einem Meeting. **2** *a* Frau Schuster spricht gerade/grad auf der anderen Leitung. *b* Ich verbinde Sie mit Herrn Hauser. *c* Könnte Frau Schuster Sie in zehn Minuten zurückrufen? **3** Ich rufe morgen nochmal an. **4** Ich rufe nachher nochmal an. / Ich probiere es nachher nochmal.

P 89 ▶ **1** Wie geht es Ihnen? **2** Danke vielmals. Ich bin sehr knapp mit Zeit im Moment.

P 90 **Pr 1** *a* hätte gern; *b* möchte gern/würde gern, Mein Name ist; *c* Ich hätte gern, gesprochen, war der Name. **2** Guten Tag, Firma, Wie geht es.

P 90 ▶ *a* ii; *b* iv, (v); *c* i; *d* vi.

P 91 ▶ between 3.30 and 4 (*zwischen halb vier und vier*).

P 92 **Pr** *Sie* Guten Tag, Herr Schmidt. *Sie* 15.00 Uhr ist schlecht. Wäre 16.00 Uhr möglich? *Sie* Alles klar. In Feldkirchen ist das? *Sie* Danke schön! Auf Wiederhören!

P 93 **Re 1** *a* nimmt; *b* sieht; *c* spricht; *d* beträgt; *e* läuft. **2** *a* im; *b* an; *c* in; *d* bei; *e* von; *f* für; *g* in. **3** *a* Guten Tag, hier ist (*student's name*), Firma (*student's company*). *b* Ich rufe nachher nochmal an. *c* Ich würde gern Herrn Grodtke sprechen. / Könnte ich bitte Herrn Grodtke sprechen? / Ich hätte gern Herrn Grodtke gesprochen. *d* Herr Sazinski ist gerade weg/leider nicht da. *e* Moment, bitte (mal). *f* Herr/Frau/Dr. (*name*) spricht gerade auf der anderen Leitung. *g* Wie war der Name noch?

P 94 ▶ *a* Psion hand-held computer (*Ich habe ihm den HC, unser mobiles Datenerfassungsgerät, beschrieben.*); *b* send Herr Schröder the documentation (*Ich wollte ihm die Unterlagen schicken.*); *c* Mr Nohr (*Vielleicht weiß der Herr Nohr etwas davon.*); *d* Mr Steib (*Ich verbinde Sie nochmal weiter zu unserem Herrn Steib.*); *e* that week (*Wir müssen uns ganz dringend diese Woche treffen.*); *f* details, terms of purchase, etc. (*um ins Detail zu gehen, zu welchen Konditionen Sie einkaufen können usw.*).

P 94 🔊 PSION GMBH, BAD HOMBURG

Herr Grodtke Guten Tag, hier ist Grodtke, Firma Psion. Ich hätte gern Herrn Schröder gesprochen.

Telefonistin Der ist leider heute nachmittag nicht im Haus. Um was geht's denn?

Herr Grodtke Es ging darum, daß ich ihm den HC, unser mobiles Datenerfassungsgerät, beschrieben habe, und ich wollte ihm die Unterlagen schicken; das hab' ich dann auch getan.

Telefonistin Bleiben Sie mal 'n Augenblick dran. Vielleicht weiß der Herr Nohr etwas davon. Kleinen Moment, bitte . . .

Herr Grodtke Das ist möglich. Danke.

Telefonistin Hallo!

Herr Grodtke Ja.

Telefonistin Ich verbind' Sie nochmal weiter zu unserem Herrn Steib. Ganz kleinen Moment, bitte, ja?

Herr Grodtke Danke schön.

Telefonistin Bitte.

Herr Steib Steib.

Herr Grodtke Guten Tag, Herr Steib! Grodtke mein Name, Firma Psion. Herr Steib, ich hab' schon mehrfach mit dem Herrn Schröder gesprochen.

Herr Steib Ja?

Herr Grodtke Es ging um mobile Datenerfassung. Herr Schröder hatte mich gebeten, ihm Unterlagen zu schicken. Was ich getan hab'. Und er sagte: Okay, wir müssen uns ganz dringend diese Woche treffen, um ins Detail zu gehen, zu welchen Konditionen Sie einkaufen können usw. Jetzt ist leider der Herr Schröder nicht da. Wissen Sie Genaueres über das Projekt?

P 94 **Pr 1** Herr/Frau/Dr. (*name*) ist leider heute nicht da/weg/nicht im Haus. **2** Um was geht es denn? **3** Bleiben Sie mal einen Augenblick dran./Moment, bitte (mal). **4** Ich verbinde Sie (weiter). **5** *a* Guten Tag, hier ist (*student's name*), Firma (*student's company*). *b* Ich bin (*student's job*) und bin zuständig für den Bereich (*student's area of responsibility*). *c* Unsere Firma ist ein führendes Unternehmen in der Branche (*sector*). *d* Sie hat ihren Hauptsitz in/Unsere Zentrale ist in (*town/city*). *e* Wir haben (*number of*) Zweigstellen/Geschäftsstellen und (*number of*) Niederlassungen in (*names of countries*).

P 95 ▶ *a* about two years earlier (*Die Poststrukturreform, die vor etwa zwei Jahren stattgefunden hat.*); *b* it was put under the

158

management of Telekom (*Die Telekom stellt das Netz zur Verfügung und managt den Telefondienst.*); **c** from Telekom or from private dealers (*Die Endgeräte – Telefonapparate, Faxgeräte... – kann der Kunde entweder von der Telekom kaufen oder von jedem beliebigen privaten Händler erwerben.*); **d** mobile radio network (*Wo wir Konkurrenz haben, das ist der Mobilfunksektor.*); **e** Telekom and Mannesmann (*Im Mobilfunksektor gibt es zwei Anbieter für das digitale Mobilfunknetz. Die Telekom bietet das D1-Netz an, und Mannesmann bietet das D2-Netz an.*).

P 95 🔊 TELEKOM, MÜNCHEN

Herr Sahla Die Rede ist von der Deregulierung. Wie ist der Stand in der Bundesrepublik auf diesem Gebiet?

Herr Kraus Der Stand ist der, daß auf Grund der Poststrukturreform in Deutschland, die vor etwa zwei Jahren stattgefunden hat, die Telekom das Netz zur Verfügung stellt und den Telefondienst managt. Während die Endgeräte, die an das Netz angeschlossen werden können, sei es Telefonapparate, Faxgeräte, Datenendgeräte, mobile Kommunikationseinrichtungen, die kann der Kunde entweder von der Telekom kaufen oder aber auch von jedem beliebigen privaten Händler erwerben oder auch dort mieten.

Herr Sahla Aber so etwas wie zum Beispiel in den Vereinigten Staaten, wo es eine ganze Reihe von Mitbewerbern gibt, das ist hier nicht in Aussicht gestellt?

Herr Kraus Im Moment noch nicht, was den Telefonsektor anbelangt. Hier hat eben die Telekom über ganz Deutschland hinweg das Monopol. Wo wir Konkurrenz schon haben, das ist der Mobilfunksektor. Im Mobilfunksektor gibt es zwei Anbieter für das digitale Mobilfunknetz. Die Telekom bietet das D1-Netz an, und Mannesmann bietet das D2-Netz an.

P 95 **Pr** *a* stellt, Verfügung; *b* Aussicht gestellt; *c* bietet, an.

P 96 **Pr 1** *a* the beep (*Startton*); *b* twice (*Nennen Sie möglichst zweimal Ihren Namen.*); *c* slowly and clearly (*Sprechen Sie dabei langsam und deutlich.*); *d* the reason for your call (*Geben Sie ggf. den Grund Ihres Anrufes an.*); *e* to give your phone number and code (*Und nicht vergessen: Ihre Telefonnummer und Vorwahl angeben!*). **2** Guten Tag, hier ist (*student's name*), Firma (*student's company*). (*day*), (*date*), (*time*). Es geht um (*reason, eg* unser Produkt, unser Gespräch am...). Könnten Sie mich bitte zurückrufen? Meine Telefonnummer ist (*number*), Vorwahl (*code*). Vielen Dank. Auf Wiederhören! **3** Guten Tag, Frau Schumann. Hier ist (*student's name*), Firma (*company*). Meine Telefonnummer ist (*number*), Vorwahl (*code*). Ich bin heute zwischen (*time*) und (*time*) zu erreichen. **4** Bitte sprechen Sie nach dem Startton/Piepton.

P 97 ▶ *a* by means of a new overlay network (*Mit einem neuen Overlaynetz haben wir in kürzester Zeit die schlechten Verbindungen zwischen alten und neuen Bundesländern spürbar verbessert.*); *b* 50 000 (*Die Zahl der Ost-Westverbindungen wurde von rund 1450 vor der Wende auf 50 000 Ende 1991 gesteigert.*); *c* 500 000 (*Im Osten wurde die Zahl der Telefonanschlüsse pro Jahr annähernd verzehnfacht – auf 500 000.*).

P 97 **Pr** *f* (*neue Verbindungen für den wirtschaftlichen Aufschwung.*); *d* (*Telekom hatte sich schon für das erste Jahr sehr viel vorgenommen.*); *b* (*Die Erwartungen der Öffentlichkeit, der Wirtschaft, der Politik.*); *a* (*die Zahl der Ost-Westverbindungen*); *c* (*die Zahl der Telefonanschlüsse im Osten*); *e* (*Wir haben damit ein wichtiges Ziel für 1991 erreicht.*).

159

P 98 ❓ *a* iii; *b* v; *c* i; *d* iv; *e* ii. **2** if not all the pages have come through (*Haben Sie alle Seiten gut erhalten? Wenn nicht, nehmen Sie bitte mit uns Kontakt auf.*).

UNIT 8: ES GEHT UM ...

P 99 ▶ **1** mobile data acquisition units (*Wir sind ein Systemhaus, das sich auf mobile Datenerfassungsgeräte spezialisiert hat.*). **2** to persuade Mr Biegner to offer his customers his software together with Psion's products (*Ich möchte erreichen, daß Herr Biegner unsere Produkte und seine Software dem Kunden anbietet.*). **3** through advertisements in trade journals (*Ich hatte mehrere Anzeigen in Fachzeitschriften über Psion-Geräte gesehen.*). **4** a future-oriented unit (*Wir sind auf der Suche nach einem zukunftsweisenden Gerät.*). **5** yes (*Ich würde schon sagen, daß das Gespräch erfolgreich war.*).

P 100 **Pr 1** Vielleicht zeigen Sie mir mal das Produkt. **2** *a* Die Firma X hat sich auf Computer spezialisiert. *b* ...auf Pharmazeutika... *c* ...auf Bekleidung... *d* ...auf die Herstellung von Fenstern... *e* ...auf Chemikalien... You could also use beschäftigt sich ausschließlich mit, *eg:* *a* Die Firma X beschäftigt sich ausschließlich mit Computern. **3** *a* Ja, Herr (*name*), wir haben ja zusammen telefoniert. *b* eg Unsere Firma ist also in der (*name of sector*)-Branche tätig. *c* Wir haben uns auf (*product*) spezialisiert. *d* eg for the Psion Series III: Die Serie III ist ein handlicher, bedienungsfreundlicher Taschencomputer. *e* eg for the Psion Series III: Die Serie III hat einen Wordprocessor. Das Gerät hat Multi-Task-Funktion. Es hat eine hohe Speicherkapazität. Es hat eine Back-up-Batterie. Es hat einen Display. Es hat eine deutsche Tastatur/ein deutsches Keyboard. *f* Das Gerät kostet (*price*). / Wir gehen – je nachdem, welche Sonderwünsche Sie einbringen – von einem momentanen Verkaufspreis von (*price*) aus. *g* Sie müßten mit einer Lieferzeit von (*delivery time*) Tagen/Wochen/Monaten rechnen.

P 101 ▶ **1** 10 am (*heute, wie vereinbart, um 10 Uhr.*). **2** two: i service agreement between PR and the service units and the subsidiaries (*Es geht um die Leistungsvereinbarung...*) ii cost-cutting measures (*Zum zweiten geht es darum, Einsparmöglichkeiten zu finden.*). **3** the service agreements, cost-cutting (*Kann ich mal Sie, Herr Buchhorn, fragen, ob Sie zu den Leistungsvereinbarungen einen Kommentar abgeben möchten, oder wo Sie eine Chance sehen, noch Einsparungen vorzunehmen?*). **4** that he offers his readers an important product (*Jeder Zeitungsmann ist davon überzeugt, ein wichtiges Produkt dem Leser anzubieten.*). **5** because Mr Buchhorn is short of time and cost-cutting affects his area of responsibility (*Da Sie in Zeitdruck sind und es Ihren Bereich betrifft, können wir die Geschäftsordnung umdrehen.*). **6** statement of costs from January to September of that year (*Das ist eine Kostenaufstellung von Januar bis September dieses Jahres.*).

P 102–103 **Pr 1** *a* Ich habe eine Unterlage vorbereitet. *b* Ich habe mit Kunden telefoniert. *c* Ich habe Kaffee bestellt. *d* Ich habe die Geschäftsordnung vorbereitet. *e* Ich habe eine Unterlage/die Unterlagen verteilt. **2** Es freut mich / Ich freue mich, daß Sie (alle) gekommen sind. **3** *a* Es geht (also) um Problemlösungen. *b* ...das Vertriebsnetz. *c* ...die Tochtergesellschaften. *d* ...die neue Zentrale. *e* ...den Verkaufspreis. *f* ...die neue Ausstellung. *g* ...die Preisliste. *h* ...den Umsatz. *i* ...die Lieferzeiten. **4** *a* Man benötigt qualifizierte Mitarbeiter, um ein gutes Produkt herzustellen. *b* Man braucht Geld, um eine Firma aufzubauen. *c* Wir benötigen Auslandsvertretungen, um weltweit Erfolg zu haben. *d* Man benötigt gute Exponate, um eine erfolgreiche Messe zu veranstalten. **5** *a* Gute Mitarbeiter sind vorhanden. *b* Die Mittel sind vorhanden. *c* Das Geld ist vorhanden. *d* Gute Exponate sind vorhanden. (*You could also say:* *a* Es sind gute Mitarbeiter vorhanden. *etc.*). **6** *a* Vielen Dank, daß Sie alle gekommen sind. *b* Es geht (also) um (*subject of meeting*). *c* Zum zweiten geht es um (*second subject*). *d* Wir können die Geschäftsordnung umdrehen. *e* Ich habe eine Unterlage vorbereitet. **7** *a* Ich bin davon überzeugt. / Ich bin überzeugt, daß . . .; *b* Meines Erachtens . . .; *c* Darf ich (Sie) (mal) kurz unterbrechen? *d* Mein Vorschlag ist/wäre . . . *e* Kann ich Sie mal fragen, ob Sie zu diesem Thema einen Kommentar abgeben möchten/etwas sagen möchten? *f* Herzlichen Dank für das Verständnis. *g* Wir müssen das zur Kenntnis nehmen.

P 103 ► **1** Mr Harms arranges for Ms Baasner to arrange it (*Kann ich Ihnen einen Kaffee besorgen?*). **2** presumably a secretary (*Frau Baasner, könnten Sie vielleicht dem Sekretariat Bescheid sagen . . .*). **3** the biscuits (*Bitte die Kekse nicht vergessen!*).

P 104 **Pr 1** Kein Problem! **2** Bitte . . . nicht vergessen! / Vergessen Sie es bitte nicht! **3** *a* Kann ich Ihnen einen Tee besorgen? *b* . . . einen Kaffee besorgen? *c* . . . ein Mineralwasser besorgen? *d* . . . einen Saft besorgen?

P 104 ► **1** that there are many older employees (*Mir ist insbesondere aufgefallen, daß Sie doch sehr viel ältere Mitarbeiter haben.*). **2** the age profile of the employees and the accounting system (*Diesen Punkt sollten wir im Detail diskutieren. Auch den Bereich des Rechnungswesens, denn da sind noch Verbesserungsmöglichkeiten vorhanden.*).

P 105 **Pr 1** *a* Ich habe die Firma X besichtigt. *b* Der Geschäftsführer hat mir die Firma gezeigt. *c* Die Firma wurde 1930 gegründet. / Die Firma ist 1930 gegründet worden. *d* Die Firma beschäftigt heute 120 Mitarbeiter. *e* Sie macht einen Umsatz von 2,5 Millionen Mark. *f* Der Sitz befindet sich in Hamburg. *g* Die Firma stellt Fenster her. *h* Ich habe (mir) einige Bereiche im Detail angeschaut. *i* Ich habe die Lackierhalle gesehen. *j* Ich habe die Mitarbeiter gesehen. **2** *a eg* Herr Sackmann hat (sich) (die) Entstehungsgeschichte, die Übernahme der PGH und die Finanzierung der GmbH angeschaut. *b* Er hat (sich) insbesondere die rechtliche Strukturierung und die steuerlichen Aspekte angeschaut. *c* Herrn Sackmann ist insbesondere aufgefallen, daß die Firma sehr viel(e) ältere Mitarbeiter hat. *d* Seines Erachtens sind im Bereich der Mitarbeiter und des Rechnungswesens Verbesserungsmöglichkeiten vorhanden. / Seines Erachtens gibt es . . . Verbesserungsmöglichkeiten. / Er glaubt, daß . . . vorhanden sind. *e* Er glaubt, daß die Firma den Schritt in die Privatisierung sehr gut geschafft hat.

P 105 ► **1** *a i* F; *ii* T (*Ich hielt die Ratschläge von Herrn Sackmann (für) sehr interessant/wichtig.*); *iii* F. *b i* T (*der glückliche Umstand des Neubeginns*); *ii* F; *iii* T (*da spielt eben unsere Vergangenheit noch eine Rolle*); *iv* F. **2** because they went through forty years of planned economy and shortages (*Wenn man 40 Jahre Planwirtschaft und Mangel gemeinsam durchgestanden hat, dann kann man sich nicht auf einmal von denen, die diesen Weg auch mit uns gegangen sind, wie Ballast trennen.*).

P 106 **Pr 1** Ich hielt die Ratschläge von Herrn/Frau/Dr.

(*name*) für sehr interessant/wichtig. **2** Ich glaube, . . . **3** *a* halte; *b* sieht. **4** *a* Herr Oschatz hielt die Ratschläge für sehr interessant. *b* Er sieht/sah vieles rein aus der Sicht des Altbundesländlers. *c* Er sah manches zu ökonomisch. *d* Herr Oschatz wird viele Ratschläge berücksichtigen. *e* Er fühlt sich moralisch gegenüber den älteren Mitarbeitern verpflichtet. *f* Diese Verpflichtung/Dies könnte ökonomisch hemmend wirken.

P 108–109 **Re 1** *a* mobil; *b* sehen; *c* kurz; *d* das Verständnis; *e* interessant. **2** *a* Wie heißt der Marketing-Manager/die Marketing-Managerin, bitte? *b* . . . der Projektleiter/die Projektleiterin . . .? *c* . . . die Sekretärin . . .? *d* . . . der Pressereferent/die Pressereferentin, . . .? *e* . . . der Filmproduzent/die Filmproduzentin, . . .? *f* . . . der Kollege/die Kollegin, . . .? *g* . . . der Geschäftsführer/die Geschäftsführerin . . .? **3** *a ii* Grüß Gott! Ich hätte gern Herrn Dr. Probst gesprochen. *iii* Okay, ich probiere es morgen nochmal. *b iv* Guten Tag! Bin ich bei der Pressestelle Systems? *v* Ich möchte gern Herrn Dr. Probst sprechen. *c i* Könnten Sie mich bitte mit Dr. Probst verbinden? **4** *a* Das Auto befindet sich auf dem Parkplatz. *b* Der Hauptsitz befindet sich in Mainz. *c* Die Tür befindet sich bei dem/beim Aufzug. *d* Das Restaurant befindet sich in dem/im Zentrum. *e* Das Büro befindet sich in der zweiten Etage. *f* Die Kasse befindet sich bei dem/beim Eingang. **5** *a* besuchen; *b* übernehmen; *c* strukturieren; *d* finanzieren; *e* mitarbeiten; *f* verbessern; *g* privatisieren; *h* untersuchen; *i* diskutieren; *j* rechnen; *k* lösen; *l* besichtigen.

P 109 ► **1** Tuesday at 10 am, and participants will be informed about the room (*Gut. Wir sehen uns dann am Dienstag um zehn Uhr. Der Raum wird allen noch bekanntgegeben*). **2** Ms Baasner (*Sie benachrichtigen die Hausverwaltung, damit wir einen Raum zur Verfügung haben.*). **3** postpone his appointment with the typesetters (*Ich habe am kommenden Dienstag um 10 Uhr einen Termin in der Setzerei. Ich werde diesen Termin verlegen auf Dienstag nachmittag um 15 Uhr.*).

P 109 (6) DEUTSCHE BP AG, HAMBURG
Herr Harms   Ich hab' Sie alle heute zusammengerufen, damit wir uns über einen Termin verständigen, bei dem wir dann über das PR-Budget sprechen wollen. Und zwar geht es heute eigentlich nur darum, den Ort und den Zeitpunkt festzulegen, wann es uns am besten allen paßt. Ich schlage vor, daß wir das in der nächsten Woche machen. Am Dienstag vielleicht. Um 10 Uhr. Den Raum müßten wir noch festlegen. Frau Baasner, würden Sie vielleicht einen Raum zur Verfügung stellen, beziehungsweise einen Raum mieten. Und die andere Frage, generell, wie sieht das bei Ihnen mit den Terminen aus?
Frau Heuck   Also, nächsten Dienstag 10 Uhr würde mir passen.
Frau Baasner   Ja, mir würde der Termin auch passen.
Herr Harms   Und Sie benachrichtigen die Hausverwaltung, damit wir dann auch einen Raum zur Verfügung haben. Vielleicht hier im Kern 5K13 oder 4K13, das spielt, glaube ich, in diesem Falle keine Rolle. Nochmal das Thema: Es geht also um die Leistungsvereinbarung und das PR-Budget. Die Leistungsvereinbarung zwischen dem Bereich PR und den Service-Einheiten und den Tochtergesellschaften, denen wir unsere Leistungen andienen. Herr Buchhorn, haben Sie da noch einen Termin?

Herr Buchhorn Also, ich hab' am kommenden Dienstag um 10 Uhr einen Termin in der Setzerei, aber wegen der Wichtigkeit dieses Themas werde ich diesen Termin verlegen auf Dienstag nachmittag um 15 Uhr.
Herr Harms Gut. Wir sehen uns dann am Dienstag um 10 Uhr. Der Raum wird allen noch bekanntgegeben.
Frau Heuck Gut.

P 110 Pr 1 *a* Bitte benachrichtigen Sie den Geschäftsführer/die Geschäftsführerin. *b* ...die Sekretärin. *c* ...den Projektleiter/die Projektleiterin. *d* ...den Ingenieur/die Ingenieurin. *e* ...die Vertretungen/die Vertreter. **2** *a* Zehn Uhr würde mir passen. *b* Nächsten Mittwoch würde mir passen. *c* Morgen würde mir passen. *d* Der Ort würde mir passen. *e* Der Termin/Die Zeit würde mir passen. **3** *a* Ich habe um acht Uhr fünfzehn einen Termin mit einem Kollegen/einer Kollegin. *b* Ich habe heute einen Termin in der Fabrik. *c* Ich habe um zwölf Uhr dreißig/halb eins einen Termin in der PR-Abteilung. *d* Ich habe um vierzehn Uhr einen Termin mit einem Kunden/einer Kundin. *e* Ich habe um fünfzehn Uhr dreißig/halb vier einen Termin in der Pressestelle. *f* Ich habe nächsten Freitag einen Termin bei der Messegesellschaft. **4** *a* Ich werde diesen/den Termin auf Mittwoch verlegen. *b* ...auf zwölf Uhr dreißig/halb eins verlegen. *c* ...auf nächste Woche verlegen. *d* ...auf nächsten Monat verlegen. *e* ...auf morgen verlegen. **5** *a* Wir sehen uns dann am Donnerstag. *b* ...im Mai. *c* ...nächstes Jahr. *d* ...am Montag. *e* ...im März. **6** *a* Das Datum wird allen noch bekanntgegeben. *b* Die Zeit... *c* Der Raum/Das Zimmer... *d* Der Ort... *e* Der Termin...

P 111 Modernste Hilfsmittel ▶ 1 a company specializing in orthopaedic equipment and rehabilitation (*Orthopädie- und Rehatechnik*); artificial limbs (*Die Firma fertigt Prothesen.*). **2** 41 (*41 Angestellte sind in der Firma beschäftigt.*).

P 111 Pr 1 *d, h, e, k, c, j, g, l, b, m, f, a, i.* **2** *a* Die Orthopädie- und Rehatechnik Dresden GmbH fertigt Prothesen und bietet eine breite Auswahl modernster Hilfsmittel – vom Rollstuhl bis zum Kompressionsstrumpf. *b* Das Unternehmen wurde von vier Mitarbeitern der Abteilung technische Orthopädie der MedAk gegründet. *c* Die Gründer investierten eine Million Mark in das neue Unternehmen. *d* Der Betrieb ist 1000 Quadratmeter groß. *e* Die Firma beschäftigt 41 Angestellte. *f* Brustprothesen sind das Spezialgebiet. *g* (Ein besonderer Service:) Eine Psychotherapeutin betreut die Frauen bei der Prothesen-Anpassung.

P 111 Ich würde ... ▶ 1 informing and inviting (*die Deutsche BP AG veranstaltet am Mittwoch, dem 9. Oktober 1991, ein Energie-Seminar in Magdeburg. Ich möchte Sie hierzu herzlich einladen.*). **2** It says *Anlage* at the end of the letter. **3** *a* das Schreiben; *b* Sehr geehrter; *c* veranstalten; *d* mit freundlichen Grüßen; *e* beifügen (*füge ... bei*); *f* sich freuen (*ich würde mich freuen*).

UNIT 9: DER KUNDE IST KÖNIG

P 113 ▶ 1 respectable, corresponding to *Mittlere Reife* or *Abitur* in the old *Länder* (*Wir erwarten einen ordentlichen Schulabschluß, der in etwa der Mittleren Reife bzw. dem Abitur in den alten Bundesländern entspricht.*). **2** an interview (*ein schriftlicher*

Eignungstest ... Läuft das zufriedenstellend, führen wir anschließend noch ein persönliches Gespräch.) **3** a contract (*Wenn das positiv am Ende abgelaufen ist, unterbreiten wir ein Vertragsangebot.*).

P 114 Pr 1 danach, anschließend. **2** *e, c, a, d, b.* **3** personality, manner, social skills (*Persönlichkeit, Auftreten, Kontaktfähigkeit.*).

P 114 ▶ 1 because he provides the money for the company to work with (*Letztendlich bringt uns der Kunde das Geld, mit dem wir arbeiten können.*). **2** by charging interest on loans (*das Geld, mit dem wir Kredite rausgeben können, um über den Zinsgewinn, den wir dabei machen, dann auch als Unternehmen Gewinn zu machen.*). **3** (financial) services (*Wir verkaufen Dienstleistungsprodukte.*). **4** the car (*Auto, PKW*), the tennis racket (*Tennisschläger*). **5** employees' salaries (*um letztendlich Ihre Ausbildungsvergütung und mein Gehalt zahlen zu können*).

P 115 Pr 1 *a* Wir verkaufen Dienstleistungsprodukte. *b* Der Kunde ist das Wichtigste für die Dresdner Bank. *c* Die Dresdner Bank ist ein gewinnorientiertes Unternehmen. **2** *a* dem; *b* der; *c* der; *d* das; *e* der; *f* dem. **3** *a* n., sing., dat.: Gespräch; *b* m., sing., nom.: Schulabschluß; *c* m., sing., nom.: Eignungstest; *d* n., sing., nom.: Unternehmen; *e* m., sing., nom.: Teil; *f* n., sing., dat.: Geld.

P 115 ? because of confidentiality (*wegen der Diskretion*).

P 116 ▶ 1 *a* he was very nervous (*Ich war sehr nervös, vor allem bei dem Vorstellungsgespräch.*); *b* by chance (*durch Zufall*) *c* he was very surprised (*sehr überrascht*). **2** 500 marks a month gross (*Im ersten Lehrjahr verdiene ich 500 Mark brutto.*). **3** two and a half years (*Meine Lehrzeit dauert zweieinhalb Jahre.*). **4** *a* vor allem; *b* durch Zufall; *c* eigentlich.

P 116 Pr 1 *a* die Schulausbildung: die Schule, die Ausbildung; *b* das Vorstellungsgespräch: die Vorstellung, das Gespräch; *c* der Bankkaufmann: die Bank, der Kaufmann; *d* die Berufsschule: der Beruf, die Schule; *e* das Lehrjahr: die Lehre, das Jahr. (The gender of the last noun in the compound determines its gender.) **2** *a* Ich war überrascht. *b* Ich war nervös. *c* Ich hatte nicht damit gerechnet. **3** *a* Ich war eigentlich/vor allem überrascht. *b* ...nervös. **4** geschickt, gerechnet.

P 117 ▶ *a* contact with customers (*der Umgang mit den Kunden*), dealing with money (*der Umgang mit dem Geld*), investing money (*das Anlegen des Geldes*); *b* it is one of the leading banks in Germany (*Die Dresdner Bank ist eins der führenden Unternehmen in Deutschland.*), the bank was the quickest (*Ich habe mich an vielen Instituten beworben, und sie war halt einfach schneller.*); *c* practical/theoretical (*in der Bank direkt am Schalter arbeiten. Und die Berufsschule wird auch sehr interessant werden.*); *d* her own branch (*Natürlich hat jeder einen Traum – von einer eigenen Filiale vielleicht.*).

P 118 Eins der führenden Unternehmen Pr 1 *a* Das Anlegen des Geldes interessiert mich. *b* Die Ausbildung... *c* Das Wertpapiergeschäft... **2** *a* Unsere Firma war besser. *b* ...langsamer. *c* ...billiger. *d* ...teurer. *e* ...interessanter. *f* ...wichtiger. **3** *a* Die Firma X hat ihren Sitz in der Nähe von Berlin. *b* ...Hamburg. *c* ...München. *d* ...Bremen. *e* ...Essen. *f* ...Köln. **4** Ausbildung (*Ich stelle mir eine interessante Ausbildung vor, in der viel Praxis vorherrschen wird.*), Bereiche (*Ich werde viel Neues kennenlernen in Bereichen, die wir bisher noch nicht gekannt hatten.*). **5** Ich weiß es nicht (genau).

P 118 ▶ *a* T (*Das erste ist, daß wir viel Praxis haben.*); *b* F (*Daß wir viel Praxis haben, das gefällt mir*). *c* F (*Und auch, daß viel mit uns gearbeitet wird – auch in Seminaren usw.*); *d* T (*daß wir schon Übung haben für Kundengespräche und Ähnliches. Und das finde ich gut.*).

P 118 **Viel Praxis** **Pr 1** Das gefällt mir. Das finde ich gut. **2** *a* Angeln gefällt mir. / Angeln gefällt mir nicht. *b* Musik . . . *c* Theater . . . *d* Kino . . . *e* Lesen . . . *f* Fotografieren . . . *g* Reisen . . . *h* Autofahren. *i* Sport . . . Or: Angeln finde ich gut/nicht gut. *etc.*

P 119–120 **Re 1** *a* Was für eine Schulausbildung haben Sie? *b* Wie lange dauert die Lehrzeit? *c* Nach welchen Kriterien wurden die neuen Lehrlinge ausgewählt? *d* Warum haben Sie sich für die Dresdner Bank entschieden? **2** *a* Wie lange dauert die Ausbildung/Lehre? *b* . . . die Schulausbildung. **3** *a* Wo wohnen Sie? *b* Woher kommen Sie? *c* Wie alt sind Sie? *d* Was für einen Schulabschluß haben Sie? *e* Wie lange dauert die Lehrzeit? **4 Thomas Barth:** *a* Der erste Auszubildende heißt Thomas Barth. *b* Er ist 16 Jahre alt. *c* Er kommt aus Dresden. **Ramona Krause:** *a* Die zweite Auszubildende heißt Ramona Krause. *b* Sie ist 16 Jahre alt. *c* Sie kommt aus einer Stadt in der Nähe von Dresden. **Claudia Birnbaum:** *a* Die dritte Auszubildende heißt Claudia Birnbaum. *b* Sie ist 18 Jahre alt. *c* Sie kommt aus Dresden. **Questions:** *a* Wie heißt der/die Auszubildende? *b* Wie alt ist er/sie? *c* Woher kommt er/sie? **5** *a* Maßgebend für meine Auswahl sind die Schulzeugnisse. *b* . . . ist die Schulausbildung. *c* . . . ist sein/ihr Alter. **6** *a* Ich bin in erster Linie für die Pressestelle zuständig. *b* . . . für die Produktion zuständig. *c* . . . für das Büro zuständig. *d* . . . für die Ausbildung zuständig. *e* . . . für die Lehrlinge zuständig. **7** *a* Der Sitz unserer Firma befindet sich/ist in (*name of town/city*). *b* Wir stellen (*name of product*) her. / Wir verkaufen (*name of product/service*). *c* Unsere Firma macht/hat einen Jahresumsatz von (*amount*). / Der Jahresumsatz beträgt (*amount*). *d* Wir haben (*number*) Tochtergesellschaften/ Niederlassungen/Filialen. *e* Die Firma beschäftigt (*number*) Mitarbeiter. **8** *a* Ich heiße (*name*). / Mein Name ist (*name*). *b* In meiner Freizeit gehe ich (*eg* ins Kino/Theater), spiele ich (*eg* Golf/Fußball), reise ich. *c eg* Ich lese gern und ich bin begeisterter Golfspieler/begeisterte Golfspielerin. *d* Meine Hobbys sind (*eg* Fotografieren, Sport – Pferdesport, Segeln, Tennisspielen, und natürlich Golf!) *e* Ich komme aus (*town/city*). *f* Ich liebe meine Stadt.

P 120 **?** **1** *a* Betrag; *b* Währung; *c* Betrag in Buchstaben; *d* Ort; *e* Datum; *f* Unterschrift; *g* an ___ oder Überbringer; *h* Konto-Nr. (*Konto-Nummer*); *i* Scheck-Nr. (*Scheck-Nummer*).

P 121 ▶ **1** *a* natural manner, good-humoured, committed (*eine sehr natürliche junge Dame, die überall gute Laune versprüht und sich sehr stark auch in der Praxis engagiert*); *b* positive captivating manner, good presentation skills (*Ramona Krause fängt mit ihrer Art und Weise Menschen positiv ein und kann sich sehr gut präsentieren.*); *c* maturity, confidence for his age (*Er ist trotz seines Alters schon sehr reif und souverän.*). **2** in selling (*Der Bereich Verkaufsverhalten ist der Bereich, an dem wir arbeiten müssen. Da besteht noch ein Nachholbedarf.*). **3** a service company (*Das ist nicht das, was wir von einem Dienstleistungsunternehmen verstehen.*).

P 121 🔊 DRESDNER BANK AG, DRESDEN
Herr Kreimeier Claudia Birnbaum ist eine sehr natürliche junge Dame, die überall eigentlich gute Laune versprüht und sich sehr

stark auch in der Praxis engagiert. Ramona Krause ist eigentlich die Schaltermitarbeiterin, Kundenberaterin schlechthin, die ich mir vorstelle. Sie fängt mit ihrer Art und Weise Menschen positiv ein und kann sich sehr sehr gut präsentieren. Thomas Barth ist einer der jüngsten. Er ist erst 16. Und er ist trotz seines Alters schon sehr sehr reif und souverän.

Frau Wachholz Und gibt es irgendwelche Bereiche, an denen die Lehrlinge jetzt noch arbeiten müssen?
Herr Kreimeier Nun, ich glaube, daß der Bereich Verkaufsverhalten sicherlich noch der Bereich ist, an dem wir arbeiten müssen. Sie haben hier nicht verkauft. Hier kamen Kunden in die Bank, um Anträge zu stellen, um vorzusprechen. Und diese Anträge wurden genehmigt oder abgelehnt. Das ist nicht das, was wir von einem Dienstleistungsunternehmen verstehen. Wir wollen unseren Kunden zu seiner Zufriedenheit bedienen. Der Kunde ist König. Und dazu gehört auch aktives Verkaufsverhalten. Und da besteht sicherlich noch 'n Nachholbedarf.

P 122 ▶ **1** organizing the apprenticeship (examination) system: overseeing the training in companies, holding the exams, issuing the certificate (*Die Industrie- und Handelskammern organisieren den gesamten Prüfungsverlauf. Wir überprüfen die Unternehmen, ob sie zu dieser Ausbildung geeignet sind. Und wir nehmen die Examina ab. Und wir stellen ein Zeugnis aus.*). **2** bank clerk (*Bankkaufmann*).

P 122 🔊 INDUSTRIE- UND HANDELSKAMMER, MÜNCHEN
Herr Alberts In der beruflichen Ausbildung, wo zum Beispiel ein angehender Bankkaufmann zwei oder drei Jahre Lehrling ist bei einer Bank und gleichzeitig im Dualsystem in einer Berufsschule einmal in der Woche Unterricht erteilt bekommt, organisieren die Industrie- und Handelskammern den gesamten Prüfungsverlauf. Wir begleiten den Auszubildenden während dieser zwei oder drei Jahre. Wir überprüfen die Unternehmen, ob sie zu dieser Ausbildung geeignet sind. Und wir nehmen die Examina ab. Und wir stellen ein Zeugnis aus, das in ganz Deutschland anerkannt ist. Und dies für alle gewerblichen und kaufmännischen Berufe. So haben wir zum Beispiel im letzten Jahr 14.000 Auszubildende allein im Bereich München und Oberbayern geprüft und ihnen ein Zeugnis, ein Abschlußzeugnis übergeben.

P 122 **Pr** *d, f, c, b, h, g, a, e.*

P 123 ▶ **1** *b* (*bis zu 4.000 Mark pro Woche.*). **2** *b* (*kostenfrei*). **3** *c* (*An weltweit rund 9,4 Millionen Akzeptanzstellen sind Sie mit Ihrer DresdnerCard ein gerngesehener Kunde oder Gast.*).

P 124 **Pr 1** *a* kostenlos, kostenfrei; *b* das laufende Konto; *c* rund um die Uhr; *d* der Geldautomat; *e* die Geheimzahl; *f* bargeldlos; *g* die Kaution. **2** *b, f, h, j, i, e, a, d, g, c.*

UNIT 10: EIN MITTELSTÄNDISCHES UNTERNEHMEN

P 125 ▶ **1** 13 years (*nach 13 Jahren Fremde*). **2** AEG (*Allgemeine Elektricitäts-Gesellschaft*). **3** because he couldn't find a suitable job (*Ich habe versucht, eine adäquate Stelle zu finden. Die gab es nicht hier in der Umgebung.*). **4** 70 000 marks (*Das waren 70.000 Mark, die ich bekommen habe.*).

P 126 Pr 1 a Herr Walter kommt aus Fluorn-Winzeln. **b** Fluorn-Winzeln befindet sich im Schwarzwald. **c** Er ist in Fluorn (Winzeln) geboren. **d** Er war bei (der) AEG beschäftigt. **e** Er ist danach in seine Heimat zurückgezogen. **f** Es gab keine adäquate Stelle/Arbeit in der Umgebung. **g** Und er hat dann seine Firma gegründet. **h** Er hat das Kapital von der Bank bekommen. **i** Sein Vater hat für ihn gebürgt. **2 a** Mein Name ist (*student's name*). **b** Ich bin am (*date*) geboren. **c** Ich bin in (*place*) geboren. **d** Ich bin (*number*) Jahre alt. **e** Ich habe eine Ausbildung/Lehre als (*name of job*) gemacht. / Ich habe (*subject*) studiert. **f** Ich bin (*name of profession*) von Beruf. / Ich bin (*job*). **g** Ich arbeite bei der Firma (*name of company*). / Ich bin beschäftigt bei der Firma (*name of company*). **h** Ich arbeite als (*position*). **i** Ich bin zuständig für (*area of responsibility*). **j** Der Sitz unserer Firma befindet sich in (*town/city*). / Die Firma hat ihren Sitz in (*town/city*). **k** Wir stellen (*name of product*) her. / Wir verkaufen Dienstleistungen. **l** Die Firma beschäftigt (*number*) Angestellte/Mitarbeiter. **m** Der Jahresumsatz beträgt (*amount*). / Unsere Firma macht einen Jahresumsatz von (*amount*). **n** Wir haben (*number*) Tochtergesellschaften. / Wir haben ein Vertriebsnetz mit (*number*) Geschäftsstellen. / Wir haben (*number*) Produktionsstätten. **o** Meine Hobbys sind (*names of hobbies*). **p** Meine Adresse ist (*address*). Meine Telefonnummer ist (*telephone number*).

P 127 ▶ In Fluorn geboren. Bei AEG (*Entwicklung*). Zurück nach Fluorn. Gründet . . . Betrieb.

P 127 Pr a Herbert Walter ist 1935 in Fluorn geboren. **b** Er ist in Fluorn in die Volksschule gegangen und hat eine Mechanikerlehre in Oberndorf und ein Fernstudium in Mathematik gemacht. In Stuttgart machte er dann ein Abendstudium in Maschinenbau, bis zum Abschluß Maschinenbauingenieur. **c** Er hat zunächst als Werkzeugmacher in der Schweiz gearbeitet. **d** 1961 war seine Heirat. **e** 1966 ist er nach Fluorn zurückgezogen. **f** Dann hat er in der Scheune des elterlichen Hauses seine eigene Firma gegründet. **g** Ab 1975 hat er Erodiermaschinen entwickelt. **h** Ab 1978 fing die Firma mit dem Vertrieb eigener Produkte an. **i** 1988 kam Götz Klusmann als Gesellschafter und kaufmännischer Geschäftsführer. **j** Am ersten ersten 1990 begann die Beteiligung von Okuma.

P 128 Die zündende Idee ▶ 1 on a trip to Ireland (*Die Idee zu einer solchen Maschine kam bei einer Reise nach Irland.*). **2** immediately on his return, three years before the interview (*Das war vor drei Jahren. Ich habe dann nach meiner Rückkehr direkt eine Patentanmeldung gemacht.*).

P 128 Pr a Herbert Walter ist vor drei Jahren nach Irland gefahren. **b** Er hat nach einer/der zündenden Idee gesucht. **c** Er ist durch Frankreich zur Fähre gefahren. **d** Bevor er an der Fähre war, hat er die Idee gehabt. **e** Dann hat er eine Patentanmeldung gemacht. **f** In der Zwischenzeit hat er die Maschine entwickelt.

P 128 Computergesteuert ▶ 1 three (*auf einer Drehbank hergestellt; in der Erodiermaschine eingespannt; entweder gedreht oder gefräst oder geschliffen*). **2** fully-automated, computerized, round the clock (*Bei der neuen Maschine ist es so, daß diese ganze Arbeit, vollautomatisch computergesteuert gemacht wird. Die Maschine kann rund um die Uhr arbeiten.*).

P 129 Pr 1 Old method: *b, d, f, i.* New method: *a, c, e, g, h.* **2 a** Das ist die bisherige Methode. **b** Die Arbeit wird vom Werkzeugmacher gemacht. **c** Die Elektrode wird auf einer Drehbank hergestellt. **d** Die Elektrode wird in der Erodiermaschine eingespannt. **e** Die Elektrode wird in der Erodiermaschine entweder gedreht oder gefräst oder geschliffen. **f** Das ist die neue Methode. **g** Hier wird die Arbeit vollautomatisch gemacht. **h** Die Elektrode wird in der EDEM-Maschine hergestellt. **i** Elektroden werden rund um die Uhr gefertigt.

P 129 ▶ 1 production area, development (*unser Betrieb, wo die Maschinen hergestellt werden; die Entwicklung . . .*). **2** seven years (*Ich arbeite jetzt seit sieben Jahren hier.*). **3** she can work part-time (*Hier habe ich die Möglichkeit, halbtags zu arbeiten.*).

P 130 Eine große Familie Pr 1 a Am Wochenende spiele ich Golf. **b** . . . gehe ich in die Berge. **c** . . . gehe ich wandern. **d** . . . spiele ich Tennis. **e** . . . bin ich begeisterter Segler. / gehe ich gern segeln. **f** . . . gehe ich ins Kino. **g** . . . treibe ich Sport. **h** . . . lese ich gern. **2 a** Ich arbeite seit einem Jahr hier. **b** . . . seit zwei Jahren hier. **c** . . . seit zehn Jahren hier. **d** . . . seit vierzehn Jahren hier. **e** . . . seit fünfundzwanzig Jahren hier. **3 a** Ich habe eine Ausbildung zum Kaufmann. **b** . . . zum Werkzeugmacher. **c** . . . zum Bankkaufmann. **d** . . . zur Sekretärin. **e** . . . zum Buchhalter/Wirtschaftsprüfer. **f** . . . zum Ingenieur. **g** . . . zum Techniker. **h** . . . zum Steuerberater (*You can add* **-in** *to a male form and substitute* **zur** *for* **zum** *to make a female profession. Instead of* **zum/zur** *you could also use* **als***.*). **4 a** Ich arbeite am Wochenende. **b** . . . samstags. **c** . . . halbtags. **5 a** Frau Krapfl ist von Beruf technische Zeichnerin. Sie arbeitet seit sieben Jahren bei Exeron. Ihre Ausbildung zur technischen Zeichnerin hat dreieinhalb Jahre gedauert. Sie hat ein Kind mit (*or von*) fünf Jahren. Sie arbeitet gern bei Exeron, weil sie die Möglichkeit hat, halbtags zu arbeiten. **b** Ich bin von Beruf (*profession/trade*). Ich arbeite seit (*number*) Jahren bei (*name of company*). Meine Ausbildung als/zum/zur (*job*) hat (*number*) Jahre gedauert. Ich habe (*number*) Kind(er) mit/von (*age(s)*). Ich arbeite gern bei (*company*), weil ich die Möglichkeit habe, (*reason*). **c** see a.

P 130 ▶ 1 Mr Klusmann: marketing, finance (*Meine Funktionen liegen im Bereich Marketing und Finanzen.*). **Mr Walter:** production, engineering and technology (*Herr Walter macht Produktion, Technik und Technologie.*). **2** if it has two heads or two hearts (*Wenn ein Unternehmen zwei Köpfe hat oder zwei Herzen, dann kann das in der Regel nicht lange gut funktionieren.*).

P 130 Kopf und Herz Pr 1 Diese Lösung halte ich für ideal. **2 a** Ich bin zuständig für Planung. **b** . . . Organisation. **c** . . . Öffentlichkeitsarbeit. **d** . . . Werbung. **e** . . . Ausbildung. **3 a** Meine Funktionen liegen im Bereich Marketing. **b** . . . Werbung. **c** . . . Produktion. **d** . . . Verkauf. **e** . . . Einkauf. **f** . . . Management. **4 a** Ich heiße (*name*). / Mein Name ist (*name*). Ich bin (*profession*). Ich bin beschäftigt bei der Firma (*company*). / Ich arbeite für die/bei der Firma (*company*). Ich arbeite als (*position*). Meine Funktionen liegen im Bereich (*functions*). **b** Er/Sie heißt (*name*). / Sein/Ihr Name ist (*name*). Er/Sie ist (*profession*). Er/Sie ist beschäftigt bei der Firma (*company*). / Er/Sie arbeitet für die/bei der Firma (*company*). Er/Sie arbeitet als (*position*). Seine/Ihre Funktionen liegen im Bereich (*function(s)*).

P 131 ▶ 1 as one of the largest producers of machine tools (*Okuma ist einer der weltgrößten Hersteller von Werkzeugmaschinen.*) **2** a strong high-tech partner in the area of spark erosion (*Okuma suchte einen leistungsfähigen High-Tech-Partner auf dem Gebiet der Senkerosion.*).

P 131 Pr 1 *a* Die Firma X ist führend auf dem Gebiet Werkzeugmaschinen. ***b*** ... Filmproduktion. ***c*** ... Hormontherapie. ***d*** ... Chemie/Chemikalien. ***e*** ... Wertpapiere/Wertpapiergeschäft. **2 *a*** leistungsfähig; ***b*** zahlungsfähig; ***c*** wettbewerbsfähig; ***d*** konkurrenzfähig.

P 133 Re 1 *a* Ich werde mich nächsten Freitag bei Ihnen melden. ***b*** Ich werde Sie morgen anrufen. ***c*** Ich werde nächsten Monat einen Termin ausmachen. ***d*** Ich werde Ihnen am Montag ein Fax schicken. ***e*** Ich werde Sie am sechsten April besuchen. **2 *a*** habe, gemacht; ***b*** habe, gesehen; ***c*** hat, gegeben; ***d*** bin, gefahren. **3 *a*** sich; ***b*** uns; ***c*** sich (*mich or uns* would in fact also be possible); ***d*** mich; ***e*** sich; ***f*** mich. **4 *a*** Können Sie mir bitte helfen? ***b*** Können Sie mir die Uhrzeit sagen? ***c*** Können Sie mir den Weg sagen?

P 133 ▶ 1 medium-sized company (*Die Firma Herbert Walter ist ein mittelständisches Unternehmen.*). **2** it is particularly good at innovation (*Die Firma Walter ist ein Unternehmen, das sich durch besondere Innovationsfreudigkeit auszeichnet.*). **3** throughout Europe (*die Exeron-Maschine, die europaweit bekannt ist*).

P 133 🄶 HERBERT WALTER GMBH

Frau Wachholz Könnten Sie vielleicht für uns einmal kurz die Firma Herbert Walter charakterisieren?

Herr Möller Also, die Firma Herbert Walter ist ein mittelständisches Unternehmen, wie die meisten kleineren Werkzeugmaschinen-Firmen in der Bundesrepublik, und ich glaube auch in ganz Europa. Und die Firma Walter ist ein Unternehmen, das sich durch besondere Innovationsfreudigkeit auszeichnet gegenüber vielen Wettbewerbern. Das zeigt sich auch schon an dem Gesicht der Exeron-Maschine, die ja europaweit bekannt ist. Es ist eine äußerst handlings-freudige Maschine. Es liegt wahrscheinlich daran, weil der Inhaber, oder die Inhaber, äußerst praxisnah sind. Herr Walter kommt ja selbst aus der Branche und hat eine riesige Erfahrung auf dem speziellen Gebiet, die er jetzt in seine Konstruktionen einbringt.

P 134 Innovationsfreudig Pr 1 *g* (*ein mittelständisches Unternehmen*); ***c*** (*wie die meisten kleineren Werkzeugmaschinen-Firmen in der Bundesrepublik*); ***e*** (*besondere Innovationsfreudigkeit*); ***b*** (*Das zeigt sich auch schon an dem Gesicht der Exeron-Maschine.*); ***a*** (*Es ist eine äußerst handlings-freudige Maschine.*); ***d*** (*Die Inhaber sind äußerst praxisnah.*); ***f*** (*Herr Walter kommt ja selbst aus der Branche und hat eine riesige Erfahrung auf dem speziellen Gebiet.*); ***h*** (*Er bringt diese Erfahrung in seine Konstruktionen ein.*). **2 *a*** Die Herbert Walter GmbH ist ein mittelständisches Unternehmen. ***b*** Die meisten (anderen) kleineren Werkzeugmaschinen-Firmen in der Bundesrepublik sind (auch) mittelständische Unternehmen. ***c*** Die Firma Walter zeichnet sich durch besondere Innovationsfreudigkeit aus. ***d*** Die Exeron-Maschine zum Beispiel ist europaweit bekannt. ***e*** Es ist eine äußerst handlings-freudige Maschine. ***f*** Die Inhaber sind sehr praxisnah. ***g*** Herbert Walter kommt selbst aus der Branche. ***h*** Er bringt seine Erfahrung in seine Konstruktionen ein.

P 134 ▶ 1 at the back of the hall on the right (*Das ist das kleine Gerät im Hallen-Hintergrund, etwas auf der rechten Seite.*). **2** on the right, in the middle (*Diese konventionellen Erodiermaschinen befinden sich auf der rechten Hallenseite, etwa in der Mitte.*). **3** Okuma's horizontal machining centre (*Schließlich befindet sich außerhalb der Halle das Horizontal-Bearbeitungszentrum von Okuma.*).

P 134 🄸 HERBERT WALTER GMBH

Prof. Schekulin Liebe Gäste, ich darf Sie nochmal um Ihre Aufmerksamkeit bitten. Wir zeigen Ihnen im Hallen-Hintergrund das Exeron-Minicenter in der Ausführung der dentalen Funkenerosion zum Erodieren von Brücken und Kronen. Das ist das kleine Gerät im Hallen-Hintergrund, etwas auf der rechten Seite. Ferner zeigen wir Ihnen – und Sie werden staunen –, wir haben noch konventionelle Erodiermaschinen. Diese konventionellen Erodiermaschinen Exeron 102, 103 und 104 befinden sich auf der rechten Hallenseite, etwa in der Mitte. Und schließlich, und last not least, befindet sich außerhalb der Halle ein sehr interessantes Objekt, nämlich das Horizontal-Bearbeitungszentrum von Okuma, die MC 400H – mit Sicherheit das modernste horizontale Bearbeitungszentrum, das es im Augenblick überhaupt gibt. Vielen Dank für Ihre Aufmerksamkeit!

P 134 Wir zeigen Ihnen... Pr 1 Liebe Teilnehmer/ Gäste, ich darf Sie um Ihre Aufmerksamkeit bitten. **2** Vielen Dank für Ihre Aufmerksamkeit!

P 134 ? FRG's global market share for different types of machine – excluding the former GDR (*Deutsche Maschinen; Anteile der Bundesrepublik Deutschland am Weltmarkt in % – 1989, alte Bundesländer*)

P 135 ▶ 1 under licence (*Okuma wird die Senkerodierzentren von Walter in Lizenz fertigen.*). **2** expansion of their range of machine tools, expansion of customer base, production site in Europe (*Für Okuma bedeutet diese Kooperation eine Erweiterung der Werkzeugmaschinenpalette. Okuma erweitert damit auch seinen Abnehmerkreis und sichert sich einen Produktionsstandort im Herzen der EG.*). **3** high-tech partner with worldwide sales network (*Die Walter-Gruppe gewinnt mit dieser Zusammenarbeit einen High-Tech-Partner mit weltweitem Vertrieb.*). **4** 100 (*Die Walter-Gruppe hat 100 Beschäftigte.*). **5** 50 per cent (*Okuma hat 50 Prozent des Kapitals an der exeron Erodiertechnologie GmbH.*).

P 136 Pr 1 *g, d, b, h, e, i, c, a, f.* **2 *a*** Herbert Walter GmbH ist ein mittelständischer Werkzeugmaschinenhersteller/ Erodiermaschinenhersteller. Okuma ist eine führende japanische Werzeugmaschinengruppe. ***b*** Die Walter-Gruppe hat 100 Beschäftigte. Die Firma erreichte 1990 bei einem 25%-igen Wachstum einen Jahresumsatz von fast 30 Mio. DM. ***c*** Okuma Japan gilt als weltweit führender Hersteller von zerspanenden Werkzeugmaschinen. ***d*** Diese Kooperation bedeutet für Okuma eine Erweiterung der Werkzeugmaschinenpalette (um technisch anspruchsvolle Erodiermaschinen). Die Firma erweitert damit ihren Abnehmerkreis und sichert sich einen Produktionsstandort im Herzen der EG. ***e*** Die Walter-Gruppe gewinnt mit dieser Zusammenarbeit einen High-Tech-Partner mit weltweitem Vertrieb. ***f*** Okuma hat 50 Prozent des Kapitals an der Exeron Erodiertechnologie GmbH. Im Rahmen der Zusammenarbeit wird Okuma die Senkerodierzentren von Walter in Lizenz fertigen und in Japan und anderen Märkten vertreiben.

GLOSSARY

The **Glossary** gives translations of all the German words in **German means Business** in context.

Nouns The definite article in front of the noun shows its gender. The plural form is in brackets:
der Anfang (¨e) *start, beginning*
ie: Anfänge *beginnings*

With nouns that don't have the normal case endings (see p 139), the genitive singular form is given in brackets before the plural:
der Name *(sing. gen. -ns) (-n) name*
ie: Namens *of the name*

Compounds Some compound nouns have been omitted, where their meaning can be deduced easily from the component parts.

Verbs Any vowel changes are given in the order (present tense), past tense, past participle (see p 143):
aussehen *(sep.)* (ie), a, e *to look (like), appear*
ie: er/sie/es/man sieht aus, sah aus, ausgesehen
The vowel of the present tense is omitted when it's the same as in the infinitive form (see p 143).

(sep.) indicates that the verb is separable (see p 143).

(sein) indicates that the verb takes **sein** as an auxiliary (see p 144):
anreisen *(sep.)* (sein) *to arrive*

sich in front of the verb indicates that the verb is reflexive (see p 143).

Verbs are given with commonly associated prepositions:
(sich) anpassen *(sep.)* (an) *to adapt (itself/oneself) (to)*

Abbreviations

(f.) feminine	*(m.)* masculine
(n.) neuter	
(sing.) singular	*(pl.)* plural
(nom.) nominative	*(acc.)* accusative
(gen.) genitive	*(dat.)* dative
(coll.) colloquial	*(lit.)* literally
(sep.) separable	*(sth.)* something

A

ab *from (see also sep. verbs with* ab)
abdecken *(sep.) to cover*
der Abend (-e) *evening*
das Abendessen (-) *supper*
abends *in the evening(s)*
das Abendstudium *evening classes, part-time degree course*

aber *but, however;* oder aber *or alternatively*
der Abfall (¨e) *waste (material)*
das Abfallholz (¨er) *waste wood*
die Abgase *(pl.) exhaust emissions*
abgeben *(sep.)* (i), a, e *to give (up)*
abgelaufen *proceeded*
abgelehnt *rejected*
abgerundet *rounded*
abgeschliffen *ground, rubbed down*
abgeschlossen *finished*
abgeschnitten *cut, trimmed*
abgetrennt *divided*
abheben *(sep.),* o, o *to withdraw, emphasize*
abholen *(sep.) to collect*
das Abitur *Abitur*
die Abkürzung (-en) *abbreviation*
ablaufen *(sep.)* (äu), ie, au (sein) *to proceed*
ablehnen *(sep.) to reject*
abnehmen *(sep.)* (nimmt ab), nahm ab, abgenommen *to administer, decrease*
der Abnehmer (-) *customer, purchaser*
der Abnehmerkreis (-e) *customers*
abrunden *(sep.) to round (off)*
ABS = Antiblockiersystem *(antilock system)*
die Absage (-n) *rejection*
der Absatz (¨e) *sale(s)*
die Absatzplanung *sales planning*
abschleifen *(sep.),* schliff ab, abgeschliffen *to grind/rub down*
abschließen *(sep.),* schloß ab, abgeschlossen *to lock, finish*
der Abschluß (-üsse) *qualification*
das Abschlußzeugnis (-se) *leaving certificate*
abschneiden *(sep.),* schnitt ab, abgeschnitten *to trim, do (well)*
absetzen *(sep.) to sell*
absolut *absolute(ly), complete(ly)*
die Abstimmung (-en) *agreement*
die Abteilung (-en) *department*
abtragen *(sep.)* (ä), u, a *to erode*
abtrennen *(sep.) to divide, separate*
abwaschbar *washable*
die Abwicklung (-en) *processing, administering, administration*
die Access *Access (card)*
ach *oh*
acht *eight*
achten *to respect;* achten auf *to pay attention to, note*
das Achten *respecting, paying attention*
achtundzwanzig *twenty-eight*
der Ackerschlepper (-) *tractor*
adäquat *suitable*
die Administrierung (-en) *administration*
die Adresse (-n) *address*
die AEG = Allgemeine Elektricitäts-Gesellschaft
das Afrika *Africa*
die AG *(comparable with) Plc (see* Aktiengesellschaft)
die Agentur (-en) *agency*

ähnlich *similar*
der, die, das Ähnliche (-n) *(the) similar (thing/one)*
die Akademie (-n) *academy, college*
die Akte (-n) *file*
die Aktie (-n) *share*
die Aktiengesellschaft (-en) *public company, joint-stock company*
aktiv *active*
die Aktivität (-en) *activity*
aktuell *current(ly), up to date*
die Akzeptanzstelle (-n) *outlet*
akzeptieren *to accept*
all, alle, allem, allen, aller, alles *(to/from/for/of) all, every;* alle *everybody;* alles *everything, all;* alles andere *everything else;* vor allem *above all, mainly, first and foremost, particularly;* aller Art *every type/kind;* alles klar *okay*
die Allee (-n) *avenue*
allein(e) *alone, only itself, however*
alleinig *sole, only*
allerdings *of course, (al)though, admittedly, however*
das Allerheiligen *All Saints' Day*
allgemein *general(ly), in general*
als *when, as, than;* sowohl...als auch *both...and;* als letztes *finally;* mehr als *more than*
also *so, therefore, that is, well, ie*
alt *old*
das Altbundesland (¨er) *Land of the former West Germany*
der Altbundesländer (-) *person from the old FRG, Wessi*
das Alter (-) *age*
älter (als) *older (than)*
altersbedingt *related to old age*
am = an dem *(see an)*
das Amerika *America*
der Amerikaner (-) *American (one)*
AMK = Ausstellungs-Messe-Kongress-GmbH
der Ammersee *(Lake) Ammersee*
amtlich *official(ly)*
an *at, on, onto, to, of, by, in (see also sep. verbs with an);* am Anfang *at the beginning, initially;* am Freitag *on Friday;* am besten *the best;* am Bankwesen *in banking*
die Analyse (-n) *analysis*
anbelangen *(sep.) to concern*
anbelangt *concerns, concerned*
anberaumen *(sep.) to plan*
anberaumt *planned*
anbieten *(sep.),* o, o *to offer, sell*
der Anbieter (-) *supplier*
anbringen *(sep.),* brachte an, angebracht *to bring, fix, attach*
andere, anderem, anderen, anderer, anderes *(to/from/for/of) other(s);* aus den Fehlern anderer *from the mistakes of others*
der, die, das andere *(the) other (one)*
ändern *to change, alter*
anders *different(ly);* anders als alle anderen *different from all the others*

anderswo *somewhere else*
andienen *(sep.) to force on*
anerkannt *recognized*
anerkennen *(sep.), a, a to recognize*
anfallen *(sep.) (fällt an), fiel an, angefallen (sein) to occur, accumulate, be obtained*
der Anfang (¨e) *start, beginning*
anfangen *(sep.) (ä), i, a to begin*
die Anforderung (-en) *requirement*
die Anfrage (-n) *enquiry*
die Angabe (-n) *specification*
angeben *(sep.) (i), gab an, angegeben to give, specify, boast*
das Angebot (-e) *offer, product range, proposal; Angebot an range of*
angebracht *attached, appropriate*
angedient *forced on*
angefangen *begun*
angehängt *associated with*
angehend *prospective*
die Angelegenheit (-en) *matter*
das Angeln *angling, fishing*
angenehm *pleasant, convenient*
angenommen *assumed*
angereist *arrived*
angeschaut *looked at*
angeschlossen *connected, followed*
angestellt *employed*
der/die Angestellte *(sing. gen. -n) (-n), ein Angestellter (the) employee (salaried), white-collar worker*
angewandt *applied (see anwenden)*
angucken *(sep.) to look (at)*
die Anhängerkupplung (-en) *tow bar*
anhängen *(sep.) to be associated with*
(sich) anhören *(sep.) to hear, listen to*
der Anlaß (¨sse) *occasion*
die Anlage (-n) *system, plant; Anlage Enclosure*
anlegen *(sep.) to invest*
das Anlegen *investment*
anmelden *(sep.) to register*
annähernd *almost, approximately*
annehmen *(sep.) (nimmt an), nahm an, angenommen to assume*
(sich) anpassen *(sep.) (an) to adapt (itself/oneself) (to)*
die Anpassung (-en) *fitting, adjustment*
anreisen *(sep.) (sein) to arrive*
der Anruf (-e) *(phone) call*
der Anrufbeantworter (-) *answerphone*
anrufen *(sep.), ie, u to ring up, call*
der Anrufer (-) *caller*
ans = an das
sich anschauen *(sep.) to look at, inspect*
anschließen *(sep.), schloß an, angeschlossen to connect*
sich anschließen *(sep.), schloß an, angeschlossen to have the same*
anschließend *then, finally*
der Anschluß (¨sse) *connection*
anschreiben *(sep.), ie, ie to write to*
die Anschrift (-en) *address*
(sich) ansehen *(sep.) (ie), sah an, angesehen to look at, regard*

ansonsten *otherwise*
ansprechen *(sep.) (i), a, o to speak to, mention, address*
der Anspruch (¨e) *claim, approach*
anspruchsvoll *sophisticated*
anstellen *(sep.) to employ*
der Anteil (-e) *proportion, share, holding*
der Antrag (¨e) *application (form)*
die Antwort (-en) *answer*
anwenden *(sep.), wandte an, angewandt to apply*
die Anzahl (-en) *number*
die Anzeige (-n) *advertisement*
anzubieten *see anbieten*
der Anzug (¨e) *suit*
anzusehen *see ansehen*
der Aperitif (-s) *aperitif*
der Apfel (Äpfel) *apple*
die Apotheke (-n) *chemist, pharmacy*
der Apotheker (-) *chemist, pharmacist*
die Apothekerin (-nen) *chemist, pharmacist (f.)*
der Apparat (-e) *phone, extension, apparatus, equipment*
der Apparatebau *equipment construction*
der Appetit *appetite*
die Applikation (-en) *application*
der April (-e) *April; im April in April*
die Arbeit (-en) *work, job, task*
arbeit' = arbeite
arbeiten *to work*
das Arbeiten *work, working*
die Arbeitskraft (¨e) *worker, wage earner*
der Architekt *(sing. gen. -en) (-en) architect*
Argentinien *Argentina*
argentinisch *Argentinian*
der Ärger *anger, trouble*
die Armaturen *(pl.) accessories, fittings*
die Art (-en) *kind, way, sort, type*
der Artikel (-) *article, product, item*
das Arzneimittel (-) *drug*
der Arzt (¨e) *doctor*
die Ärztin (-nen) *doctor (f.)*
Asien *Asia*
der Aspekt (-e) *aspect*
der Assistent *(sing. gen. -en) (-en) assistant*
die Assistentin (-nen) *assistant (f.)*
das Atelier (-s) *atelier, studio*
der Atlantikdorsch (-e) *Atlantic cod*
die Atmosphäre (-n) *atmosphere*
attraktiv *attractive*
der, die, das attraktivste *(the) most attractive (one)*
auch *also, as well, either, again; sowohl...als auch both...and; oder aber auch or else*
auf *on (to), in (to), to, for, at (see also sep. verbs with auf); auf die Dauer in the long term; auf welchen Namen in whose name; auf keinen Fall certainly not; auf dem Gebiet in the area; auf der Welt in existence; auf Grund der*

because of the; von rund...auf *from about...to*
aufbauen *(sep.) to construct, build*
das Aufbauen *construction, erection*
aufbewahren *(sep.) to keep, look after*
aufbringen *(sep.), brachte auf, aufgebracht to find, summon up*
der Aufenthalt (-e) *stay*
auffallen *(sep.) (ä), fiel auf, aufgefallen (sein) to notice; mir ist aufgefallen I noticed*
die Aufgabe (-n) *task, job, function*
das Aufgabengebiet (-e) *area of responsibility*
aufgebaut *built, erected*
aufgefallen *noticed*
aufgegriffen *taken up*
die Aufgeschlossenheit *receptiveness*
aufgestapelt *stacked up*
aufgreifen *(sep.), griff auf, aufgegriffen to take up; BP hat dieses Thema aufgegriffen BP addressed this issue*
aufklappen *(sep.) to open (up)*
der Aufkleber (-) *sticker*
aufmachen *(sep.) to open*
aufmerksam *alert*
die Aufmerksamkeit (-en) *attention*
aufnehmen *(sep.) (nimmt auf), nahm auf, aufgenommen to take up; nehmen Sie...Kontakt auf get in touch*
der Aufschwung (¨e) *upswing, upturn*
der Aufsichtsrat (¨e) *supervisory board*
aufstapeln *(sep.) to stack up*
aufsteigen *(sep.), ie, ie (sein) to climb up, move up, be upgraded*
aufstellen *(sep.) to set up*
auftauchen *(sep.) (sein) to surface*
aufteilen *(sep.) to divide up*
der Auftrag (¨e) *order, commission; Aufträge tätigen to generate orders*
das Auftreten *occurrence, appearance*
auftreten *(sep.) (tritt auf), a, e (sein) to occur, arise, appear*
aufwendig *expensive, complex*
die Aufwendung (-en) *expense; entsprechend auch hoch die Aufwendungen dafür the costs (expenditure) are equally great*
der Aufzug (¨e) *lift*
der Augenblick (-e) *moment*
der August (-e) *August*
aus *from, out of, made of (see also sep. verbs with aus); aus den Fehlern anderer from the mistakes of others; aus meiner Erfahrung from my experience; in England ist man auf den praktischen Aspekt aus, daß in England people are geared to the practical aspect that; aus Fernost from the Far East*
ausbilden *(sep.) to train, educate*

die Ausbildung (-en) *education, training*

sich auseinandersetzen (*sep.*) (mit) *to discuss, address an issue*

die Ausfuhr (-en) *export*

die Ausführung (-en) *model, design*

ausfüllen (*sep.*) *to fill in*

die Ausgabe (-n) *expenditure, edition*

die Ausgangszeit (-en) *departure*

ausgeben (*sep.*) (i), a, e *to pay out, spend; das viele Geld auszugeben to spend all that money*

ausgefüllt *filled in*

ausgehen (*sep.*), ging aus, ausgegangen (sein) (von) *to start out (from), proceed on the basis of*

ausgehend (von) *departing (from)*

ausgenutzt *used, made use of*

ausgeprägt *developed*

ausgesehen *looked like, appeared*

ausgesprochen *exceptional(ly), really*

ausgestattet *equipped*

ausgewählt *selected, chosen*

der Ausgleich (-e) *balance*

ausgleichen (*sep.*), i, i *to make up for, compensate for*

die Auskunft (¨e) *directory enquiries, information*

ausländisch *foreign*

die Auslandsvertretung (-en) *foreign agent/representative*

ausnutzen (*sep.*) *to use, exploit*

sich ausprägen (*sep.*) *to be present/developed; die Hierarchie ist nicht so dominant ausgeprägt the hierarchy is not so strongly developed*

ausreichen (*sep.*) *to be sufficient*

ausreichend *sufficient, enough*

die Ausrüstung (-en) *equipment*

ausschließlich *exclusive(ly)*

ausschreiben (*sep.*), ie, ie *to invite tenders for*

der Ausschuß (¨sse) *committee, confederation*

aussehen (*sep.*) (ie), a, e *to look (like), appear; es sieht gut aus it looks good*

außen *outside, exterior, external(ly)*

der Außenhandel *export(s)*

außenstehend *outside, external*

außer *except (for)*

außerdem *besides, in addition, also*

außerhalb *outside*

äußerst *extremely*

die Aussicht (-en) *prospect; nicht in Aussicht gestellt not on the cards*

ausstatten (*sep.*) (mit) *to equip (with)*

ausstellen (*sep.*) *to exhibit*

der Aussteller (-) *exhibitor*

die Ausstellung (-en) *exhibition*

das Australien *Australia*

ausüben (*sep.*) *to practise, carry out*

die Auswahl (-en) *selection, choice*

auswählen (*sep.*) *to select*

der Ausweis (-e) *identity card, papers*

auswerten (*sep.*) *to evaluate*

die Auswertung (-en) *analysis*

auszahlen (*sep.*) *to pay out; sich Geld auszahlen lassen to withdraw money*

sich auszeichnen (durch) (*sep.*) *to be characterized/marked (by)*

der/die Auszubildende (*sing. gen.* -n) (-n), ein Auszubildender *trainee, apprentice*

auszugeben *see* ausgeben

autark *self-sufficient(ly)*

das Auto (-s) *car*

die Autobahn (-en) *motorway, autobahn*

die Auto-Extras (*pl.*) *car accessories*

das Autofahren *driving (a car)*

der Autofahrer (-) *driver*

die Automatik (-en) *automatic transmission/gearbox*

automatisch *automatic(ally)*

das Automobil (-e) *automobile, car*

die Autopapiere (*pl.*) *car papers*

der Azubi (-s) = Auszubildende

B

das Bad (¨er) *bath(room), spa*

die Bahn (-en) *train, rail, railway*

der Bahnhof (¨e) *station*

bald *soon*

der Ballast (-e) *ballast*

banal *banal*

die Bank (¨e) *bench*

die Bank (-en) *bank*

das Bankgeschäft (-e) *banking (business/transaction)*

die Bankkauffrau (-en) *bank clerk (f.)*

der Bankkaufmann (¨er) *bank clerk (m.)*

die Bankleitzahl (-en) *bank sort code*

das Bankwesen *banking*

BAP = Betriebs- und Absatzplanung

bar *cash*

das Bargeld *cash*

bargeldlos *cashless*

das Basilikum *basil*

die Batterie (-n) *battery*

der Bau (-ten) *construction, building*

das Bauelement (-e) *component*

bauen *to build, construct, produce*

der Baum (¨e) *tree*

die Baustoffmaschinen (*pl.*) *construction-materials machines*

der *or* das Bauteil (-e) *component*

das Bauwerk (-e) *building*

das Bauwesen *construction*

der Bayer (*sing. gen.* -n) (-n) *Bavarian*

bayerisch *Bavarian*

Bayern *Bavaria*

der Bazillus (Bazillen) *bacterium, bug*

beachten *to take note of*

beantworten *to answer*

bearbeiten *to machine, process, work, approach/deal with; der lokale Markt muß speziell bearbeitet werden the local*

market must be approached in a special way

bearbeitet *machined, approached*

die Bearbeitung (-en) *machining, processing, craftsmanship*

die Bearbeitungsmaschine (-n) *machine tool*

das Bearbeitungszentrum (-zentren) *machining centre*

beauftragen *to commission*

der Bedarf (-e) (an) *need (for)*

bedeuten *to mean*

bedeutend *significant, important*

die Bedeutung (-en) *meaning, importance*

bedienen *to serve*

der Bediener (-) *operator*

bedienungsfreundlich *user-friendly*

die Bedingung (-en) *condition*

beeindrucken *to impress*

beeindruckt *impresses, impressed*

die Beere (-n) *berry*

befallen *to overcome, assail*

sich befassen (mit) *to be concerned (with)*

sich befinden, a, u *to be (located)*

befolgen *to follow*

die Befragung (-en) *survey, opinion poll*

begann *began (see* beginnen*)*

begeistert *fanatical(ly), enthusiastic*

der Beginn (-e) *beginning, start*

beginnen, a, o *to begin*

begleiten *to accompany*

begreifen, begriff, begriffen *to understand, realize*

begreiflich *understandable; begreiflich machen to explain*

begrüßen *to greet, welcome*

behandeln *to treat*

behandelt *treats, treated*

beherrschen *to master*

behilflich *helpful; gerne sind wir behilflich we are pleased to help*

die Behinderten-Einrichtungen (*pl.*) *facilities/toilets for the disabled*

die Behörde (-n) *authority*

bei *at, near, with, for, when, in the case of, on the point of (see also* beifügen*); bei uns in our/the company; bei Ihnen (for/from/to/ with) you; beim Essen at lunch; bei Sport in the case of sport; bei der Verarbeitung during processing; bei Tag und bei Nacht day and night; bei der Firma Price Waterhouse at Price Waterhouse; beim Besichtigen der Betriebe when looking round the businesses*

beide(s) *both*

beifügen (*sep.*) *to enclose*

die Beilage (-n) *side-dish*

beim = bei dem (*see* bei)

das Bein (-e) *leg*

beinhalten *to include*

das Beispiel (-e) *example; zum Beispiel for example, eg*

beispielsweise *for example*
bekannt *well-known, familiar*
bekanntgeben (sep.) (i), a, e *to make known, inform*
bekanntgegeben *made known*
die Bekleidung *clothing, garment(s)*
bekommen, a, o *to get, receive; daß kaum Zimmer zu bekommen sind that there are scarcely any rooms to be had*
sich belaufen (äu), ie, au (auf) *to amount (to)*
die Belegschaft (-en) *team, workforce*
das Belgien *Belgium*
beliebig *any, to your requirements*
beliebt *popular*
bemerken *to note, notice*
bemerkt *notes, notices, noted, noticed*
die Bemerkung (-en) *remark*
bemühen *to bother*
sich bemühen (um) *to try (to obtain)*
benachrichtigen *to inform*
benötigen *to require, be necessary*
benutzen/benützen *to use*
die Benutzerdaten (pl.) *user data*
das Benzin (-e) *petrol*
beraten (ä), ie, a *to advise, give advice*
beraten *advise, advised*
der Berater (-) *adviser, consultant*
die Beraterin (-nen) *adviser, consultant (f.)*
die Beratung (-en) *consultancy, service*
die Beratungsfunktion (-en) *advisory function*
berechnen *to calculate*
der Bereich (-e) *area, sector, industry*
die Bereitstellung (-en) *loading*
der Berg (-e) *mountain*
der Bericht (-e) *report*
berieseln *to sprinkle*
berieselt *sprinkles, sprinkled*
Berliner *of Berlin, Berlin*
berücksichtigen *to take account of*
der Beruf (-e) *job, trade, profession*
beruflich *professional(ly); berufliche Tätigkeit job*
die Berufsausbildung (-en) *vocational training*
das Berufsbild (-er) *job (description)*
die Berufsorganisation (-en) *professional/trade organization*
die Berufsschule (-n) *vocational (training) college*
berühmt *famous*
besäumen *to edge*
besäumt *edges, edged*
beschäftigen *to employ, occupy*
sich beschäftigen (mit) *to deal with, occupy/concern oneself with, do*
beschäftigt *employs, employed*
der/die Beschäftigte (sing. gen. -n) (-n), ein Beschäftigter *(the) employed person, employee; die Beschäftigten workforce*

der Bescheid (-e) *information, message; Bescheid sagen to tell, inform*
die Bescheidenheit (-en) *modesty*
beschicken (mit) *to load (with)*
beschickt *loads, loaded*
beschränken *to restrict*
beschränkt *limited*
beschreiben, ie, ie *to describe*
das Besichtigen *tour*
besichtigen *to inspect, tour*
der Besitzer (-) *holder, owner*
der, die, das besondere *(the) special (one)*
der, die, das Besondere *(the) special thing/one*
die Besonderheit (-en) *special feature; es gibt Besonderheiten in den Nuancen there are special nuances*
besonders *particularly, especially*
besorgen *to obtain, get*
besprechen (i), a, o *to discuss*
die Besprechung (-en) *meeting*
besser (als) *better (than)*
der, die, das beste *(the) best (one/thing)*
bestehen, bestand, bestanden *to be, exist; bestehen aus to consist of*
bestellen *to book, order, appoint*
bestellt *orders, ordered, booked*
die Bestellung (-en) *order*
am besten *best*
bestimmen *to establish, determine*
bestimmt *establishes, established*
bestimmt *particular(ly), certain(ly)*
die Bestimmung (-en) *regulation, rule*
der Besuch (-e) *visit*
besuchen *to visit*
der Besucher (-) *visitor*
der Besucherausweis (-e) *visitor's pass*
die Besucherin (-nen) *visitor (f.)*
der/die Besuchte (sing. gen. -n) (-n), ein Besuchter *person visited*
sich beteiligen (an) *to take part (in)*
die Beteiligung (-en) (an) *investment, stake, holding (in)*
beten *to pray, ask*
betonen *to emphasize*
die Betonung (-en) *emphasis*
der Betrag (⏜e) *amount (of money)*
betragen (ä), u, a *to amount to, be*
betreffen (betrifft), betraf, betroffen *to affect, concern*
betreffend *concerned*
betreiben, ie, ie *to pursue; hier wird ganz bewußt Importförderung betrieben imports are promoted quite consciously here*
betreuen *to take care of, support*
betreut *supports, supported*
die Betreuung *(customer) support*
der Betrieb (-e) *business, company, firm*
betrieben *carried out*
das Betriebsklima (-s) *working atmosphere*
die Betriebsplanung (-en) *operations planning*
der Betriebsrat (⏜e) *works council*

die Betriebswirtschaft *business studies/administration, macro-economics*
bevor *before*
sich bewähren *to prove oneself/itself*
bewährt *proven, established*
bewegen *to move*
sich bewegen *to move, operate, range*
bewegt *moves, moved, operated*
sich bewerben (i), bewarb, beworben (an) *to apply (to)*
der Bewerber (-) *applicant*
die Bewerbung (-en) *application*
der Bewohner (-) *citizen*
beworben *applied*
bewußt *conscious, intentional(ly)*
das Bewußtsein *awareness, consciousness*
bezahlen *to pay*
beziehungsweise (bzw.) *or (rather)*
der Bezug (⏜e) *reference; in Bezug auf with respect/reference to*
Bhf. = Bahnhof
das Bier (-e) *beer, lager*
bieten, o, o *to offer, present*
sich bieten, o, o *to present it/him/herself*
das Bild (-er) *picture, image; wir machen uns ein Bild über we gain an idea/impression of*
die Bild(-Zeitung) *Bild (national newspaper, tabloid)*
bilden *to form*
die Bildung *education, culture*
billig *cheap, cost-effective, low-cost*
bin *am (see sein); ich bin Ingenieur I am an engineer; ich bin gefahren I went*
der Binnenmarkt (⏜e) *internal/single market; europäischer Binnenmarkt single European market*
bis *until, till, (up) to, through, before, by; bis zu up to; bis zum Beginn to the start; bis hin zum through to the; bis jetzt up to now; vom...bis zum from...to*
bisher *up to now*
bisherig *previous(ly), up to now*
bißchen: ein bißchen *a (little) bit*
bislang *up to now*
bitte *please; bitte (schön) you're welcome; bitte schön you're welcome, here you are; bitte schön? yes, can I help you?*
die Bitte (-n) *request*
bitten, bat, gebeten (um) *to ask (for)*
das Blatt (⏜er) *leaf, piece, sheet, page*
der Blattsalat (-e) *lettuce*
der Blattspinat *spinach*
bleiben, ie, ie (sein) *to stay, remain*
blicken (auf/in) *to look (to/into)*
blieben *remained (see bleiben)*
das Blümchen (-) *little flower*
das Boot (-e) *boat*
die Boot/boot *Boat Show*
die Bootmesse (-n) *boat exhibition/show*
der Bord: an Bord *on board (ship)*

168

die Botschaft (-en) *message, embassy*
die Boulevardzeitung (-en) *tabloid*
brachten *brought (see bringen)*
die Branche (-n) *sector*
das Brasilien *Brazil*
braten (ä), ie, a *to fry*
brauch' = brauche
brauchen *to need, require*
bräucht' = bräuchte
BRD = Bundesrepublik
  Deutschland *FRG*
breit *wide*
die Breite (-n) *width*
der Breitreifen *wide tyre*
brennen, brannte, gebrannt *to
  burn*
das Brennholz *firewood*
der Brennstoffhandelsverband *fuel
  traders' association*
der Brief (-e) *letter*
bring' = bringe
bringen, brachte, gebracht *to
  bring; bringen auf to achieve*
britisch *British*
die Broschüre (-n) *brochure*
das Brot (-e) *bread*
die Brücke (-n) *bridge*
die Brühe (-n) *consommé*
die Brust (¨e) *chest, breast*
die Brustprothesen (*pl.*) *artificial
  breasts*
brutto *gross*
der BTX = Bildschirmtext *interactive
  videotext*
büßen *to pay/atone (for)*
das Buch (¨er) *book*
buchen *to book*
der Buchhalter (-) *bookkeeper/
  accountant*
die Buchhalterin *bookkeeper/
  accountant (f.)*
die Buchhaltung *accounts/book-
  keeping department*
der Buchstabe (*sing. gen.* -ns) (-n)
  letter (of the alphabet)
buchstabieren *to spell*
das Budget (-s) *budget*
das Buffet (-s) *buffet*
das Bulgarien *Bulgaria*
der Bund (¨e) *federation*
die Bundesbahn *German (lit. Federal)
  Railway, railway, rail*
die Bundesbank (-en) *Bundesbank,
  central bank (lit. federal bank)*
das Bundesgebiet (-e) *Federal Republic*
das Bundesland (¨er) *(federal) Land/
  state*
die Bundespost *(German lit. Federal)
  Post Office*
der Bundesrat (¨e) *Bundesrat, upper
  house*
die Bundesrepublik *Federal Republic*
die Bundesstelle (-n) *federal office*
der Bundestag *Bundestag, lower house*
der Bundesverband (¨e) *federal
  association*
bunt *bright, brightly coloured; bunt
  gemischt (lit. colourfully) mixed*

bürgen *to stand surety*
die Bürgschaft (-en) *surety*
das Büro (-s) *office*
die Bürokauffrau (-en) *office
  clerk/clerical worker (f.)*
der Bürokaufmann (¨er) *office
  clerk/clerical worker (m.)*
die Bürokraft (¨e) *office clerk/clerical
  worker*
die Bürokratie (-n) *bureaucracy*
der Bus (-se) *bus, coach*
Buß-: Buß- und Bettag *day of
  penitence*
die Butter *butter*
die BVG = Berliner Verkehrsgesellschaft, *now* Verkehrsbetriebe
bzw. = beziehungsweise

C

ca. = circa *about (see also zirka)*
das Café (-s) *café*
die CDH = Centralvereinigung
  Deutscher Handelsvertreter-
  und Handelsmakler-Verbände
  *Federation of German Commercial
  Agents and Brokers*
der Chairman (Chairmen) *chairman*
der Champagner (-) *champagne*
der Champignon (-s) *mushroom*
die Chance (-n) *chance*
charakterisieren *to characterize*
die Chemie *chemicals (industry)*
der Chemiekonzern (-e) *chemicals
  company*
die Chemikalie (-n) *chemical*
chemisch *chemical*
das Chile *Chile*
das China *China*
der Chip (-s) *chip (computer)*
circa *approximately, around, about*
der Club (-s) *club*
CNC *computerized numerical
  control*
Co. *Co. (company)*
der Cocktail (-s) *cocktail*
die Cognacsauce (-n) *cognac sauce*
der Computer (-) *computer*
computergesteuert *computer
  controlled, computerized*
die Creme (-s) *cream*
die Crevette (-n) *prawn*
die Currysahne (-n) *curry cream*

D

d. = der
D = Deutschland
das D-Netz (-e) *mobile phone network*
da *here, there, since, because*
dabei *with you, during this (process)*
dafür *for it/them, that is why*
daher *therefore, hence*
damals *at that time, then*
die Dame (-n) *woman, lady*
damit *with it/them/this, so (that)*
der Damm (¨e) *dyke, road*
dämpfen *to steam*

die Dämpfgrube (-n) *steam vat*
die Dampfmaschinen (*pl.*) *steam
  engines/machines*
danach *after that/this*
das Dänemark *Denmark*
der Dank *thanks, gratitude;* vielen/
  herzlichen Dank *many thanks*
danke *thank you;* danke
  sehr/schön *thank you (very
  much)*
danken *to thank;* ich danke
  herzlich *thank you very much*
dann *then, also*
daran *at/on/about/in it/them*
darauf *on/of it/them;* sich darauf
  einstellen *to adapt to that*
daraus *out of it/them, from it/them*
darf *may (see dürfen)*
darf's = darf es
darin *in it/them*
darstellen (*sep.*) *to show, present*
darüber *over/about it/them;
  darüber hinaus additionally*
darum *about (it/them/that);* es
  ging darum *it was about*
das *the, this, that, these, which, who
  (see der);* was ist das? *what is
  it/that?* das ist *this is;* sind das...?
  are they...? das heißt *that is, ie*
daß *that; so daß so that;* ich hoffe,
  daß *I hope that*
die Daten (*pl.*) *data*
das Datenendgerät (-e) *data terminal*
die Datenerfassung (-en) *data
  acquisition*
das Datenerfassungsgerät (-e) *data-
  acquisition unit, hand-held
  computer*
die Datensicherheit *data security*
die Datenverarbeitung *data
  processing*
die Datenverarbeitungszentrale (-n)
  data-processing centre
das Datum *date*
die Dauer *period of time*
dauern *to last, take;* wie lange
  dauern die Lehre? *how long does
  the training last?*
davon *about/of it/them;* davon
  überzeugt, daß *convinced that*
dazu *in addition (to it/them), for/to
  it/this/that, with*
dazugehören (*sep.*) *to belong to*
dazugehörend *belonging to*
die DDR = Deutsche Demokratische
  Republik *GDR*
deck' = decke
das Deckblatt (¨er) *cover page/sheet*
decken *to cover, finance (see also
  abdecken)*
dein *your (familiar)*
dem *(to/from) the/whom, which (see
  der)*
demnächst *soon*
die Demokratie (-n) *democracy*
demokratisch *democratic(ally)*
demonstrieren *to demonstrate*
den *the, which, whom (see der)*

denen *(to) which/whom, those*
denken, dachte, gedacht *to think;*
   denken an *to think about/of*
denn *as, because, for, then*
dennoch *still*
dental *dental*
der *the, this, who, which, it, that,*
   he; einen Zug, der *a train which*
die Deregulierung (-en) *deregulation*
deren *their, whose, of which*
dergleichen *that kind of (thing)*
derjenige, diejenige, dasjenige,
   diejenigen (pl.) *the person (who)*
derzeit *at present*
des *of the, which, whom (see* der)
deshalb *therefore*
das Design (-s) *design*
dessen *his, its, whose, of which/that*
desto: je...desto *the...the*
deswegen *therefore, because of*
das Detail (-s) *detail*
deutlich *significant(ly), clear(ly)*
deutsch *German*
das Deutsch *German*
das Deutsch *German (language)*
der/die Deutsche *(sing. gen.* -n) (-n), ein
   Deutscher *(the) German*
   (person/thing/one)
das Deutschland *Germany*
der Dezember (-) *December*
   Di. = Dienstag
dich *you (* familiar)
die *the, this, those, who, which, it,*
   that, she, they (see der)
der Dienst (-e) *service*
der Dienstag (-e) *Tuesday*
dienstags *on Tuesdays*
der Dienstleister (-) *service company*
die Dienstleistung (-en) *service*
dies, diese, diesem, diesen, dieser,
   dieses *(to/from/for/of) this/these,*
   this/these (thing(s)/one(s))
die Dieselmotorisierung (-en)
   diesel engine/power
digital *digital(ly)*
der Dillschaum *dill sauce*
   DIN = Deutsche Industrienorm
das Ding (-e) *thing, function*
   Dipl.-Ing. = Diplom-Ingenieur
   Dipl.-Kfm. = Diplom-Kaufmann
das Diplom (-e) *degree, diploma*
der Diplom-Ingenieur (-e)
   engineer
die Diplom-Ingenieurin (-nen)
   engineer (f.)
die Diplom-Kaufleute *sales people*
der Diplom-Kaufmann (¨er)
   salesman, business-school
   graduate
direkt *direct(ly)*
direkter (als) *more direct(ly)*
   (than)
die Direktion (-en) *management,*
   manager's office
die Direktionsabteilung (-en)
   administrative department
die Disko (-s) *disco*
die Diskretion *confidentiality*

die Diskussion (-en) *discussion*
diskutieren *to discuss*
diskutiert *discusses, discussed*
der/das Display (-s) *display*
divers *diverse, different, various*
   DM = Deutsche Mark
die D-Mark (-) *(German) mark*
   Do. = Donnerstag
doch *yet, but, nevertheless, certainly*
der Doktor (-en) *doctor*
dokumentieren *to document*
der Dollar (-s) *dollar*
die Domäne (-n) *domain*
dominant *dominant(ly)*
der Donnerstag (-e) *Thursday;* am
   Donnerstag *on Thursday*
donnerstags *on Thursdays*
das Doppelzimmer (-) *double room*
das Dorf (¨er) *village*
dort *there*
   Dr. (= Doktor) *Dr*
   Dr. med. *Dr of medicine*
der Draht (¨e) *wire, line*
das Drahterodieren *(CNC) wire*
   cutting
die Drahterodiermaschine (-n)
   wire cutting machine
dran = daran
dranbleiben (sep.), ie, ie (sein) *to*
   hold the line
drauf = darauf
die Drehbank (¨e) *lathe*
drehen *to turn*
sich drehen (um) *to revolve around*
das Drehen *turning*
die Drehmaschine (-n) *lathe*
drei *three*
dreieinhalb *three and a half*
dreimal *three times*
dreißig *thirty*
der, die, das dreizehnte *(the) thirteenth*
Dresdner *of Dresden, Dresden*
der Dresdner *person from Dresden*
das Dressing (-s) *dressing*
drin = darin
dringend *urgent(ly)*
der, die, das dritte *(the) third (one)*
das/ein Drittel (-) *third*
der Druck *pressure*
der Drucker (-) *printer*
die Druckerei *printer, printing*
drunter *under*
du *you (* familiar)
das Dualsystem (-e) *dual system*
durch *through, by, on the basis of*
   (see also sep. verbs with durch)
durchaus *thoroughly, definitely*
durchdacht *thought through*
durchdenken, durchdachte,
   durchdacht *to think through*
durchführen (sep.) *to carry out*
durchgehen (sep.), ging durch,
   durchgegangen (sein) *to go*
   through
durchgestanden *went/gone through*
durchstehen (sep.), stand durch,
   durchgestanden *to go through*
durchstellen (sep.) *to put through*

die Durchwahl (-en) *direct line*
dürfen (a), u, u *to be allowed to, to*
   have to, may, must; darf nicht
   must not
die Dusche (-n) *shower*
Düsseldorfer *(of) Düsseldorf*

E

eben *just, after all, precisely*
ebenfalls *also*
ebenso *just as, as well*
echt *genuine(ly), really*
das Eck (-e) *corner*
die Ecke (-n) *corner*
die EDEM = Electrical Discharge and
   Electrode Milling *(machine)*
die EDM = Electrical Discharge
   Machining
   EG = Erdgeschoß *(ground floor)*
die EG = Europäische Gemeinschaft
   EC (European Community)
ehe *before*
ehemalig *former*
eher *rather, more*
das Ei (-er) *egg*
eigen, eigene, eigenem, eigenen,
   eigener, eigenes *(its, his, her,*
   their) own, unique
die Eigenart (-en) *idiosyncrasy, quirk*
der Eigenbetrieb (-e) *public utility*
die Eigenentwicklung (-en) *in-house*
   development/innovation
die Eigenproduktion (-en) *in-house*
   production
die Eigenschaft (-en) *characteristic*
eigentlich *actually, really, rather*
der Eigner (-) *owner, proprietor*
der Eignungstest (-s) *aptitude test*
ein, eine, einem, einen, einer,
   eines *(to/from/for/of) a, one,*
   (the) right person, somebody (see
   also sep. verbs with ein)
die Einbahnstraße (-n) *one-way street*
der Einbau (-ten) *installation*
einbauen (sep.) *to install, build in*
einbringen (sep.), brachte ein,
   eingebracht *to (wish to)*
   incorporate/include, apply
eindeutschen (sep.) *to adapt to the*
   German market
eineinhalb *one and a half*
einfach *simple (-ly), really, easy*
   (-ily)
einfacher (als) *simpler, easier (than)*
einfallen (sep.) (ä), ie, a (sein) *to*
   think of, occur
einfangen (sep.) (ä), i, a *to captivate*
einführen (sep.) *to introduce, import*
der Eingang (¨e) *entrance, input*
die Eingangszeit (-en) *time of arrival*
eingebaut *built-in, installed*
eingeben (sep.) (i), a, e *to enter*
eingehen (sep.), ging ein,
   eingegangen (sein) (auf) *to go*
   into, give attention to
eingeladen *invited*
eingereicht *handed in*
eingeschickt *sent in*

eingeschränkt *restricted*
eingespannt *gripped, clamped*
eingetragen *registered*
die Einheit (-en) *unit, unity*
einige, einigem, einigen, einiger,
    einiges *(to/from/for/of) some*
der Einkauf (¨e) *purchase (department)*
einkaufen *(sep.)* *to purchase*
der Einkäufer (-) *buyer*
einladen *(sep.)* ä, u, a *to invite*
die Einladung (-en) *invitation*
einleiten *(sep.)* *to introduce, insert*
einlösen *(sep.)* *to cash*
einmal *once, really, first of all*
die Einnahme (-n) *receipts, income*
einnehmen *(sep.)* (nimmt ein),
    nahm ein, eingenommen
    to take up
einreichen *(sep.)* *to hand in, submit*
die Einrichtung (-en) *installation*
eins *one*
einschicken *(sep.)* *to send in*
einschränken *(sep.)* *to restrict*
einspannen *(sep.)* *to grip, clamp
    (into)*
einsparen *(sep.)* *to save*
die Einsparmöglichkeit (-en)
    possibility for cost-cutting
die Einsparung (-en) *economy, saving*
einstellen *(sep.)* *to adjust, employ*
sich einstellen (auf) *to adjust (oneself)
    (to)*
die Einstellung (-en) *adjustment,
    position*
einstufen *(sep.)* *to classify*
sich eintragen *(sep.)* (ä), u, a *to register*
eintreten *(sep.)* (tritt ein), trat ein,
    eingetreten (sein) *to enter*
der Eintritt (-e) *entry*
der Einwohner (-) *inhabitant*
einzeln *individual(ly), single*
das Einzelunternehmen (-) *single
    company*
das Einzelzimmer (-) *single room*
einzigartig *unique*
einzudeutschen *see eindeutschen*
die Eisenbahn (-en) *rail, railway*
elegant *elegant(ly)*
elektrisch *electrical(ly)*
die Elektrode (-n) *electrode*
der Elektrofilter (-) *electric filter*
die Elektronik *electronics*
elektronisch *electronic(ally)*
das Element (-e) *element*
elf *eleven*
der, die, das elfte *(the) eleventh (one)*
elitär *elitist*
der, die, das Elitäre *(the) elite thing/one*
elterlich *parental*
das Elternhaus (¨er) *family home*
emotional *emotional(ly)*
die Emotionalität (-en) *emotion-
    ality, emotional quality*
der Empfang (¨e) *reception*
empfangen (ä), i, a *to receive*
der Empfänger (-) *recipient, To*
die Empfangsdame (-n) *receptionist*

die Empfangssekretärin (-nen)
    receptionist
empfehlen (ie), a, o *to recommend*
empfinden, a, u *to feel*
die Endbearbeitung (-en)
    finishing
das Ende (-n) *end, finish*
enden *to end*
das Endgerät (-e) *terminal*
endlich *final(ly)*
die Energie (-n) *energy*
eng *tight(ly), close(ly), narrow*
das Engagement (-s) *commitment*
sich engagieren *to be involved,
    committed*
engagiert *committed, enthusiastic*
das England *England, Britain, UK*
der Engländer (-) *Englishman*
die Engländerin (-nen) *English-
    woman*
englisch *English, British*
entrinden *to strip (bark)*
sich entscheiden, ie, ie (für) *to decide
    (on)*
die Entscheidung (-en) *decision*
der Entscheidungsträger (-) *decision-
    maker, opinion leader*
entschieden *decided(ly),
    considerable*
sich entschließen, o, o *to decide*
entschlossen *decided*
sich entschuldigen *to apologize;*
    entschuldigen Sie *excuse me*
entsprechen (i), a, o *to correspond
    (to), conform (to)*
entsprechend *corresponding(ly), in
    accordance with*
entstanden *emerged (see
    entstehen)*
entstehen, entstand, entstanden
    (sein) *to emerge, come into being*
die Entstehungsgeschichte (-n)
    company history/origin
entweder...oder *either...or*
entwerten *to validate*
der Entwerter (-) *validator*
(sich) entwickeln *to develop, evolve*
das Entwickeln *development,
    developing*
entwickelnd *developing*
entwickelt *develops, developed*
der, die, das Entwickelte *(the)
    developed one/thing*
der Entwickler (-) *design engineer,
    inventor*
die Entwicklung (-en)
    development
das Entwicklungsland (¨er)
    developing country
er *he, it*
das Erachten *opinion; meines
    Erachtens in my opinion*
die Erde (-n) *earth*
das Erdgeschoß (-sse) *ground floor*
das Erdöl *oil*
das Ereignis (-se) *event*
erfahren (ä), u, a *to experience*

die Erfahrung (-en) *experience;
    aus/nach meiner Erfahrung
    from/in my experience*
die Erfassung (-en) *acquisition*
der Erfolg (-e) *success*
erfolgreich *successful(ly)*
erfordern *to demand*
erfordert *demands, demanded*
erfreulich *pleasing(ly), gratifying(ly)*
erfreulicherweise *happily*
sich ergeben (i), a, e *to result, arise*
das Ergebnis (-se) *result*
erhalten (ä), ie, a *to receive, obtain*
erhalten *receive, received*
sich erholen *to relax*
erklären *to explain*
die Erklärung (-en) *explanation*
sich erkundigen *to enquire*
erleben *to experience*
erleichtern *to make easy*
die Erleichterung (-en) *relief*
ermöglichen *to make possible*
ernst *serious(ly)*
die Ernte (-n) *harvest*
das Erodieren *(spark) erosion, EDM,
    electrical discharge machining*
erodieren *to erode*
die Erodiermaschine (-n) *(spark)
    erosion machine, EDM machine*
die Eröffnung (-en) *opening*
die Erosion (-en) *(spark) erosion,
    electrical discharge machining*
erreichen *to achieve, attain, reach*
erreicht *achieves, achieved*
erscheinen, ie, ie (sein) *to appear*
erschienen *appeared*
erst *first, only, not until*
der Erstaussteller (-) *first-time exhibitor*
der, die, das erste *(the) first (one)*
erstens *first of all, first(ly)*
erteilen *to give, place, commission*
erteilt *gives, given (see erteilen)*
der/die Erwachsene *(sing. gen. -n) (-n), ein
    Erwachsener adult*
(sich) erwarten *to expect, anticipate*
die Erwartung (-en) *expectation*
erweitern *to expand*
erweitert *expands, expanded*
die Erweiterung (-en) *expansion*
erwerben (i), a, o *to buy, purchase*
erwischen *to catch, get; wer
    von...erwischt wird anyone who
    catches (lit. is caught by)*
erwischt *catches, caught*
der, die, das Erwünschte *(the) desirable
    thing/one*
erzeugen *to produce, create, generate*
das Erzeugnis (-se) *product*
erzielen *to achieve, attain*
es *it, there; es gibt there is/are*
essen (ißt), aß, gegessen *to eat*
das Essen (-) *meal, food*
    Estland *Estonia*
sich etablieren *to get/become
    established*
die Etage (-n) *floor, storey*
    etc. *etc.*

etwa *approximately, around, about;*
in etwa *approximately*
etwas *something, anything, rather;*
etwas Ungewöhnliches
something unusual; etwas, was
something that
euch *(to) you (*familiar*)*
das Europa *Europe;* in ganz Europa *in*
the whole of Europe
europäisch *European*
europaweit *all over Europe*
der Euroscheck (-s) *Eurocheque*
e.V. = eingetragener Verein
eventuell *possible (-ly), any*
Examina *(pl.) exams*
die Ex-DDR *ex-GDR*
exklusiv *exclusive(ly)*
exotisch *exotic(ally)*
das Exponat (-e) *exhibit*
der Export (-e) *export*
der Exporteur (-e) *exporter*
exportieren *to export*
der Exportkaufmann (¨er) *export*
trader/salesman/clerk
der Exportleiter (-) *head of exports*
der Exportmarkt (¨e) *export market*
exportorientiert *export-oriented*

F

die Fabrik (-en) *factory*
der Fabrikant *(sing. gen. -en) (-en)*
manufacturer
das Fach (¨er) *subject, trade, specialist*
der Facharbeiter (-) *skilled worker*
die Fachmesse (-n) *(specialist) trade fair*
die Fachpresse (-n) *trade press*
die Fachzeitschrift (-en) *trade journal*
fähig *capable*
der Fahrausweis (-e) *ticket*
die Fähre (-n) *ferry*
das Fahren *driving*
fahren (ä), u, a (sein *or* haben) *to*
go (by vehicle), travel, drive, run;
ich bin gefahren *I went;* ich habe
gefahren *I've sailed*
der Fahrer (-) *driver*
die Fahrkarte (-n) *ticket*
die Fahrt (-en) *journey*
das Fahrzeug (-e) *vehicle*
der Faktor (-en) *factor*
der Fall (¨e) *case;* auf jeden Fall *in any*
case; auf keinen Fall *certainly not*
fallen (ä), ie, a (sein) *to fall, decrease*
falsch *false, wrong*
die Fama *reputation*
familiär *family, friendly*
die Familie (-n) *family*
die Familienplanung (-en) *family*
planning
fangen (ä), i, a *to catch*
fängt *see* fangen, anfangen
fantastisch *fantastic(ally)*
der Fasching (-e *or* -s) *carnival*
fast *almost, practical(ly)*
die Fastnacht *carnival*
das Fax (-e) *fax*
das Faxgerät (-e) *fax machine*
die Faxnummer (-n) *fax number*

die FAZ = Frankfurter Allgemeine
Zeitung
der Februar (-e) *February*
fehlen *to be lacking, be missing*
der Fehler (-) *mistake, error*
der Feiertag (-e) *public/bank holiday*
fein *fine, (very) good*
das Feld (-er) *field, area, sphere*
der Feldsalat (-e) *lamb's lettuce*
der Fendant *Fendant (white wine*
from the Swiss canton of
Valais)
das Fenster (-) *window*
der Fensterheber: elektrische
Fensterheber *electric windows*
der Fensterplatz (¨e) *window seat*
fern *far, distant, remote*
ferner *further*
Fernost *Far East*
fernsehen *(sep.) (ie), a, e to watch*
television
das Fernsehen *television*
der Fernsehfilm (-e) *television film*
der Fernsprecher (-) *telephone*
das Fernstudium *distance-learning*
degree course
fertig *finished, ready*
fertigen *to manufacture*
die Fertigung (-en) *manufacture*
die Fertigungskontrolle (-n)
production control
fest *fixed, firm(ly)*
festgestellt *established*
festlegen *(sep.) to lay down, establish*
die Festplatte (-n) *hard disk*
feststellen *(sep.) to establish, find*
festzulegen *see* festlegen
das Filet (-s) *fillet*
die Filiale (-n) *branch (office)*
der Film (-e) *film*
der Filter (-) *filter*
die Filteranlage (-n) *filter system*
die Finanz (-en) *finance, financial*
finanzieren *to finance*
die Finanzierung (-en) *finance*
find' = finde
finden, a, u *to find, consider*
(findet...statt *see* stattfinden*);*
das finde ich gut *I think that is*
good
sich finden, a, u *to be found*
fing *see* fangen, anfangen
die Firma *(Firmen) firm, company*
der Firmengründer (-) *company*
founder
der Fisch (-e) *fish*
fischen *to fish*
das Fischen *fishing*
die Fläche (-n) *surface, land, area, site*
die Flasche (-n) *bottle*
das Fleisch *meat*
flexibel *flexible (-ly)*
fliegen, o, o (sein) *to fly*
das Fliegen *flying*
der Flughafen (¨) *airport*
das Flugzeug (-e) *aeroplane, aircraft*
der Fluß *(Flüsse) river*
flüssig *liquid*

die Flüssigkeitspumpen *(pl.) liquid*
pumps
folgen (sein) *to follow;* einer
Einladung folgen *to accept an*
invitation
folgend *(the) following*
der Ford *Ford (car)*
fordern *to demand*
fördern *to promote, challenge*
die Fördertechnik *conveyor technology*
die Forderung (-en) *demand*
die Förderung (-en) *promotion*
die Form (-en) *shape, form, design,*
mould, die
der Formenbau *mould/die making*
das Formular (-e) *form*
formulieren *to formulate*
forschen *to research*
der Forscher (-) *researcher*
die Forschung (-en) *research*
der Forst (-e) *forest*
das Fotografieren *photography*
die Fotokopie (-n) *photocopy*
Fr. = Freitag
die Fracht (-en) *freight, load*
die Frage (-n) *question, issue, matter*
fragen *to ask (for), demand*
Frankfurter *of Frankfurt, Frankfurt*
das Frankreich *France*
der Franzose *(sing. gen. -n) (-n)*
Frenchman
die Französin (-nen) *Frenchwoman*
französisch *French*
fräsen *to mill*
die Fräsmaschine (-n) *milling machine*
die Frau (-en) *woman, wife, Mrs, Ms*
das Fräulein *(- or -s) young woman,*
Miss
frei *free (of charge), vacant*
freiberuflich *self-employed*
der Freitag (-e) *Friday*
freitags *on Fridays*
die Freizeit (-en) *leisure (time)*
fremd *foreign*
der/die Fremde *(sing. gen. -n) (-n) foreign*
person, stranger
die Fremde *foreign parts, abroad*
der Fremdenverkehr *tourism*
der Fremdenverkehrsverein (-e)
tourist office
die Fremdfirma (-firmen)
(foreign/outside/another) company
die Fremdsprache (-n) *foreign language*
die Freude (-n) *joy, happiness*
freudig *happy (-ily), friendly, easy*
sich freuen (über) *to be pleased (about);*
sich freuen auf *to look forward to;*
(es) freut mich *I'm pleased*
der Freund (-e) *friend*
freundlich *friendly;* Mit freundlichen Grüßen *Yours sincerely*
frisch *fresh(ly)*
der Frisör (-e) *hairdresser, barber*
frites: Pommes frites *(pl.) chips*
froh *happy, happily*
der Fronleichnam *Corpus Christi*
die Frucht (¨e) *fruit*
fruchtbar *fruitful*

früh *early*
früher *in the past (see also* früh*)*
der, die, das frühere *(the) earlier (one)*
das Frühjahr (-e) *spring*
der Frühling (-e) *spring*
das Frühstück (-e) *breakfast*
das Frühstücksbuffet (-s) *breakfast buffet*
frühzeitig *early, timely*
füge...bei *(see* beifügen*)*
fühl' = fühle
sich fühlen *to feel (oneself)*
fuhr *went (see* fahren*)*
führen (zu) *to lead, organize (see also* durchführen*); ein Gespräch führen to have a conversation/interview*
das Führen: das Führen der Händler-akten *managing dealer files*
führend *leading, major*
der Führerschein (-e) *driving licence*
die Führung *management*
füllen *to fill, stuff*
das Fundbüro (-s) *lost property office*
die Funds *(pl.) funds*
fünf *five*
der, die, das fünfte *(the) fifth (one)*
fünfundvierzig *forty-five*
der Funk *radio*
die Funkenerosion (-en) *spark erosion, EDM, electrical discharge machining*
das Funktelefon (-e) *mobile phone*
die Funktion (-en) *function, position*
funktionell *functional(ly)*
funktionieren *to function, work*
funktioniert *functions, functioned*
für *for; was für ...? what kind of...?*
fürs = für das
der Fußball *football*

G

gab: es gab *there was/were (see* geben*)*
gäbe: gang und gäbe *usual*
gab's = gab es
galvanotechnisch *(electro)plating*
gang: gang und gäbe *usual*
der Gang (-̈e) *gear, aisle*
ganz *quite, whole, entire(ly), really, very; ganz in der Nähe nearby; ganz genau to be precise; im großen und ganzen by and large; in ganz Europa in the whole of Europe*
der, die, das Ganze *(the) whole question*
gar: gar nicht *not (at all)*
die Garage (-n) *garage, car park*
die Garantie (-n) *guarantee, warranty*
garantieren *to guarantee*
garantiert *guarantees, guaranteed*
die Garderobe (-n) *cloakroom*
der Garten (-̈) *garden*
gartenfrisch *fresh*
der Gast (-̈e) *guest*
der Gasthof (-̈e) *inn*
geändert *changed (see* ändern*)*
gearbeitet *worked (see* arbeiten*)*

gebaut *built (see* bauen*)*
geben (i), a, e *to give, be; es...gibt there is/are; es gab there was/were; es wird...geben there will be; wenn der Umstand gegeben ist when you have the circumstances*
das Geben *give, giving; ein Geben und Nehmen a give and take*
gebeten *asked (see* bitten*)*
das Gebiet (-e) *area, region, sector*
geboren *born*
gebraten *fried (see* braten*)*
gebraucht *used (see* brauchen*)*
die Gebühr (-en) *fees, dues*
gebürgt *stood surety (see* bürgen*)*
die Geburt (-en) *birth*
das Geburtsdatum (-daten) *date of birth*
der Geburtsort (-e) *place of birth*
der Geburtstag (-e) *birthday*
gedämpft *steamed (see* dämpfen*)*
gedreht *turned (see* drehen*)*
die Geduld *patience*
geehrt: Sehr geehrter *Dear*
geeignet *suitable*
gefahren *gone, driven (see* fahren*)*
gefallen *decreased (see* fallen*)*
gefallen (ä), ie, a *to please; das gefällt mir I like that; das gefällt mir nicht I don't like that*
gefragt *demanded (see* fragen*)*
gefräst *milled (see* fräsen*)*
geführt *led, managed (see* führen*)*
gefüllt *filled, stuffed (see* füllen*)*
gegangen *gone (see* gehen*)*
gegeben *given (see* geben*)*
gegen *against, around; so gegen halb vier at around half past three*
die Gegend (-en) *district*
gegenüber *opposite, to, towards, in comparison with; gegenüber den Unternehmen with respect to the companies*
gegründet *founded (see* gründen*)*
geh' = gehe
gehabt *had; haben...gehabt had, have had (see* haben*)*
das Gehalt (-̈er) *salary, pay*
geheim *secret(ly)*
das Geheimnis (-nisse) *secret*
die Geheimzahl (-en) *PIN number*
gehen, ging, gegangen (sein) *to go, walk, sell (see also* eingehen*); wenn es geht if possible; links gehen keep moving on the left; wie geht es Ihnen? how are you? es geht/ging um it is/was about*
gehören *to belong, be part of; dazu gehört part of that is*
gehört *belongs, belonged, heard (see* gehören, hören*)*
geht's = geht es
gekannt *known (see* kennen*)*
gekennzeichnet *identified (see* kennzeichnen*)*
gekommen *come (see* kommen*)*
gekürzt *shortened (see* kürzen*)*
gelagert *stored (see* lagern*)*

das Gelände (-) *site, complex*
gelb *yellow*
das Geld (-er) *money, payment*
der Geldautomat *(sing. gen. -en)* (-en) *cash dispenser*
gelegentlich *occasionally, sometimes*
gelegt *laid (see* legen*)*
geleistet *carried out (see* leisten*)*
gelernt *trained, qualified (see* lernen*)*
gell? (coll.) *isn't it?*
gelten (i), a, o *to apply (to), be; gelten als to be*
gemacht *made, done (see* machen*)*
die Gemeinde (-n) *local authority*
gemeinsam *together, communal*
die Gemeinschaft (-en) *community*
gemischt *mixed (see* mischen*)*
das Gemüse (-) *vegetable(s)*
genannt *called (see* nennen*)*
genau *right, careful(ly), precise(ly)*
der, die, das Genauere (-n) *(the) more precise (thing/one)*
genehmigen *to approve*
genehmigt *approves, approved*
der Generalkonsul (-e) *General Consul*
das Generalkonsulat (-e) *General Consulate*
die Generation (-en) *generation*
generell *general(ly)*
genommen *taken (see* nehmen*)*
genug *enough*
genügen *to be sufficient, meet, satisfy*
genügend *sufficient(ly)*
geöffnet *open, opened (see* öffnen*); geöffnet täglich open daily/every day; ist am Samstag geöffnet is open on Saturday*
das Gepäck *left luggage*
die Gepäckaufbewahrung (-en) *left luggage*
gepreßt *pressed (see* pressen*)*
geprüft *tested, inspected (see* prüfen*)*
gerad' = gerade
gerade *just, at the moment, exactly, precisely*
geradeaus *straight on*
geradezu *virtually, almost, really*
das Gerät (-e) *machine, unit, device*
gerechnet *reckoned (see* rechnen*)*
das Gericht (-e) *dish, court*
gering *low, restricted*
der, die, das geringe *(the) low (one)*
geringer *lower (see* gering*)*
gerissen *torn (see* reißen*)*
gern(e) *like (to); ich lese gern I like reading*
gerngesehen *welcome*
gesagt *said (see* sagen*)*
gesamt *whole, overall, entire, total*
das Gesamtinteresse *overall interest*
geschaffen *created (see* schaffen*)*
geschafft *managed (see* schaffen*)*
das Geschäft (-e) *business, shop*

die Geschäftsbedingungen *(pl.)* *terms and conditions of business*
geschäftsführend *managing, executive*
der Geschäftsführer (-) *managing director, general manager*
die Geschäftsführerin (-nen) *managing director, general manager (f.)*
die Geschäftsführung (-en) *(board of) management*
die Geschäftsleitung (-en) *(board of) management*
die Geschäftsleute *(pl.)* *business people*
der Geschäftsmann (¨er) *businessman*
die Geschäftsordnung (-en) *agenda*
die Geschäftsreise (-n) *business trip*
die Geschäftsstelle (-n) *sales office*
geschah *happened (see geschehen)*
geschaut *looked (see schauen)*
geschehen (ie), a, e (sein) *to happen*
der Geschenkartikel (-) *gift*
die Geschichte (-n) *history, thing(s)*; so eine Geschichte *something like that*
geschichtlich *historical(ly)*
das Geschichtliche *history*
geschliffen *ground (see schleifen)*
geschlossen *closed (see schließen)*
das Geschnetzelte *slices of meat stewed in a sauce*
geschnitten *cut (see schneiden)*
geschrieben *written (see schreiben)*
gesehen *seen (see sehen)*
die Gesellschaft (-en) *company, society;* Gesellschaft mit beschränkter Haftung (GmbH) *private (limited) company*
der Gesellschafter (-) *shareholder, partner*
die Gesellschaftsform (-en) *legal form of a company*
gesetzlich *legal(ly)*
gesichert *secured*
das Gesicht (-er) *face, appearance*
gesorgt *ensured (see sorgen)*
das Gespräch (-e) *conversation, meeting, interview*
gesprochen *spoken (see sprechen)*
gestalten *to design*
gestaltet *designed*
gesteigert *increased, risen (see steigern)*
gestellt *placed (see stellen)*
gestern *yesterday*
gesteuert *controlled, automated*
gestoßen *pushed (see stoßen)*
gestrichen *deleted (see streichen)*
gesucht *sought (see suchen)*
getan *done, made (see tun)*
das Getränk (-e) *drink, beverage*
die Getränkekarte (-n) *wine list*
getrennt *separated (see trennen)*
das Getriebe (-) *gears, gearbox*
getrocknet *dried (see trocknen)*
gewählt *chosen (see wählen)*
gewähren *to provide*

gewährleisten *to ensure, guarantee*
gewerblich *industrial, technical*
die Gewerkschaft (-en) *(trade) union*
gewesen *been, gone (see sein)*
der Gewinn (-e) *profit, prize;* Gewinn- und Verlustrechnung *profit and loss account*
gewinnen, a, o *to win, gain*
gewinnorientiert *profit-oriented*
die Gewinnzone (-n) *net income area (area of profit in breakeven analysis)*
gewöhnt (an) *used/accustomed (to)*
geworden *become, turned into (see werden)*
ggf. = gegebenenfalls *where relevant*
gibt *see geben*
gilt *see gelten*
ging *went (see gehen)*
glänzen *to shine*
das Glas (¨er) *glas*
die Glasbranche (-n) *glass sector*
die Glaskeramiken *(pl.)* *glass ceramics*
die Glaswerke *(pl.)* *glass works*
glaub' = glaube
glauben *to think, believe*
gleich *immediate(ly), just*
der, die, das gleiche *(the) same (one)*
gleichgültig *irrespective, indifferent*
gleichzeitig *simultaneous(ly)*
glücklich *happy*
die GmbH (-s) = Gesellschaft mit beschränkter Haftung
das Gold *gold*
das Golf *golf*
der Golfclub (-s) *golf club*
der Golfspieler (-) *golf player*
der Gott (¨er) *god, God*
der Grad (-e) *degree, level*
grad *just, at the moment*
greifen, griff, gegriffen *to grip, reach (see also herausgreifen)*
die Grenze (-n) *border*
der Grieche (*gen. sing.* -n) (-n) *Greek (person)*
das Griechenland *Greece*
die Griechin (-nen) *Greek (f.)*
der Grill (-s) *grill, barbecue*
Grönländer *from Greenland*
groß *big, large, much, tall;* im großen und ganzen *overall*
großartig *splendid(ly)*
das Großbritannien *Great Britain*
die Größe (-n) *size, parameter, factor*
die Größenordnung (-en) *order of (magnitude)*
größer (als) *bigger/greater (than)*
die Großstadt (¨e) *city, conurbation*
der, die, das größte *(the) biggest (one)*
größtenteils *largely, mainly*
grün *green*
der Grund (¨e) *reason, basis;* im Grunde (genommen) *basically;* auf Grund der *because of the*
gründen *to found, establish*
der Gründer (-) *(company) founder*
der Grundsatz (¨e) *basis*

grundsätzlich *basic(ally), in/on principle, always*
die Gründung (-en) *founding*
das Gründungskapital *start-up capital*
das Gründungsland (¨er) *country of foundation*
die Gruppe (-n) *group*
der Gruppenleiter (-) *supervisor*
die Gruppenleitung (-en) *team supervision/management*
der Gruß (¨e) *greeting*
grüßen *to greet;* grüß Gott *hallo, good morning/afternoon/evening*
GS = geprüfte Sicherheit
gültig *valid*
der/das Gummi *rubber*
gut *good, well*
das Gymnasium (-ien) *grammar school*

H

hab' = habe
haben (hat), hatte, gehabt *to have (also used to form the perfect and pluperfect of other verbs);* ich hätte gern *I would like*
die Haftung (-en) *liability*
das Hähnchen (-) *chicken, cockerel*
die Hähnchenbrust (¨e) *chicken breast*
halb *half;* halb sechs *half past five*
die Halbpension (-en) *half-board*
halbtags *halfdays(s), part-time*
die Halle (-n) *(exhibition/production) hall*
die Hallenseite (-n) *side of the hall*
hallo *hello*
halt *just, simply*
halt' = halte
halten (ä), ie, a *to hold, consider;* ich halte...für *I consider*
die Hand (¨e) *hand;* in die Hand nehmen *to pick up*
der Handball *handball*
der Handel *trade, commerce*
handeln (mit) *to trade (with/in)*
sich handeln (um) *to concern;* es handelt sich um *it is*
das Handelsblatt *Handelsblatt (newspaper for business)*
die Handelskammer (-n) *chamber of commerce;* (see Industrie)
der Handelsmakler (-) *broker (see CDH)*
der Handelsreferent (*sing. gen.* -en) (-en) *commercial attaché*
der Handelstag *see Industrie*
der Handelsvertreter (-) *agent (see CDH)*
die Handelsvertretung (-en) *agent*
der Händler (-) *agent, dealer, buyer*
handlich *convenient, compact*
handlings-freudig *easy to use*
das Handwerk *trade, craft*
der Handwerker (-) *skilled worker, craftsman*
Hannover *Hanover*
hart *hard, tough*
härter *harder (see hart)*
hat *has (see haben)*

hätt' = hätte
hatte *had (see* haben*)*
hätte *had, would have (see* haben*)*
die Haube (-n) *bonnet, hood*
Haupt- *main*
die Hauptkasse (-n) *main cashier's office*
der Hauptschulabschluß (-üsse) *basic school-leaving certificate (15–16)*
die Hauptschule (-n) *intermediate school (10–15)*
der Hauptsitz (-e) *head office, headquarters*
das Hauptwerk (-e) *main plant/factory*
das Haus (¨er) *house, home, company;* im Hause *in the company/office;* zu Hause *at home*
die Hausfrau (-en) *housewife;* ,,Hausfrauen Art" *home-made*
der Haushalt (-e) *budget, household*
die Haushaltsplanung (-en) *budget planning*
hausintern *in-house*
die Haustechnik *domestic appliances*
die Hausverwaltung (-en) *property management, administration*
der HC = Handheld-Computer
die Hebebühne (-n) *lifting platform*
heilig *holy,* Heilige Drei Könige *Twelfth Night*
der Heiligabend *Christmas Eve*
die Heilkunde *medical science, medicine*
die Heimat *home country/town*
der Heimatort (-e) *home town/village*
die Heirat (-en) *marriage*
heiraten *to get married*
heißen, ie, ei *to be called, to mean*
helfen (i), a, o *to help*
das Hemd (-en) *shirt*
die Hemdtasche (-n) *shirt pocket*
hemmend *restrictive*
her *here, from (see also* herstellen*)*
heran *to(wards)*
herankommen *(sep.),* kam heran, herangekommen (sein) (an) *to get (at)*
herantreten *(sep.)* (tritt heran), trat heran, herangetreten (sein) (an) *to approach*
heraus *out (see also* herausgreifen, herauskriegen*)*
die Herausforderung (-en) *challenge*
herausgegriffen *identified*
sich herausgreifen *(sep.),* griff heraus, herausgegriffen *to identify*
herauskriegen *(sep.) to find out, get*
der Herbst (-e) *autumn*
herein *in;* herein! *come in!*
hergestellt *produced, manufactured*
die Herkulesarbeit (-en) *Herculean/massive task*
der Herr *(sing. gen.* -(e)n*)* (-en) *Mr, man*
die Herrenbekleidung (-en) *menswear*
herrschen *to reign, be*
herstellen *(sep.) to manufacture, produce*

das Herstellen *manufacturing*
der Hersteller (-) *manufacturer*
die Herstellung (-en) *manufacture, production*
herum *around, about;* so um die zwanzig rum *around twenty*
herumreisen *(sep.)* (sein) *to travel around*
das Herz *(sing. gen.* -ens*)* (-en) *heart*
herzlich *sincere(ly), warm*
herzustellen *see* herstellen
Hessen *Hesse, Hessian*
heute *today, now, nowadays;* heute morgen *this morning*
heutig *today's, present*
heutzutage *nowadays, currently*
hielt *held, took (see* halten*)*
hier *here*
die Hierarchie (-n) *hierarchy*
hierher *here*
hierherkommen *(sep.),* kam hierher, hierhergekommen (sein) *to come here*
hierzu *with this, in connection with this*
hiesig *local, here*
das *or die* High-Tech *high-tech*
die Hilfe (-n) *help;* erste Hilfe *first aid*
hilfreich *helpful(ly)*
das Hilfsmittel (-) *device, equipment*
der Himmel (-) *heaven*
die Himmelfahrt (-en) *Ascension Day;* Mariä Himmelfahrt *Assumption*
die Himmelsrichtung (-en) *compass point*
hin *to, there (see also* hinziehen*);* Hin und Her *to and fro*
hinaus *out;* darüber hinaus *additionally*
hinein *in, into*
hingezogen *drawn, attracted (see* hinziehen*)*
hinten *behind;* da hinten durch *through over/back there*
hinter *behind*
der, die, das hintere *(the) rear (one)*
hinterfragen *to analyze*
der Hintergrund (¨e) *background*
hinweg: über...hinweg *right across...*
der Hinweis (-e) *pointer, advice*
hinziehen *(sep.),* zog hin, hingezogen (zu) *to draw (to), attract*
hinzu *also, in addition*
das Hobby (-s) *hobby*
hoch *high(ly), senior*
die Hochbahn (-en) *overhead railway*
das Hochdeutsch *standard German*
hochentwickelt *highly developed*
hochgeharzt *(highly) resinated*
höchst *highly;* im höchsten Maß *to maximum extent*
der, die, das höchste *(the) highest (one), extremely*
am höchsten *highest*

die Hochtechnologie (-n) *high-tech*
hochzivilisiert *highly civilized, industrialized*
der Hof (¨e) *court, courtyard*
hoffen *to hope*
höher (als) *higher (than)*
holen *to fetch*
Holland *Holland, The Netherlands*
Hollandaise *hollandaise*
holländisch *Dutch*
hol's = hole es
das Holz (¨er) *timber, log, wood*
die Holzbearbeitungsmaschinen: Holzbe- und -verarbeitungsmaschinen *(pl.) wood-processing machines*
das Holzfenster (-) *wooden window*
der Holzvorrat (¨e) *stock(pile) of wood*
hören (von) *to hear (from), listen*
horizontal *horizontal(ly)*
die Hormontherapie (-n) *hormone therapy*
das Hors d'oeuvre (-s) *starter*
die Hose (-n) *(pair of) trousers*
das Hotel (-s) *hotel*
hoteleigen *hotel-owned*
das Huhn (¨er) *chicken, hen*
der Humor *humour*
der Hund (-e) *dog*
hundert *hundred*

I

ich *I*
ideal *ideal*
die Idee (-n) *idea*
die Identifikation (-en) *identification*
identifizieren *to identify*
identisch *identical(ly)*
die Identität (-en) *identity*
ihm *(to) him/it*
ihn *him, it*
ihnen, Ihnen *(to/from) them/you* (formal*), they*
Ihr(e) *your (*formal*)*
ihr(e) *her, its, their*
im = in dem
das Image (-s) *image*
immens *immense*
immer *always, more and more;* immer wieder *again and again;* immer mehr *more and more;* immer noch *still*
immerhin *after all*
die Immobilien *(pl.) property, real estate*
der Import (-e) *import*
der Importeur (-e) *importer*
die Importförderung (-en) *promotion of imports*
importieren *to import*
in *in, into, on;* im Moment *at the moment;* in erster Linie *primarily;* im Jahr *a year*
der Individualtourismus *individual tourism*
individuell *individual(ly)*
das Indonesien *Indonesia*

die Industrie (-n) *industry, industrial;*
Industrie- und Handels-
kammer *chamber of industry and
commerce;* Industrie- und
Handelstag *Association of
German Chambers of Industry and
Commerce*
die Industriekauffrau (-en) *industrial
clerk (f.), industrial saleswoman,
manager*
der Industriekaufmann (¨er)
*industrial clerk, industrial
salesman, manager*
das Industrieland (¨er) *industrialized
country*
industriell *industrial(ly)*
der Industrieverband (¨e) *industrial
association*
die Information (-en) *information*
die Informationsbroschüre (-n)
publicity brochure
das Informationsmaterial (-ien)
information, publicity material
die Informationsstelle (-n)
information point
informieren *to inform*
sich informieren (über) *to get
information, find out (about)*
die Infrastruktur (-en)
infrastructure
der Ingenieur (-e) *engineer*
die Ingenieurin (-nen) *engineer (f.)*
der Inhaber (-) *proprietor*
inkl. (= inklusive) *incl. (including)*
inklusive *inclusive(ly), including*
innen *inside, interior*
die Innenstadt (¨e) *(town/city) centre*
die Innentasche (-n) *inside pocket*
innerhalb *within, in, inside (of)*
die Innovation (-en) *innovation*
innovationsfreudig *innovative*
die Innovationsfreudigkeit *enthusiasm
for innovation*
innovativ *innovative(ly)*
ins = in das
die Insassenversicherung (-en)
passenger insurance
insbesondere *especial(ly)*
insgesamt *overall, altogether, in all*
insofern *in so far*
installieren *to install*
das Institut (-e) *institution, bank*
intensiv *intensive(ly), focused*
der Intercity (-s) *intercity (train)*
interessant *interesting, important*
das Interesse (-n) *interest*
interessieren *to interest*
sich interessieren (für) *to be/become
interested (in)*
interessiert (an) *interests, interested
(in)*
international *international(ly)*
investieren *to invest*
die Investition (-en) *investment*
das Investmentland (¨er)
investment country
der Investor (-en) *investor*
inzwischen *now*

irgend *some, any;* irgend etwas
something/anything
irgendwann *sometime*
irgendwelche *some/any*
irgendwie *somehow, anyhow*
irgendwohin *somewhere, anywhere*
das Irland *Ireland*
das Island *Iceland*
ist *is (see sein)*
das Italien *Italy*
der Italiener (-) *Italian*
die Italienerin (-nen) *Italian (f.)*
italienisch *Italian*

J

ja *yes, what's more, after all, of course*
die Jacht (-en) *yacht*
die Jacke (-n) *jacket*
das Jackett (-s) *jacket*
das Jahr (-e) *year*
der Jahresumsatz (¨e) *annual
turnover/sales*
die Jahreszeit (-en) *season*
das Jahrhundert (-e) *century*
jährlich *annual(ly)*
das Jahrtausend (-e) *millennium*
das Jahrzehnt (-e) *decade*
Jan. = Januar
der Januar *January;* im Januar *in
January*
das Japan *Japan*
japanisch *Japanese*
je *according (to);* je nach(dem)
depending on; von je *each;*
je...desto *the...the*
jede, jedem, jeden, jeder,
jedes *(to/from/for/of)
any/each/every/everyone;* jeder
Art *of all kinds*
jederzeit *at any time*
jedoch *however, but*
jemand *someone, anyone*
jetzt *now, still;* bis jetzt *up to now*
der Julei (-s) *July (on the phone)*
der Juli (-s) *July;* im Juli *in July*
Julienne *(vegetable) julienne*
jung *young*
jünger (als) *younger (than) (see
jung)*
junggeblieben *youthful*
der, die, das jüngste *(the) youngest (one)*
der Juni (-s) *June;* im Juni *in June*
der Juno (-s) *June (on the phone)*
der Jus *juice*

K

der Kaffee (-s) *coffee*
die Kalbsleber (-n) *calves' liver*
das Kalbssteak (-s) *calves' steak*
kalibrieren (auf) *to calibrate (to)*
kalt *cold*
kam *came (see* kommen*)*
das Kanada *Canada*
kann *can (see* können*)*
das Kännchen (-) *pot (of coffee/tea)*
die Kapazität (-en) *capacity*
das Kapital (-e) *capital*
der Karfreitag (-e) *Good Friday*

der Karneval (-e *or* -s) *carnival*
die Karte (-n) *ticket, card*
das Kartentelefon (-e) *cardphone*
die Kartoffel (-n) *potato*
der Kartoffelschnee *puréed potato*
die Käseauswahl (-en) *cheese board*
die Kasse (-n) *ticket office, cashier's
counter, cash desk, till*
der Katalog (-e) *catalogue*
der Katalogverkauf (¨e) *catalogue sale*
katholisch *Catholic*
der Kauf (¨e) *purchase*
kaufen *to buy, purchase*
die Kauffrau (-en) *saleswoman, clerical
worker (f.)*
das Kaufhaus (¨er) *department store*
die Kaufleute *sales people, clerks*
der Kaufmann (¨er) *salesman, (sales)
clerk, trader*
kaufmännisch *commercial*
kaum *scarce(ly), hardly*
die Kaution (-en) *deposit .*
kein, keine, keinem, keinen,
keiner, keines *(to/from/
for/of) no, none, no one*
keinerlei *no, none*
der *or* das Keks (- *or* -e) *biscuit*
der Kellner (-) *waiter*
die Kellnerin (-nen) *waitress*
kennen, kannte, gekannt *to know*
kennenlernen *(sep.) to get to know*
die Kenntnis (-se) *knowledge;* zur
Kenntnis nehmen *to accept*
das Kennzeichen (-) *sign, registration*
kennzeichnen *to identify*
die Keramik (-en) *ceramics*
der Kern (-e) *core*
das Keyboard (-s) *keyboard*
Kfm. = Kaufmann
Kfz. = Kraftfahrzeug
die KG (-s) = Kommanditgesellschaft
das Kind (-er) *child*
der Kindergarten (¨) *kindergarten*
das Kino (-s) *cinema*
die Kirche (-n) *church*
die Klappe (-n) *flap, lid*
klar *clear(ly), simple (-ly)*
der, die, das Klare: sich im Klaren
sein *to be clear*
die Klasse (-n) *class*
klein *small, little, short*
knapp *scarce, short (of time)*
knüpf' = knüpfe
knüpfen *to make*
der Kohl *cabbage*
der Kollege (*sing. gen.* -n) (-n)
colleague
die Kollegin (-nen) *colleague (f.)*
Köln *Cologne*
komm' = komme
das Komma (-s) *comma, point*
die Kommanditgesellschaft (-en)
limited partnership
der Kommanditist (*sing. gen.* -en) (-en)
limited partner
kommen, kam, gekommen
*(sein) to come, go, reach,
arrive at (see also* heran-, hierher-,

zurückkommen*)*; kommen auf *to come to, be placed on;* kommen aus *to come from;* kommen zu *to give rise to, come about*

kommend *coming (see* kommen*)*

der Kommentar *statement, comment*

die Kommunikation *communication(s)*

die Kommunikationseinrichtungen (*pl.*) *communications equipment*

kommunistisch *communist*

der Komplementär (-e) *personally liable partner, general partner*

komplett *complete(ly), fully*

kompliziert *complex, complicated*

die Komponente (-n) *component*

der Kompressionsstrumpf (¨e) *elastic stocking*

der Kompressor (-en) *compressor*

die Kondition (-en) *condition*

die Konferenz (-en) *conference*

die Konferenztechnik *conference equipment*

der Kongreß (Kongresse) *conference*

der König (-e) *king*

das Königreich (-e) *kingdom*

die Königscrevetten (*pl.*) *king prawns*

die Konkurrenz (-en) *competition*

konkurrenzfähig *competitive*

können (kann), konnte, gekonnt *can, to be able*

könnt' = könnte *(see* können*)*

die Konsequenz (-en) *consequence*

die Konstruktion (-en) *design*

der Kontakt (-e) *contact;* nehmen Sie bitte mit uns Kontakt auf *please get in touch, please call*

die Kontaktfähigkeit (-en) *social skills*

kontaktfreudig *outgoing*

kontaktieren *to contact*

das Konto (Konten) *account*

die Kontrazeption *contraception*

kontrovers *controversial(ly)*

konventionell *conventional(ly)*

sich konzentrieren (auf) *to concentrate (on), focus (on)*

das Konzept (-e) *concept, design*

die Konzeption (-en) *concept(ion)*

der Konzern (-e) *concern, company*

die Kooperation (-en) *cooperation*

koordinieren *to coordinate*

der Kopf (¨e) *head*

körperbehindert *disabled*

die Kosten (*pl.*) *costs*

kosten *to cost*

die Kostenaufstellung (-en) *breakdown of costs*

die Kosteneinsparung (-en) *cost saving*

kostenfrei *free of charge*

kostenlos *free of charge*

köstlich *delicious*

die Kraft (¨e) *force, power*

der Kraftfahrer (-) *truck/lorry driver*

das Kraftfahrzeug (-e) *(powered) vehicle*

die Kraftzentrale (-n) *power plant*

krank *ill;* ich bin krank *I am ill*

die Krankenkasse (-n) *health-insurance scheme/company*

der Krankenschein (-e) *health-insurance voucher*

die Krankheit (-en) *disease, illness*

die Kräuterrahmsauce (-n) *cream sauce with herbs*

der Kredit (-e) *loan, credit*

das Kreditinstitut (-e) *bank*

die Kreditkarte (-n) *credit card*

die Kreisstadt (¨e) *district town*

das Kreuzworträtsel (-) *crossword*

die Krevette (-n) *prawn*

kriegen *to get (see also* herauskriegen*)*

das Kriterium (Kriterien) *criterion*

kritisch *critical(ly)*

die Krokette (-n) *croquette*

die Krone (-n) *crown*

der Kuchen (-) *cake*

die Kultur (-en) *culture, heritage*

der Kunde (*sing. gen.* -n) (-n) *customer*

die Kundenberaterin (-nen) *customer adviser (f.)*

der Kundendienst (-e) *customer service*

das Kundengespräch (-e) *contact with customers, presentation*

die Kundin (-nen) *customer (f.)*

künftig *future, prospective*

die Kunst (¨e) *art*

die Kunstgewerbebranche (-n) *arts and crafts (sector)*

das Kunstharzpreßholz (¨er) *resin-treated compressed wood*

künstlich *artificial*

die Kunststadt (¨e) *historic city*

der Kunststoff (-e) *plastic(s)*

die Kunststoffmaschinen (*pl.*) *plastics machines*

der Kurfürst (*sing. gen.* -en) (-en) *Elector*

kurz *short, brief*

die Kürze *shortness;* in Kürze *shortly*

kürzen *to shorten, cut*

der, die, die kürzeste: in kürzester Zeit *very quickly, in no time*

die Kürzung (-en) *cut (in funds)*

L

das Labor (-s *or* -e) *laboratory*

lackieren *to paint*

die Lackiererei (-en) *paint shop*

die Lackierhalle (-n) *paint shop*

laden (lädt), lud, geladen *to load (see also* einladen*)*

der Laden (¨) *shop, boutique*

der Ladendiebstahl (¨e) *shop-lifting*

die Lage (-n) *position, site, situation*

die Lagenhölzer (*pl.*) *laminated wood (products)*

lagern *to store*

das Land (¨er) *Land, state, country*

die Landeswährung (-en) *local currency*

die Landschaft (-en) *countryside*

die Landstraße (-n) *trunk road*

lang *long*

lange *long;* nicht lange *not for long*

die Länge (-n) *length*

langjährig *long-standing*

langsam *slow(ly)*

lassen (läßt), ließ, gelassen *to let, leave, allow, have something done;* wie Kollegen sich aus dem Bankautomaten die Pfunde haben auszahlen lassen *how colleagues withdrew (lit. had themselves paid out) pounds from the cash dispenser*

last: last not least *last but not least*

der Lastkraftwagen (-) *or* LKW *truck*

der Lauf (¨e) *course;* im Laufe des Jahres *over the year*

laufen (äu), lief, au (sein) *to run, walk, go (see also* ablaufen*)*

laufend *running, current*

die Laune (-n) *mood*

laut *noisy (-ily), loud(ly)*

das Leben (-) *life*

leben (mit) *to live (with)*

die Lebenserwartung (-en) *life expectancy*

lecker *delicious*

legen (auf) *to lay (on) (see* Wert*)*

der Lehrbrief *apprenticeship certificate*

die Lehre (-n) *training scheme, apprenticeship*

lehren *to teach*

das Lehrjahr (-e) *(academic) year*

die Lehrkraft (¨e) *teacher, teaching staff*

der Lehrling (-e) *trainee, apprentice*

die Lehrzeit (-en) *(period of) apprenticeship, training period*

leicht *light, easy*

das Leichtmetallrad (¨er) *light-alloy wheel*

leiden, litt, gelitten *to deteriorate*

leider *unfortunately*

leisten *to carry out, achieve*

die Leistung (-en) *service, power, performance, achievement*

das Leistungsangebot (-e) *range of services*

leistungsfähig *competitive(ly), successful(ly), powerful(ly)*

die Leistungsvereinbarung (-en) *service agreement*

leiten *to lead, be in charge of*

der Leiter (-) *head, manager (*lit. *leader)*

die Leitung (-en) *line, management*

lernen *to learn, train*

lesen (ie), a, e *to read*

das Lesen *reading*

der Leser (-) *reader*

die Leseratte (-n) *enthusiastic reader*

Lettland *Latvia*

der, die, das letzte *(the) last (one), past;* als letztes *as the last thing*

letztendlich *finally, in the end*

letztlich *in the end, final(ly)*

die Leute (*pl.*) *people, staff, personnel*

lieb *kind, dear (see also* gern*)*

lieben *to love*

lieber (als) *preferably, rather*

lieblich *sweet (for wine)*

am liebsten *best of all, most of all, ideally*
lief *see* laufen, ablaufen
die Lieferfirma (-firmen) *supplier*
liefern *to deliver, provide, supply*
die Lieferzeit (-en) *delivery time*
liegen, a, e *to lie, be (situated)*
ließ *let (see* lassen*)*
die Linie (-n) *line;* in erster Linie *primarily*
der, die, das linke *left(hand)*
links *(on/to the) left;* links gehen *keep moving on the left*
die Literatur (-en) *literature*
Litauen *Lithuania*
die Lizenz (-en) *licence;* in Lizenz *under licence*
der LKW (-s) = Lastkraftwagen *truck*
der Lohnerodierbetrieb (-e) *contract (spark) erosion business*
lokal *local(ly)*
lösen *to solve, remove, purchase*
die Lösung (-en) *solution*
die Lust *inclination*

M

'm = dem
m = Meter
machen *to make, do, carry out, produce, spend, be, be responsible for;* Gewinn machen *to make a profit;* Freude machen *to give enjoyment;* Geschäfte machen *to do business;* ich mache Produktion *I am in charge of production*
mag *like(s) (see* mögen*)*
die Mahlzeit (-en) *meal;* Mahlzeit! *enjoy your meal!*
der Mai *May;* im Mai *in May*
der Maifeiertag (-e) *spring bank holiday, Labor Day*
der Makler (-) *broker*
mal = einmal *(coll.) once, at that time, originally, just;* bleiben Sie mal dran *(just) hold the line*
das Mal (-e) *time;* das erste Mal *(for) the first time;* letztes Mal *last time*
man *one, you, we, they, people*
das Management (-s) *management*
managen *to manage*
der Manager (-) *manager*
die Managerin (-nen) *manager (f.)*
manch, manche, manchem, manchen, manches *several/some (things)*
manchmal *sometimes*
die Mandelcreme (-s) *almond cream*
der Mangel (-) *shortage, defect*
der Mann (-er) *man*
die Mannschaft (-en) *crew, team*
manuell *manual(ly)*
der Maraschino (-s) *maraschino*
die Mark (-) *mark (German currency)*
das Mark *beef marrow*
das Marketing *marketing*
der Markt (-e) *market, (super)store*
die Markteinführung (-en) *launch*

die Marktnische (-n) *market niche*
der März *March;* im März *in March*
die Maschine (-n) *machine, machinery*
der Maschinenbau *mechanical engineering*
der Maschinenlieferant (*sing. gen.* -en) (-en) *machinery supplier*
das Maß (-e) *measure;* im höchsten Maß *to maximum extent*
maßgebend *decisive*
maßgeschneidert (auf) *tailored (to)*
die Maßnahme (-n) *measure*
das Material (-ien) *material*
die Mathematik *mathematics*
das Matjesfilet (-s) *herring fillet*
die Mauer *the Wall*
mbH *see* GmbH
die Mechanikerlehre (-n) *apprenticeship as a machinist*
Mecklenburg-Vorpommern *Mecklenburg and West Pomerania*
das Medaillon (-s) *medallion*
die MedAk = Medizinische Akademie *medical academy*
die Medien (*pl.*) *media*
das Medikament (-e) *medication, drug*
die Medizin *medicine*
das Meeting (-s) *meeting*
der Meeting-Point (-s) *meeting point*
mehr (als) *more (than);* nicht mehr *no longer;* mehr und mehr/immer mehr *more and more*
mehrere *several*
mehrfach *several times*
die Mehrwertsteuer *Value-Added Tax*
mein, meine, meinem, meinen, meiner, meines *(to/from/for/of) my;* meines Erachtens *in my opinion*
meinen *to think, be of the opinion;* wie wir meinen *in our opinion*
die Meinung (-en) *opinion;* wir sind der Meinung, daß *we think that (lit. are of the opinion)*
meist *most(ly);* die meiste Zeit *most of the time*
der, die, das meiste *(the) most*
der Meister (-) *master craftsman, instructor, supervisor, foreman*
sich melden *to get in touch, contact;* ich werde mich bei Ihnen melden *I will contact you*
die Melone (-n) *melon*
das Melonenschiffchen (-) *slice(s) of melon (lit. little ship(s))*
der Mensch (*sing. gen.* -en) (-en) *person;* Menschen (*pl.*) *people*
merken *to notice*
das Merkmal (-e) *feature*
die Messe (-n) *trade fair*
das Messe-Center (-) *fair centre*
das Messegelände (-) *trade-fair complex*
die Messegesellschaft (-en) *(trade) fair company*
messen (mißt), maß, gemessen *to measure (see also* ausmessen*)*
der Messestand (-e) *trade-fair stand*
die Messezeit (-en) *trade-fair period*

der Metallic-Lack *metallic paint*
der or das Meter (-) *metre*
die Methode (-n) *method*
mich *me*
die Miete (-n) *rent;* wir sind hier zur Miete *we are renting here*
mieten *to rent*
das Mietverhältnis (-se) *tenancy*
der Mietwagen (-) *hire car*
die Milch (-e) *milk*
die Milliarde (-n) *1,000,000,000, thousand million, billion, milliard*
die Million (-en) *1,000,000, million*
die Minderheit (-en) *minority*
mindestens *at least*
das Mineral (-e) *mineral*
das Mineralöl (-e) *(mineral) oil*
das Minicenter (-) *minicentre*
die Minute (-n) *minute*
Mio. = Millionen
mir *to/for/from me*
mischen *to mix*
mit *with (see also* mitarbeiten, mitbringen, mitziehen*)*
mitarbeiten (*sep.*) *to cooperate*
der Mitarbeiter (-) *employee, colleague (lit. co-worker),* pl.: *personnel*
die Mitarbeiterin (-nen) *employee/colleague (f.)*
die Mitarbeiterzahl (-en) *number of employees*
der Mitbewerber (-) *fellow applicant*
mitbringen (*sep.*), brachte mit, mitgebracht *to bring with (him/her/them...)*
miteinander *with each other*
das Mitglied (-er) *member*
der Mittag (-e) *midday*
das Mittagessen (-) *lunch*
die Mitte (-n) *centre, middle, mid*
das Mittel (-) *means, resources*
der Mittelstand (-e) *small and medium-sized companies (50 to 5000 people)*
mittelständisch *medium-sized*
Mittlere: die Mittlere Reife *Mittlere Reife (vocational qualification (age 16-17))*
der Mittwoch (-e) *Wednesday*
mittwochs *on Wednesdays*
MMG = Münchener Messe- und Ausstellungsgesellschaft mbH
Mo. = Montag
mobil *mobile*
der Mobilfunk *mobile phone (network)*
mobilisieren *to mobilize*
die Mobilität *mobility*
möcht' = möchte
möchte *would like (see* mögen*)*
die Mode (-n) *fashion*
das Modell (-e) *model*
die Modellpalette (-n) *range of models*
modern *modern, up-to-date*
der, die, das modernste *(the) most modern/up-to-date (one), latest*
mögen (mag), mochte, gemocht *to like (to);* ich möchte (gern) *I would like*

möglich *possible*
die Möglichkeit (-en) *possibility, opportunity, option*
möglichst *if possible;* möglichst kurz *as short as possible*
der Moment (-e) *moment;* im Moment *at the moment, now;* Moment, bitte *just a moment*
momentan *momentary (-ily), at the moment*
der Monat (-e) *month*
das Monopol (-e) *monopoly*
der Montag (-e) *Monday;* am Montag *on Monday*
montags *on Mondays*
moralisch *moral(ly)*
die Morchel (-n) *morel (mushroom)*
morgen *tomorrow, (on) the next day;* heute morgen *this morning*
der Morgen (-) *morning*
morgens *in the morning(s)*
der Motor (-en) *engine*
die Motorisierung *engine, power unit*
Mrd. = Milliarde
die Mühe (-n) *effort;* sich Mühe geben *to put in/make an effort*
multi-europäisch *multi-European*
multinational *multinational*
die Multi-Task-Funktion (-en) *multi-task function, multi-tasking*
München *Munich*
Münch(e)ner *of Munich, Munich*
die Münze (-n) *coin*
die Musik *music*
muß *must, have to (see* müssen*)*
müssen (muß), mußte, gemußt *must, to have to*
mußte *had to (see* müssen*)*
müßte *would have to, had to, should (subjunctive)*
das Muster (-) *sample (see* stellen*)*
die MwSt. *VAT (see* Mehrwertsteuer*)*

N

'n = ein, einen
nach *to, after, according to, in accordance with, in conformity with, following, about, for, in;* nach Hamburg *to Hamburg;* nach links *to the left;* nach rechts *to the right, turn right;* je nach *according to;* nach wie vor *still, now as ever;* nach unserer Erfahrung *according to our experience;* nach meiner Rückkehr *after my return*
nachdem *since, after;* je nachdem *depending on (which)*
die Nachfrage (-n) *demand*
nachher *after(wards), later*
der Nachholbedarf *need to catch up*
der Nachmittag *afternoon*
nachmittag *afternoon*
nachmittags *(in the) afternoons*
der Nachname (*sing. gen.* -ns) (-n) *surname*
die Nachspeise (-n) *dessert*
der, die, das nächste *(the) next/nearest*
nächstfolgend *next*

die Nacht (⸚e) *night*
der Nachteil (-e) *disadvantage*
der Nachtisch (-e) *dessert*
nah *near*
die Nähe *nearness, closeness;* in der Nähe (von) *near (by)*
näher (als) *nearer (than);* nähere Auskünfte geben *to give more detailed information*
das Nahrungsmittel (-) *food*
der Name (*sing. gen.* -ns) (-n) *name*
die Namensverbindung (-en) *name (combination)*
nämlich *namely, that is, ie, you see*
nannte *called (see* nennen*)*
national *national(ly)*
die Natur (-en) *nature*
naturgemäß *naturally*
das Naturheilverfahren (-) *naturopathy*
natürlich *natural(ly), of course*
der Naturstoff (-e) *natural material*
Nauticus: Virus Nauticus *nautical virus*
der Nazi (-s) *Nazi*
'ne = eine
neben *besides, in addition, next to, apart from*
das Nebenbüro (-s) *subsidiary office*
nebenstehend *opposite*
nee = nein
nehm' = nehme
nehmen (nimmt), nahm, genommen *to take, use, have (see also* auf-, zunehmen*)*
das Nehmen *taking (see* Geben*)*
nein *no*
'nem = einem
'nen = einen
nennen, nannte, genannt *to call, name, give (name);* als dritte Säule ist zu nennen *the third 'pillar' to be mentioned is*
das Nennen *naming*
sich nennen, nannte, genannt *to be called*
'ner = einer
nervös *nervous(ly)*
nett *nice*
netto *net(t)*
das Netz (-e) *net(work)*
das Netzwerk (-e) *net(work), mains*
neu *new(ly)*
der Neubeginn (-e) *new beginning/start*
das Neubundesland (⸚er) *former GDR Land*
der/die/das Neue *(the) new thing;* viel Neues *many new things*
der, die, das neu(e)ste *(the) newest/latest*
das Neujahr (-e) *New Year*
neun *nine*
nicht *not, none;* überhaupt nicht *not at all;* nicht nur...sondern auch *not only...but also;* nicht zuletzt *last but not least*
der Nichtraucher (-) *non-smoker*

nichts *nothing*
die Niederlande *Netherlands*
die Niederlassung (-en) *branch, subsidiary*
Niedersachsen *Lower Saxony*
niedlich *pretty*
niedrig *low, compact*
nimmt *see* nehmen, zunehmen
die Nische (-n) *niche*
das Niveau (-s) *level, standard*
noch *still, even, as well, yet;* noch (einmal) *again;* noch nicht *not yet;* immer noch/noch immer *still;* weder...noch *neither...nor*
nochmal *again, once more, further*
der Nord(en) *north, (the) North*
der Nordpol *North Pole*
Nordrhein-Westfalen *North Rhine-Westphalia*
die Norm (-en) *standard*
die Normung (-en) *standardization*
das Norwegen *Norway*
nötig *essential*
notwendig *necessary, essential*
der November (-) *November*
Nr. = Nummer
die Nuance (-n) *nuance;* es gibt Besonderheiten in den Nuancen *there are special nuances*
null *zero*
die Null (-en) *zero*
numerisch *numerical(ly)*
die Nummer (-n) *number*
nun *well, now*
nunmehr *now*
nur *only, and, just;* nur noch *only*
Nürnberg *Nuremberg*
nutzen *to use, utilize*
nützlich *useful(ly)*

O

ob *whether*
oben *above, at the top*
oberbayerisch *Upper Bavarian*
Oberbayern *Upper Bavaria*
die Oberflächentechnik (-en) *surface technology*
das Obergeschoß (-sse) *storey*
die Oberpostdirektion *regional post office (administration)*
das Objekt (-e) *object, phenomenon*
der Obstsalat (-e) *fruit salad*
oder *or;* oder aber auch *or else;* entweder...oder *either...or*
der OEM = Original Equipment Manufacturer
offen *open(ly)*
sich offenbaren *to be obvious*
offensiv *offensive(ly)*
öffentlich *public*
die Öffentlichkeit *(general) public*
die Öffentlichkeitsarbeit (-en) *public relations (work)*
offiziell *official(ly)*
öffnen *to open (up)*
oft *often*
OG = Obergeschoß
ohne *without*

okay *okay*
der Ökonom (*sing. gen.* -en) (-en) *economist*
ökonomisch *economical(ly)*
der Oktober (-) *October*
das Öl (-e) *oil*
der Omnibusbetrieb (-e) *bus company*
online *online*
der Opel (-) *Opel (car model)*
die Operation (-en) *operation*
die Optik *optics, appearance*
optimistisch *optimistic(ally)*
die Optoelektronik *optoelectronics*
oral *oral(ly)*
ordentlich *orderly, respectable*
ordnen *to order, organize, arrange*
die Ordnung (-en) *order* (das geht) in Ordnung *that's fine*
die Organisation (-en) *organization*
organisieren *to organize*
der Ort (-e) *place, site*
die Orthopädie *orthopaedic(s)*
Oschatz *Oschatz (surname and town in Saxony)*
der Ost(en) *east, (the) East*
Ostberlin *East Berlin*
das Ostern (-) *Easter*
das Österreich *Austria*
das Osteuropa *Eastern Europe*
das Overlaynetz (-e) *overlay network*

P

paar: ein paar *a couple, some, a few*
das Paar (-e) *pair, couple*
die Palette (-n) *range*
das Palm-Top-Gerät (-e) *palm-top unit*
das Papier (-e) *paper*
die Paprikastreifen (*pl.*) *strips of peppers*
der Park (-s) *park*
parken *to park*
das Parkhaus (¨er) *multi-storey car park*
der Parkplatz (¨e) *parking space*
der Parkschein (-e) *parking ticket*
der Parkschein-Automat (*sing. gen.* -en) (-en) *parking-ticket machine*
der Parmaschinken (-) *Parma ham*
der Partner (-) *partner*
das Partnerland (¨er) *partner (country)*
die Partnerschaft (-en) *partnership*
der Paß (Pässe) *passport*
passen (paßt) *to suit, go*; müßte passen *ought to go*; wann es uns allen paßt *when it suits us all*
das Paßwort (¨er) *password*
die Patentanmeldung (-en) *patent application*
die Pension (-en) *boarding house*
perfekt *perfect(ly)*
die Person (-en) *person*
die Personalabteilung (-en) *personnel department*
der Personalausweis (-e) *ID card*
die Personalverwaltung (-en) *personnel administration*
die Personen (*pl.*) *people (see* Person)

die Personengesellschaft (-en) *partnership, unlimited company*
der Personenkraftwagen (-) *car*
die Personenversicherung (-en) *personal insurance*
persönlich *personal(ly)*
die Persönlichkeit (-en) *personality*
der Pfeffer (-) *pepper*
der Pfennig (-e) *pfennig*
der Pferdesport (-e) *riding*
das Pfingsten *Whitsun, Pentecost*
das Pflanzenschutzmittel *pesticide*
das Pfund (-e) *pound*
die PGH = Produktionsgenossen-schaft des Handwerks (*former GDR*) *trade/craft cooperative*
die Pharma *pharmaceuticals (division)*
die Pharmazeutika (*pl.*) *pharmaceuticals*
die Pharmazie (-n) *pharmaceuticals*
phenolgeharzt *phenol-resinated*
die Philosophie (-n) *philosophy*
Piccata *piccata (sour lemon sauce)*
der Piepton (¨e) *beep*
piiiep *beep*
die Pille (-n) *(the) pill*
die Pionierarbeit (-en) *pioneering work*
der PKW = Personenkraftwagen
planen *to plan*
die Planung (-en) *planning*
die Planwirtschaft *planned/command economy*
die Platte (-n) *panel*
das Plattenformat (-e) *panel format, size of the panel(s)*
der Platz (¨e) *place, seat, square*
platzen (sein) *to split, crack*
die Platzkarte (-n) *seat (reservation)*
plazieren *to place*
das Plus *plus*; ein Plus an *more*
plus *plus*
der Polder (-) *platform*
das Polen *Poland*
polieren *to polish*
die Politik *policy, politics*
die Polizei (-en) *police*
der Polsterstoff (-e) *upholstery*
Pommes: Pommes frites (*pl.*) *chips*
der Port *port*
das Portugal *Portugal*
das Porzellan (-e) *porcelain, china*
positiv *positive(ly)*
die Post *post (office)*
das Postamt (¨er) *post office*
das Postfach (¨er) *post box (PO box)*
die Postleitzahl (-en) *post code, zip code*
die Poststrukturreform (-en) *structural reform of the postal services*
potentiell *potential(ly)*
das Potpourri (-s) *potpourri*
die PR *PR (Public Relations)*
praktisch *practical(ly), virtually, more or less*
praktizieren *to practise*
(sich) präsentieren *to present (oneself)*

der Präsident (*sing. gen.* -en) (-en) *president*
die Praxis *practice, experience*
praxisnah *practical(ly)*
die Präzisionswerkzeuge (*pl.*) *precision tools*
der Preis (-e) *price*
die Preisänderung (-en) *price change*
preisgünstig *cost-effective, low-cost*
preiswert *value for money, low-cost*
die Presse (-n) *press (machine), the press (newspaper industry)*
die Presse-Information (-en) *press release* (lit. *information*)
die Presseabteilung (-en) *press department/office*
die Pressearbeit *press relations*
pressen (preßt), preßte, gepreßt *to press*
der Presseraum (¨e) *press room*
der Pressereferent (*sing. gen.* -en) (-en) *press officer*
der Pressesprecher (-) *press officer*
die Pressestelle (-n) *press office*
prima *first class, excellent, great*
das Prinzip (-ien) *principle*
prinzipiell *in/on principle, basically*
die Priorität (-en) *priority*
Priv. = privat
privat *private(ly)*
privatisieren *to privatize*
die Privatisierung (-en) *privatization*
das Privatkundengeschäft (-e) *retail banking*
pro *per*; pro Person *per person*
probieren *to try*
probier's = probiere es
das Problem (-e) *problem*
problemlos *without problem*
die Problemlösungen (*pl.*) *solutions to problems*
der Producer (-) *producer*
das Produkt (-e) *product, material*
das Produktdesign (-s) *product design*
die Produktgruppe (-n) *product group*
die Produktion (-en) *production*
der Produktionsstandort (-e) *production facility*
die Produktionsstätte (-n) *production facility*
der Produzent (*sing. gen.* -en) (-en) *producer*
produzieren *to produce*
Prof. = Professor
der Professor (-en) *professor*
das Programm (-e) *programme, program, product range*
das Projekt (-e) *project*
der Projektleiter (-) *project manager*
die Promotion (-en) *doctorate, PhD*
der Prospekt (-e) *brochure*
die Prothese (-n) *artificial limb*
das Protokoll (-e) *report*
die Provision (-en) *commission*
das Prozent (-e) *percent; %-igen percentage*
der Prozentsatz (¨e) *percentage*

prüfen *to inspect, examine, test, audit*
die Prüfung (-en) *inspection, exam(ination), test, audit*
der Prüfungsverlauf (-̈e) *examination/testing procedure*
die Psychotherapeutin (-nen) *psychotherapist (f.)*
der Punkt (-e) *point, dot, factor*
pünktlich *punctual(ly), on time*
die Putenbrust (-̈e) *turkey breast*
putzen *to clean*

Q

der *or* das Quadratmeter (-) *square meter*
die Qualifikation (-en) *qualification*
qualifiziert *qualified*
die Qualität (-en) *quality*
qualitativ *qualitative(ly)*
die Quantität (-en) *quantity*
die Quelle (-n) *source*
die Quittung (-en) *receipt*

R

der Rahmen (-) *frame; im Rahmen in the course/context (of), during*
der Rat *advice*
das Rathaus (-̈er) *townhall*
der Ratschlag (-̈e) *(piece of) advice*
der Raucher (-) *smoking, smoker*
der Raum (-̈e) *room, area*
raus = heraus *or* hinaus
rausgehen (*sep.*), ging raus, rausgegangen (sein) *to go out*
die Reaktion (-en) *reaction*
die Realisierung (-en) *realization, implementation*
die Realschule (-n) *vocational school (10 to 16)*
die Recherchen (*pl.*) *research*
rechnen *to calculate, count (amount); rechnen mit to reckon with; ich hatte nicht damit gerechnet I hadn't reckoned on that*
der Rechner (-) *computer*
rechnergeführt *computerized*
die Rechnung (-en) *bill, invoice*
das Rechnungswesen *accountancy, book-keeping, accounting*
das Recht (-e) *law, right*
recht *right, rather, quite; ich hatte damit recht I was right*
der, die, das rechte *right(hand)*
rechtlich *legal(ly)*
rechts *(on/to the) right (see links)*
die Rechtsabteilung (-en) *legal department*
die Rechtsform (-en) *legal structure*
die Rede (-n) *speech*
reden (über) *to talk, speak (about)*
die Reform (-en) *reform*
der Reformationstag (-e) *Reformation Day*
die Regel (-n) *rule, convention; in der Regel as a rule, generally*

die Regierung (-en) *government*
regional *regional*
der Regisseur (-e) *(film/theatre) director*
REHA (= Rehabilitation) *rehabilitation*
die Rehabilitationshilfen (*pl.*) *rehabilitation aids*
die Rehabilitationsmittel (*pl.*) *rehabilitation equipment*
reibungslos *seamless(ly)*
reif *mature*
die Reife (-n) *maturity; (see Mittlere)*
die Reihe (-n) *row, series, a number of*
rein = herein, hinein; in die Speichermedien rein sollen *in(to) which storage media are intended to go*
rein *pure(ly), clean*
reingelegt *laid*
reinlegen (*sep.*) *to lay in(to)*
der Reis *rice*
die Reise (-n) *journey*
das Reisebüro (-s) *travel agent*
die Reisebürokauffrau (-en) *travel agent (f.)*
das Reisen *travel(ling)*
reisen (sein) *to travel (see also anreisen, herumreisen)*
reißen, riß, gerissen (haben *and* sein) *to tear, rip; uns aus der Hand gerissen torn out of our hands*
die Reistimbale (-n) *rice timbale (a savoury mousse made with rice)*
reizvoll *attractive(ly)*
die Reklamation (-en) *complaint, customer service/care (department)*
relativ *relative(ly)*
relevant *relevant*
der Repräsentant (*sing. gen.* -en) (-en) *representative*
repräsentieren *to represent*
die Republik (-en) *republic*
reservieren *to reserve, book*
die Reservierung (-en) *reservation*
das Restaurant (-s) *restaurant*
restaurieren *to restore*
der Reststoff (-e) *residue*
der Rhein *(River) Rhine*
Rheinland-Pfalz *Rhineland-Palatinate*
richtig *correct(ly), right*
die Richtung (-en) *direction*
der Riese (*sing. gen.* -n) (-n) *giant*
die Riesencrevette (-n) *king prawn*
die Riesennachfrage (-n) *massive demand*
der Riesennachholbedarf *massive need to catch up*
riesig *massive, huge*
das Rinderfilet (-s) *fillet steak*
die Rinderkraftbrühe *beef consommé*
roh *raw*
die Rolle (-n) *role, roll; das spielt keine Rolle that is not important*
der Rollstuhl (-̈e) *wheelchair*

das Röntgenkontrastmittel (-) *X-ray contrast medium*
der Rosé (-s) *rosé*
der Rosenmontag (-e) *Monday preceding Ash Wednesday*
die Rösti (*pl.*) *fried grated potatoes*
die Röstzwiebel (-n) *fried onion(s)*
rot *red*
die Rückforderungsansprüche (*pl.*) *restitution claims*
die Rückkehr *return*
der Rückruf (-e) *return (phone) call*
die Rückseite (-n) *overleaf*
der Ruf (-e) *(phone) call, reputation*
ruf' = rufe
rufen, rief, gerufen *to call, ring (see also zurückrufen, anrufen)*
ruhig *quiet, easily*
rum = herum
Rumänien *Rumania*
rumreisen = herumreisen
rund *about, around, approximately; rund rum around here*
der Rundfunk *radio*
russisch *Russian*
das Rußland *Russia*

S

's = es
der Sachbearbeiter (-) *clerk*
die Sachbearbeiterin (-nen) *clerk (f.)*
die Sache (-n) *thing*
Sachsen *Saxony*
Sachsen-Anhalt *Saxony-Anhalt*
der Saft (-̈e) *juice*
sagen *to say, tell (see also zusagen)*
sah *saw (see sehen)*
die Sahne *cream*
die Sahnehaube (-n) *cream topping*
die Saison (-s) *season*
das Sakko (-s) *jacket*
der Salat (-e) *salad, lettuce*
das Salz (-e) *salt*
die Salzkartoffel (-n) *boiled potato(es)*
der Samstag (-e) *Saturday*
samstags *on Saturdays*
der Satz (-̈e) *sentence, message*
sauber *clean*
saubermachen (*sep.*) *to clean*
die Sauce (-n) *sauce*
sauer *sour*
die Sauerstofftherapie (-n) *oxygen therapy*
die Säule (-n) *column, pillar*
sautieren *to fry*
die S-Bahn (-en) *S-Bahn, suburban rail network*
schaffen, schuf, geschaffen *to create*
schaffen, schaffte, geschafft *to accomplish, manage (to do sth.)*
der Schalter (-) *counter*
die Schaltermitarbeiterin (-nen) *counter clerk (f.)*
schätzungsweise *approximate(ly)*
schauen *to look, see*
das Schaufenster (-) *shop window*

der Scheck (-s) *cheque;* zahlen Sie gegen diesen Scheck *pay against this cheque the sum of*

der Schecktext *cheque text*

die Scheibe (-n) *slice*

scheinen, ie, ie *to appear, seem*

scheitern (sein) (an) *to founder (due to)*

die Scheune (-n) *barn*

schicken *to send*

das Schiebedach (¨er) *sunroof*

das Schiff (-e) *ship*

die Schinkenstreifen (*pl.*) *strips of ham*

schlaflos *sleepless*

schlagen (ä), u, a *to hit, strike*

schlecht *bad*

schlechthin *the epitome of*

schleifen, schliff, geschliffen *to grind, rub down*

die Schleifmaschine (-n) *grinder*

schlicht *simple (-ly), clear(ly)*

schließen, o, o *to close, conclude (see also* anschließen*)*

schließlich *final(ly)*

der Schlüssel (-) *key*

schmutzig *dirty*

schneiden, schnitt, geschnitten *to cut (see also* abschneiden*)*

schnell *fast, quick(ly)*

schneller (als) *faster (than)*

schnellstens *as fast/soon as possible*

schnurlos *cordless*

schon *already, yet;* das wär's schon *that is all;* ich würde schon sagen *yes, I would say so*

schön *beautiful(ly), nice, good;* danke schön *thank you;* bitte schön *you're welcome, here you are;* bitte schön? *yes, can I help you?* schönen guten Tag *(a very) good morning/afternoon*

das Schottland *Scotland*

das Schreiben (-) *letter*

schreiben, ie, ie *to write (see also* anschreiben, ausschreiben*)*

schrieb *wrote (see* schreiben*)*

schriftlich *written, in writing*

der Schritt (-e) *step*

der Schulabschluß (¨-üsse) *school qualification/result*

die Schulausbildung (-en) *school education, schooling*

die Schulden (*pl.*) *debts*

die Schule (-n) *school*

das Schulzeugnis (-se) *school certificate*

Schwaben *Swabia*

schwäbisch *Swabian*

schwanken *to fluctuate*

schwarz *black*

der Schwarzwald *Black Forest*

Schweden *Sweden*

das Schwein (-e) *pig, pork*

das Schweinefilet (-s) *fillet of pork*

die Schweiz *Switzerland*

der Schweizer (-) *(the) Swiss person/thing/one*

schwer *heavy (-ily), difficult*

schwierig *difficult*

die Schwierigkeit (-en) *difficulty*

sechs *six*

der, die, das sechste *(the) sixth (one)*

sechsundvierzig *forty-six*

der See (-n) *lake*

das Segeln *sailing*

segeln *to sail*

sehen (ie), a, e *to see, look (see also* aussehen*);* das wird immer gerne gesehen *that always creates a good impression*

sich sehen (ie), a, e (als) *to see oneself/each other (as) (see also* umsehen*)*

sehr *very, so much, a lot;* sehr viel *a lot (of);* danke sehr *thank you*

sei *is, be, are (subjunctive) (see* sein*);* sei es *whether they are*

sein (ist), war, gewesen (sein) *to be (also used to form the perfect, pluperfect and passive of other verbs)* bin *am;* ist *is;* sind *are;* war *was;* gewesen *been, gone;* wäre(n) *were, would be;* man ist auf den praktischen Aspekt aus *people are geared to the practical aspect;* er ist zu erreichen *he can be reached*

sein, seine, seinem, seinen, seiner, seines *his, (to/from/for/of) him/its*

seit *since, for*

seitdem *since (then)*

die Seite (-n) *side, page*

seitens *on the part of*

das Sekretariat (-e) *office, secretarial duties*

die Sekretärin (-nen) *secretary (f.)*

der Sekt (-e) *sparkling wine*

der Sektor (-en) *sector*

die Sekunde (-n) *second*

selber *or* selbst *self, myself, yourself, himself, herself, itself, etc.*

selbst *even (see also* selber*)*

die Selbständigkeit *independence*

selbstverständlich *naturally, of course*

selten *seldom*

das Seminar (-e) *seminar*

die Sendeanstalt (-en) *broadcasting network/station*

senden *to send*

die Senkerodiermaschine *diesinking/ spark-erosion machine*

die Senkerodierzentren (*pl.*) *diesinking/spark-erosion centres*

die Senkerosion *diesinking/spark erosion*

das Sensorfeld (-er) *sensor field*

der September (-) *September*

die Serie (-n) *series, (mass/volume) production*

der Service *service*

die Servolenkung *power steering*

(sich) setteln (sein) *to settle*

setzen *to use, set (see also* einsetzen*)*

die Setzerei (-en) *typesetter*

der Sherry (-s) *sherry*

sich *(to/from/for/of) oneself, himself, herself, itself, yourself, yourselves, themselves (also used with reflexive verbs, eg* sich melden*);* in sich *in itself;* von sich aus *in itself*

sicher *secure(ly), safe(ly), reliable (-ly), certain(ly), of course*

die Sicherheit (-en) *safety, certainty;* mit Sicherheit *certainly;* geprüfte Sicherheit *safety-tested*

das Sicherheits-Bremssystem (-e) *antilock braking system*

sicherlich *certain(ly)*

sich sichern *to secure (for oneself)*

die Sicht *(point of) view*

sichtbar *visible (-ly)*

sie *she, her, it, they, them*

Sie *you (formal)*

sieben *seven*

siebzehn *seventeen*

sich siedeln *to settle*

sieht's = sieht es

das Silvester (-) *New Year's Eve*

sind *are (see* sein*)*

der Sinn (-e) *sense, meaning, point*

die Situation (-en) *situation*

der Sitz (-e) *seat, head office, headquarters*

sitzen, saß, gesessen (haben *or* sein) *to sit, have the head office*

der Sitzplatz (¨-e) *seat*

die Sitzschale (-n) *seat shell/mould*

die Sitzung (-en) *meeting*

das Skandinavien *Skandinavia*

Slowakisch: Slowakische Republik *Slovak Republic*

so *so, thus, such that, (like) this, about, as;* so..., daß... *in such a way that;* so daß *so that;* so...wie *just as;* es ist so *it is like this*

sofort *immediately;* ab sofort *from now*

die Software (-s) *software*

sogar *even*

sogenannt *so-called, known as*

der Sohn (¨-e) *son*

solch, solche, solchem, solchen, solches *such;* all solche Geschichten *all that kind of thing*

soll *should, is, has to (see* sollen*)*

sollen (soll), sollte, gesollt *to be supposed to/intended/destined to, to be, should (see also* rein*)*

soll's = soll es *(see* sollen*)*

somit *thereby, therefore*

der Sommer (-) *summer*

die Sonderausstattung (-en) *special equipment, extras*

sondern *but, on the contrary*

die Sonderwünsche (*pl.*) *special wishes/requirements*

der Sonnabend (-e) *Saturday*

der Sonntag (-e) *Sunday*

sonntags *on Sundays*

sonst *otherwise, usually, else*

sorgen (für) *to ensure (that), take care (of), work for*

das Sortiment (-e) *product range*

die Soße (-n) *sauce*
souverän *confident*
sowie *and, as well as*
sowohl: sowohl...als auch *both...and*
das Spanien *Spain*
der Spanier (-) *Spaniard*
die Spanierin (-nen) *Spaniard (f.)*
die Sparte (-n) *product group*
spät *late*
später (als) *later (than), future*
spätestens *at the latest, not later than*
die Spätzle (pl.) *spätzle (similar to pasta)*
der Speck *ham, bacon*
der Spediteur (-e) *freight forwarder*
die Spedition (-en) *carriage, shipping, forwarding agent, freight forwarder*
der Speicher (-) *storage, memory*
die Speichermedien (pl.) *storage media*
die Speise(n)karte (-n) *menu*
das Spektrum (-tren) *range, spectrum*
das Spezialgebiet (-e) *specialist area*
das Spezialglas (¨er) *special glass*
spezialisieren *to specialize*
sich spezialisieren (auf) *to specialize (in)*
speziell *special(ly)*
spezifisch *specific(ally)*
das Spiel (-e) *game*
spielen *to play*
der Spieß (-e) *skewer, (roasting) spit*
der Spinat *spinach*
die Spitzenprodukte (pl.) *top products*
die Spitzentechnologien (pl.) *top technologies*
der Sport *sport(s)*
die Sprache (-n) *language*
sprechen (i), a, o *to say, speak, talk*
der Sprecher (-) *speaker*
die Sprechzeiten (pl.) *surgery hours*
die Spur (-en) *trace, track, lane*
spürbar *discernible*
spüren *to feel, notice*
der Staat (-en) *state, nation*
staatlich *government-owned, state*
die Staatsregierung (-en) *(state) government*
die Stabilität *stability*
die Stadt (¨e) *town, city*
der Stahl (¨e) *steel*
der Stahlformenbauer (-) *steel mould/die maker (also trade journal)*
der Stamm (¨e) *trunk, log*
stammen (aus) *to originate (from)*
der Stand (¨e) *exhibition stand, position*
der Standard (-s) *standard (see Norm)*
der Standort (-e) *location*
stark *strong(ly), powerful(ly), highly; sehr stark zu Hause a very strong presence*
die Stärke (-n) *strength, thickness*
stärker (als) *stronger (than)*
der Startton (¨e) *(starting) signal, beep*
statt *instead of (see also stattfinden)*
stattfinden (sep.), a, u *to take place*
stattgefunden *taken place*
staunen *to be astonished*

das Steak (-s) *steak*
stehen, stand, gestanden (sein or haben) *to stand, be*
steigen, ie, ie (sein) *to increase*
steigend *increasing(ly)*
steigern *to increase*
stell' = stelle
die Stelle (-n) *place, position, job, department; übergeordnete Stelle higher level of management*
stellen *to place, put, be, make (see also sich vorstellen); ich bekomme Muster gestellt I receive free samples; um Anträge zu stellen in order to place applications*
sich stellen *to face up to; BP hat sich ihrer Verantwortung gestellt BP faced up to its responsibility*
der Stellenwert (-e) *value, status*
die Steuer (-n) *tax*
der Steuerberater (-) *tax adviser, accountant, book-keeper*
steuerlich *(relating to) tax*
steuern *to control*
stieß *pushed (see stoßen)*
stimmen *to be so, to be true/right*
die Stimmung (-en) *atmosphere, morale*
der Stock (¨e) *floor, storey*
das Stockwerk (-e) *floor, storey*
der Stoff (-e) *material, fabric; es muß schon ein Stoff sein it certainly has to be fabric*
stoßen (stößt), stieß, gestoßen *to push; stoßen (auf) to come up with an idea*
die Straße (-n) *street, road(way)*
die Straßenbahn (-en) *tram*
die Strategie (-n) *strategy*
strategisch *strategic(ally)*
streichen, strich, gestrichen *to cross out*
streng *strict(ly)*
die Strickwaren (pl.) *knitwear*
die Struktur (-en) *structure*
strukturieren *to structure*
die Strukturierung (-en) *structure, structuring*
der Strumpf (¨e) *stocking*
das Stück (-e) *piece, unit*
die Studie (-n) *study*
das Studium *(university) course of studies*
die Stunde (-n) *hour*
die Suche *search; die Suche nach the search for*
suchen *to search (for)*
der Süd(en) *south, (the) South*
süddeutsch *south German; 'Süddeutsche Zeitung' (national newspaper, liberal)*
südost *south-east*
die Suppe (-n) *soup*
die Symbiose (-n) *symbiosis*
das System (-e) *system*

T

der Tag (-e) *day; (schönen) guten Tag (a very) good morning/afternoon*
der Tagesausweis (-e) *day pass*
die Tageszeitung (-en) *daily paper*
tagsüber *during the day*
die Tagung (-en) *conference*
der Tagungsverlauf (¨e) *conference programme*
der Tannenbaum (¨e) *fir tree, Christmas tree*
die Tasche (-n) *pocket, bag*
die Tasse (-n) *cup*
die Tastatur (-en) *keyboard*
tätig *active; tätig sein to be active*
tätigen *to effect (see Auftrag)*
die Tätigkeit (-en) *activity*
tatsächlich *in fact, in practice*
tauchen *see auftauchen*
tausend *thousand*
das Taxi (-s) *taxi*
das Team (-s) *team*
Techn. = Technischer
die Technik (-en) *engineering, technology, technique*
der Techniker (-) *engineer*
die Technikerin (-nen) *engineer (f.)*
technisch *technical(ly)*
die Technologie (-n) *technology*
technologisch *technological(ly)*
der Tee (-s) *tea*
der *or* das Teil (-e) *part; zum Teil (in) part, partly*
der Teilnehmer (-) *participant, delegate*
teilweise *partly*
Tel. = Telefon
das Telefax (-e) *fax*
das Telefon (-e) *telephone*
der Telefonanschluß (-üsse) *telephone connection*
der Telefonapparat (-e) *handset*
der Telefondienst (-e) *telephone (answering) service*
telefonieren *to phone*
das Telefonieren *telephoning*
telefonisch *by telephone*
die Telefonistin (-nen) *telephonist (f.)*
die Telefonsekretärin (-nen) *telephonist (f.)*
die Telefonzelle (-n) *telephone box*
die Telefonzentrale (-n) *switchboard*
das Telegramm (-e) *telegram*
das Teletex *teletex*
das Telex (-e) *telex*
die Temperatur (-en) *temperature*
das Tennis *tennis*
der Tennisschläger (-) *tennis racket*
der Termin (-e) *appointment*
der Test (-s) *test*
teuer *expensive*
der Text (-e) *text*
die Textilien (pl.) *textiles*
das Theater (-) *theatre*
das Thema (Themen) *subject, topic*
die Theorie (-n) *theory*
Thüringen *Thuringia*
die Tiefgarage (-n) *underground garage/car park*

der Tip (-s) *tip*
der Tisch (-e) *table*
Tlx. = Telex
die Tochter (⸚) *daughter, subsidiary*
die Tochtergesellschaft *subsidiary*
das Tochterunternehmen (-)
    subsidiary (lit. daughter company)
die Toilette (-n) *WC, toilet, lavatory*
toll *great, smashing, zappy,*
    incredible
die Tomate (-n) *tomato*
die Tomatenspaghetti *spaghetti with*
    tomato sauce
total *total(ly)*
der Totensonntag (-e) *Sunday before*
    Advent to commemorate the dead
der Tourismus *tourism*
der Tourist (sing. gen. -en) (-en) *tourist*
traditionell *traditional(ly)*
tragen (ä), u, a *to carry, wear*
der Transport (-e) *transport*
der Traum (⸚e) *dream*
traurig *sad(ly)*
(sich) treffen (i), a, o *to meet*
treiben, ie, ie *to go in for; Sport*
    treiben to go in for sports; wenn
    man mit Deutschen Handel
    treiben will if you want to do
    business with Germans
der Trend (-s) *trend*
der Trendartikel (-) *fashionable article*
sich trennen von *to separate (oneself)*
    from, jettison
treten (tritt), trat, getreten (sein) *to*
    tread (see also auf-, herantreten)
das Trinkbare: etwas Trinkbares
    something drinkable
trinken, a, u *to drink*
das Trinkgeld (-er) *tip*
tritt *treads (see treten)*
trocken *dry*
der, die, das trockne *(the) dry (one)*
trocknen *to dry*
trotz(dem) *despite, in spite of*
Tschechisch: Tschechische
    Republik *Czech Republic*
tschüs *bye, see you*
tun (tut), tat, getan *to do, deal with*
sich tun (tut), tat, getan *to happen*
die Tür (-en) *door*
die Turbine (-n) *turbine*
der Turm (⸚e) *tower*
der TÜV = Technischer
    Überwachungsverein *TÜV*
    (German Technical
    Inspectorate)
der Typ (-en) *type*
typisch *typical(ly)*

U

u. = und
die U-Bahn (-en) *U-Bahn,*
    underground (train), subway
üben *to practise (see also ausüben)*
über *about, with, above, over, from,*
    more than, away (see also sep. verbs
    with über); über 120 Jahre more
    than 120 years; übers Geschäft
    reden talk about business; übers
    Jahr over the year
überall *everywhere*
überbacken *baked under the grill*
der Überbringer (-) *bearer*
übergeben (i), a, e *to hand over*
übergeordnet *higher, superior*
überhaupt *at all, single; überhaupt*
    nicht not at all
sich überlegen *to consider*
der Übermut *high spirits*
die Übernahme (-n) *takeover, purchase*
übernehmen, übernimmt,
    übernahm, übernommen *to*
    take over
überordnen (sep.) *to place above*
überprüfen *to inspect, test,*
    examine
überraschen *to surprise*
übers = über das
die Übersicht (-en) *overview*
die Überwachung (-en) *monitoring*
überweisen, überwies,
    überwiesen *to transfer*
überzeugen (von) *to convince (of);*
    ich bin davon überzeugt, daß I
    am convinced that
üblich *common, usual, standard*
übrig *remaining; im übrigen*
    incidentally
die Übung (-en) *practice, exercise*
die Uhr (-en) *hour, clock, watch; um*
    sechs Uhr at six o'clock
die Uhrenwerkstatt (⸚en) *clockmaker's*
    (workshop)
die Uhrzeit (-en) *time*
die Ukraine *Ukraine*
der Ultraschall *ultrasound*
um *at, for, in, by (see also sep. verbs*
    with um); um...zu in order to;
    sechs Uhr at six o'clock; es geht
    um it is about; um...zahlen zu
    können in order to be able to pay...;
    so um die zwanzig rum around
    twenty
umbenennen (sep.), benannte um,
    umbenannt *to re-name*
umdrehen (sep.) *to turn*
    (round/over), reverse
umfangreich *comprehensive(ly)*
umfassen, umfaßte, umfaßt *to*
    comprise, include, cover
umfassend *comprehensive(ly)*
der Umgang (mit) *contact, dealings*
    (with)
die Umgangsformen (pl.) *manners*
umgangssprachlich *colloquial(ly)*
die Umgebung (-en) *surrounding area*
umgehend *immediate(ly), direct(ly)*
umgesehen *looked around*
umlegen (mit) *to surround (with)*
umreißen, umriß, umrissen *to*
    outline
ums = um das
der Umsatz (⸚e) *turnover, sales*

das Umsatzvolumen (- or -volumina)
    sales volume, turnover
sich umschauen (sep.) *to look around*
sich umsehen (sep.), sah um,
    umgesehen *to look around*
der Umstand (⸚e) *circumstance, state*
umsteigen (sep.), ie, ie (sein)
    (auf) to change over, switch (to)
die Umwandlung (-en) *change*
die Umwelt *environment*
der Umweltschutz *environmental*
    protection
unabhängig *independent(ly)*
unbekannt *unknown*
und *and; und so weiter (usw.) and*
    so on, etc.; und zwar that is
das Ungarn *Hungary*
ungefähr *about, approximately*
ungeheuer, ungeheu(e)re
    massive(ly), high(ly)
ungewöhnlich *unusual(ly)*
der, die, das Ungewöhnliche *(the)*
    unusual (thing/one)
unglücklich *unhappy (-ily)*
universell *universal(ly)*
die Universität (-en) *university*
uns *(to) us, for us, ourselves*
unser, unsere, unserem, unseren,
    unserer, unseres *(to/from/*
    for/of) our
der Unsicherheitsfaktor (-en) *element*
    of uncertainty
unten *below, under, at the bottom*
unter *under, beneath, among*
unterbrechen (i), a, o *to interrupt*
unterbreiten *to make, issue*
unterbringen (sep.), brachte unter,
    untergebracht *to accommodate*
untereinander *between them/us*
sich unterhalten (unterhält), unter-
    hielt, unterhalten (über)
    to discuss, talk, converse (about)
die Unterlage (-n) *document(ation)*
unterm = unter dem
unternehmen *to undertake*
das Unternehmen (-) *company,*
    enterprise, undertaking, operation
unternehmerisch *corporate*
der Unterricht (-e) *lesson, teaching*
(sich) unterscheiden, ie, ie *to distinguish*
    (itself/oneself)
der Unterschied (-e) *difference*
unterschiedlich *variable, various*
unterschreiben, ie, ie *to sign*
unterschrieben *signed*
die Unterschrift (-en) *signature*
unterstützen *to support*
die Unterstützung (-en) *support*
untersuchen *to examine*
die Untersuchung (-en) *examination*
unterteilen *to (sub)divide*
unwichtig *unimportant*
der Urlaub (-e) *holiday(s)*
die Urlaubsorte (pl.) *holiday resorts*
ursächlich *causal(ly), properly*
USA *USA*
usw. (= und so weiter) *etc.*

V

die Vakuumpumpen (*pl.*) *vacuum pumps*
variabel *variable (-ly)*
der Vater (∸) *father*
veranstalten *to organize, hold*
die Verantwortung (-en) *responsibility (see also sich stellen)*
die Verarbeitung (-en) *process(ing)*
der Verband (∸e) *association, union, federation, society*
verbessern *to improve*
die Verbesserung (-en) *improvement*
verbinden, verband, verbunden *to connect, link*
die Verbindung (-en) *connection*
verbreiten *to spread*
verdienen *to earn*
der Verein (-e) *association*
vereinbaren *to agree; wie vereinbart as agreed*
die Vereinbarung (-en) *agreement*
vereinigt *united; Vereinigtes Königreich United Kingdom (UK); die Vereinigten Staaten The United States (of America)*
vererben *to leave (to)*
verfeinern *to refine, round off*
verfügen (über) *to have access (to), have (at one's disposal)*
die Verfügung *disposal; zur Verfügung haben/stellen to have/ make available; zur Verfügung stehen to be available*
die Vergangenheit (-en) *past*
vergessen (vergißt), vergaß, vergessen *to forget*
der Vergleich (-e) *comparison*
vergleichbar *comparable (-ly)*
das Verhalten (-) *behaviour*
das Verhältnis (-se) *relation(ship)*
der Verkauf (∸e) *sale, sales (office/department)*
verkaufen *to sell*
das Verkaufshaus (∸er) *sales outlet*
der Verkaufspreis (-e) *purchase/ retail price*
der Verkaufsprofi (-s) *professional salesperson*
das Verkaufsverhalten *sales strategy (-ies)*
der Verkehr *traffic, transport*
das Verkehrsamt (∸er) *tourist office*
die Verkehrsbetriebe (*pl.*) *transport system/services*
das Verkehrsmittel (-) *(means of) transport*
die Verkehrstechnik *traffic engineering*
das Verkehrsunternehmen (-) *transport company*
der Verkehrsverein (-e) *tourist office*
das Verkehrswesen *transport*
der Verlag (-e) *publisher*
verlegen (auf) *to postpone (to)*
die Verlustrechnung: *see Gewinn*
vermehrt *increasing(ly)*
vermieten *to rent*
die Vermietung (-en) *rental, lease*

die Vermittlung (-en) *operator, exchange*
die Verpackungsmaschinen (*pl.*) *packaging machines*
verpflichten *to oblige*
verpflichtet *obliged, responsible*
verschieden *various, different*
die Versicherung (-en) *insurance*
der Versicherungsschutz *insurance protection*
sich versorgen (mit) *to obtain*
sich verspäten *to be late; ich habe mich verspätet I'm late*
versprechen (i), a, o *to promise*
das Versprechen (-) *promising, promise*
versprochen *promised*
versprühen *to radiate*
verstanden *understood (see verstehen)*
verständigen *to notify, advise*
sich verständigen *to agree*
das Verständnis *understanding*
verständnisvoll *(full of) understanding*
versteh' = verstehe
verstehen, verstand, verstanden *to understand*
das Verstehen *understanding*
sich verstehen, verstand, verstanden (als) *to see oneself (as)*
versuchen *to try, attempt*
verteilen *to distribute, hand round*
der Vertrag (∸e) *contract*
vertraglich *contractual(ly)*
das Vertragsangebot (-e) *contract offer*
vertreiben, ie, ie *to sell, market*
vertreten (vertritt), a, e *to represent*
der Vertreter (-) *agent, representative*
die Vertreterin (-nen) *representative (f.)*
die Vertretung (-en) *agent, agency, sales/representative office*
der Vertrieb (-e) *sales (department), selling*
die Vertriebsgesellschaft (-en) *distributor/sales company*
der Vertriebsinnendienst (-e) *in-house sales department/office*
die Vertriebszentrale (-n) *sales centre*
die Verwaltung (-en) *administration*
verzehnfachen *to increase tenfold*
verzichten (auf) *to go/do without*
viel, viele, vielem, vielen, vieler, vieles *much, (as) many, all; sehr viel a lot (of); vieles many things; das viele Geld all that money*
der, die, das viele *(the) many (thing(s)/ one(s))*
vielleicht *perhaps*
vielmals *many times*
vielseitig *many-sided*
vier *four*
viereinhalb *four and a half*
der, die, das vierte *(the) fourth (one)*
der/ein Viertel (-) *(a) quarter, district*
die Viertelstunde (-n) *quarter of an hour*

vierzig *forty*
die VIP *VIP (Very Important Person)*
das *or* der Virus (Viren) *virus*
die Visitenkarte (-n) *business card*
das Volk (∸er) *people, nation*
die Volksrepublik: Volksrepublik China *People's Republic of China*
die Volksschule (-n) *elementary school*
der Volkstrauertag (-e) *day of mourning*
voll *complete, full(y)*
vollautomatisch *(fully) automatic(ally), automated*
völlig *complete(ly)*
die Vollkaskoversicherung (-en) *fully-comprehensive insurance*
die Vollpension *full board*
die Vollständigkeit *completeness*
vollversichert *fully insured*
das Volumen (- *or* Volumina) *volume*
vom = von dem *of/from the, date*
von *of, from, by (von is a common title indicating noble forebears eg Michaela von Asen); von einem Apotheker gegründet founded by a pharmacist; vom...bis zum from...to*
vor *before, in front of, on, ago; vor allem above all, mainly; vor 20 Jahren 20 years ago; nach wie vor still, now as ever*
vorbehalten: Preisänderungen vorbehalten *prices subject to change*
die Vorbemerkung (-en) *introductory remark*
vorbereiten (sep.) *to prepare*
die Vorbereitung (-en) *preparation*
das Vorbild (-er) *model, example*
der Vordergrund (∸e) *foreground*
vorführen (sep.) *to demonstrate*
vorgedruckt *(pre-)printed*
vorgehen (s), ging vor, vorgegangen (sein) *to act, go on/forward, proceed; mit der gleichen Konzeption vorgehen to proceed on the same basis*
vorgenommen *planned, undertaken (see vornehmen)*
vorgesehen *conceived, planned*
der/die Vorgesetzte (-n), ein Vorgesetzter *superior*
das Vorhaben (-) *plan*
vorhanden *available; die Mittel sind vorhanden the resources are available*
vorher *before(hand), previous(ly)*
vorherrschen (sep.) *to predominate*
die Vorlaufzeit (-en) *run-up, preliminary/preparatory time*
vorliegen (sep.), lag vor, vorgelegen *to be known/ available*
der Vormittag (-e) *morning*
vorn *at the front*
der Vorname (*sing. gen.* -ns) (-n) *first name, forename*

185

vornehmen (*sep.*) (nimmt vor), nahm vor, vorgenommen *to carry out*

sich vornehmen (*sep.*) (nimmt vor), nahm vor, vorgenommen *to undertake, plan*

der Vorschlag (⸚e) *suggestion*

vorschlagen (*sep.*) (schlägt vor), schlug vor, vorgeschlagen *to suggest*

die Vorschrift (-en) *regulation*

die Vorspeise (-n) *starter, hors d'oeuvre*

vorsprechen (*sep.*) (i), a, o *to attend for interview, call on*

der Vorstand (⸚e) *board of management*

die Vorstandsassistentin (-nen) *assistant to the board of management (f.)*

die Vorstandssekretärin (-nen) *secretary to the board of management (not company secretary) (f.)*

vorstellen (*sep.*) *to present, introduce*

sich vorstellen (*sep.*) *to introduce oneself*

sich vorstellen (*sep.*) *to imagine, envisage;* ich stelle mir eine interessante Ausbildung vor *I anticipate an interesting training*

die Vorstellung (-en) *requirement, wish, presentation*

das Vorstellungsgespräch (-e) *interview*

der Vorteil (-e) *advantage*

die Vorwahl (-en) *dialling code*

vorzu- *see* vornehmen, vorsprechen, vorstellen

der Vorzug (⸚e) *advantage*

W

die Wachsjacke (-n) *waxed jacket*

das Wachstum *growth*

wacklig *shaky*

der Wagen (-) *car*

die Wahl (-en) *choice, selection*

wählen *to choose, select, elect*

wahnsinnig *incredible (-ly)*

wahr *true*

während *while, during, whereas*

wahrscheinlich *probably, very likely*

die Währung (-en) *currency*

das Wälzlager (-) *roller bearing*

die Wand (⸚e) *wall*

wandern (sein) *to walk, hike;* wandern gehen *to go walking/ hiking*

wann *when*

war *was (see* sein*)*

wär' = wäre; wär's = wäre es

die Ware (-n) *product, goods*

wäre *would be (see* sein*)*

waren *were (see* sein*)*

warm *warm*

die Wärme *heat*

wärmedämmend *heat-absorbing*

warten *to wait, service*

warum *why*

was *what, that, something, which;* was für ein...? *what type of...?* etwas, was *something which*

das Wasser (-) *water*

das Wassersportmesseereignis (-se) *water-sports event*

das WC (-s) *WC, toilet, lavatory*

wechseln *to change, vary*

wecken *to wake up*

weder: weder...noch *neither...nor*

der Weg (-e) *path, way, route, method*

weg *away, out (see also* weggehen*)*

wegen *because of, due to*

weggehen (*sep.*), ging weg, weggegangen (sein) *to go out/away*

das Weihnachten (-) *Christmas*

weil *because*

der Wein (-e) *wine*

das Weinfest (-e) *wine festival*

die Weise (-n): Art und Weise *manner*

weiß *white*

weiß *know(s) (see* wissen*)*

weit *far (away), wide;* so weit es geht *as far as possible*

weiter *further, more;* und so weiter *and so on*

der, die, das weitere *other(s), further*

weiterhin *in addition, still*

weiterleiten (*sep.*) (an) *to forward, pass on (to)*

welche, welchem, welchen, welcher, welches *(to/from/ for/of) which, some, them*

die Welt (-en) *world*

der Welt-Maschinist (*sing. gen.* -en) (-en) *world-class machine-tool manufacturer*

der, die, das weltgrößte *biggest in the world*

der Weltumsatz (⸚e) *world turnover/ sales*

weltweit *worldwide*

die Wende *the breaching of the Wall*

wenig *little, few*

wenigstens *at least*

wenn *if, when*

wer *who*

die Werbeagentur (-en) *advertising agency*

der Werbeleiter (-) *advertising manager/director*

die Werbeleiterin (-nen) *advertising manager/director (f.)*

die Werbung (-en) *advertising, advertisement*

werd' = werde

werden (wird), wurde, worden (sein) *is, will (auxiliary verb to form future and passive);* ich werde mich bei Ihnen melden *I will contact you;* die Schiffe werden in England produziert *the ships are produced in England*

werden (wird), wurde, geworden (sein) *to become, turn out;* die Messe wird größer *the fair is getting bigger*

die Werft (-en) *shipyard, dock*

das Werk (-e) *works, factory, company*

die Werkstatt (⸚en) *workshop*

der Werkstoff (-e) *material*

die Werkzeitung (-en) *company newspaper*

das Werkzeug (-e) *tool*

der Werkzeugbau *tool making*

der Werkzeugmacher (-) *toolmaker*

die Werkzeugmaschine (-n) *machine tool*

der Wert (-e) *value;* Wert legen auf *to place importance on*

die Wertarbeit (-en) *craftsmanship*

das Wertpapier (-e) *security*

das Wertpapiergeschäft (-e) *securities business/trading*

das Wesen *being, nature, entity*

wesentlich *essential(ly), important*

der West(en) *west, (the) West*

westlich *westerly*

der Wettbewerb (-e) *competition*

der Wettbewerber (-) *competitor*

wettbewerbsfähig *competitive*

der Whisky (-s) *whisky*

wichtig *important*

wichtiger (als) *more important (than)*

die Wichtigkeit (-en) *importance*

der, die, das Wichtigste *the most important (thing)*

der, die, das wichtigste *(the) most important (one)*

wie *how, as, like, as if;* nach wie vor *still, now, as ever;* wie weit *how far, to what extent;* wie heißen Sie? *what is your name?* wie lange? *how long?*

wieviel/wie viele *how much/many;* wie immer *as always;* wie vereinbart *as agreed;* ebenso...wie *both...and;* wie wir meinen *in our opinion;* wie ich hierherkam *when I came here*

wieder *again, back;* immer wieder *again and again, frequently*

Wiederhören: (auf) Wiederhören! *goodbye (on the phone)*

Wiederschauen: (auf) Wiederschauen! *goodbye*

Wiedersehen: (auf) Wiedersehen! *goodbye (lit. until we meet again)*

wieviel *how much/many;* wie viele *how many*

will *want(s) (see* wollen*)*

willkommen *welcome*

das Willkommen (-) *welcome*

der Winter (-) *winter*

wir *we*

wir's = wir es

wird *is (see* werden*)*

wirken *to act, work, have an effect*

wirklich *real(ly), in fact*

der Wirkstoff (-e) *active substance*

die Wirtschaft (-en) *economy, trade and industry*

wirtschaftlich *economic(ally), financial(ly), cost-effective*

der Wirtschaftsprüfer (-) *auditor (comparable with chartered accountant)*

die Wirtschaftsprüfungsgesellschaft (-en) *auditing company, auditors*
wissen (weiß), wußte, gewußt *to know (a fact)*
die Wissenschaft (-en) *science(s)*
wo *where;* wo ist der Hauptsitz? *where is the head office?* wo es...gibt *where there are...*
die Woche (-n) *week*
das Wochenende (-n) *weekend*
woher *from which, where from*
das Wohl *health, welfare;* zum Wohl! *Cheers!, good health!*
wohlwissend *well aware*
wohnen *to live*
wollen (will), wollte, gewollt *to want (to)*
wollt' = wollte
worden *was/were (see* werden*)*
der Wordprocessor (-en) *wordprocessor*
wunderbar *wonderful*
der Wunsch (¨e) *wish, demand*
wünsch' = wünsche
wünschen *to wish*
würd' = würde
wurde *was, has been (see* werden*)*
würde *would (see* werden*)*

Z

die Zahl (-en) *number, digit*
zahlen *to pay*
zählen (zu) *to belong (to), be among*
zählend (zu) *numbering among*
zahlreich *numerous*
der, die, das Zahlreiche *(the) numerous thing/one*
die Zahlung (-en) *payment*
zahlungsfähig *solvent*
die Zahlungsfrist (-en) *time limit for payment*
der Zahn (¨e) *tooth*
der Zahnarzt (¨e) *dentist*
die Zahnärztin (-nen) *dentist (f.)*
z.B. = zum Beispiel
zehn *ten*
das Zeichen (-) *sign, symbol, reference, ref.;* Ihr Zeichen *your ref.*
die Zeichnerin (-nen) *draughtswoman*
die Zeichnung (-en) *drawing*
zeigen *to show*
sich zeigen *to emerge, show, be evident;* das zeigt sich...an *this...shows in*
die Zeile (-n) *line*
die Zeit (-en) *time, period;* zu jeder Zeit *at all times;* zur Zeit *at present*
die Zeitfrage (-n) *matter of time*
zeitgemäß *modern, contemporary*
der Zeitpunkt (-e) *time;* Ort und Zeitpunkt *place and time*
der Zeitraum (¨e) *space of time*
die Zeitung (-en) *newspaper*
der Zeitungsmann (¨er) *journalist*
zentral *central, centralized*
die Zentrale (-n) *centre, head office, headquarters*
die Zentralverriegelung *central locking*

das Zentrum (Zentren) *centre*
der Zeppelin (-e) *zeppelin, air ship*
zerspanen *to machine, cut*
zerspanend *machining, cutting*
das Zeugnis (-se) *certificate*
ziehen, zog, gezogen *to pull, take, move;* Konsequenzen ziehen *(to) take the consequences*
das Ziel (-e) *aim, objective, target, goal*
das Zimmer (-) *room*
der Zins (-en) *interest*
der Zinsgewinn (-e) *interest*
zirka *approximate(ly), about*
der Zoo (-s) *zoo*
zoologisch: Zoologischer Garten *zoological garden*
zu *to, at, too, on (see also* zulassen, zulegen, zusagen*);* um zu *in order to;* zu teuer *too expensive;* zu genauen Zeiten *at precise times;* Sie haben uns beauftragt,...zu finden *you commissioned us to find...;* um...zahlen zu können *in order to be able to pay...;* bis zu *up to;* zum Erodieren *for eroding;* zum Thema *(on the) subject (of);* zum Beispiel *for example;* zu Hause *at home*
das Zubehör *accessory, accessories*
der Zucker (-) *sugar*
zuerst *(at) first, firstly*
der Zufall (¨e) *chance*
zufrieden *satisfied*
die Zufriedenheit *satisfaction*
zufriedenstellend *successful(ly), satisfactorily*
der Zug (¨e) *train;* im Zuge *as a result (of)*
zugleich *at the same time, concurrent(ly), simultaneous(ly)*
der Zugriff (-e) *access*
zuhören (sep.) *to listen*
die Zukunft *future*
zukünftig *future*
zukunftsweisend *future-oriented*
sich zulegen (sep.) *to get;* ich werde mir eine zulegen *I will get one*
zuletzt *last(ly);* nicht zuletzt *last but not least*
zum = zu dem *to the (see* zu*)*
zumindest(ens) *at least*
zunächst *first (of all), initial(ly)*
zündend *initial*
zunehmen (sep.) (nimmt zu), nahm zu, zugenommen *to increase*
zunehmend *increasing(ly)*
zur = zu der
Zürcher *Zurich, of Zurich*
zurück *back (see also sep. verbs with* zurück*)*
zurückgezogen *drawn/moved back*
zurückkehren (sep.) (sein) *to return*
zurückkommen (sep.), kam zurück, zurückgekommen (sein) *to return*
zurückrufen (sep.), rief zurück,

zurückgerufen *to ring back*
zurückziehen (sep.), zog zurück, zurückgezogen *to draw back;* (sein) *to move back*
zurückzurufen *see* zurückrufen
die Zusage (-n) *acceptance*
zusagen (sep.) *to appeal*
zusammen *together (see also sep. verbs with* zusammen*)*
die Zusammenarbeit *cooperation*
zusammenarbeiten (sep.) *to work together, work with, cooperate*
zusammengerufen *called together*
zusammengeschlossen *amalgamated*
zusammenrufen (sep.), riefen zusammen, zusammengerufen *to call together*
sich zusammenschließen (sep.), schloß zusammen, zusammengeschlossen *to amalgamate;* haben sich zusammengeschlossen *amalgamated*
zusammensein (sep.) (bin zusammen), war zusammen, bin zusammengewesen (mit) *to be together (with)*
zusätzlich *additional(ly), extra*
der Zuschlag (¨e) *supplement*
zustande: zustande kommen *to occur, come about*
zuständig (für) *responsible (for)*
zutreffen (sep.) (trifft zu), traf zu, zugetroffen *to apply, be true*
zutreffend *true, applicable*
zuverlässig *reliable (-ly)*
der Zwang (¨e) *compulsion, pressure*
zwangsläufig *inevitable (-ly)*
zwanzig *twenty*
der, die, das zwanzigste *(the) twentieth (one)*
zwar *indeed, although, actually, in fact;* zwar...aber *although...but;* und zwar *that is*
zwei *two*
zweieinhalb *two and a half*
das Zweier-Sekretariat (-e) *two-person office*
die Zweigstelle (-n) *branch office*
zweimal *twice, two times*
die Zweit-Sekretärin (-nen) *second/assistant secretary*
der, die, das zweite *(the) second (one);* zum zweiten *secondly*
zweitens *second(ly)*
der, die, das zweitgrößte *(the) second largest (one)*
zweiundzwanzig *twenty-two*
die Zwiebel (-n) *onion*
zwischen *between*
das Zwischenergebnis (-se) *interim result*
die Zwischenzeit (-en) *meantime*
zwo *two (on the phone)*
zwölf *twelve*
der, die, das zwölfte *twelfth*
der Zyklonfilter (-) *cyclone filter*